FORGOTTEN
FOUNDATIONS OF
BRETTON WOODS

FORGOTTEN FOUNDATIONS OF BRETTON WOODS

International Development
and the Making of the Postwar Order

Eric Helleiner

CORNELL UNIVERSITY PRESS   ITHACA AND LONDON

First published 2014 by Cornell University Press
First printing, Cornell Paperbacks, 2016

Library of Congress Cataloging-in-Publication Data

Helleiner, Eric, 1963– , author.
   Forgotten foundations of Bretton Woods : international development and the
making of the postwar order / Eric Helleiner.
      pages cm
   Includes bibliographical references and index.
   ISBN 978-0-8014-5275-8 (cloth : alk. paper)
   ISBN 978-1-5017-0437-6 (pbk. : alk. paper)
   1. United Nations Monetary and Financial Conference (1944 : Bretton
Woods, N.H.) 2. International finance—History—20th century. 3. Economic
development—History—20th century. I. Title.
   HG3881.H4177   2014
   338.9109'045—dc23   2013045238

Cornell University Press strives to use environmentally responsible suppliers
and materials to the fullest extent possible in the publishing of its books. Such
materials include vegetable-based, low-VOC inks and acid-free papers that are
recycled, totally chlorine-free, or partly composed of nonwood fibers. For further
information, visit our website at www.cornellpress.cornell.edu.

Contents

Preface

This book offers an unconventional interpretation of the birth of the postwar international economic order. At least, it was unconventional to me until I came upon some archival material well over a decade ago that generated the research path that led me to write this book. Like many others, I had long assumed that international development goals and North-South relations played little role in the creation of the Bretton Woods system. After many years of digging through archives and other sources, I have become convinced that they were much more important to the origins of that system than is usually acknowledged. These are forgotten foundations of Bretton Woods and they are not just of historical interest. They deserve to be remembered at a time that there is much discussion about how to reconcile the existing liberal international economic order with the development aspirations of emerging Southern powers. The Bretton Woods architects addressed this issue squarely and creatively "at the creation," and they included representatives from many of the key emerging economic powers of today such as Brazil, China, India, and Mexico.

Many people have helped me in this project. I am very grateful to various archivists working in the institutions mentioned in the reference list who shared their wisdom and provided invaluable assistance. I have also been lucky to work with a remarkable group of students who provided valuable research assistance and insights: Asim Ali, Geoff Cameron, Taarini Chopra, Judit Fabian, Athanasia Limperatos, Masaya Llavaneras-Blanco, Troy Lundblad, Ian Muller, Stefano Pagliari, Antulio Rosales, Anastasia Ufimtseva, Verónica Rubio Vega, and J. Ricardo Tranjan. Ricardo deserves special recognition for his valiant efforts on a trip to locate Paraguayan archival material that appears to have been lost to the historical record. Thanks, too, to staff at the Banco Central del Paraguay for their assistance with his efforts.

Thanks to many others who provided helpful commentary, reactions, sources, and advice on various aspects of the argument. They include Manmohan Aggarwal, Jacquie Best, James Boughton, Gerry Boychuk, Benedicte Bull, Tom Callaghy, Greg Chin, Andy Cooper, Bob Cox, Roy Culpepper, Ed Dosman, Alan Dye, Michael Edelstein, Ted Fertik, Ed Friedman, Kevin Gallagher, Patti Goff, Mui Pong Goh, Derek Hall, Jason Hecht, Gerry Helleiner, Kathy Hochstetler, Harold James, Miles Kahler, Robert Keohane, Jonathan Kirshner, John Kleeberg, Akinoba Kuroda, Kathryn Lavelle, Kari Levitt, Brad Lewis, Odette Lineau, Charles Lipson,

Perry Mehrling, Bessma Momani, James Morrison, Ananya Mukherjee-Reed, Craig Murphy, John Odell, Paul Poast, Tony Porter, Laura Randall, Eric Raunchway, Emily Rosenberg, John Sanbrailo, Kurt Schuler, James Scott, Irvine Stone, Andrew Thompson, Gail Triner, Ryan Touhey, Richard von Glahn, Hongying Wang, David Weiman, Rorden Wilkinson, Ngaire Woods, as well as many other participants in seminars where I presented aspects of this work at Columbia University, Cornell University, Harvard University, the History of Economics Society, McMaster University, Oxford University, Princeton University, the Rockefeller Foundation's Bellagio Centre, Sciences Po, the University of Chicago (the PIPES seminar), the University of Ottawa, the University of Southern California, the University of Tokyo, the University of Warwick, and the University of Waterloo. To any people I have overlooked, please accept both my apologies and my thanks.

I am also particularly grateful to Roger Haydon for all his insights and cheerful encouragement as well as to two anonymous reviewers of this manuscript for their very helpful comments and suggestions. Gavin Lewis and Susan Specter also provided extremely useful editorial advice. Many thanks, too, to the Social Sciences and Humanities Research Council of Canada, the Canada Research Chairs Program, and the Trudeau Foundation for helping to fund the research underlying this book. And finally this book is dedicated to the three people who have made the most important contributions to it: Jennifer, Zoë, and Nels. Jennifer has listened and reacted to my ideas about this history (and much else) for a very long time; Zoë and Nels have spent almost their whole lives with this project and sometimes wondered why someone could possibly be so interested in a faraway forest called Bretton Woods. Thanks to each of them for their wonderful patience, intelligence, humor, support, and love of life, which have been constant sources of inspiration.

Abbreviations

BIS	Bank for International Settlements
CFF	Compensatory Financing Facility
CFR	Council on Foreign Relations
ECLA	Economic Commission for Latin America
FBI	Federation of British Industries
FRBNY	Federal Reserve Bank of New York
GATT	General Agreement on Tariffs and Trade
IAB	Inter-American Bank
IADB	Inter-American Development Bank
IBRD	International Bank for Reconstruction and Development
ICU	International Clearing Union
IDA	International Development Association
IFEAC	Inter-American Financial and Economic Advisory Committee
IMF	International Monetary Fund
ISI	import-substitution industrialization
ITO	International Trade Organization
KMT	Kuomintang
NIEO	New International Economic Order
OPEC	Organization of the Petroleum Exporting Countries
RBI	Reserve Bank of India
RFC	Reconstruction Finance Corporation
RIIA	Royal Institute of International Affairs
SUNFED	Special UN Fund for Economic Development
TVA	Tennessee Valley Authority
UNCTAD	UN Conference on Trade and Development

FORGOTTEN FOUNDATIONS OF BRETTON WOODS

INTERNATIONAL DEVELOPMENT AND THE NORTH-SOUTH DIALOGUE OF BRETTON WOODS

The Bretton Woods conference is justly famous for creating the foundations for the postwar international financial system. Delegates from countries around the world met at the Mount Washington Hotel in New Hampshire in July 1944 to establish a new multilateral legal framework for financial relations. They also created two institutions—the International Monetary Fund (IMF) and the International Bank for Reconstruction and Development (IBRD)—that remain at the center of global financial governance today. These arrangements, in turn, were underpinned by an innovative "embedded liberal" vision that sought to reconcile a commitment to liberal multilateralism with new interventionist economic practices that had become influential across the world during the 1930s.[1]

The Bretton Woods negotiations have also attracted many critics over the years. One of the most consistent criticisms has concerned their treatment of international development issues and the concerns of poorer (or "Southern") countries.[2] The Bretton Woods agreements are commonly portrayed as a product

---

1. For embedded liberalism, see Ruggie 1982. Ruggie describes how this ideology infused not just the international financial discussions of Bretton Woods but also international trade negotiations after the conference. Trade issues occasionally arise in the analysis here, but the main focus is on the international financial issues addressed directly by the Bretton Woods conference itself.

2. In this book, the term "Southern countries" is used interchangeably with "poorer countries." The term came into vogue during the 1970s when it was used to refer to the coalition of poorer countries that presented a distinctive perspective on global economic issues from those of wealthier "Northern" countries. In the historical discussions examined in this book, a number of terms were used to describe poorer countries, such as "less developed," "undeveloped," "underdeveloped,"

of Anglo-American negotiations between 1942 and 1944 in which development issues received little attention and Southern voices were largely absent. This historical narrative has reinforced arguments that the Bretton Woods system has long privileged the narrow interests and perspectives of the rich "North" over those of the South.

This book offers a very different interpretation of the origins and content of the Bretton Woods agreements. It shows how international development goals—that is, those aiming to provide official international support for the economic development of Southern countries[3]—were widely discussed during the negotiations that led up to the 1944 Bretton Woods agreements. These discussions inspired many innovative proposals to create a more development-friendly international financial order than had existed in the past. Not all of these proposals found their way into the final Bretton Woods agreements, but some important ones did. Far from neglecting international development goals, the Bretton Woods negotiations should be recognized for their pioneering role in incorporating these goals into a liberal multilateral financial architecture for the first time.

Furthermore, officials from Southern countries played a more active and significant role in shaping and supporting the Bretton Woods outcomes than conventional wisdom suggests. Particularly important were Latin American policymakers who worked closely with US officials from the late 1930s onward—well before the Anglo-American negotiations of 1942–44 began—to build a new pattern of international financial relations that favored their aspirations for state-led development. Policy innovations arising from this US–Latin American financial partnership helped prepare the ground for the Bretton Woods negotiations, and Latin American officials and analysts continued to be active participants in the discussions that led to the 1944 agreements themselves. Officials and thinkers from other poorer parts of the world—especially China, India, and eastern Europe—also strongly backed the development content of Bretton Woods. The Bretton Woods negotiations were thus much more than just an Anglo-American affair. They took place against a wider political background that included a rather extensive North-South dialogue that was in fact the first of its kind to shape the global financial order.

This book thus offers a significant reinterpretation of the birth of the postwar international economic order. Its unconventional history calls attention to the overlooked international development content of the Bretton Woods

---

"depressed," "non-industrialized," "industrializing," "poor," "capital poor," "capital-needy," "low income," "economically backward" and "backward" (the latter was sometimes used in quotation marks, e.g. in Berle 1941a).

3. "Official," that is, in contrast to a much longer tradition of international nongovernmental development initiatives. This definition deliberately sidesteps the issue of what the economic "development" of Southern countries might mean.

agreements as well as to the neglected North-South dimensions of the negotiations that generated that content. These are, I argue, the forgotten foundations of Bretton Woods. The goal of the book is to reveal them and bring them to light.

Why has this history been forgotten? One reason may be that the scholars who helped establish the conventional wisdom on this topic did not have access to the range of archival material that I draw on here. But it may also be because the world changed quite dramatically in the immediate aftermath of the Bretton Woods conference. Very quickly after the war, US officials turned their backs on much of the development content of the Bretton Woods agreements for reasons described in the final chapter of this book. This turn of events set the stage for Southern policymakers and analysts to see the Bretton Woods order as a Northern-dominated arrangement that was ill-suited to their state-led development strategies. By the 1970s, Southern dissatisfaction had escalated into widespread calls for a New International Economic Order (NIEO) to reform the Bretton Woods system in a more development-oriented direction. In this charged political context, both supporters and critics of the NIEO overlooked the fact it resurrected many ideas that had been discussed during the Bretton Woods negotiations.

If this history might have been useful to participants in the NIEO debates, it is also relevant to the current moment. We are living in an era when the North-South dimensions of the global financial system are once again becoming politically contentious. Many policymakers and analysts from increasingly powerful emerging economies are demanding better representation in global financial governance as well as specific reforms to the global financial system to further their state-led development goals. This book provides a reminder that efforts to reconcile liberal multilateralism with the state-led developmental goals of poorer countries were in fact at the center of the politics that created the postwar international financial order. Indeed, many of the key emerging economic powers today—Brazil, China, India, and Mexico—helped to build the forgotten development foundations of Bretton Woods.

The historical analysis here also sheds new light on current scholarly debates about international development's history and meaning. Many contemporary scholars assert that international development was born with US President Truman's 1949 inauguration speech and the early Cold War priorities of Western policymakers. In some "postdevelopment" scholarship, this historical narrative is used to support a broader critique that international development has been, from its very origins, a neo-imperialist political project of powerful capitalist countries.[4]

---

4. See for example Escobar 1995, Rist 1997, Sachs 1990 and 1992. Some of this literature claims that the concept of development itself originated in the Truman era, but this view has been effectively critiqued by Cowen and Shenton 1996.

While skepticism about the post-1949 international development experience may be justified, this critique rests on a flawed history of the origins of international development, which was neither invented by the Truman administration nor a product of the Cold War. International development has a deeper history, in which the US–Latin American financial partnership of the late 1930s and early 1940s and the subsequent Bretton Woods negotiations played an important part. Moreover, much of the push for international development in this earlier period came from Southern officials and analysts, and many of the pioneers in this period (including those from the United States) saw its content rather differently than Truman and his advisers. The politics of the birth of international development, in other words, are more complicated than the critique suggests.

Common Views of Bretton Woods

Before I outline this book's arguments, it is worth reviewing some of the common views about the role of international development and Southern countries in the Bretton Woods negotiations.[5] Typical of conventional wisdom are the views of Richard Gardner who pioneered the study of the negotiations in his important book *Sterling-Dollar Diplomacy*.[6] Gardner argues the Bretton Woods agreements resulted largely from Anglo-American negotiations in which the question of how to assist the development of poorer countries "was not recognized as a major issue in the postwar planning."[7] His more specific discussion of the creation of the IMF reinforces this point: "the delegates at Bretton Woods gave little thought to the Fund's potential impact on the less-developed countries."[8] Gardner even downplays the significance of the creation of the International Bank for Reconstruction *and Development* at the conference: "There was simply no conception of the vast needs of the less developed countries and of the role the Bank should play in meeting them. Indeed, the Bank was conceived mainly as an institution for reconstruction. Incredible as it seems today, the word 'development' did not even appear in Harry White's first draft circulated within the US Treasury Department."[9]

---

5. Given the following criticisms of existing literature, I hasten to add that my own early work on Bretton Woods also neglected the development content of Bretton Woods and the role of Southern countries in the negotiations; Helleiner 1994, chap. 2. Mea culpa.
6. Initially published in 1956, a revised version of his book was published in 1980 (Gardner 1980).
7. Gardner 1985, 30.
8. Gardner 1980, xxi.
9. Gardner 1985, 30. See also Gardner 1996, 202.

Gardner's view of the Bank's original purpose is shared by others. For example, in a prominent book analyzing the Bretton Woods institutions, geographer Richard Peet argues:

> The IBRD was a mere afterthought. What little exchange there was concerning the IBRD centred on its possible role in the post-war reconstruction of Europe. On the few occasions that poor countries were—briefly—mentioned, issues such as poverty never came up. Indeed, such were the preoccupations of the Europeans and Americans at the time that labels such as "poor countries," or the more critical term "underdeveloped countries," did not exist as functional geographical categories—countries outside Europe and North America were referred to as "the colonies."[10]

The most recent comprehensive history of the Bank comes to a similar conclusion about its intended role. Echoing Gardner, the authors of this history argue that the first US draft of a proposal for a bank written in early 1942 by Harry Dexter White "made no mention of development."[11] They point out that in the subsequent international negotiations leading up to the Bretton Woods conference, the Bank also received much less attention than the IMF and conclude that "development arrived almost by accident and played a bit role at Bretton Woods."[12] In their earlier history of the World Bank, Edward Mason and Robert Asher also suggest that "the distinction between developed and less developed and between north and south—the special problems of the 'third world'—had scarcely swum into the ken of postwar planners."[13]

Existing scholarship has also often downplayed the role of Southern countries in the creation of the Bretton Woods system. Economist Gerald Meier, a leading authority on the history of development thinking, describes the dynamics of the Bretton Woods negotiations as follows: "Most of the developing countries were still colonies, and only a relatively few, mainly independent nations of Latin

---

10. Peet 2009, 127.

11. Kapur, Lewis, and Webb 1997, 57.

12. Kapur, Lewis, and Webb 1997, 68. See also Benjamin 2007, 12–14. Better than many other analysts, Kapur, Lewis, and Webb do mention briefly the push by India and some Latin American countries for more focus on development issues at Bretton Woods. They also cite President Roosevelt's interest in addressing poverty abroad (1997, 60, 61 n.16, 65–66), although they argue that he "was ahead of his audience and of the political mood in 1944" and that his message "was glossed over at Bretton Woods" (1997, 66, 69). They also quote US Treasury Secretary Henry Morgenthau's comment that "poverty, wherever it exists, is menacing to us all," but argue that no one at the time stated that "development assistance was in the self-interest of the giver." They add: "There were allusions to the importance of developing the resources available in undeveloped areas, by which delegates meant, principally, raw materials" (1997, 69).

13. Mason and Asher 1973, 4.

America, were invited. The political power lay with the United States and Britain, and from the outset it was apparent that issues of development were not to be on the Bretton Woods agenda."[14] Like many other scholars, he also cites a comment from the British negotiator John Maynard Keynes dismissing the role of many poorer countries invited to the meeting, arguing that they "clearly have nothing to contribute and will merely encumber the ground. . . . The most monstrous monkey-house assembled for years."[15]

Meier also argues that Southern countries themselves did not press for development issues to be included in the Bretton Woods plans: "At Bretton Woods, the developing countries tended to view themselves more as new, raw-material-producing nations and less as countries with general development problems. Comprehensive strategies of development and policies to accelerate national development were yet to be identified."[16] In Meier's view, it was thus not only American and British officials who "were not directly interested" in development during the negotiations. As he puts it, "even most of the representatives of LDCs [less developed countries] seemed unconcerned."[17]

Some of the more detailed descriptive accounts of the overall Bretton Woods negotiations identify specific issues raised by Southern governments, but their analyses still center on the role of Britain and the United States.[18] The most recent of these accounts, Benn Steil's *The Battle of Bretton Woods*, reinforces this tendency, focusing very heavily on the Anglo-American relationship, and even suggesting at one point that "other than the United States, United Kingdom, and Canada, few delegations came equipped to make intellectual contributions to the architecture of the fund or the bank."[19] The downplaying of Southern contributions is also apparent in John K. Horsefield's important documentary volume that reproduces the original Bretton Woods plans of the United States,

---

14. Meier 1984b, 9.

15. Meier 1984b, 9. Meier (1984a, 11–12) also echoes the arguments that the early drafts of the IBRD gave little attention to development issues and that the bank received little attention in the negotiations. For other references to Keynes's remark, see Meier 1984a, 11; Kapur, Lewis, and Webb 1997, 62; Toye and Toye 2004, 23; Benjamin 2007, 15–16; Peet 2009, 49. The remark's significance is discussed in chapter 8 below.

16. Meier 1984b, 9.

17. Meier 1984a, 13. Despite these arguments, Meier does acknowledge that India and some Latin American countries lobbied for some development provisions (1984a, 13–14, 20). He also cites Roosevelt's desire to see "freedom from want," as well as the UN Charter's commitment to promote "higher standards of living" and "development," but argues that the Bretton Woods conference "remained largely immune from these aspirations" (Meier 1984b, 9). In addition, he notes that "elements of what would now be called a 'New International Economic Order' were proposed by some economists who were examining the structure of the postwar world" but he argues that they were "not yet differentiating between North and South" (Meier 1984a, 17).

18. In addition to Gardner's book, detailed histories of the Bretton Woods negotiations can be found in Van Dormael 1978, Eckes 1975, Horsefield 1969a, Mikesell 1994, and Steil 2013.

19. Steil 2013, 229.

British, Canadian, and French governments while neglecting those of the Chinese government.[20] A widely read 1993 historical volume titled *A Retrospective on the Bretton Woods System* also says little about the role of Southern countries in the creation of Bretton Woods. Significantly, though, one of its editors, Michael Bordo, makes the important point in his introductory chapter that one of the key remaining questions to be addressed by historians is "how did the nonindustrialized world relate to the Bretton Woods system?"[21]

From political science, John Ruggie's seminal article on the significance of the ideology of embedded liberalism—a term he first coined—also devotes little attention to the development content of the Bretton Woods negotiations. In a very insightful analysis, Ruggie demonstrates how US and British negotiators set out to build a multilateral financial order that, unlike the gold standard, "would be predicated upon domestic interventionism." Under this "compromise" of embedded liberalism, countries would commit to stable exchange rates and current account convertibility, while their domestic economies would be cushioned "against the strictures of the balance of payments" by multilateral rules allowing adjustable exchange rates and capital controls as well as by the IMF's provision of short-term balance of payments support. But in Ruggie's analysis, the relevant "domestic interventionism" was a kind developed by industrialized countries. As he puts it, the ideology of embedded liberalism was informed by a "shared legitimacy of a set of social objectives to which the industrial world had moved," objectives that were focused on full employment and the provision of social security.[22] Little attention is devoted the new interventionist practices emerging in poorer countries at this time that were aimed at promoting economic development.

In a book published just after his 1982 article, Ruggie does note that the IBRD's concessional lending to developing countries instituted "the concept of an international role in the development process."[23] But he suggests that Keynes was focused more on the development of "the world economy" than on the development of poorer countries specifically. Citing India's unsuccessful effort to get a reference to "development" goals explicitly included in the IMF's charter, Ruggie asserts that specific references to the development of developing countries "were systematically excluded from the Final Acts."[24] Other political scientists have echoed this point, suggesting that, while IBRD's articles of agreement

---

20. Horsefield 1969b.
21. Bordo 1993, 85.
22. Ruggie 1982, 393, 395, 398.
23. Ruggie 1983b, 8.
24. Ruggie 1983c, 430.

"do mention (but do not emphasize) assisting countries in raising standards of living, they do not mention or target poor countries in particular."[25]

Much recent scholarship exploring the origins of international development has also overlooked the importance of development issues in the Bretton Woods negotiations. This analysis often focuses on the importance of Truman's January 1949 inauguration speech in which he declared that "we must embark on a bold new program for making the benefits of our scientific advances and industrial progress available for the improvement and growth of underdeveloped areas."[26] For many postdevelopment scholars inspired by discourse analysis, Truman's speech changed world history by inventing, or at least popularizing, the term "underdeveloped." In the context of the birth of the Cold War, the term is seen to have justified US intervention in poorer countries by suggesting that these countries needed external help to promote development.[27] As Gustavo Esteva puts it, "Underdevelopment began, then, on January 20, 1949. On that day, two billion people became underdeveloped."[28] Like others working in this tradition, Arturo Escobar argues that the results of this new international development project were disastrous: "the discourse and strategy of development produced its opposite: massive underdevelopment and impoverishment, untold exploitation and oppression."[29]

Some scholars who stress the importance of the Truman speech and the early Cold War in the birth of international development acknowledge that there were precursors. For example, Esteva argues that the term "underdevelopment" was probably "invented" in 1942 by Wilfred Benson, a former official of the International Labour Organization. But he suggests that "the expression found no further echo, neither with the public nor with the experts" until Truman's speech.[30] Another important scholar working in this tradition, Gilbert Rist, also notes briefly how the League of Nations showed some limited interest in international development, but his historical narrative jumps from this episode to Truman's speech which, he states, truly *inaugurated the 'development age.'*"[31] Escobar (who argues that the term "underdevelopment" "did not exist before 1945") also shows some awareness of two phenomena that are at the core of the analysis here: the Roosevelt administration's Good Neighbor policy and Latin American

---

25. Finnemore 1997: 206.

26. Quoted in Rist 1997, 71.

27. See especially Escobar 1995; Rist 1997; and Sachs 1990 1992.

28. Esteva 1992, 7.

29. Escobar 1995, 4.

30. Esteva 1992, 7. Benson's role is also mentioned by Sachs (1990) and Rist (1997, 73 n. 5).

31. Rist 1997, 71. Italics in original. In addition to discussing the reference to "development" in the League's charter, Rist (1997, 65–66) mentions the League's technical assistance to China in the 1930s. That assistance was requested by China—a request that does not square well with Rist's overall view of the Northern origins of international development.

development aspirations during the 1930s and 1940s.[32] But he overlooks their significance to the origins of international development by neglecting their role in generating the US–Latin American financial partnership and Bretton Woods negotiations.

A Different Perspective

The findings here offer a quite different perspective from that of the conventional wisdom in three respects: the degree of US and other Northern support for international development, the role of Southern countries, and the origins of international development.

Northern Support for International Development

To begin with, throughout the Bretton Woods negotiations, US negotiators saw international development as a priority issue on the agenda of postwar international financial planning. Despite claims to the contrary, archival evidence shows that White's earliest drafts of the IBRD did assign the Bank a mandate to promote "development" (he uses the term). The IBRD's final articles of agreement also do explicitly mention the goal of promoting the development of poor countries; the first formal purpose of the Bank includes "the encouragement of the development of productive facilities and resources in less developed countries." In addition, American policymakers did not view the IBRD as an "afterthought." They always saw the Bank's creation as a crucial complement to the Fund in postwar international financial planning. More time was devoted to the Fund during the Bretton Woods negotiations simply because its design was more complicated and its provisions were more controversial.

More generally, far from ignoring international development, White's early postwar plans were in fact particularly ambitious in addressing this topic. Anticipating some of the NIEO agenda in the 1970s, White outlined innovative provisions for long-term international development finance, compensatory short-term balance of payments financing, debt restructuring, commodity price stabilization, the control of capital flight, and support for infant industry trade protection in Southern countries.[33] Although not all of White's proposals found

---

32. Escobar 1995, 31, 28–32.
33. For these and other reasons, I take a different view from Steffek (2006) who argues that the ideology of the "redistributive multilateralism" of the NIEO contrasted with, and represented a challenge to, the ideology of embedded liberalism. Steffek's argument rests on an analysis of the GATT

their way into the final Bretton Woods agreements, his commitment to international development was widely shared in the US government throughout the 1942–44 period. So was his commitment to what Toye and Toye call "*procedural multilateralism,*" which provided many poorer countries with a formal role in the negotiation of the Bretton Woods order and in its subsequent administration.[34]

The origins of White's initial plans have sometimes puzzled scholars, particularly since he produced initial drafts extremely quickly after an initial request from Morgenthau in mid-December 1941.[35] Drawing on detailed primary material, this book demonstrates that these proposals built directly on a number of initiatives that White and other US officials had launched in the late 1930s to support Latin American state-led development ambitions. These initiatives were part of Roosevelt's broader Good Neighbor policy toward the region. and they even included the negotiation of a multilateral lending institution in 1939–40—the Inter-American Bank (IAB)—whose central mandate was to promote economic development in the region and whose features anticipated some of those of the IMF and IBRD. These initiatives pioneered core features of White's initial proposals, including their development provisions.

Keynes is often seen as the intellectual father of Bretton Woods because he developed his first postwar plan before White in 1941 and because of his greater intellectual stature at the time. Rather than "catching up" to Keynes, however, White and other US officials were ahead of him in developing key features of Bretton Woods within the inter-American context.[36] US–Latin American financial relations in the late 1930s and early 1940s, in other words, played a crucial role in setting the stage for the initial US Bretton Woods proposals. And international development issues were at the center of those relations.

It is also important to recognize that US policymakers saw the ideology of embedded liberalism as having both a Northern and a Southern side. Although

---

trade regime; he devotes almost no attention to the Bretton Woods negotiations and their financial content. In fact, however, as we shall see, redistributive multilateralism was part of the ideology of embedded liberalism from the start. Steffek also argues that Southern countries remained outside of the embedded liberal system because their governments did not have the same capacity to cushion their citizens against the disruptive domestic effects of international markets that Northern government had. Yet as will also be shown, US officials worked actively at the time of Bretton Woods to strengthen this domestic cushioning capacity of Southern governments. In other words, they recognized this problem and explicitly sought to remedy it as part of the construction of the new embedded liberal order.

34. Toye and Toye 2004, 18. Emphasis in the original.

35. For example, Ikenberry (1992, 300) describes their origins as "unclear" while Moggridge (1992, 684) writes that "the exact origins of White's monetary plan are somewhat mysterious."

36. The image of White "catching up" to Keynes can be found in Van Dormael 1978. For another analysis that highlights how White came to his ideas very independently of Keynes, see Boughton 2002, 2004.

the ideology sought to reconcile liberal multilateralism with new kinds of domestic interventionism, the kinds of interventionism emerging from the experience of the Great Depression differed in Northern and Southern countries. In the North, supporters of embedded liberalism sought to reconcile liberal multilateralism with new commitments to social security and Keynesian full employment policies. But US officials also were determined to marry liberal multilateralism with new state-led development policies that had become influential across Latin America and many other poorer regions of the world during the 1930s. These policies were more focused on promoting rising living standards, rapid economic growth, and latecomer industrialization than on creating a welfare state and full employment.

United States officials worked actively to accommodate these distinctive preferences of Southern countries in the postwar planning process. The embedded liberal vision was thus aimed at pioneering a new model for both North–North and North–South financial relations. One way that US officials sought to meet the distinctive needs of Southern countries was through the IBRD's role in mobilizing international development lending. But American policymakers also viewed the design of the IMF through a development lens. They thought that the Fund's provision of short-term balance of payments finance would be particularly helpful for commodity-exporting countries that were vulnerable to seasonal fluctuations and commodity price swings. They also saw the Fund's endorsement of adjustable exchange rates and capital controls as useful for Southern governments seeking to bolster their capacity to promote their countries' rapid economic development.

Indeed, at the same time that they were negotiating the Fund's creation, US officials pioneered a new kind of financial advisory mission that was explicitly designed to strengthen this capacity by encouraging wide-ranging domestic monetary and financial reforms in Southern countries. The first two missions of this kind were led by White to Cuba in 1941–42 (during which he apparently wrote his first draft of the IBRD) and by Robert Triffin (of the Federal Reserve Board) to Paraguay in 1943–44. During and in the immediate wake of the Bretton Woods negotiations, White, Triffin, and other US financial advisers backed development-oriented domestic monetary and financial reforms in a number of other Southern countries—primarily in Latin America, but also in other countries that had attended Bretton Woods such as the Philippines and Ethiopia. The activities of this new breed of US "money doctor" complemented the establishment of the Fund perfectly. While the latter created a new multilateral framework that was permissive of national development policies, the former helped build domestic institutional capacity to enable those policies to be pursued. In this way, they reinforced at the domestic level the development foundations of Bretton Woods.[37]

What explains the US interest in promoting international development from the late 1930s through the Bretton Woods negotiations? Particularly important was the strategic goal of offsetting the Nazi threat, first in Latin America during the late 1930s and early 1940s and then worldwide once the United States joined World War II in late 1941. By offering to back the development aspirations of Southern governments, US officials helped secure alliances and provide a wider moral purpose to the Allied cause in the war, particularly at a time when fascist (and communist) ideals provided alternative routes to development from the preferred US model. As John Ikenberry argues in his analysis of the Bretton Woods negotiations, many US officials sought to legitimate US power in the postwar world by promulgating "a postwar system that would have a normative appeal to elites in other nations."[38] The promotion of international development did indeed hold much appeal for many Southern elites at this time.

American support for international development also grew out of some values of Roosevelt's New Deal, especially the belief that the provision of economic security to individuals was a key foundation for political stability. During his presidency, Roosevelt increasingly projected this idea into the international arena, arguing that the reduction of poverty abroad was a key pillar for international peace. Support for this goal was only reinforced by the broad concern of many New Dealers for the poor and for social justice. The antipathy of New Dealers toward New York financial elites and past US imperialist practices also encouraged their support for Latin American development goals as well as their interest in learning from Latin American experience. The willingness of New Dealers to challenge neoclassical economics and accept a greater role for government in economic life also led them to be more open to exploring the distinctive problems of Southern economies and to experimenting with new public initiatives at the international level to address those problems, often building on their own domestic experiences such as with the Tennessee Valley Authority.[39]

Finally, many US officials argued that their support for international development also served the country's economic interests. Particularly prominent were arguments that the development of Southern countries would help foster new export markets and new opportunities for investment. Underlying these

---

37. The significance of these US financial advisory missions in this period has been largely overlooked in existing literature, although see Cullather 1992, 80; Alacevich and Asso 2009; and Helleiner 2009.

38. Ikenberry 1992, 320.

39. For the broader case that the New Deal's endorsement of greater state intervention in the domestic economy led to interest in international economic activism, see Burley 1993; Ikenberry 2011, chap. 5; Patrick 2009.

arguments was often a vision of a new international division of labor in which capital-intensive US manufacturing firms would help foster import substitution industrialization in the South by exporting capital goods and establishing branch plants behind Southern tariff walls. Although those firms provided some support for that vision, the international development initiatives and goals of US government officials often proved controversial within the broader US business community. Opposition from the New York financial community, in particular, often blocked or diluted them.

The United States was not alone among wealthy countries in backing the incorporation of development goals within postwar international plans. Policymakers from other wealthy countries such as Canada, the Netherlands, and Australia did so too. Despite the claims made in some scholarship, even British officials expressed support for international development goals throughout the Bretton Woods negotiations from Keynes's initial 1941 drafts onward. This often reflected similar strategic and economic interests as in the United States, as well as some ideational motivations that paralleled New Deal values, particularly among figures in the Labour Party. Keynes and many other British officials did not, however, take up the cause of international development with the same enthusiasm as many of the US counterparts, and British officials actively tried to thwart development-oriented monetary reforms in countries such as Ethiopia (see chapter 8).

The Role of the South

Conventional wisdom has also unfairly downplayed the role of Southern countries in the creation of the Bretton Woods system. It is certainly the case that many Southern countries today were colonies at the time of the conference and thus unrepresented (although India was an important exception).[40] But many others were present. The attendees included officials from nineteen Latin American countries (all but Argentina),[41] four African countries (Egypt, Ethiopia, Liberia, and South Africa), and five delegations from the Asian continent (China, India, Iran, Iraq, and the Philippines). Also represented were four countries from eastern Europe (Czechoslovakia, Greece, Poland, and Yugoslavia), a region that many (including its representatives) saw at the time as facing similar economic problems to those of other poor regions. Meier argues that "relatively few" developing

---

40. The status of colonies also generated an interesting discussion within the US delegation at the conference (see chapter 7 opening).

41. Bolivia, Brazil, Chile, Colombia, Costa Rica, Cuba, Dominican Republic, Ecuador, El Salvador, Guatemala, Haiti, Honduras, Mexico, Nicaragua, Panama, Paraguay, Peru, Uruguay, Venezuela.

countries were invited, but if these jurisdictions are added up, they comprise a large majority—thirty-two of the total forty-four—of those formally represented at the conference.[42] Even if one might question whether all these delegations represented "developing countries,"[43] it seems fair to argue that a substantial majority of the countries represented at Bretton Woods fell in this group.

It is true that some of these Southern delegations included only one or two people.[44] But many others had more representatives, and some were quite large, such as the delegations from China (33 people), Brazil (13), Cuba (10), India (8, although half of these were British officials), Peru (8), Chile (9), Poland (8), and Mexico (7). Indeed, the size of the Chinese delegation—representing the world's most populous Southern independent country—was second only to that of the United States (45), while Brazil's was tied with Canada for the fourth largest behind Britain (15). Moreover, if all the individuals involved in the delegations from the thirty-two Southern jurisdictions are added, the total comes to 173 people, which is considerably more than the 140 in the delegations from the other twelve countries represented.[45] It is also worth noting that the head of the Mexican delegation was invited to chair one of the three commissions around which the Bretton Woods conference discussion was organized (the other two were chaired by White and Keynes).

In addition to their numbers, Southern delegates made many very substantial contributions to the conference discussions, as the transcripts of the conference make very clear.[46] During the meeting, these delegates derived some leverage from the fact that US officials were keen for the agreements to be ratified by as many countries as possible in order to bolster their legitimacy. The sizeable representation of Southern governments at the meeting also provided them with

---

42. In addition to the forty-four formal delegations at the conference, the Danish minister to the United States also attended in a personal capacity at the invitation of the United States (Denmark's government was Nazi-controlled and there was no government-in-exile) (Schuler and Rosenberg 2012, 108; Fuchs 1974b, 24). The other countries represented at Bretton Woods were the United States, the Soviet Union, the United Kingdom, three other British dominions (Australia, Canada, New Zealand), and six other West European countries (Belgium, France, Iceland, Luxembourg, Netherlands, Norway).

43. For example, Kapur, Lewis, and Webb (1997, 66) note that within Latin America, Argentina (which was not at the conference), Uruguay, and Venezuela had per capita incomes higher than much of Europe.

44. One-person delegations included those from Bolivia, Guatemala, Honduras, and Yugoslavia. Two-person delegations came from Ecuador, Haiti, Panama, Paraguay, and Uruguay.

45. These numbers are drawn from Schuler and Rosenberg 2012, appendix A. They include not just the official delegates but also all the secretaries, advisers, experts, consultants, and assistants associated with the various delegations. There were also many others at the conference who were not associated with specific delegations, such as members of the conference secretariat, individuals representing international organizations, as well as media and other observers. According to Horsefield (1969a, 89), 730 people attended the conference in total.

46. See Schuler and Rosenberg 2012; US State Department 1948.

concrete potential voting power. Many issues were settled without formal voting, but when votes were taken, each government had one vote with majorities
deciding the outcome. In this situation, delegates were well aware that the bloc
of nineteen Latin American countries in particular had almost enough votes to
decide any issue on its own.[47] As we shall see, the views of Latin American delegates were often very cohesive and they had a particularly significant impact in
the following areas: reinforcing and strengthening the importance of the Bank's
development mandate; creating the possibility for more generous IMF balance
of payments support for commodity exporting countries (the "waiver" clause);
and securing a conference resolution calling for a future international agreement
relating to commodity marketing and pricing.

The influence of delegates from Latin America and other parts of the South
should not be overstated. United States officials kept tight control of the proceedings and sought to avoid votes on issues where US goals might not be served.[48]
Many of the provisions of the Bretton Woods agreements that found favor
among Southern delegates—such as provisions for development loans, adjustable exchange rates, and capital controls—were also backed by the United States,
Britain, or both, making it difficult to say that Southern contributions to the
conference discussions changed the final outcome in decisive ways in many areas.
It is important to recognize, however, that Southern officials actively lobbied for
these provisions and saw them as important for their development goals.

Some Southern initiatives did not achieve their intended results because they
encountered opposition at the conference. India's effort to introduce "development" content into the Fund's mandate was one of the most prominent such
initiatives. Interestingly, however, opposition to India's proposal came not just
from the United States and Britain but also from Brazil which worried about
overlap with the Bank's mandate. The episode highlighted the fact that Southern
governments—with the important exception of Latin American governments—
did not present much of a unified front at the conference. To be sure, there was
widespread recognition of the common structural problems facing poorer countries, and some Chinese voices spoke initially in 1943 of the need to rally "weaker
nations" and become "the leader of undeveloped countries" in the discussions.[49]
But in contrast to the politics of the NIEO, there is not much explicit coalition
building between Latin American governments and representatives of other poor
regions of the world during the Bretton Woods negotiations.

---

47. See chapter 6.
48. See for example Steil 2013, 212; MD, book 753.
49. Quotes from Tsu-yee Pei in May 1943, who would become a Chinese delegate at Bretton
Woods.

The contribution of Southern officials to the negotiation of the Bretton Woods agreements was not restricted to their participation in the 1944 conference. Through their involvement in the inter-American financial initiatives of the late 1930s and early 1940s, Latin American policymakers helped pioneer key ideas and practices that laid the groundwork for the early US Bretton Woods plans, particularly their development content. China, Brazil, and Mexico were also part of an inner core of countries (along with the Soviet Union) consulted by American and British officials on postwar international financial plans from 1942 onward. American and British policymakers also consulted with many other Southern countries bilaterally and in smaller groupings throughout the negotiation process. In these consultations and at the Bretton Woods conference itself, Southern officials were much more than simply passive observers. They offered detailed commentary on, and contributions to, the content of postwar international financial plans. Latin American analysts—particularly Raúl Prebisch—also played an important role in influencing the content of the new US financial advisory missions that reinforced the Bretton Woods development foundations.

In their various inputs to the postwar planning discussions, Southern officials and analysts stressed that they were centrally concerned with how postwar international financial plans could further their general "development" aspirations (and once again, they used this term). At this time (and contrary to some of the common arguments discussed above), many Southern policymakers were strongly committed to the goal of raising their countries' living standards through comprehensive state-led economic development and industrialization strategies. In some Southern countries, the breakdown of the world economy in the 1930s had already acted as a catalyst for industrialization, and policymakers sought to reinforce this trend with active state support. The experience of the Great Depression had bolstered this goal by revealing the vulnerability of commodity exporters to volatile (and declining) commodity prices as well as to agricultural protectionism in Northern markets. The depression also undermined the legitimacy of liberal ideology and policies, opening the door to more statist economic policies—a phenomenon only reinforced by the examples abroad of the centrally planned industrialization of the Soviet Union, the economic growth of fascist powers such as Germany and Italy, and the growing support for economic planning in the US and Britain.

The push for industrialization also reflected Southern strategic concerns, particularly given the uncertain international security environment of the time. Industrialization was associated with power—just as it had been in the nineteenth century for late industrializers such as the United States, Germany, and Japan that had feared British domination. Many countries saw "late-late" industrialization strategies as a way to avoid subordination in the increasingly unequal world created by the second industrial revolution under way in the leading economies. Industrialization and broader national economic development also promised to help reduce economic dependence on foreign countries more generally.

The growing interest in active development policies also emerged out of a heightened awareness of widening international inequality between industrialized countries and the rest. Observers at the time commented on how intensifying communication links across the world were contributing to this growing awareness.[50] The production of new international statistics also played a role. For example, a widely noticed survey in the mid-1930s by the League of Nations concluded that two-thirds of the world's population had inadequate diets.[51] Colin Clark's 1939 book *Conditions of Economic Progress* also drew on national income statistics to compare living standards across the world. As Heinz Arndt notes, "for the first time, the gulf between living standards in the rich and the poor countries of the world was brought home in hard statistical terms." Arndt also calls attention to the International Labour Organization's work in the 1930s comparing levels of consumption in areas such as food, clothing, housing, medical care, and education in countries around the world.[52]

In the nineteenth century, poorer countries seeking to catch up economically had focused on national economic strategies, often inspired by Friedrich List's advocacy of state-led industrialization. Now, many Southern officials and analysts began to consider how the international community could play a role in assisting their national development initiatives. Encouraged by broader questioning of liberal orthodoxy at the time, they gave particular attention to roles that involved replacing, supplementing, and regulating international market actors. This thinking was also prompted by the fact that international organizations had assumed a much more prominent place in the landscape of world politics.

Also significant was the recognition of the enormity of the task of catching up economically to the leading powers. While late industrialization could be accomplished through national initiative, successful late-late industrialization might require international assistance. Modern day Listians, in other words, might need to combine nationalism with internationalism.[53] Figures such as Prebisch and China's Sun Yat-sen, whose ideas play an important role in this book, represented this combination well.

---

50. See League of Nations 1939, 9; Bonné 1945, 1; Nurkse 1944, 203, as well as passages quoted in this book.

51. Lee 2010, 112.

52. Arndt 1987, 35, 35–36. See also Alcalde 1987, 77–81.

53. The contrast should not be overstated since List himself saw his policies as a first step toward a long-term goal of a "union of nations" and a "universal society." That goal, he argued, could not be successful unless countries were of more equal power. His protectionist policies for weaker countries were aimed at generating greater inter-national equality (Helleiner 2002, 313–14).

The attraction of seeking international support for national development initiatives would, of course, be enhanced if there existed willing foreign partners for this project. Roosevelt's New Deal United States presented just such a partner. Latin American governments were the first to take up this opportunity in the late 1930s and early 1940s. Despite some skepticism arising from the history of US intervention in their region, many Latin American officials appreciated Roosevelt's Good Neighbor policy and recognized the potential value of developing coalitions with American New Dealers who shared some of their values. Out of this recognition emerged some key transnational expert coalitions between reform-minded economists from both Latin America and the United States who were interested in development issues.[54] These coalitions helped to drive the international development content of some of the key initiatives in the late 1930s and early 1940s and the Bretton Woods negotiations.

Their role parallels that of transnational expert coalitions—led by Keynes and White—that Ikenberry has identified as facilitating the Anglo-American dimensions of the Bretton Woods negotiations.[55] While the Keynes-White axis shared a commitment to Keynesian full employment policies and social security goals, US and Latin American economists came together around a common belief in new development thinking. As we shall see, Triffin and Prebisch emerged as particularly central figures within this axis in the process of pioneering a new model of financial advising for Southern countries.

While the US–Latin American financial partnership emerged in the late 1930s, officials from other poorer regions of the world also came to recognize the potential of an international development partnership with the United States (and other Northern countries) once the Bretton Woods negotiations began. Their backing of the negotiations was linked to an understanding that the Bretton Woods agreements would favor their development goals. For example, the IBRD's development-lending role was strongly supported not just by Latin American officials but also by policymakers from China, India, and eastern Europe. Many Southern officials—like their US counterparts—also saw various aspects of the IMF's articles of agreement as favoring their "development" objectives, such as its provision of balance of payments assistance and its support for exchange rate adjustments and capital controls. For the same reason, many Southern countries welcomed the kinds of domestic financial and monetary reforms recommended by White, Triffin, and US officials during, and in the immediate wake of, the Bretton Woods negotiations.

---

54. For another analysis that emphasizes the role of coalitions between US and Latin American reformers in driving the Good Neighbor initiatives more generally in this period, see Cobbs 1992.

55. Ikenberry 1992.

In all these contexts, Southern officials often pointed out that the development problems facing their countries were distinctively different from economic issues facing industrialized countries, and they lobbied hard to have their countries' unique needs recognized in the postwar world. These contributions to the discussions were reminiscent of those made by Southern representatives during the 1960s and 1970s. Of course, the geographical breadth of the Southern representation in the Bretton Woods negotiations was much narrower than in international economic discussions of that later period, since vast areas of the poorer regions of the world remained under colonial rule. Still, the content of Southern inputs into the debates—and the broader North-South axis of much of the discussion at the Bretton Woods conference—anticipated later dynamics in striking ways.

The Origins of International Development

In light of this analysis, it is clear that international development was not invented by Truman's inauguration speech and Cold War politics. The Bretton Woods negotiations were a clear predecessor. Those negotiations, in turn, were predated by other development-related initiatives that served as a backdrop for the Bretton Woods discussions. The most important of these were the initiatives associated with the US–Latin American financial partnership that had such an important influence on the development content of Bretton Woods. Even earlier advocacy of international development came from Sun Yat-sen, whose 1918 book *International Development of China* inspired the Chinese official position at Bretton Woods as well as some American thinkers in the 1940s. As noted above, the League of Nations also backed some limited international development activities. In addition, new British interest in colonial development in the interwar period may have helped to shape the country's support for some of the development provisions of Bretton Woods.

Truman was not even the first to popularize the term "underdeveloped." On the contrary, that term was used widely in American and British policy debates during the early 1940s (with some uses also predating Benson's alleged invention of the term).[56] Further complicating the claims of postdevelopment scholarship is the fact that some Southern officials also used the term before Truman's speech. At the Bretton Woods conference itself, Indian delegates even attempted to insert it in the Fund's articles of agreement. To further their development goals, the

---

56. The use of the term by Paul Rosenstein-Rodan in 1944 in discussions within Britain's Royal Institute of International Affairs (see chapter 9) is particularly noteworthy given that Esteva (1992, 7) explicitly mentions him as someone who did not use the term.

Indian delegation proposed that the Fund's mandate should include the following phrase: "to assist in the fuller utilisation of the resources of economically underdeveloped countries."[57] In this context, the politics were the opposite of those suggested by postdevelopment scholars. Rather than the term "underdeveloped" being invoked by US officials to justify intervention in Southern countries, it was used by Southern officials as part of an effort to demand greater international support for their development goals. Moreover, the initiative to insert this wording in the Fund's mandate was blocked by US officials (who feared that the Fund's lending mandate might then overlap with that of the Bank).

The development content of the Bretton Woods negotiations was also different from what Truman endorsed. While the latter focused primarily on the provision of technical assistance, the former was more ambitious in the specific ways described above and in its broad support of state-led development strategies. The international development project thus had a wider set of meanings in its early years than the Truman-centered view presented in much current scholarship.[58] To be sure, the breadth of the meanings should not be overstated. Most of the participants in the discussions examined in this book saw "development" as a national project of industrialization and modernization designed to catch up to the leading economies. Very few prominent officials or political leaders—Gandhi was an exception—questioned this basic model in the broader way that postdevelopment scholarship does today. Still, within the limits of this framework, the Bretton Woods vision was much more supportive of a role for the public sector in achieving development goals—at the national and international level—than the Truman-centered view allows.

The politics generating the international development content of Bretton Woods were also not quite the same as those identified in prominent postdevelopment literature. It is certainly true that US policymakers saw this content as serving their country's strategic and economic interests. But the key strategic threat that drove much of the US policy innovation in this era was the Nazi threat in the late 1930s and early 1940s rather than the Cold War of Truman's era. Indeed, the Cold War had the effect of diluting, rather than strengthening, the US commitment to international development for reasons explained in the concluding chapter. In addition, US officials were more inclined in this earlier period to see their country's economic interests served by a new international division of labor involving extensive Southern industrialization. Also important was the fact that US support for international development at this time was influenced

---

57. US State Department 1948, 23.
58. See also Cullather 2000, 650; Cooper and Packard 1977, 10. This case also reinforces Corbridge's (2007) broader argument about the need to recognize the plurality of development ideologies.

strongly by the values of the New Deal. Indeed, if a US president was to be chosen as a pioneer of international development, Franklin Roosevelt deserves the title much more than Truman.

Southern officials and analysts also played an active role in pioneering this earlier international development initiative. In much postdevelopment scholarship, the South appears largely as a passive recipient of an international development project foisted upon it by Northern powers driven by economic and Cold War imperatives. During the US–Latin American initiatives of the late 1930s and early 1940s and the Bretton Woods negotiations, however, Southern officials and analysts played a significant role in shaping, and actively assisting in, the birth of the project of international development. Indeed, they were a major source of the demand for this innovation in world politics.

There is a certain irony in the neglect within postdevelopment literature of the agency of these Southern figures. Postdevelopment scholars critique much existing development analysis for portraying those living in the South as "lacking in historical agency,"[59] but their own understanding suffers from the same weakness. Indeed, important pioneers of international development from poorer regions of the world receive little or no attention in prominent postdevelopment analyses of the origins of international development, including not just figures such as Sun and Prebisch but also others such as Leon Baranski, Chintaman Deshmukh, Antonio Espinosa de los Monteros, Paul Rosenstein-Rodan, Victor Urquidi, and Eduardo Villaseñor, to name a few.[60]

Postdevelopment scholars might respond by questioning the content of the ideas put forward by these individuals. For example, Escobar downplays the significance of the ideas of Latin American economists such as Prebisch who were associated with the Economic Commission for Latin America (ECLA) in the late 1940s and 1950s, on the grounds that they did not pose a "radical challenge" to dominant Northern discourse since they were still committed to a "modernization process" and "development remained in essense, in the eyes of these economists, a process of capital accumulation and technical progress."[61] The same criticism would likely be leveled against the ideas of Southern analysts described here since they were very similar to those of ECLA economists. But it would be incorrect to argue that these ideas were simply derivative of Northern thinking. The international flow of ideas also went from South to North, with a number of

59. Escobar 1995, 8.

60. For example, of these names, only Prebisch is cited in the index of Rist (1997, 109, 113). Escobar (1995, 72, 90–91) mentions only Prebisch and Rosenstein-Rodan briefly.

61. Escobar 1995, 81. Escobar (1995, 63, 74, 76–80) is also critical of the ideas of the Caribbean economist Arthur Lewis, who was a Southern advocate of development policies along similar lines as Prebisch and others in the early 1940s.

Southern officials and analysts—such as Sun and Prebisch—influencing Northern ideas about international development in this period. Ideas also flowed among the poorer regions, as in the cases of eastern European influence on Latin American development thinking, the sharing of ideas among Latin Americans, and the mutual learning among eastern European intellectuals and officials living in Britain during the war.[62]

Even more important is the fact that Southern development goals responded less to the international ideational or discursive environment (which is a key focus of postdevelopment analysis) than to a number of new structural material circumstances facing Southern countries: the traumatic depression experience, the international strategic uncertainties of the time, and widening international inequalities. In these circumstances, officials and thinkers in different poorer parts of the world appeared to arrive independently—and almost simultaneously—at the view that industrialization and economic modernization were needed to reduce their countries' economic and strategic vulnerability. Given the scale of the task they faced and the growing density of the international institutional landscape, they were also prompted to consider whether international support for their goals could help boost living standards and their countries' economic development more quickly. Far from being a tool of oppression, the discourse of international development appeared to these Southern officials and analysts as a potential source of support for national empowerment and advancement.[63]

Building on Previous Scholarship

The arguments here thus challenge much conventional wisdom, but I do not break entirely new ground. My interest in this aspect of the origins of the Bretton Woods system began when, in the course of researching another project, I stumbled across some US archives from the early 1940s that discussed international development issues. After exploring further archival evidence, I read wider secondary literature on this period and found a number of existing analyses that

---

62. See also Love 1996.

63. See also Cooper and Packard 1977, 4; Cooper 1997, 84. In the second edition of the influential postdevelopment book *The Development Dictionary*, Wolfgang Sachs acknowledges that the Southern demand for development was understated in the first, 1992 edition: "Looking at *The Development Dictionary* today, it is striking that we had not really appreciated the extent to which the development idea has been charged with hopes for redress and self-affirmation. It certainly was an invention of the West, as we showed at length, but not just an imposition on the rest. On the contrary, as the desire for recognition and equity is framed in terms of the civilizational model of the powerful nations, the South has emerged as the staunchest defender of development." He also notes: "Self-defense against the hegemonic powers has been an important motive of the drive for development until today" (Sachs 2010, viii–ix).

picked up, and contributed to, important parts of the story I was reading in the archives. The relevant scholarship is referenced and discussed in the chapters that follow, but four particularly useful bodies of scholarship are worth noting at the outset.

To begin with, this book builds on the work of some historians of the Bretton Woods negotiations who have touched on various themes developed here. Important insights have been drawn from some analyses of specific Southern country experiences during the negotiations, such as those of China, India, Mexico, and Brazil.[64] The significance of the US–Latin American partnership for the Bretton Woods experience has also been identified by a few scholars.[65] Drawing on extensive archival evidence, I here extend their analyses and also examine in more detail the broader politics that generated the development dimensions of that partnership and its link to Bretton Woods.

Second, this book is not the first to locate the birth of international development earlier than Truman's speech. Scholars such as Heinz Arndt, Amy Staples, and Elizabeth Borgwardt have identified US and British wartime planning as the key origin.[66] Others have found earlier sources in US thinking and policy innovations during the interwar years as well as in changing British colonial practices in that same period.[67] Drawing insights from these important works, I explore the important role of the Bretton Woods negotiations in the emergence of international development in greater detail.[68] I also seek to widen the geographical focus beyond the United States and Britain, the main focus of these analyses, in order to explore the views of policymakers and analysts from poorer countries. In addition, I call attention to an issue that is quite overlooked in these analyses: the significance of US–Latin American financial relations in the late 1930s and early 1940s for the origins of international development.[69]

For the latter task, the book draws considerably on a third body of literature: historical analyses of Roosevelt's Good Neighbor policy toward Latin America

---

64. These various country-specific analyses are cited in chapters 6,7, and 9.

65. See especially Bordo and Schwartz 2001; Oliver 1975; Boughton 2004. See also references in chapter 2.

66. Arndt 1987, Staples 2006, Borgwardt 2005.

67. See for example Alcalde 1987, Cullather 2010, Ekbladh 2010, Hodge 2007, Havinden and Meredith 1993.

68. The interesting analyses of both Staples and Borgwardt each devote a chapter to the Bretton Woods planning process. A discussion of Bretton Woods is largely absent from Ekbladh's important book which cites the conventional wisdom that the IBRD's development mandate arrived "almost by accident" (Ekbladh 2010, 90). Alcalde (1987, 175–76) also downplays the development content of Bretton Woods.

69. Of these works cited above, Alcalde's impressive (and often neglected) analysis devotes the most attention to the Good Neighbor policy (1987, 119–31) and Southern views more generally, although his focus is still on the US and British roles in backing the idea of economic development.

in the late 1930s and early 1940s. Some historians have identified this policy's significance in pioneering international development practices, but the link between the Good Neighbor policy and the Bretton Woods negotiations has been overlooked.[70] I focus on two key aspects of the Good Neighbor policy that were critical to this link and that have received less attention in historical literature: the 1939–40 effort to establish the IAB and the US financial advisory missions to Latin America that began in 1941. The analysis here of the relationship between the Good Neighbor policy and Bretton Woods also devotes considerable attention to the Latin American activities of some US policymakers, such as Harry Dexter White and Robert Triffin, who have been quite neglected in general histories of the Good Neighbor policy.[71]

Finally, in broadening the focus beyond the United States and Britain, I draw inspiration from the work of several scholars who have analyzed the growing development focus of Southern officials and analysts in the 1930s and early 1940s. One such scholar is Joseph Love, whose important analysis shows how development aspirations in this period emerged not just from Northern sources but also from eastern European and Latin American economists.[72] For Latin America, other indispensable sources for this line of argument are Edgar Dosman's recent biography of Prebisch as well as Sarah Babb's analysis of the origins of developmental economic thought in Mexico.[73] Also important is Margherita Zanasi's work on China's interwar development thought and policy, which includes a critique of the assumption in postdevelopment scholarship that Southern governments were simply passive spectators of early international development initiatives.[74] While these analyses highlight the need to explore the Southern origins of international development, they are not focused on the importance of the Bretton Woods process itself.

Overview

The focus in the first three chapters is on the creative financial partnership between US and Latin American policymakers that emerged during the late

---

70. For recognition of the policy's significance in pioneering international development, see Cobbs 1992, 2–3; Grow 1981, 36; Adamson 2005. For the wider literature, see references in the chapters 1–3.

71. For example, neither White nor Triffin is even listed in the indexes of important books on the Good Neighbor policy such as Gellman 1979 and Pike 1995.

72. Love 1996.

73. Dosman 2008, Babb 2001.

74. See especially Zanasi 2007, 146. See also Zanasi 2006.

1930s and early 1940s and helped prepare the ground for the building of the development foundations of Bretton Woods. Chapter 1 explores the motivations that inspired this financial partnership on both the US and the Latin American sides. It also provides an overview of a number of the initiatives that grew out of this partnership before the entry of the United States into World War II, from US lending for short-term Latin American currency stabilization and long-term development purposes in 1938–39 to the more ambitious initiatives of 1940 to stabilize the prices of major commodity exports, renegotiate external debts, and promote regional economic cooperation.

The next two chapters provide a detailed analysis of two initiatives in this period that were particularly important in setting the scene for Bretton Woods. The first was the negotiation of the IAB in the fall of 1939 and spring of 1940 by the US and Latin American governments. The IAB's charter had an explicit mandate to promote Latin American development and some of its provisions acted as important precedents for White's first drafts of the IMF and the World Bank. The second was the US financial advisory mission sent to Cuba under White's leadership in 1941–42. The mission backed the Cuban government's development goals by recommending an overhaul of the country's monetary system through de-dollarization and the creation of a new governmentally controlled central bank that could pursue a more activist monetary policy aimed at domestic needs.

Both the IAB proposal and the Cuban mission were slightly ahead of their time. Despite support from the Roosevelt administration and many Latin American governments, the IAB was never created because it failed to receive US Congressional approval. The Cuban mission encountered opposition from US financial interests as well as from various Cuban opponents who succeeded in delaying the adoption of its recommendations by the Cuban Congress. Despite these failures, both the IAB initiative and the Cuban mission served as key precursors for the Bretton Woods negotiations. The IAB project pioneered a new kind of multilateral public financial institution, while the Cuban mission's advice set a precedent for a new model of money doctoring that worked to realize embedded liberal values in Southern countries. Many of the key figures involved in these initiatives also went on to play leading roles in Bretton Woods planning.

If the US-Latin American financial partnership prepared the ground, US plans for the postwar international financial order played a critical role in building the foundations for the Bretton Woods agreements. Drawing on detailed analysis of primary materials, chapter 4 corrects the common misconception that White's early proposals displayed no interest in development issues. Those proposals built directly on the experience of the US–Latin American initiatives of the late 1930s and early 1940s, and he and other US policymakers also had a Latin American audience clearly in mind in developing the early drafts. While some of the ambition of White's original development proposals was watered down by internal US government discussions in 1942–43, the core US commitment to international development remained strong throughout the negotiations leading up to the Bretton Woods conference. It was also widespread across many branches of the Roosevelt administration as well as among influential Americans outside of government.

US support for international development manifested itself during the Bretton Woods negotiations in yet other way, discussed in chapter 5. In 1943–44, the US Federal Reserve responded to a request from Paraguay for a financial advisory mission to help create a new national currency and central bank. Under Robert Triffin's leadership, the mission provided similar advice to that of White's Cuban mission, but now argued explicitly that this would help reinforce, at the domestic level, the goals of the Bretton Woods agreements. In this work, Triffin also did much more than White to reach out for advice and assistance to Latin American experts, most notably Prebisch. Triffin was also more successful than White had been in Cuba: his advice was immediately adopted by the Paraguayan government which saw its monetary reforms as key for its developmental ambitions.

Latin American governments were active players in the Bretton Woods negotiations, showing particular interest in how postwar plans could help them achieve their development aspirations. In chapter 6, we see them playing an important role in protecting and strengthening the IBRD's development mandate which they saw as a direct follow-on from the stillborn IAB. They were also strong supporters—on development grounds—of the IMF's balance of payments lending and its provisions for exchange rate adjustments and capital controls, as well as of a conference resolution endorsing future negotiations to address international commodity marketing and pricing. Latin American support for the Bretton Woods vision was also apparent in the widespread interest that Triffin's 1943–44 Paraguayan mission received across the region. After returning from Paraguay, Triffin was kept busy for several years responding—sometimes in consultation with Prebisch—to a number of Latin American governments' requests for him to emulate his work for Paraguay in their countries.

Chapter 7 examines the support for the development content of Bretton Woods that came from the only two East Asian countries represented at the conference: China and the Philippines. During the Bretton Woods negotiations, China was seen by US officials as one of the four great powers that would help govern the postwar world, and the Chinese government used this status to lobby for a postwar international financial order that would assist its ambitious state-led development goals. In so doing, it drew explicit inspiration from a deeper legacy than that of any other country: Sun Yat-sen's 1918 proposals. This objective found favor well beyond the Kuomintang government that represented

China at Bretton Woods; US officials discovered after the conference that even the leadership of the rival Chinese Communist Party shared it. Representatives of the Philippines played a much more low-key role during the Bretton Woods negotiations, but soon after the conference they linked their participation in the Bretton Woods system to United States–supported domestic monetary reforms of the kind that White and Triffin had promoted in Latin America. These reforms highlighted another way in which the Good Neighbor financial partnership generated innovations of wider geographical relevance for the construction of the development foundations of Bretton Woods.

Keynes and many other British officials also favored the inclusion of international development goals in the postwar international financial order. As explained in chapter 8, however, Britain did not take a leadership role in this area and the interest of many of its officials in development issues during the Bretton Woods negotiations was much more lukewarm than that of US officials (as well as that of some officials from other higher-income countries such as the Netherlands, Canada, and Australia). The British also did not show the same enthusiasm as US officials for development-oriented monetary reforms. The contrast between US and British views on this issue was particularly stark in regard to one of the countries that attended the Bretton Woods conference: Ethiopia.

Chapter 9 discusses the much greater enthusiasm for the international development content of Bretton Woods among officials and analysts from two regions with close links to Britain at this time: eastern Europe and India. A number of individuals from eastern Europe living in Britain at the time of the war (some representing governments-in-exile) put together ambitious international development plans to encourage state-led industrialization and rising living standards in their region. These proposals found their way into British (and US) postwar planning discussions as well as into the Bretton Woods negotiations themselves through the participation of eastern European governments. The demand for international development also came from India, which was represented at the Bretton Woods conference partly by Indians and partly by British officials because of its status as a British colony. Like eastern European and Latin American officials, many Indians had ambitious development goals for their soon-to-be-independent country and they backed the development content of Bretton Woods negotiations in hopes that it could provide international support for their domestic plans.

In a concluding chapter, I briefly explore the fate of the development foundations of Bretton Woods. United States support for the international development goals of Bretton Woods quickly unraveled as a result of domestic political shifts following Roosevelt's death in 1945 and changing strategic priorities, particularly the onset of the Cold War. Two of the major Southern supporters of the

Bretton Woods development content—(mainland) China and eastern Europe—also ceased to be part of the Bretton Woods system in the early Cold War years. Those Southern governments that remained expressed their frustrations with the lack of international support for their development goals and their calls for reform were soon echoed by others when decolonization in Africa and Asia accelerated during the 1950s and 1960s, culminating in demands for the NIEO by the early 1970s. Some modest international economic reforms emerged from this period that built upon the development foundations of Bretton Woods, but Bretton Woods itself was rarely invoked. Although support for the NIEO collapsed in the early 1980s, North-South debates about reforming the global financial system are reemerging with the present-day shifts in economic power, once again bringing relevance to the forgotten foundations of Bretton Woods.

GOOD NEIGHBORS PREPARE THE GROUND

It is widely recognized that Franklin Delano Roosevelt ushered in a new chapter in US–Latin American relations when he renounced military intervention in the region soon after coming into office in 1933. Less well known is the fact that his Good Neighbor policy expanded in the late 1930s and early 1940s to include a more active idea of an inter-American financial partnership designed to promote economic development across Latin America, which in turn pioneered new policies and ideas that prepared the ground for the construction of the international development foundations of Bretton Woods.

The new US interest in promoting Latin American development stemmed from a complex mix of economic interests, strategic goals, and New Deal values. Latin American policymakers welcomed US support for increasingly their ambitious development aspirations, particularly since the support came from US officials who publicly rejected past imperialist practices. Working together, US and Latin American officials generated creative financial initiatives, some bilateral and others regionwide. However, the Good Neighbor financial partnership encountered powerful critics—particularly within the United States—whose opposition undermined the ambitions of the partnership and also foreshadowed criticism of the Bretton Woods plans a few years later.

Political Origins of the Partnership

To understand the origins of the Good Neighbor financial partnership, it is necessary first to recognize the impact of the Great Depression on Latin American economic policymaking. The global economic crisis of 1929–33 severely affected Latin American countries, most of which had been heavily dependent during the 1920s on commodity exports as well as on private capital inflows. The collapse of export markets, commodity prices, and foreign investment dealt these economies a serious blow and undermined existing liberal economic policy regimes.[1] During the crisis and in its immediate wake, many Latin American governments abandoned the gold standard, defaulted on external debts, imposed exchange controls, and increased state involvement in the domestic economy by offering public assistance to distressed businesses and societal groups.

During the lead-up to World War II, domestic criticism of the laissez-faire, export-oriented economic policies of the past intensified. Latin American critics of economic liberalism—on both the left and the right of the political spectrum—argued that those policies had left their countries unprotected from global economic instability and locked into dependence on their raw material exports. They called for statist and nationalist economic policies that would focus more squarely on the goal of national economic development via greater public ownership, import-substitution industrialization (which had already been accelerating in some Latin American countries with the collapse of the world economy), and the promotion of larger domestic markets as well as improved social conditions and living standards. As the international security situation became more uncertain in the late 1930s, these interventionist policies were also backed for the strategic reason that they could enhance national power and autonomy. The outbreak of World War II in September 1939 intensified this trend and also challenged liberal economic regimes in new ways as trade with Europe collapsed. With unsold agricultural surpluses, import shortages, and general economic upheavals, even quite liberal Latin American governments were prompted to intervene in their domestic economies to a much greater degree than they had done in the past.[2]

Scholars emphasize how the new support for state-led development and industrialization objectives emerged more as a practical response to changing material circumstances facing Latin America at the time than out of the influence of a coherent new theoretical or ideological paradigm.[3] But in calling for greater state intervention in the economy, some Latin American analysts and policymakers drew broad inspiration from Roosevelt's New Deal and the Keynesian revolution in economics. The heightened criticism of Latin America's dependence on commodity exporting was also reminiscent of the ideas of nineteenth-century critics of economic liberalism such as Friedrich List. Some Latin Americans on

---

1. Diaz-Alejandro 1988.
2. See for example, Gilderhus 2000, 104–7; Rock 1994.
3. Love 1996, 120; Sikkink 1991, 53.

the left were also attracted by the example of the Soviet Union's policies that appeared to be transforming a largely poor and agricultural country into a major industrial power in a very short period of time. As Michael Grow points out, the emergence of fascist governments in Europe also offered to some Latin Americans on the right a "supremely developmentalist ideology" in which the international economic system was depicted as "a ruthless and dangerously unstable arena, crowded with nations competing for wealth and status."[4]

United States Strategic and Economic Interests

It was in fact the fear of growing Nazi influence in Latin America that provided the crucial catalyst for US officials to begin to develop the idea of the Good Neighbor financial partnership. In addition to exporting fascist ideology, the German government began in 1934 an aggressive economic campaign to expand trade with Latin America via exclusive trade agreements, export subsidies, barter, and promises of high prices for Latin American exports. The campaign produced a large increase in German–Latin American trade, often at the expense of US exports to the region. This concerned many Roosevelt administration officials who saw US exports to Latin America as an important component of their efforts to promote a US economic recovery.[5] United States policymakers also became increasingly concerned about challenges to US security interests as Germany intensified diplomatic efforts to build stronger political and military ties with the region in the late 1930s. Latin America was an important source of various strategic raw materials for US defense production, a source whose importance was growing as Japan expanded its influence across Asia in the late 1930s and early 1940s. United States officials also worried that support for the Nazis and fascist ideology might be substantial in a number of Latin American countries. After the outbreak of World War II, US policymakers even became concerned about possible German military incursions into Latin America.[6]

From the late 1930s onward, American officials increasingly saw a new financial partnership with Latin America as an important tool for meeting the German challenge. They hoped US encouragement for Latin American development goals would cultivate alliances in the region as well as offset the appeal of Nazi ideology. It would also secure and expand export markets for US firms, particularly those producing the capital goods that could assist Latin American efforts to build up local industrial production of consumer goods. After the outbreak

---

4. Grow 1981, 11.
5. Gardner 1964; Gellman 1979; Green 1971; Grow 1981; Pike 1995.
6. Green 1971, chap. 4; Friedman 2003; Haglund 1984.

of World War II, many US policymakers came to see the creation of a more integrated economic bloc with Latin America as a mechanism to exclude Germany, secure US economic interests in the region, reorient Latin American economies after the loss of European markets, and build closer inter-American political cooperation.

In addition to serving these goals, the new partnership with Latin America helped to address US concerns about how increasingly unorthodox economic policies in Latin America—coming from both left- and right-wing governments—could threaten American economic interests more generally. Latin America was not just an export market and a source of important commodities but also a profitable investment location for many US businesses. As Latin American economic policies moved in increasingly statist and nationalist directions, some of these US economic interests were threatened directly, a point brought home clearly by the 1937 Bolivian and 1938 Mexican confiscations of US oil companies' property. By offering help for more moderate development goals of Latin American governments, US policymakers hoped to promote political and economic stability and offset the appeal of more radical economic ideologies.[7]

New Deal Values

Historians argue that the Roosevelt administration's interest in the Good Neighbor financial partnership stemmed not just from US strategic or economic interests but also from the values of the New Deal.[8] Many New Dealers saw Latin American experiments in state-regulated capitalism as similar to their own initiatives within the United States, and thus deserving of support. During his 1936 visit to Brazil, Roosevelt described the Vargas regime as having introduced a "South American New Deal."[9] He also saw Mexican President Cárdenas as a kindred spirit.[10] More generally, historian Frederick Pike writes of "the common ground that American and Latin American intellectuals found in condemning business civilization" at this time, and argues that "without that convergence, there could have been no Good Neighbor policy."[11]

The belief of New Dealers in greater government intervention in the economy also encouraged them to explore how the public sector could take on the role of

---

7. For the various US motivations, see Gardner 1964, Gellman 1979, Green 1971, Grow 1981, Pike 1995.

8. See especially Gellman 1979, Pike 1995, Wood 1961, Rivas 2002.

9. Quoted in Weis 2000, 138.

10. Stiller 1987, 96. For the affinity perceived between Cardenas' regime and the New Deal by US officials, see also Cullather 2010, 50–1.

11. Pike 1995, 15.

promoting international development. They had already experimented with government initiatives aimed at generating rising standards of living in poor regions within the United States. The best-known was the Tennessee Valley Authority (TVA), an ambitious regional development program overseen by a government-sponsored public corporation involved in activities ranging from public health and education to hydroelectric power development and agricultural improvement. Its apparent success encouraged US policymakers to consider "international TVA" initiatives to raise living standards abroad through a more liberal form of planning that was different from the communist and fascist variety.[12] Many initiatives examined here reflect the willingness of New Dealers to turn to the public sector in promoting Latin America's development in other ways as well.

The New Deal economists involved in the Good Neighbor financial partnership (and Bretton Woods planning) also often favored the Keynesian revolution that was under way in the economic discipline at the time. Although Keynes wrote relatively little about development issues, Albert Hirschman and others have highlighted how he indirectly encouraged new interest in development economics by asserting that neoclassical ideas applied only in certain contexts. Through his rejection of the "monoeconomic" claim of neoclassical economics to universal validity, Keynes legitimized inquiries into the distinctive problems of Southern countries.[13] This openness to, and indeed enthusiasm for, the study of the distinctive economic difficulties facing Latin American economies characterized many of the New Deal economists involved in the Good Neighbor policy.

In addition, some New Dealers saw the project of extending financial assistance to Latin America as an opportunity to transfer their humanitarian concern for the poor onto the international stage. For example, historian Darlene Rivas has called attention to the role of "humanitarian and moral impulses" in driving US policy toward Latin America in this period.[14] As Roosevelt told a group of skeptical business reporters in early 1940, the new US support for Latin American development was designed to "give them a share." Historian David Green notes how Roosevelt made clear that this "share" was to include "both a share of decision-making authority in inter-American economic concerns and a share of the wealth being developed from Latin America's vast resources by private and public capital."[15]

For many New Dealers, the sense of solidarity with Latin America was reinforced by their antipathy toward the New York financial community. Before the

---

12. Ekbladh 2010, chap. 2.
13. Hirschman 1981. See also Singer 1984, 277; Toye 1987, 39–40; Babb 2001, 7.
14. Rivas 2002, 7.
15. Green 1971, 38.

1930s, US officials had commonly attributed Latin America's economic problems to Latin Americans themselves. As James Park puts it, "this collective wisdom held that Latin Americans were a racially inferior people handicapped by an authoritarian, medieval cultural legacy and by a tropical setting inimical to progress."[16] The depression, however, led many New Dealers to see Latin Americans in a new light, as victims of the same New York financial elite that they blamed for America's economic troubles.[17] Senate hearings in 1933–34 that investigated the lending practices of New York financiers during the 1920s only reinforced this perspective.[18] The committee's counsel, Ferdinand Pecora, attracted widespread and sympathetic attention across the country with his analysis of the corruption and greed associated with Wall Street loans to Latin America, reinforcing growing criticisms of militarism and exploitation associated with the pre-1930s dollar diplomacy of the US government toward the region. As antibanker discourses mixed with anti-imperialist ones, many Americans saw support for Latin America as an opportunity to correct past wrongs in US economic relations with the region.[19]

The extent to which US popular perceptions of Latin America shifted during this period was apparent in the late 1930s when "a craze for things Latin American swept the country" and Hollywood films "displayed an almost reverential attitude towards things Latin American."[20] As we shall see, many of the US officials involved in the Good Neighbor financial partnership were also keenly interested in learning from Latin American experience rather than seeing themselves as experts bringing superior knowledge. In this period, American expert analyses of Latin American poverty also increasingly emphasized the role of external factors—rather than domestic ones—such as foreign exploitation and the region's dependence on one or two export commodities. Analyses of the latter sometimes even drew links to the US farming experience during the depression. For example, in a 1940 Congressional debate on US loans to Latin America, one analyst pointed out that "these are commodity countries. Many of them are in the kind of trouble Kansas would have been in if it were an independent nation and dependent wholly on its wheat crop."[21]

Finally, interest in international development policies was encouraged by the New Deal's emphasis on individual economic security. Borgwardt notes that a

---

16. Park 1995, 3.
17. Pike 1995.
18. Pike 1995, 29.
19. Rosenberg 2003.
20. Park 1995, 132, 143. Park notes that the US government also actively encouraged this interest in Latin America as part of the Good Neighbor policy.
21. Quoted in Park 1995, 148.

"dominant motif" of the New Deal was its focus on "security for individuals" and the "connection between individual security and the stability and security of the wider polity."[22] As the Nazi threat in Latin America grew, Roosevelt began to internationalize this idea, arguing that the promotion of rising living standards in the region could help promote political stability and peace in the Americas in a high-profile speech to an important inter-American conference in Buenos Aires in December 1936. The conference had been conceived by influential foreign policy adviser Sumner Welles to encourage inter-American solidarity against fascism, and it "amounted to his [Roosevelt's] debut on the international stage."[23] Here is the rationale that Roosevelt provided at the conference for promoting rising living standards abroad: "Through democratic processes we can strive to achieve for the Americas the highest possible standard of living conditions for all our people. Men and women blessed with political freedom, willing to work and able to find work, rich enough to maintain their families and to educate their children, contented with their lot in life and on terms of friendship with their neighbors will defend themselves to the utmost but will never consent to take up arms for a war of conquest."[24] This link between rising living standards and international peace was one that would become even more prominent in New Deal plans for the postwar world during the early 1940s.

Opposition within the United States

Not everyone in the United States agreed with the new US economic policy toward Latin America.[25] New York financial interests—often led by W. Randolph Burgess of National City Bank, as we shall see—were particularly critical. Many conservative bankers saw the new policy as an extension into foreign economic policy of misguided New Deal interventionist economics in ways that dangerously "politicized" international economic relations and encouraged departures from free-market policies abroad. United States financiers were also concerned that new public-sector lending to Latin America would cut into their own business in the region, and that the US government should not assist countries that had defaulted on their payments until these countries had reached settlements with creditors.

The politics of Latin American debt settlements had in fact become increasingly intractable by the late 1930s, with approximately half of Latin American

---

22. Borgwardt 2005, 78.
23. O'Sullivan 2008, 23. See also Schwartz 1987, 122.
24. Quoted in Gantenbein 1950, 176.
25. See especially Green 1971, chap. 3; Pike 1995.

countries still in default in 1938. When the Roosevelt administration had come to power in 1933, it had taken the position that the US government would not be directly involved in any efforts to collect the Latin American debts of private US citizens. To avoid any appearance of dollar diplomacy, it had created the Foreign Bondholders Protective Council in late 1933 to act as an independent body to negotiate debt settlements with Latin American governments in a "disinterested" manner independent from Wall Street influence.[26] By the late 1930s, however, the council's own financial difficulties led it to come under the influence of bondholders who were reluctant to discuss with debtors any reduction in the principal of outstanding debts.[27] In the aftermath of the Bolivian and Mexican confiscations of US properties, many US corporations with direct investments in the region also joined the bondholders in opposing economic assistance for countries that had not settled with investors, a position that found some support in Congress and among more conservative members of the Roosevelt administration.[28]

Corporate opposition to the new US–Latin American financial partnership should not be overstated. As we shall see, Nelson Rockefeller assembled a group of reform-minded business leaders who were very much in favor of partnership.[29] By the late 1930s, some large US industrial firms backed import-substitution industrialization in Latin America because it created new export markets for their machinery and new opportunities for foreign investment via the establishment of manufacturing subsidiaries behind local tariff walls to produce for local markets.[30] United States officials were well aware of these divisions within the business community.[31]

Another source of opposition to the Good Neighbor financial partnership consisted of isolationists in Congress such as Republicans Arthur Vandenberg and Robert Taft.[32] They objected to the spending of public money abroad, and their critiques were often wrapped up with broader opposition to the interventionist economic policies of the New Deal that was similar to that of many US bankers. Concerns about the statist nature of US overtures to Latin America were

---

26. Quote from White House statement of October 20, 1933 announcing the creation of the council, quoted in Corbett to Knoke, December 9, 1939, p. 8, ISF, box 152. See Adamson 2002.

27. Wallich to Sproul, March 6, 1942, ISF, box 152; Bemis 1943, 339–40; Green 1971, 21, 40–41; Pike 1995, 246; Blum 1965, 52–58; Gellman 1979, 41.

28. Langer and Gleason 1970, 207; Gellman 1979, 156.

29. Rivas 2002.

30. Maxfield and Nolt 1990, 55–56.

31. See for example Schmidt, Spiegel, and Hanson, "Protection and Promotion by the United Government of American and Financial Interests in Foreign Countries," April 18, 1939, p. 5, CFHDW, box 2, file 13.

32. See for example Pike 1995, 36–38; Green 1971, 67–68; Gellman 1979, 2, 12; Blum 1965, 50; Patterson 1972, 190, 192, 196.

also expressed by other Republicans and by conservative Democrats in Congress. Even within the Roosevelt administration itself, more conservative figures such as Jesse Jones (who headed the Reconstruction Finance Corporation from 1932 and then served as commerce secretary between 1940 and 1945) were skeptical of the role of the public sector in international lending.[33] Many officials in the State Department were also often viewed at this time as sympathetic to Wall Street interests and, more generally, as "still largely in thrall to its tradition of interventionism and instinctive disdain for Latin Americans."[34] Frederick Pike observes that, in a kind of "anticipatory McCarthyism," J. Edgar Hoover also worried that US policy toward Latin America had been, in Pike's words, "taken over by un-American radicals," and that "the Good Neighbor policy had become hopelessly 'soft' on, hopelessly accommodating to, Latin American statism that was tantamount to disguised communism."[35]

In addition, specific initiatives associated with the Good Neighbor policy were sometimes thwarted by bureaucratic rivalries within the Roosevelt administration. The administration was notorious for its internal turf battles, and policy coherence toward Latin America in the late 1930s and early 1940s was often undermined by struggles between Secretary of State Cordell Hull and Treasury Secretary Henry Morgenthau, as well as rivalries within the State Department itself between Hull and Welles.[36] As a result of New Deal reforms, US foreign financial policy in this period was also frequently characterized by three-way tensions between the Treasury Department, the board of governors of the Federal Reserve system, and the Federal Reserve Bank of New York.

The Latin American Side

How was the idea of the Good Neighbor financial partnership received in Latin America? As we shall see, some of the specific international and domestic initiatives that US policymakers supported in the late 1930s and early 1940s were ones that Latin American policymakers had sought for some time, and they welcomed the new willingness of US policymakers to support these initiatives. They were also pleased that US officials appeared to recognize the new "development" priorities of governments across the region. As Cuban professor Herminio Portell Villa told a US audience in July 1941, "we [Latin Americans] don't want to continue with the colonial economy that we have. We think we are as worthy as the

---

33. Pike 1995, 242.
34. Quote from Friedman 2003, 79. For Wall Street sympathies, see Adamson 2002, 2005.
35. Pike 1995, 202, 203.
36. Kimball 1991, Gellman 1979.

United States to round out our economic structure and to have a higher standard of living in our countries, as you have here." United States help with Latin American industrialization was particularly welcomed. As the director of Mexico's Universidad Obrera, Alejandro Carrillo, told the same audience: "If you believe that Latin-Americans wish to continue producing only raw materials for United States manufacturing industries and remain in that condition forever, you are certainly mistaken. No such opinion prevails in any Latin-American center."[37]

At the official level, US backing for Latin American industrialization objectives played an important role in securing support in the region for the Good Neighbor financial partnership. One of highest-profile examples came in 1940 when the United States offered to assist the building of Brazil's huge steel plant at Volta Redonda with a loan and technical assistance. Since the authoritarian turn of Brazil's president Getúlio Vargas in 1937 and especially since the outbreak of war, he had committed to more nationalist and interventionist economic policies, including state-directed industrialization. In its foreign economic policy, his government played the United States and Germany off against each other. For example, the US offer of help with the Volta Redonda project came at a time when Brazil was also negotiating for assistance from Germany, and it was designed to signal broadly the seriousness of the US commitment to Latin American development.[38] When Brazil accepted the offer and moved firmly into an alliance with the United States, the US support for Latin America's first steel mill became "a symbol of inter-American cooperation, US accommodation of economic nationalism." The architect of Brazil's alliance with the United States at this time was foreign minister Osvaldo Aranha, who had been one of the strongest advocates of economic nationalism and industrialization throughout the 1930s, and who came to see Roosevelt's Good Neighbor policy as furthering those goals.[39]

Mexico provides another interesting example of a major Latin American power endorsing the Good Neighbor financial partnership. Since President Lázaro Cárdenas came to power in 1934, Mexican economic policy had turned in an increasingly nationalist direction, culminating in the expropriation of foreign oil and land holdings in 1938. By mid-1940, however, the long-standing and powerful finance minister Eduardo Suárez (who oversaw the expropriation) had become a strong advocate of closer ties with the United States. Within the Cárdenas administration, he was a leading critic of orthodox economic thinking who favored more activist and nationalist development policies often inspired by Keynesian and New Deal thinking. Suárez played an important role in convincing

---

37. Norman Wait Harris Memorial Foundation 1941, 133, 138.
38. Hilton 1979, 219; Skidmore 1967, 44–45; McCann 1974, chap. 7.
39. Quote from Weis 2000, 141. See also p. 134.

his government colleagues that closer ties with the United States could be used to strengthen Mexican development and industrialization.[40] Those economic ties grew much closer in 1941 after the signing of an agreement that included compensation for the petroleum and land expropriation. Suárez was later selected for the high-profile role of chairing of one of the three "commissions" at the Bretton Woods conference.

Not everyone in Latin America was as supportive of new US policies toward the region. Many Argentine officials distrusted the intentions of the US government and were suspicious that American officials favored Brazil.[41] After the United States joined World War II in December 1941, its relations with Argentina deteriorated further when the latter refused to break off diplomatic relations with the Axis powers—a decision that left it as the only Latin American country not invited to Bretton Woods.[42]

As we shall see, there were also domestic groups in other countries across Latin America who expressed concerns about the Good Neighbor financial partnership. Criticism sometimes came from economic interests that benefited from older patterns of US–Latin American relations or from opponents on ideological grounds of initiatives to expand state intervention in their domestic economies. At the same time, those attracted to fascist or communist ideas felt that the partnership did not go far enough in assisting interventionist policies. Even among supporters, there was some lingering skepticism about US goals in light of past American policy toward the region.[43] As one US official involved in the Good Neighbor financial partnership later acknowledged, "Latin America continually questioned the permanence of our interest, suspecting that the co-operative activity was designed to meet specific short-term requirements of our foreign policy and would shortly be abandoned."[44]

But many in the region also held out hope that a new era in US–Latin American relations was possible, given that New Deal officials themselves offered trenchant critiques of past US behavior in the region. If US officials were now willing to assist more beneficial "development" with public funds, many Latin Americans welcomed the change. As Professor Carrillo put it in 1941,

> we in Mexico are very much opposed to free-lance capitalists coming into the country and investing money in any way they think best,

---

40. Schuler 1998, 18, 22. For Suárez's biography, see Dávila 1977.
41. McCann 1974, 7–8.
42. Argentina finally broke off relations in January 1944 and declared war in March 1945. See Woods 1979.
43. See for example Inman 1944, 3–4.
44. Hanson 1950, 66.

because we believe that that type of investment would tend to disrupt Mexican economic life instead of helping to develop it. . . . [But] if American capital investment is to be a government affair between the United States and the respective governments of Latin-America, I am sure that Mexico, for one, will be more than willing to go into a venture like this.[45]

What Initiatives?

Early efforts to create the Good Neighbor financial partnership appeared between late 1938 and mid-1939 when the Roosevelt administration began to extend financial assistance to the region in the form of short-term loans to support currency stabilization and longer-term loans to assist specific Latin American state-sponsored development projects. Within the State Department, Sumner Welles was the major supporter of this public lending program largely because of his concerns about growing Axis influence in the region. His appointment as Under Secretary of State in 1937 was part of an effort by Roosevelt—whose friend Welles had been for decades—to bring the State Department more into line with New Deal priorities.[46] Another close colleague of Roosevelt, Treasury Secretary Morgenthau, was also very keen on US public assistance for Latin America. In late 1938, he had argued that the United States needed a "financial Monroe Doctrine" to counter Axis influence in the region.[47]

Another enthusiast in the Treasury was Harry Dexter White who was serving at this time as the influential director of the department's Division of Monetary Research, a position he had assumed in March 1938.[48] White's background and views deserve more detailed attention because of his lead role in this period and in the Bretton Woods negotiations. Born to Russian immigrants, White had earned a Ph.D. from Harvard in 1930 at the age of thirty-eight, and he had then taught briefly at a Wisconsin college before joining the Treasury in 1934. Like Morgenthau, White was an "ardent New Dealer" who had shown an early willingness to challenge orthodox economic thinking.[49] For example, in his Ph.D. (which had won the prestigious Wells Prize at Harvard and was published in

---

45. Norman Wait Harris Memorial Foundation 1941, 112–13.
46. Stiller 1987, 96. For Welles's influence and views more generally, see O'Sullivan 2008; Friedman 2003, 78–79; Pike 1995, 202–4; Woods 1979, 23–24.
47. Quoted in Rees 1973, 75. See also Blum 1965, 50.
48. Rees 1973, 74–75, 100; Green 1971, 46.
49. Quote from Van Dormael 1978, 42.

1933), White had questioned neoclassical arguments favoring free capital move-ments.[50] At the height of the Great Depression in 1932, he had also advocated countercyclical fiscal policies to boost employment, several years before Keynes published his *General Theory*.[51] The unorthodox nature of his thinking should not be overstated; he placed a high value on price stability and monetary disci-pline. Indeed, one of his colleagues in the US government later commented that "he was probably the most conservative monetary force in the world during his period in the Treasury Department."[52]

After joining the Treasury, White quickly gained the trust of Morgenthau and he proved to be effective bureaucratic operator. He also made many enemies because of his strong personality and often very gruff style. Even Morgenthau acknowledged years later that White "could be disagreeable . . . quick tempered, overly ambitious, and power went to his head."[53] His role in US policymaking became even more controversial after the war because of accusations that he was a Soviet spy. There is no doubt that White—like many other New Dealers—saw the Soviet Union as an important ally for the United States in the antifascist wartime struggle and the postwar world. In a 2004 book analyzing the issue of White's possible espionage role, Bruce Craig discusses how some of White's sub-ordinates in the Treasury, as well as individuals with whom he had close friend-ships, were involved in spying for the USSR.[54] Craig argues that accusations that White himself actively subverted US foreign policy in various episodes are exag-gerated, but he concludes that there is "little doubt that White was involved in 'a species of espionage'" which involved sharing of information.[55] Several recent

50. White 1933, 301, 311–12.
51. Laidler and Sandilands 2002.
52. Emilio Collado quoted in Wilson and McKinzie (1971, 39). For White's monetary conserva-tism, see also Boughton 2002.
53. Quoted in Rees 1973, 425. For other recollections of his personality from contemporaries, see McKinzie 1972, 85; Fuchs 1974b, 10, 19–20; Oliver 1961a, 21–22; Craig 2004, 292 n. 9; Acheson 1969, 81–82; Mikesell 1994, 55, Keynes 1980b, 356.
54. The Treasury officials that Craig (2004) identifies as involved with Soviet espionage include: Solomon Adler, Frank Coe, Harold Glasser, Sonya Gold, Victor Perlo, George Silverman, Nathan Gregory Silvermaster, and William Ullman. Of these individuals, only Glasser and Coe appear in this book, and in insignificant ways. A number of these individuals were at the Bretton Woods conference itself, but I have seen no evidence that they influenced outcomes vis-à-vis the issues I am analyzing. Coe was the conference's technical secretary general while Ullman was an assistant secretary to one of the four committees of Commission II. White had also asked Silvermaster to be one of seven "techni-cal secretaries" to the US delegation, but he left after a day or two because of his health (Rees 1973, 217, 413). Although Adler does not appear on the official list of conference attendees, he turned up at Bretton Woods (recently returned from China) to help with bilateral financial negotiations between US and Chinese officials that took place on the sidelines of the conference (MD, book 752, p. 3). One other figure involved in Soviet espionage, Laurence Duggan from the State Department, appears briefly in connection with White's 1941–42 Cuban mission (see chapter 3).
55. Craig 2004, 14.

analysts have drawn stronger conclusions about White's involvement in Soviet espionage, while others question whether the evidence is fully conclusive.[56]

Whatever the truth may be, it seems unlikely that any involvement of White in Soviet espionage influenced the outcomes being analyzed here. According to Craig, there is no evidence that White had any association with Soviet intelligence between April 1938 and August 1941, the very period during which he pioneered international development policies in Latin America that are at the core of this book's analysis. Indeed, it is interesting to read a memo he wrote in mid-June 1940 in which he highlights Soviet "ideological aggression," and argues that it "becomes more dangerous in a politically unsettled world and in countries where the standard of living is low or declining."[57] Pointing out that the United States was suddenly being forced to deal with Germany, Japan, and the USSR as major world powers, White also argued in the memo that America could not have the same identity of interest with any of them as it had with France and Britain.

During the subsequent Bretton Woods negotiations, there is also little evidence that Soviet officials made any effort to support or shape the international development content that White was promoting. They contributed little to United States–led postwar planning discussions throughout 1942–43 and, when they became a little more engaged in the months leading up to the conference and during the conference itself, Mikesell points out that they displayed "an almost complete lack of interest in the broad purposes which the Fund and Bank were designed to accomplish."[58] Instead, they focused only on issues that affected them directly, such as the size of their quotas in the institutions (which helped determine voting power and access to borrowing) or their access to reconstruction loans from the Bank.[59] As Steil puts it more generally, "the broad 'White Plan' for postwar monetary reform certainly bore no imprint of Soviet monetary thinking, as there was none to speak of."[60]

Finally and most importantly, there was very wide support within US official circles for the kinds of international development policies that White advocated. President Roosevelt himself was a very strong supporter, as were many officials across various branches of the US government as well as influential business

56. For the former, see for example Haynes, Klehr, and Vassiliev 2009, 258–62; Weinstein and Vassiliev 1999, 158, 163–64, 168–69; Steil 2013. For the latter, see Boughton 2001a, 2013; Boughton and Sandilands 2003; Sandilands 2009, 131 n. 18. See also the perspectives of Mikesell (1994, 56; 2000, 55–57), who worked closely with White, as well as Rauchway 2013; Skidelsky 2000, 256–63.

57. White, untitled memo, pp.4–5, June 15, 1940, HDWP, box 9, folder 3.

58. Mikesell 1951, 106.

59. Acsay 2000, chap. 8, 9; Black 1991, 43; Bernstein 1993; Van Dormael 1978, 191–97; Mikesell 1951.

60. Steil 2013, 6.

leaders and analysts associated with groups such as the Council on Foreign Relations. In other words, this innovation in US foreign policy cannot be explained simply by White's views and action. It grew out of larger trends in US policy-making that would have driven US policy in this direction even if White had not been involved.

What prompted White's initial interest in promoting Latin American development loans? As in the cases of Welles and Morgenthau, security concerns appear to have acted as the initial catalyst. In a late March 1939 memo to Morgenthau, White argued that, without major US financial support, "Latin America will gradually succumb to the organized economic and ideological campaign now being waged by aggressor nations."[61] In another memo in early June, he pressed for a "bold program" of financial assistance to Latin America that could be an "important part of our international political program of peace, security and encouragement of democracy." In addition, he complemented the strategic rationale for support for Latin America with the economic argument that US exports to the region could be an important part of a domestic economic recovery program. He argued: "Latin America presents a remarkable opportunity for economic development. Only capital and technical skill are needed to develop the area so that it could provide for a much larger population, for a higher standard of living and a greatly expanded foreign trade."[62]

White strongly supported Latin American industrialization. For example, when Aranha and other Brazilian officials visited the United States in early 1939 seeking assistance, White urged in an internal memo that the United States extend "long-term productive loans" to promote "the industrial development of Brazil," noting that "the standard of living of the Brazilian people cannot, in our opinion, be raised until and unless Brazil embarks upon these productive investments."[63] Like many other New Dealers, White was also critical of how private foreign capital in Latin America had been in the past "directed toward exploiting those countries without adequate attention to their fundamental capacity and long-run interests."[64] Because of past problems with private investment, White became an advocate of ambitious US public lending to promote Latin American development, as we shall see in the next chapter.

---

61. White to Morgenthau, March 31, 1939, p. 2, CFHDW, box 2, file 12. He was also advocating loans to China and Russia at this time.

62. "Loans to Latin America for the Industrial Development of Latin America," pp. 1, 2, June 6, 1939, HDWP, box 5, folder 6. This document is unsigned but White's biographer Rees (1973, 103) asserts that White was the author.

63. White to Taylor, February 6, 1939, p. 4, CFHDW, box 2, file 12.

64. "Loans to Latin America," p. 5.

First Steps

To extend financial assistance to Latin America, US policymakers turned initially to the Export-Import Bank which had been created by the Roosevelt administration in 1934 to supply credit to support US exporters. After only very limited activity in its initial years, the bank's lending expanded considerably in 1938–39 to further US foreign policy goals in Latin America (and elsewhere such as in China). Loans were made to various governments to support development projects (including industrial projects) as well as currency stability.[65]

These new loans immediately attracted controversy. When the Export-Import Bank's charter came up for renewal in February 1939 in Congress, Taft and other Republicans made clear their opposition to its new Latin American lending program. While their efforts to liquidate the bank failed, these opponents did convince Congress to cap its lending at $100 million, rejecting Roosevelt's effort to increase its loans to $500 million.[66] Some officials in the State Department also sought to block lending to countries that had not settled with US bondholders, efforts that severely frustrated Morgenthau and White, particularly after Roosevelt had explicitly argued in June 1939 that "ancient frauds of the 1920's should not interfere with new sound loans under consideration."[67]

The outbreak of World War II strengthened the case for US cooperation with Latin America both because the new urgency of preventing Axis influence and because of the economic dislocations in the region caused by the war. On September 18, Assistant Secretary of State Adolf Berle wrote to Roosevelt that "we shall have to intensify our South American policy to the limit."[68] Fluent in Spanish and a member of Roosevelt's early Brains Trust, Berle had emerged as an important architect of the Good Neighbor policy in an advisory capacity earlier in the decade. Along with Hull and Welles, he had helped write Roosevelt's 1936 speech in Buenos Aires and he was proud of the New Deal's anticolonial stance, having witnessed atrocities by US troops in the Dominican Republic in 1918. At Welles's insistence, he had become assistant secretary of state in early 1938 and he now became a strong supporter of Latin American development initiatives, seeing them as an extension of the reformed capitalism he favored at home.[69]

At this time, the Roosevelt administration approved larger-scale lending to Latin America by the Export–Import Bank and asked Congress to approve an

---

65. Adams 1976, Adamson 2005.
66. Adams 1976, 250–52.
67. Quoted in Roorda 1998, 201. See also Gellman 1979, 43–44, 159–61; Adams 1976, 195–98; Blum 1965, 52–58.
68. Quoted in Langer and Gleason 1970, 206.
69. Schwartz 1987, 122,127; O'Sullivan 2008, 22; Friedman 2003, 81.

expansion in the bank's size; an increase of $100 million was finally approved in March 1940.[70] At a September 1939 summit of foreign ministers of American republics in Panama, the United States also backed a Latin American proposal to create a Washington-based Inter-American Financial and Economic Advisory Committee (IFEAC) whose members included financial experts from each country in the region.[71] Chaired by Welles, the committee had a mandate to build "close and sincere cooperation" among the American republics, and it quickly set to work to develop a proposal for an Inter-American Bank.[72] In January 1940, it also recommended the creation of an Inter-American Development Commission to encourage US–Latin American joint ventures that would "undertake the development of new lines of Latin-American production for which a new or complementary market can be found in the United States or in other Republics of the Western Hemisphere."[73] When W. Randolph Burgess's name was initially suggested as a possible US business representative on the commission, Roosevelt explicitly ruled out any New York bankers from serving and chose instead a representative from the industrial firm Westinghouse Electric Company.[74]

Ambitious US Proposals

United States financial policy toward Latin America became more ambitious in the wake of the dramatic German military victories across continental Europe in mid-1940. The victories heightened US concerns about the defense of the hemisphere as well as about economic and political turmoil in Latin America. The need for a coherent US response was only compounded when the Nazis publicized a plan for a postwar international economic order in Europe. If Latin American countries remained friendly to the Axis cause, the German government stressed, these countries might benefit from this "New Order."[75] It is frequently noted that the New Order propaganda provoked Keynes into developing his first thinking about British postwar plans in late 1940 and early 1941.[76] Less well known is the fact that the German plans also encouraged US officials to develop proposals for a more integrated economic bloc within the Americas in late May and early June of 1940.

---

70. US State Department 1957, 508–11; Adams 1976, 198–204, 215–20, 250–52.
71. For the Latin American push for this body, see Gellman 1979, 156–57.
72. US State Department 1957, 765.
73. Quoted in Green 1971, 75.
74. US State Department 1961, 374–75; Green 1971, 315.
75. Langer and Gleason 1970, 637.
76. Van Dormael 1978, chap. 1; Skidelsky 2000, 194–99.

Many of these US proposals were summarized in a June 10 memo by the State Department's Emilio Collado. Cuban-born and raised in the United States, Collado had a Harvard Ph.D. in economics and had worked with White at the Treasury in 1934–36 and then at the Federal Reserve Bank of New York before joining the State Department in 1938. He was seen there as one of the "reform-oriented" officials, along with Welles, and he had quickly become involved with the new Latin American development lending program of the Export-Import Bank, of which he was very much in favor.[77] After noting the German proposals, Collado's memo outlined "An Economic Program for the Americas" involving much closer inter-American trade and financial relations. In the trade realm, Collado suggested that the United States assist Latin American countries to adjust to the collapse of their export markets in Europe by offering tariff concessions, encouraging inter-American trade, purchasing surplus commodities, coordinating trade policy vis-à-vis outsiders, and supporting international commodity agreements that could stabilize the prices of key Latin American exports. In the monetary and financial realm, Collado called for greater US public lending for short-term balance of payments assistance and long-term development projects. He also noted that the views of Morgenthau, White, and other Treasury officials "in general coincide with those expressed in this memorandum."[78] Indeed, in a March 1940 memo to Morgenthau, White had advocated once again a large increase in lending to Latin America as well as "the establishment of the Americas as a tight economic unit."[79]

Another proposal that attracted Roosevelt's attention at this time came from a group of businessmen, economists, and lawyers outside the government who were led by thirty-two-year old Nelson Rockefeller. Long interested in the region, Rockefeller had become an advocate of US efforts to encourage a reformed "capitalism with social objectives" in Latin America.[80] On June 14, 1940 (the day that German troops entered Paris), he presented a plan for "Hemispheric Economic Defense" that was similar to Collado's, but put even more emphasis on the need to promote economic development in Latin America through technical and financial assistance, including initiatives to convert outstanding debts into local currency that could be used for investment, and to allow repayment of future debt in local currency.[81] Roosevelt liked the basic outlines of this plan as well as the possibility that Congressional opposition might be lessened by the fact that

---

77. Woods 1979, 23–24. See also Wilson and McKinzie 1971; Adams 1976, 219–20.
78. US State Department 1961, 363.
79. Quoted in Rees 1973, 103.
80. Rivas 2002, 3.
81. Langer and Gleason 1970, 632–33; Green 1971, 48; Rivas 2002, 39–41.

Rockefeller was a Republican. He hastily organized a committee of the secretaries of state, commerce, treasury, and agriculture, chaired by Berle, that backed its basic elements. The plan was then announced to the public by Roosevelt on June 21.

Opposition at home and across Latin America quickly shot down some of the more ambitious proposals in the plan, most notably the creation of an "Inter-American Trading Corporation" that would have been empowered to market surplus commodities of the region and coordinate countries' trade relations with the outside world.[82] But Welles told a July 11 meeting of the IFEAC that the United States would still support the "temporary financing and storage of export products until they can be marketed in an orderly fashion" and the "development of commodity agreements with a view to assuring the nations of this hemisphere equitable terms of trade with the rest of the world."[83] The United States subsequently empowered its Reconstruction Finance Corporation (RFC) to create new corporations that could buy strategic materials such as rubber and metals, with bilateral purchasing programs for each country. In the coffee sector, which was so important to a number of Latin American countries, the United States also worked through the IFEAC to draw up an Inter-American Coffee Agreement that was endorsed by fifteen countries in November 1940, establishing export quotas for coffee producers and guaranteeing each of them a share of the US market.[84]

Roosevelt's plan also called for "vigorous action" to be "undertaken as rapidly as possible in the broad field of development in some American Republics of new industries and production." At the July 11 IFEAC meeting, Welles told Latin American representatives that "the productive capacity of the area and the standard of living of its populations must be increased," and he asked countries to tell the IFEAC "their pressing needs and the plans which they have prepared for economic development."[85] Hull then reinforced this message at a meeting of foreign ministers of the American republics in Havana in late July, using language that highlighted his wider global vision (and that foreshadowed comments of Morgenthau at the Bretton Woods conference):

> If the standards of living of the American peoples are to be maintained at levels already achieved, and particularly if they are to be raised in accordance with the legitimate aspirations of these peoples, production

---

82. Gellman 1979, 93–94; Green 1971, chap. 4; Pike 1995, 214–16.

83. US State Department 1961, 372.

84. Green 1973, 94–95; Gilderhus 2000, 105. The signatories were Brazil, Colombia, Costa Rica, Cuba, the Dominican Republic, Ecuador, El Salvador, Guatemala, Haiti, Honduras, Mexico, Nicaragua, Peru, the United States, and Venezuela. The agreement was ratified by the United States in April 1941.

85. US State Department 1961, 370, 371, 373.

and distribution must expand, not only in this hemisphere but throughout the world. This same condition is essential to the well-being of all
other areas. For no nation or group of nations can hope to become or to
remain prosperous when growing poverty stalks the rest of the earth.[86]

To work toward this goal, Roosevelt appointed Rockefeller to head a new body
that was subsequently named the Office of the Coordinator of Inter-American
Affairs, and whose mandate was to help coordinate US policies toward Latin
America in the commercial and cultural areas.[87] Roosevelt also requested a large
expansion of the Export–Import Bank's lending capacity from $200 to $700 million just as the Havana meeting was starting. Congress approved the increase in
late September (although not without some opposition) and the bank expanded
its loans immediately, with the Brazilian steel mill loan being one of the most
prominent.[88] At the Havana meeting, Hull also invited Latin American governments to approach the US Treasury for currency stabilization loans. White (who
attended the Havana conference) then discussed details of the many requests
that were forthcoming with Latin American finance ministries, and many of the
Export-Import Bank's loans served this purpose.[89] White was also interested in
how the US Exchange Stabilization Fund could support Latin American currency
stabilization. Between 1936 and 1938, he had already begun to pioneer the use of
the ESF for short-term bilateral lines of credit for balance of payments purposes
to some Latin American countries.[90] New agreements were now reached, beginning with a November 1941 line of credit to Mexico and followed soon after by
agreements with Ecuador, Cuba, and Brazil.[91]

United States policy toward Latin American debt also shifted around this
time. In a June 15, 1940 memo, Roosevelt had instructed the interdepartmental committee studying Rockefeller's plan that the problem of "external debts
should be faced realistically and these debts should not stand in the way of constructive financial and trade assistance. Study should be given to the refunding
of these debts."[92] By the end of the year, many of the outstanding disagreements
between debtors and US bondholders had been resolved.[93] In cases where

---

86. Quoted in Gantenbein 1950, 208.
87. Cramer and Prutsch 2006; Rivas 2002, 61.
88. Becker and McClenahan, 2003, 45–59; Gellman 1979, 99, 162.
89. White to Morgenthau, August 2, 1940, CFHDW, box 3, file 17; Blum 1965, 321; Rees 1973,
104; US Senate 1941, 41.
90. Boughton 2004, 188–89; 2009, 14–15; Bordo and Schwartz 2001.
91. Earlier lines of credit had been extended to Mexico (in 1936 and 1938) and Brazil (1937)
(Henning 1999, 14, 21–22).
92. Quoted in Guerrant 1950, 161.
93. Robert Triffin, "Notes on an Investment Program for Latin America," September 25, 1942,
ISF, box 152, file: Latin America, Finance (1936–1954).

agreements had not been reached, the State Department increasingly overrode the concerns of US bondholders when considering financial assistance packages.[94] Indeed, by the spring of 1941, US government officials were discussing how the activities of the Foreign Bondholders Protective Council could be brought more in line with broader official US policy toward Latin America through personnel changes and by moving its headquarters from New York to Washington.[95] As the US government increasingly overrode the Bondholder Council's views, its activities rapidly diminished and Wall Street firms stopped supporting it.[96]

One final US policy initiative at this time will be discussed in more detail later on. In his June 21, 1940 announcement, Roosevelt had called upon US government agencies to give further attention to extension "of cooperation, when desired by other American Republics, in the strengthening of their monetary systems."[97] The extension of financial assistance was one such mechanism of cooperation, but a second one soon emerged in the fall of 1941 when the United States initiated the first of a series of ambitious financial advisory missions— responding to requests from Latin American governments—that were designed to "strengthen" Latin American monetary systems. These missions were reminiscent of US money-doctoring missions to Latin America in the 1920s, but the advice offered was now very different and in keeping with the goal of promoting "development" along the Good Neighbor lines.

These various initiatives highlighted the extent to which US policymakers were now committed to a new kind of financial (and broader economic) partnership with Latin America. The promotion of Latin American economic development was a core goal of this partnership. Latin American policymakers were not always pleased with the details of the US development initiatives. For example, they were frustrated when the Export-Import Bank wanted to finance projects that served US economic or security interests rather than their priorities. They also did not appreciate the bank's requirement that all schemes be government-guaranteed.[98] But at a more general level, the new US commitment to Latin American development goals was applauded by many in the region. The US enthusiasm for this objective was well expressed by the Treasury's Frank Southard in July 1941: "... if one goes around Washington now I think he will hear more often than any other

---

94. Gellman 1979, 161; US State Department 1962, 58, 72; Adamson 2002.
95. Green 1971, 316 n. 40. See also the growing frustration with the council's strict policies among some bondholders themselves (e.g. Norman Wait Harris Memorial Foundation 1941, 121) as well as in the Federal Reserve Bank of New York (e.g. Wallich to Sproul, March 6, 1942, p. 12, ISF, box 152.
96. Bemis 1943, 448–49.
97. US State Department 1961, 370.
98. Green 1971, 78–79.

one word in the vocabulary of the Good Neighbor enthusiasts with which that city abounds the word 'developmental' or 'development.'"[99]

In an article published a few months earlier, in March, Berle pointed out how public international lending for development contrasted with past US private investment practices in the region: "It should be the beginning of a system in which finance is the servant of exchange and development, and is adjusted to that commerce and that building which serves the various countries—in direct contrast to the older system, which insisted that the development and the commerce must serve finance, or it could not go forward."[100] In a June 1941 speech, Berle developed this theme further. Arguing that "nineteenth century economic imperialism is dead as the brontosaur," he suggested that the Export-Import Bank and the RFC "are vividly interested in whether the development is a good thing in itself." He continued: "In other words we have shifted our entire point of view. Instead of being anxious to find a place where a group of people who have privately saved money can secure a private stream of profits, we are anxious rather to find opportunities for sound development which may add to the general safety, security, and well-being of the Western Hemisphere." Because modern production techniques had created such abundance, he argued that larger markets and "a general rise in standards of living everywhere" were necessary.[101] Indeed, he argued that the ultimate goal for the Western hemisphere was that "standards of living shall approximate the highest standards in the area." And finally: "Carried to its logical conclusion, all this must require a higher degree of economic planning and, at the same time, a higher degree of open trade between the American nations. . . . In the combination of the new conceptions with the new mechanisms we have already gone a long way toward establishing the foundation of what will be the cooperative international economics of the future."[102]

Berle's final line was prophetic. As shall see, the commitment to international development being pioneered in the Good Neighbor financial partnership would find a central place in plans for the postwar international financial system. Even more intriguing was his suggestion that the "cooperative international economics of the future" would need to rest on a combination of greater planning and freer trade. This combination was one that foreshadowed the embedded liberal ideology of the Bretton Woods agreements. As we shall see, Berle was deeply involved in the early US postwar planning discussions. Before then, he was also a central figure in pioneering a concrete mechanism—the Inter-American Bank—for

---

99. Norman Waits Memorial Foundation 1941, 49.
100. Berle 1941b, 106.
101. Berle 1941a, 758–59.
102. Berle 1941a, 760–61.

operationalizing this ideology, a mechanism that served as an important precursor to the Bretton Woods institutions. In both this speech and the IAB initiative, the centrality of the commitment to international development within this conception of embedded liberalism is striking.

Several historians of the Good Neighbor policy have remarked on how US policies toward Latin America in the late 1930s and early 1940s foreshadowed US international development policies in the post-1945 world.[103] This important observation has been overlooked by those who have traced the origins of international development to the Truman speech of 1949 or even to the Bretton Woods negotiations of 1942–44. As we have seen, US policymakers in the late 1930s and early 1940s period were keenly interested in promoting Latin American economic development and they developed various important mechanisms to serve this goal: long-term loans for international development projects, short-term loans for balance of payments assistance, commodity market stabilization, and debt restructuring.

The new Good Neighbor financial partnership was born out of a unique intersection of Latin American and US political developments in this period. On the Latin American side, the Great Depression encouraged greater interest in state-led development and industrialization as a priority of economic policy. Many Latin American governments welcomed US backing for their development goals, particularly when the content and rhetoric of US support seemed to reject past practices from the era of dollar diplomacy. On the US side, a complex combination of strategic goals, economic interests, and New Deal values prompted policymakers by the late 1930s to back many of the new Latin American development aspirations. The partnership proved to be a crucial incubator for some core aspects of the Bretton Woods proposals, especially in two of its manifestations: the Inter-American Bank of 1939–40 and the Cuban financial advisory mission of 1941–42.

---

103. Grow 1981, 36; Gellman 1979, 2; Cobbs 1992, 2–3.

THE FIRST DRAFT
The Inter-American Bank

The negotiation of the Inter-American Bank was the most ambitious initiative undertaken by US and Latin American policymakers under the Good Neighbor financial partnership. Beginning in the fall of 1939, they set out to construct a multilateral financial institution that would help achieve their new partnership's goals. By April 1940, they had drafted a convention and by-laws for a publicly owned multilateral financial institution to foster regional cooperation.

Although the IAB was never established, various historians have argued that it acted as key precursor to the Bretton Woods initiative. Robert Oliver suggests that "in a sense, the Inter-American Bank plan was the first draft of subsequent plans for a Stabilization Fund and a World Bank."[1] John Horsefield agrees, noting that the IAB "clearly formed part of the background against which these drafts [of the Bretton Woods institutions] were evolved."[2] Morgenthau's biographer John Morton Blum also makes the point that the IAB initiative "gave the Americans concerned, White in particular, an experience which was to prove useful years later in the organization of postwar financial institutions."[3]

Despite these and other similar comments, historians of Bretton Woods have not undertaken a detailed analysis of the politics of the IAB negotiations.[4] The

---

1. Oliver 1975, 99. See also Oliver 1985, 19 n. 1.
2. Horsefield 1969a, 11.
3. Blum 1965, 57.
4. Oliver (1975, 92–99) provides the most detailed discussion. For other comments about the importance of the IAB, see Bordo and Schwartz 2001; Mason and Asher 1973, 16; Skidelsky 2000, 239; Bittermann 1971, 61; Steil 2013, 377–8; Rees 1973, 104.

IAB initiative is not even discussed in much depth in the historical literature on the Good Neighbor policy, with the important exception of David Green's 1971 book *The Containment of Latin America*.[5] This chapter builds on Green's work by drawing on new archival sources, providing more detail about specific features of the IAB negotiations, and stressing the IAB's broader significance for Bretton Woods (an issue that Green neglects). It is particularly noteworthy that the IAB was the first international organization to be formally negotiated whose central mandate included the promotion of international development. This innovation set the stage for the development orientation of the Bretton Woods agreements.

The Latin American Push for an Inter-American Bank

Proposals for an Inter-American Bank had been put forward by US and Latin American individuals as far back as the First International Conference of American States in 1890. Initially, the goal was to simply to facilitate payments and strengthen banking linkages through the creation of a US-incorporated bank with branches or agencies in other countries.[6] At an important December 1933 inter-American conference in Montevideo, however, several Latin American governments proposed the creation of a new international financial institution with a more ambitious mandate aimed at addressing the economic distress engendered by the Great Depression. These proposals set the stage for the development focus of the IAB initiative of 1939–40 (and the subsequent early US drafts of the Bretton Woods proposals).

The most ambitious and controversial proposal came from Mexico's foreign minister, José Manuel Puig, who called on the conference to explore "the possibility of establishing public international organizations to take care of debts negotiations and agreements, in order to exclude thereby the intervention of Bankers' Committees and to look for the interest of both debtors and creditors."[7] At the time, almost every government in Latin America had defaulted on its external debts as a consequence of the Great Depression. As the wording of Puig's proposal made clear, his proposal was designed primarily to strengthen the bargaining position of debtor countries vis-à-vis private creditors (a point reinforced by the fact that he also requested a six-to-ten-year moratorium on all foreign debt

---

5. Green 1971, 60–74.
6. See for example Gardner and Powelson 1970; Dell 1972.
7. "VII Conferencia Internacional Americana, Delegación de México" n.d., p. 2, RIC, Comm. On Initiatives, 2–4, box 5.

payments). Private creditors from many countries were organized into Bankers' Committees that negotiated with debtors with one voice in times of difficulties. Puig explicitly set out to undermine the power of the committees by transferring debt-restructuring negotiations to an international organization in which sovereign debtors and creditor *governments* were represented.

Although a number of Latin American countries favored Puig's proposal, it failed to generate the necessary level of support to be placed on the conference's agenda and it was shelved for further study.[8] Some Latin American governments feared that a public expression of support for debt restructuring might undermine their creditworthiness in the eyes of foreign investors, while the Roosevelt administration was reluctant to get involved directly in the resolution of private US loans to Latin American governments.[9]

Delegations from Peru, Uruguay, Chile, and Cuba advanced other proposals for new Pan-American international financial institutions at the Montevideo conference.[10] After extensive discussion of these various ideas, two conference subcommittees recommended the creation of an Inter-American Bank that would be empowered to grant credit facilities, "mobilize" capital, and "improve the onerous conditions in which many of the Latin American countries negotiate their foreign loans."[11] Latin American supporters of the IAB, such as Peru's Felipe Barreda Laos, argued that it would consolidate "the definite economic liberation of Latin America." The conference as a whole then passed a resolution unanimously recommending consideration at the next Pan-American Financial Conference of the creation of an IAB with purposes "to establish and promote Inter-American credit and the interchange of capital" and "to collaborate in the reconstruction of national monetary conditions." Its membership was to be confined to central bankers in order to protect the body from political influence, while a broader "Inter-American Organization" including government representatives would set "its general plan of work." The resolution also noted that the IAB's headquarters should be in a Latin American capital, an idea that Barreda Laos had argued would help "create centers of equilibrium and counterweight."[12]

---

8. Mexico's proposal was supported by Brazil, El Salvador, and Nicaragua. See "VII Conferencia"; "Committee IV, December 14, 1933," RIC, Comm. On Initiatives, 2–4, box 6.

9. Braden to Hull, January 4, 1934, in RIC, Comm. On Initiatives, 7–9, Minutes and Antecedents of Final Act, box 7.

10. Mexico also suggested the creation of a separate "central bank for the continent" that could help national central banks with international clearing and financial operations ("VII Conferencia," p. 3).

11. "Fourth and Ninth Committees: Minutes and Antecedents," n.d., p. 49, RIC, Comm. On Initiatives, 7–9, Minutes and Antecedents of Final Act, box 7.

12. "Fourth and Ninth Committees," pp. 52, 49, 54, 57.

The resolution passed the conference unanimously, but the US delegation added a reservation that the United States could not commit to participate in a future IAB. The US delegate involved in the committee discussions of the IAB, Spruille Braden, reported back to Hull that he had been surprised by how strongly Peru and Uruguay had pushed for the IAB idea. Given the wider enthusiasm for their proposals, he pointed out that it "seemed unwise for the American delegation to openly oppose these projects, particularly as it is conceivable that at some future time a central bank comparable to the International Discount Bank at Basle may prove advantageous to the Americas."[13] The latter was a reference to the Swiss-based Bank for International Settlements (BIS) that had been established in 1930 to facilitate reparations payments from World War I and encourage central bank cooperation. Although the planned Pan-American Financial Conference never took place, the IAB idea continued to be raised by Latin American governments at subsequent conferences in the 1930s, including at an inter-American meeting in Lima in late 1938 where a unanimous resolution was passed once again calling for study of the IAB idea. But the United States remained wary.[14]

The idea then finally took flight at an important Panama meeting of foreign ministers of the Americas in late September 1939 just after World War II had begun. At the Panama meeting, Mexico presented a proposal for an IAB that could: (1) act as an inter-American clearing house; (2) serve as financial agent of central banks in international capital markets; (3) assist central banks in stabilizing the internal and external value of currencies; (4) study trade, exchange, and other problems; and (5) contract with the US government to accept not just gold but also silver in settlement of international balances owed by any country.[15] United States officials suddenly showed more enthusiasm for the idea, agreeing to a resolution authorizing the establishment of the IFEAC, whose functions included the study of "the necessity of creating an inter-American institution which may render feasible and ensure permanent financial cooperation between the treasuries, the central banks and analogous institutions of the American republics."[16] The US delegation had not come to Panama intending to back the IAB proposal, but their views were changed by what David Green calls the "adamant" Latin American support for the Mexican idea.[17] The central US goal at the conference was to persuade Latin American countries to remain neutral in

---

13. Braden to Hull, January 4, 1934, p. 9, in RIC, Comm. On Initiatives, 7–9, Minutes and Antecedents of Final Act, box 7.
14. US State Department 1956, 67.
15. Villaseñor 1941, 166.
16. Quoted in Gantenbein 1950, 791.
17. Green 1971, 62.

the war and to check the growing Nazi economic and political influence in the region. United States policymakers recognized that they could cultivate goodwill in the region by signaling their support for this popular proposal.

Within the US government, some officials had in fact favored an inter-American financial institution before the Panama meeting, such as Treasury official Simon Hanson, a graduate of Harvard who had published a 1938 book that sympathetically analyzed Uruguay's extensive social reforms and state-led industrialization initiatives.[18] In June 1939, Hanson had written to White with a proposal for an institution—headquartered in Latin America—that would facilitate capital flows to Latin American countries in default by guaranteeing their new bond issues. In an echo of Mexico's 1933 proposal, Hanson also suggested that the body could select commissioners general to force debt resettlement deals on past defaults within two years. These officials were to be selected by a process in which all member countries had an equal vote so that "any suggestion of single-nation impingement upon autonomy and sovereignty is avoided." To reinforce the point, Hanson added that it was "desirable that the commissioner-generals not be State Department imperialists and that control not be limited to North Americans."[19] Hanson's frustration with US policy toward Latin American debt was apparent in another August memo when he wrote: "the President has spoken sharply about the 'ancient fraud' of Latin American loans of the twenties. . . [but] his administrators have given the bondholders the identical dollar-diplomat protection which they would have received from an administration that openly catered to bondholders."[20]

In the middle of the Panama conference, Hanson wrote to White again, pointing out that the IAB proposal under discussion could assist in debt settlement negotiations. Hanson also argued that the IAB could help float long-term loans "for the developmental activity of the less important countries in South America," although he warned that the IAB should not replace the Export-Import Bank's lending role because the United States would not control the former to the same degree. From Hanson's standpoint, the most important role the IAB could play was to provide technical assistance: "Technical assistance offered by one country carries a connotation of arrogance and penetrating imperialism which weakens its effectiveness. If the assistance comes through the Bank it is likely to be more useful to the country since the insincerity of present-senders of technicians would be eliminated, and in addition would be accepted more generously."[21]

---

18. Hanson 1938.
19. Hanson, "Proposal for a Pan American Financial Institute," June 5, 1939, p. 2, TSF, 450/81/02/03, box 65.
20. Hanson to Glasser, "Economic Implementation of the Good-Neighbor Policy," August 21, 1939, p. 1, TSF, 450/81/20/07, box 28.
21. Hanson to White, September 27, 1939, pp. 1, 2, TSF, Entry 67A1804, box 65.

White himself had also been toying with a proposal for a public bank to promote lending to Latin America several months before the Panama meeting, although he initially conceptualized this as a US government bank rather than a multilateral one. In a memo written in early June, White proposed the creation of a "government bank" with $300 million in common stock purchased by the US government and with the power to issue $700m in bonds guaranteed by the government (as well as $1 billion more if the need arose).[22] The proposal appeared to build on an idea that Morgenthau had floated the previous month for a Bank of North and South America—chartered by Congress—that could lend to Latin America in a manner that took "risks for policy reasons" and was a "good gesture" to the region.[23] At the time, White had been very supportive of the concept but argued that Morgenthau's proposed capitalization of $100 million for the bank was too low.

Under White's new proposal, the bank's "sole function" would be "to assist in promoting the long-run economic development of Latin America." It would perform this function partly by offering credits to finance US exports to Latin America and short-term gold or silver loans for monetary stability. But the bank's most important activity was to be the extension of low-interest "long-term loans for productive purposes" which would be used only to develop public works and industrial enterprises that boosted the productivity of the borrowing country. White insisted that the control of the projects would remain with Latin Americans who would also be required to provide money toward them in local currency. He also suggested that at least three-quarters of the dollar loans had to be spent in the United States and all imported goods and services used in the construction of the project had to be purchased there. White was keen to emphasize that his plan was different from past US dollar diplomacy toward the region which had meant "the exploitation of a weak country by private American commercial and industrial interests with the aid of the American government." By contrast, White argued, his program "would have as its base the development of industrial enterprises in Latin America that would be under the control and ownership of the borrowing country or their nationals," and he stressed that "there is no part of the program which envisages any action by the United States Government or threat of such action, subtle or overt, which would interfere with the inherent sovereignty and rights of those countries."[24]

---

22. "Loans to Latin America for the Industrial Development of Latin America," June 6, 1939, p. 3, HDWP, box 5, folder 6.

23. "Financial Assistance to Nicaragua (and Other Latin American Countries)," pp. 7, 5, May 4, 1939, MD, book 188.

24. "Loans to Latin America," pp. 3–4, 6.

The day after the Panama conference ended, Morgenthau asked to speak with White about his June idea.[25] With its focus on the need for both short-term and long-term lending to Latin America, White's proposal would serve as an effective template for the multilateral IAB proposal that would soon be developed under his leadership. White was not, however, involved in the initial discussions of the IAB proposal. Those took place within the IFEAC, which had become operational by mid-November with twenty-one members appointed, including Welles as chair.

The Development of the Proposal

The initial detailed work on the IAB proposal was assigned to a financial subcommittee of the IFEAC which included Welles once again as chair and the following Latin American representatives: Antonio Espinosa de los Monteros (Mexico), Carlos Guachalla (Bolivia), C. Alonso Irigoyen (Argentina), Esteban Jaramillo (Colombia), Pedro Larrañaga Montero (Peru), and Eduardo Salazar (Ecuador). Although Welles was very keen on the IAB, he placed Adolf Berle in charge of the subcommittee and of coordinating the US position on this issue. After the subcommittee's first meeting on November 17, Berle recorded in his diary that the topic of greatest interest was the creation of an inter-American financial institution.[26]

The keen interest of Latin American officials had also been evident at a meeting in Guatemala of finance ministry officials of the American republics a few days earlier. At the meeting, Mexico's Eduardo Villaseñor put forward his country's proposal for an IAB once again and he added one additional function that the bank could assume: "to act as a channel for the investment of capital which will promote sound economic development in the American Republics."[27] Villaseñor was the head of the Bank of Mexico, and as Sarah Babb notes, he was "never an orthodox central banker." In addition to helping to modernize Mexican economics in the 1930s, he was a strong advocate of the idea that the central bank had an important role to play in promoting economic development and

---

25. See note dated October 4, 1939 on front of "Loans to Latin America."
26. Berle to Welles, November 17, 1939, p. 2, BP, box 59. For Berle's role, see "November 17, 1939," BP, box 211; Berle and Jacobs 1973, 271–78, 284–91. For Welles's enthusiasm for the IAB, see for example his discussions with the Brazilian representative on the IFEAC; Penteado to Aranha, December 19, 1939, FGV, Osvaldo Aranha, cp 1939.01.17 rolo 16 fl.651; Eurico Penteado to Osvaldo Aranha, January 12, 1939, FGV, Osvaldo Aranha 16-366.
27. Villaseñor 1941, 166. See also Urquidi 1996, 33.

industrialization.[28] He carried these developmental priorities into his ideas about the IAB proposal. Other Latin American representatives at the Guatemala meeting also were keen to see the IAB proposal discussed, such as those from Brazil, Colombia, Peru, and Uruguay, and a resolution was passed urging the IFEAC to investigate the issue. The resolution reinforced Mexico's new "development" focus for the bank by declaring that it was "desirable that the necessary capital be invested for the promotion of the agricultural and industrial development of the various countries in this hemisphere."[29]

The negotiation of the IAB then proceeded quickly. By February 7, 1940, the IFEAC as a whole had agreed on a draft convention and by-laws for the bank to be submitted to governments for comment, and final texts were released publicly on April 16. Throughout the process of drafting the IAB's by-laws, US policymakers took the lead role because the United States was to be the largest contributor to the bank. As the head of international work at the Federal Reserve Board, Walter Gardner, told the board in mid-January 1940, "it had been understood by them [Latin American governments] all along that if a bank is created it would be what the United States gives them." At the same meeting, the board's director of research and statistics, Emanuel Goldenweiser, also stressed the broader political context: "[Latin American countries] would accept anything that was worked out. He said they wanted money and protection and they were enthusiastic about solidarity and offering a united front against European aggression."[30]

Who were the US officials involved in drafting the IAB? As noted above, Berle took the initial lead. He was very keen on the initiative, viewing it as an opportunity to strengthen political cooperation among the American republics.[31] Berle also saw the IAB initiative as an opportunity to implement his vision for the new kind of international finance described in the previous chapter.[32] After initial discussions within the IFEAC subcommittee, Berle decided in late November that it was not possible to proceed further without getting the Treasury involved. Berle mentioned in his diary that the task of securing Treasury cooperation was not straightforward because Morgenthau appeared to think that Welles's appointment

---

28. Babb 2001, 30–31, 58–59.

29. Quoted in Villaseñor 1941, 166. For Latin American support in Guatemala, see also US Senate 1941, 23.

30. "The following comments are from notes taken at the meeting of the Board on January 16, 1940, on the statements made by Messrs. Goldenweiser and Gardner relating to the Inter-American Bank," pp. 4, 7, CSF, 301.23-9.

31. See Gardner to Board of Governors, "The Inter-American Bank Proposal," December 20, 1939, pp. 2–3, CSF, 301.23-9.

32. "Speech of A. A. Berle, at George Washington University conference on inter-American affairs, December 5, 1939," pp. 6–7, BP, box 211.

as US representative to the IFAEC had been an insult to him.[33] At a meeting with Berle and Welles on November 28, however, Morgenthau offered full technical assistance if Roosevelt was in agreement. At the recommendation of Berle and Welles, he also agreed to involve Federal Reserve experts in the discussions.

Morgenthau's support for the proposal may have been encouraged by a memo White wrote to him that same day in which the latter outlined its potential benefits. Although the Treasury did not know the details being discussed, White assumed the IAB would be empowered to extend short-term credits to Latin America which could have the following advantages: "(a) Latin American countries may be able to borrow without waiting for difficult debt adjustments . . . (b) There would be less danger of defaulting on these obligations if the creditor were an Inter-American Bank than if it were a wealthy country, (c) The charge of dollar diplomacy would be absent." Echoing Hanson, White also argued that "the bank might build up a corps of experts who could perform a useful service in advising Latin American countries on their financial and economic problems." In addition to facilitating trade by guaranteeing private short-term credits, the bank could also "develop procedures to facilitate the granting of long-term loans and the settlement of outstanding debts."[34]

After Roosevelt expressed his strong support for the IAB proposal on December 4, White moved quickly to lead discussions on the IAB among an informal committee of officials from the Treasury (Edward Bernstein, Merle Cochran, Joseph Cotton, Harold Glasser, Simon Hanson, Winfield Riefler, Orvis Schmidt, [missing first name] Stewart, and Jacob Viner) and the Federal Reserve Board (Goldenweiser and Gardner).[35] This group quickly developed a questionnaire of thirty items that the IFEAC subcommittee agreed to send out to all Latin American republics.[36] From Berle's standpoint, White also played a critical role in convincing Morgenthau to support further work on the IAB proposal on December 15.[37]

On that same day, White produced a three-page summary of some issues discussed in the informal US committee he was leading. It outlined a bank with $100 million in capital made up of government subscriptions. Countries would be assigned a minimum subscription based on their population size but could voluntarily contribute more as long as no single government subscribed more than 25–35 percent of the total. The board of directors would consist of representatives

33. "November 28, 1939," pp. 1, 4, BP, box 211.

34. White to Morgenthau, November 28, 1939, pp. 1–2, CFHDW, box 3, file 14.

35. For Roosevelt's support, see "December 5, 1939," BP, box 211. For membership, see Gardner to Board of Governors, "The Inter-American Bank Proposal."

36. White, "Informal Committee on Consideration of Proposal to Create a Pan-American Banking Institution," December 7, 1939, JVP, box 49, folder 4.

37. "December 15, 1939," BP, box 211.

from each country with voting shares bearing "some relation to the proportion of the total capital stock held," although "the relationship is not to be directly proportional." This document did not say much about the goal of the bank's lending beyond that it should be for "productive purposes." It did point out, however, that the bank could lend only to governments, government agencies, or nongovernmental organizations whose loans were guaranteed by a government (which also had to act as the borrowing agent in those cases). Governments' servicing of these loans also had to take priority over all other external loans. In addition, the bank would be empowered to guarantee bonds floated on the private market and it could raise funds by selling its own debentures on the open market.[38]

White then worked intensely with several officials from the informal committee, particularly his assistant Edward Bernstein, to produce a detailed draft of the by-laws on January 11, 1940.[39] From the State Department, Collado also became increasingly involved at this time, playing an active role in the IAB proposal's development and subsequent promotion.[40] Although the IAB proposal was refined in various ways after this point, much of the content of White's January 11 draft appeared in the final documents that were approved in April. For this reason, Berle later argued that "the principal credit [for the IAB] ought to go to Harry White."[41]

Not all US officials were enthusiastic about the IAB idea. When Federal Reserve Bank of New York (FRBNY) officials such as Allan Sproul, George Harrison, John Williams, and Harold Roelse were finally consulted on the proposal by Collado in late March, they attacked it vigorously. In addition to predicting political difficulties with its management, they argued that the IAB would compete with the FRBNY's own foreign department and existing commercial banks. Their position may also have been influenced by the fact that New York banks were also very opposed to the IAB. But one official told Collado privately that he thought the "principal objection" of senior FRBNY officials to the IAB was that they "had not been consulted in its preparation." Indeed, Collado noted that less senior officials in the research department thought the proposal was quite good.[42]

Some US officials involved in the informal committee discussions also worried that Latin American expectations of the economic benefits of the IAB might

---

38. Quotes from White, "Outline of Tentatively Proposed Bank for American Republics," December 15, 1939, pp. 1–2, JVP, box 49, folder 4.

39. "Draft of By-Laws of a Bank to be called the Inter-American Bank," January 11, 1940, JVP, box 28, folder 11. For Bernstein's important role, see US Senate 1941, 24, and "Status of the Proposal," January 11, 1940, ISF, box 245.

40. "Status of the Proposal"; McKinzie 1974, 7; Wilson and McKinzie 1971, 10.

41. Berle and Jacobs 1973, 291. See also McKinzie 1974, 6.

42. Quote from Collado to Berle, March 29, 1940, p. 2, DSDF 710.BANK/81.

be exaggerated and that the IAB might distract attention from the necessary reforms in the region.[43] There were concerns expressed, too, about whether the IAB would be able attract good personnel and whether Latin American governments would repay loans, particularly if they had difficulties increasing exports to the United States.[44] Like Hanson in September, both Cochran and Riefler also pointed out that the United States would retain more control over lending if it performed this task unilaterally rather than through the IAB.[45]

Others saw the virtues of the IAB, however. Like Berle, some US officials noted the broader political benefit that the multilateral IAB could foster cooperation and unity across the Americas.[46] From the Federal Reserve Board, Goldenweiser and Gardner also emphasized that the IAB could improve clearing facilities for intraregional transactions and provide both short-term credit to cover temporary balance of payments deficits and long-term loans that the private sector would not make. In addition, they argued that loans extended through the IAB instead of bilaterally "would throw less onus on the United States if eventually the debtor government has difficulties in paying." They added that "advice from the bank or insistence on sound financial practices would represent the collective judgment of a group of American countries and not just the self-interest of a single creditor—the United States. It would tend to soften the charge of financial imperialism."[47]

While White and other US officials took the lead in developing the IAB proposal, the role of Latin American representatives should not be understated. Key purposes of the IAB echoed the 1939 Mexico proposals closely. The work of US officials was also informed by answers to the detailed questionnaire circulated to all participating countries in mid-December 1939. While US officials took the lead in drafting the by-laws of the bank, Jaramillo (who had been a Colombian finance minister) and Monteros (who was head of the Mexican industrial development bank Nacional Financiera) also prepared the draft convention.[48] More generally, Latin American representatives on the IFEAC participated very actively in commenting on the evolving proposal. As Collado later told a US Senate subcommittee, the IFAEC during the drafting phase "met practically every

---

43. White, "Outline of Tentatively Proposed Bank," p. 2.
44. See Gardner to Board of Governors, "The Inter-American Bank Proposal."
45. Cochran to White, December 4, 1939, p. 1, ISF, box 245; Gardner to Board of Governors, "The Inter-American Bank Proposal," p. 9. Stewart was also strongly opposed to the IAB idea from the start; White, "Outline of Tentatively Proposed Bank."
46. Hanson to White, December 7, 1939, TSF, Entry 67A1804, box 65; Goldenweiser and Gardner to Board of Governors, "The Inter American Bank proposal," January 16, 1940, p. 3, CSF, 301.23-9.
47. Goldenweiser and Gardner to Board of Governors, "The Inter American Bank proposal," p. 3. See also Oliver 1975, 94; Bemis 1943, 353.
48. "Anteproyecto de convención," January 18, 1940, BP, box 59.

day and there were very extensive discussions, in addition to which there were innumerable private discussions outside the regular formal sessions."[49] Berle was also struck by the quality of the contributions of Latin American officials within the IFEAC. After bringing White and Gardner to talk to his subcommittee in mid-December, he noted in his diary that "the Latin Americans, on the whole, have thought more deeply about this than the American experts; at all events, when we got through it seemed to me that the Latin Americans had all the honors of the discussion. Naturally, there was no point in saying this to the Treasury and Federal Reserve men."[50]

Throughout the drafting process, Latin American officials remained generally favorable to the IAB idea. There were, however, some exceptions. Peru's Larrañaga urged the IFEAC financial subcommittee to embrace more ambitious thinking, preferring that the IAB be more like a international central bank "able to issue its own credit expressed in its own money-of-account."[51] From the opposite perspective, in responding to the IFEAC questionnaire, some other Latin American governments, such as that of El Salvador and Guatemala, stated that they did not have much need for the bank.[52] The Argentine government was even less keen on the idea. As one Argentine newspaper put it, there was little point in the country contributing money to the project "as long as the hostility to its exports continues being in the United States a political banner which nobody is disposed to challenge."[53]

Innovative Features

If the IAB had been established, it would not have been world's first multilateral financial institution established through an intergovernmental convention. The BIS had earned that title in 1930. But three aspects of the IAB proposal were highly innovative in comparison to the BIS: its mandate to provide public international loans to achieve development objectives, its provisions addressing capital flight from poorer countries, and its control and ownership by governments.

---

49. US Senate 1941, 44.

50. "December 14, 1939," p. 4, BP, box 211.

51. Delegate of Peru, "Proposed Pan-American Bank," November 29, 1939, BP, box 59. See also "Memo Peru No.17, December 21, 1939," BP, box 59; Delegate of Peru, "Memorandum for the Study of Subcommittee 1: The Creation of a Pan American Bank," November 20, 1939, TSF, Entry 66A1039, box 31.

52. White to Morgenthau, January 9, 1940, TSF, Entry 67A1804, box 65.

53. Quoted in White to Morgenthau, "Foreign Economic Developments," March 12, 1940, p. 7, CFHDW, box 3, Chron 15. See also "The following comments . . . ," p. 7.

Public International Development Loans

The IAB's draft by-laws outlined an institution with maximum $100 million in capital that had nine formal purposes:

(1) Facilitate the prudent investment of funds and stimulate the full productive use of capital and credit.

(2) Assist in stabilizing the currencies of American Republics; encourage general direct exchanges of the currencies of American Republics; encourage the maintenance of adequate monetary reserves; promote the use and distribution of gold and silver; and facilitate monetary equilibrium.

(3) Function as a clearing house for, and in other ways facilitate, the transfer of international payments.

(4) Increase international trade, travel and exchange of services in the Western Hemisphere.

(5) Promote the development of industry, public utilities, mining, agriculture, commerce, and finance in the Western Hemisphere.

(6) Foster cooperation among the American Republics in the fields of agriculture, industry, public utilities, mining, marketing, commerce, transportation and related economic and financial matters.

(7) Encourage and promote research in the technology of agriculture, industry, public utilities, mining and commerce.

(8) Engage in research and contribute expert advice on problems of public finance, exchange, banking and money as they relate specifically to the problems of the American Republics.

(9) Promote publication of data and information relating to the purposes of the Bank.[54]

Many of these purposes echoed goals that the Mexican government had suggested for the IAB at the Panama conference in September 1939. A number of them were also clearly designed to help achieve the goal that Mexico had added to its proposal at the Guatemala conference in November: the promotion of economic development. Indeed, Welles argued that the IAB's support for development was its core role. Explicitly contrasting the IAB's purpose to that of the BIS, he pointed out that "its principal importance will lie in investigating and facilitating rather long-term development projects in other American republics." Only as a "secondary consequence" would the bank be involved in "the extension

---

54. Department of State 1940, 524.

of shorter-term facilities to the monetary authorities of the hemisphere to assist them in eliminating seasonal and temporary fluctuations in their exchanges."[55]

Other US officials also stressed the importance of the IAB's development mandate. In testimony before a Senate subcommittee, Collado argued that the most important role of the IAB was to promote the establishment of industries and resource development in Latin America over the longer term.[56] According to Berle, when Morgenthau had supported further work on the IAB in mid-December 1939, his reasoning was also that "such an institution might introduce a significant step in the direction of a greater cooperative responsibility in the economic and financial development of the Americas."[57] An initial January 3, 1940 draft of the IAB that Hanson helped prepare also stated very explicitly that one of the core purposes of the bank was to "assist in the movement of long-term capital for developmental purposes to regions where capital is relatively scarce and costly." The bank was to serve this purpose not just through lending and guaranteeing private loans, but also by purchasing government bonds and "offering its services to any American Republic for investigations of the feasibility of programs of public works and agricultural and industrial development, i.e., acting as a central planning agency."[58]

Latin American governments also stressed the importance of the bank's development role. White noted that Latin American governments who responded to the IFEAC's questionnaire were "unanimous" in arguing that "the bank is needed to provide long-term developmental capital to Latin America."[59] Indeed, when answering the questionnaire, several governments submitted quite detailed estimates of the support needed for specific development projects in their country.[60] One of the IAB's strongest Latin American proponents, Mexico's Villaseñor, also emphasized its development-lending role above all else. In his view, the IAB should in fact lend "only for the type of investment which leads to the economic development and improvement of the peoples of America." In his view, such lending would include assistance for public works programs, the development of factories, land improvements to increase commodity yields, hydroelectric power plants ("preferably for industrial use"), and the creation and development of hotels, steamship lines, and air routes for passenger transport.[61]

55. Welles to William Lancaster, June 11, 1940, pp. 2–3, DSDF, 710.BANK/193.
56. US Senate 1941, 49.
57. "December 15, 1939," BP, box 211.
58. Hanson to Glasser, January 3, 1940, p. 3, TSF, Entry 67A1804, box 65.
59. White to Morgenthau, "Foreign Economic Developments," p. 7. See also views of Nicaragua, Honduras, and Haiti in White to Morgenthau, January 9, 1940, TSF, Entry 67A1804, box 65.
60. Green 1971, 63.
61. Villaseñor 1941, 174, 173.

To serve its various purposes, the IAB's by-laws empowered the institution to grant "short-term, intermediate and long-term loans and credits." These loans could be granted not just to "participating governments" but also to "fiscal agencies, central banks, political subdivisions and nationals thereof." Loans with maturities over two years that were made to a "fiscal agency, central bank, political subdivision or national" had to be guaranteed by the government of the country concerned and needed that government's approval.[62] The IAB's lending mandate was thus a very wide one that encompassed both short-term currency stabilization loans (similar to those offered by the US Exchange Stabilization Fund) and longer-term development loans (similar to those of the Export-Import Bank). In effect, it was an institution that wrapped together the future functions of the IMF and the IBRD into one. The BIS had already pioneered the role of an international financial institution offering currency stabilization loans. But the idea of a multilateral financial institution offering public international long-term loans designed to promote economic development was entirely novel.

The architects of the IAB trumpeted this innovation at the time. In testimony before a Senate subcommittee in May 1941, Berle argued that its lending would be very different from those "unhappy experiences" in the past of private lending "where money was squandered or where it was used to build up some kind of rather tyrannous foreign monopoly which the country resented" and where the movements of capital were regarded as "imperialist." The goal of the IAB was to generate capital movements "following the more careful plans of the various governments involved with a view to the steady development of the country." Instead of "the old very speculative forms of finance," the IAB's lending "could be made to serve national needs."[63]

The fact that the IAB would serve national needs was reinforced by a important clause in its by-laws which stated that "the operations of the Bank shall at all times be conducted in conformity with the laws of the territory where the Bank is acting and, so far as possible, be conducted in conformity with the policies of the participating government directly concerned."[64] Welles highlighted how this protection of national policy autonomy was core to the IAB's design: "the Bank, generally speaking, may take no action which may affect a particular nation until after that nation has been given an opportunity to object to, or to give its consent, approval, or guaranty to the operation. This safeguard to the interests of individual nations is inherent in the entire plan and appears throughout the drafting."[65]

---

62. Department of State 1940, 524.
63. US Senate 1941, 20.
64. Department of State 1940, 525.
65. Welles to Lancaster, June 11, 1940, p. 4.

Recycling Flight Capital

When US officials such as Berle critiqued "speculative forms of finance," they had in mind not just the foreign lending of Wall Street but also private flight capital from Latin America that had grown considerably during the 1930s. As Berle told the US Senate subcommittee, "Latin-America is commonly said to be without capital, and, of course, that is in considerable measure true; but a part of the savings of Latin America—and there are very considerable savings—comes to the United States, and is there held on deposit in various institutions, and there is no way for a Latin-American country to get its own savings back for productive use in its own country, except by coming into the New York market or some other money market."[66]

Accordingly, a second innovative aspect of the IAB was that it was explicitly designed to recycle the foreign holdings of private Latin American citizens in the form of stable loans back to countries in the region. For this purpose, it was empowered to sell its own bonds directly to investors within those countries and to accept deposits from individual citizens across Latin America (unless the national government objected). As Gardner put it, "it was hoped that the Bank and its branches might become, by reason of its preferred position, a popular repository for Latin American funds."[67] Flight capital could then be rechanneled to the specific country from which it originated in the form of public loans for developmental purposes. In this way, the bank's lending capacity would be boosted well beyond the capital subscriptions of governments and the IAB could, in Berle's words, "take some of the strain of that [Latin American development] financing off us."[68]

The mobilization of flight capital for development was in fact identified by Berle at the start of the IFEAC's work as one of the priority roles for the IAB.[69] Gardner and Goldenweiser at the Federal Reserve were also keen to see the issue addressed.[70] At the time of the IAB's negotiation, White was very interested in the problem of "hot money" and speculative capital inflows to the United States as well.[71] He had made sure that the IFEAC questionnaire asked Latin American governments about the size of flight capital in New York within the last five

---

66. US Senate 1941, 19.
67. Gardner to Board of Governors, "The Inter-American Bank Proposal," p. 5.
68. US Senate 1941, 19.
69. Berle, "Thesis," November 20, 1939, p. 3, BP, box 59; Delegate of USA, "Memorandum," November 20, pp. 2–3, IFEAC Subcommittee 1, DSDF, 710.FEAC/143.
70. Hanson to Glasser, January 4, 1940, TSF, Entry 67A1804, box 65; Goldenweiser and Gardner to Board of Governors, "The Inter American Bank Proposal," p. 2.
71. White, "Questions on Foreign Capital in the United States," February 27, 1940, HDWP, box 3, folder 9.

years and overall.[72] Although few countries were able to provide useful estimates, US officials estimated that Latin American private balances in New York had increased from \$100 million in 1933 to over \$300 million by 1939.[73]

Some US officials, such as Hanson and Bernstein, questioned whether it was wise for the IAB to take on the role of recycling capital flight by accepting deposits. As White told Morgenthau on January 9, 1940, "the major objection is that local banks might be drained of deposits or feel that the Bank is acting as a competitor."[74] Larrañaga had also raised this concern earlier, arguing that the IAB was "going to subtract the assets of others in order to redistribute them itself . . . it will be merely a distributor of existing poverty."[75] After consulting with the Federal Reserve Board, even Gardner and Goldenweiser pointed out to Berle that "there is a danger that in accepting deposits from the public the bank might take a substantial amount of business away from local institutions or from branches of American banks in Latin America to which we have hitherto lent encouragement." Still, they and other US officials remained committed to the IAB's deposit-taking role (while warning that it should not "draw an undue amount of business away from existing commercial banks in Latin America").[76]

An Intergovernmental Institution

The third innovative feature of the IAB was that it would be owned and controlled by national governments. Although the BIS had been created by the intergovernmental Hague Convention of 1930, that agreement simply committed the Swiss government to grant a charter to the bank under which six central banks (from Belgium, Britain, France, Germany, Italy, and Japan) and one private US banking group (involving J. P. Morgan and Company, the First National Bank of New York, and the First National Bank of Chicago) became its founding members providing the initial capital. The BIS was not directly accountable to governments. The IAB was also to be established by an intergovernmental convention, but the bank's draft by-laws described an institution in which national governments subscribed to its shares, managed its operations, and were its

72. Question no. 10 in White, "Informal Committee," p. 2.

73. Goldenweiser and Gardner to Board of Governors, "The Inter American Bank Proposal"; Green 1971, 63.

74. White to Morgenthau, January 9, 1940, p. 2, TSF, Entry 67A1804, box 65. Hanson also questioned the expected benefits, arguing that the amount of capital leaving Latin America annually was no more than \$25 million and that not all of this would come to the bank. Hanson to White, January 5, 1940, and Hanson to Glasser, January 4, 1940, TSF, Entry 67A1804, box 65.

75. Delegate of Peru, "Proposed Pan-American Bank," pp. 1–2.

76. Gardner and Goldenweiser, "Suggestions Relative to Proposed Inter-American Bank," January 18, 1940, pp. 12, 4, CSF, 301.23-9.

members. As one BIS official privately noted, "what characterizes the I.A.B. and distinguishes it clearly from the BIS is that it is *an association of governments*. All pretense that monetary and credit-regulating functions of a state are segregated from its general sovereign rights and duties and are vested in an independent Bank or banking system seems to have been entirely dropped for the purposes of the I.A.B."[77]

Morgenthau and White promoted this feature of the IAB as part of the broader New Deal struggle to wrest control of financial policy away from the Wall Street elite and the FRBNY. In the wake of the 1929 stock market crash and the Great Depression, the Roosevelt administration had asserted greater centralized public control over monetary and financial issues. Regulations had been tightened over private financial firms and markets, and New Deal legislation in 1935 had shifted power within the Federal Reserve system away from the privately owned Reserve Banks to the Washington-based Federal Reserve Board whose members were all appointed by the president and confirmed by the Senate.[78] Under Morgenthau's leadership, the Treasury had also assumed a much more prominent role in US international financial policy than it had had during the 1920s when such policy had often been dominated by the FRBNY and private financial interests. The Treasury's new prominence was reinforced by the Good Neighbor policy of the late 1930s, as Morgenthau and White strongly promoted US public lending to Latin America via the Export-Import Bank and the Treasury-controlled Exchange Stabilization Fund. Berle explained to Goldenweiser how Morgenthau's insistence on a government-owned IAB needed to be seen in this context: "I think probably what you really get in the Treasury is a reflection of the classic fight between Mr. Morgenthau and the Federal Reserve Bank of New York."[79]

White had a similar perspective on the issue. After meeting him on December 8, 1939, Berle reported in his diary that White had "expressed the fear lest it [the IAB proposal] fall into the hands of the Federal Reserve which he thinks would merely throw it right back into the New York banks."[80] According to Goldenweiser, White presented a similar rationale to Latin American officials: ". . . if it [the IAB] were opened to central banks or to a Treasury designated bank then there would be the profit-making motive of the banks in the picture instead of an institution which because of its broad purposes would not be concerned

---

77. (Illegible author's name), "Inter-American Bank," April 3, 1940, p. 108, THMC, series 2 Business Papers, carton 9, folder 9.

78. The Federal Reserve Board was also formally renamed the Board of Governors of the Federal Reserve System, but the name Federal Reserve Board continued to be used.

79. "Conversation between Dr. Goldenweiser and Mr. Berle, January 25, 1940," p. 9, CSF, 301.23-9.

80. "December 8, 1939," p. 3, BP, box 211.

with profits."[81] Both Welles and Collado also supported an intergovernmental bank.[82]

Federal Reserve officials, however, opposed the idea that the IAB would be owned and controlled by governments rather than central banks. Goldenweiser urged the Federal Reserve Board to resist the Treasury's idea, declaring that he "disliked to see the Federal Reserve lose position one step after another" and that "there is greater dependability in the central banks than in South American governments."[83] Some in the Treasury, such as Cotton, Cochran, and Hanson, agreed that the bank might be better served if it was run by central bankers.[84] At the urging of the Federal Reserve Board, Gardner and Goldenweiser sent a memo to Berle in mid-January 1940 insisting that the IAB be a "central bankers' bank" which was not government-controlled. In their words, "a politically-minded group of directors untrained in banking and giving most of their time between meeting to political issues at home could easily convert the bank into a source of serious embarrassment for the United States and its South American relations."[85] They also remarked that many Latin American delegates on the IFEAC seemed to share their preference for a body controlled by central banks.[86] Indeed, in a memo to the IFEAC on November 20, 1939, Larrañaga had suggested that the bank should have "no relations with the public nor with State governments."[87]

At a January 23, 1940 meeting with Berle to discuss the letter from Gardner and Goldenweiser, Morgenthau was dismissive: "Why bother with them? They have made their recommendations and if it is up to me, I just don't accept them."[88] White also rejected the Fed's proposal on the following grounds:

> we have created an instrument here and given it enormous powers for good or evil and for us to turn it over at this stage to banking groups, it seems to me we are just going back to all the evils that we wish to avoid.... This bank, if it is successful, if it lives up to expectations with respect to power, can have a very profound degree of influence on the small countries and whether that shall be democratically used in the

---

81. This quote is taken from a description of White's views in "The following comments...," p. 6.
82. Welles to Lancaster, June 11, 1940; Collado to Secretary of State, September 7, 1943, p. 2, TSF, 450/81/02/03, box 66.
83. "The following comments...," pp. 9, 2–3.
84. Hanson to White, December 7, 1939, and Cotton, "Inter-American Bank," January 9, 1940, TSF, Entry 67A1804, box 65.
85. Gardner and Goldenweiser, "Suggestions," pp. 1, 3.
86. See also Gardner to Board of Governors, "The Inter-American Bank Proposal," p. 12.
87. Delegate of Peru, "Memorandum," p. 1.
88. MD, book 237, p. 257.

sense of attaining objectives of Government to Government or whether it shall be merely a bankers' attempt to use that to serve—not their own individual purposes but the general philosophy that they represent, I think is a very fundamental matter and I don't see how this Administration, with its whole New Deal philosophy and with its attitude toward those fundamental problems can support an institution that becomes a super-central bank.[89]

Berle was sympathetic to these arguments, and added one further "very powerful argument" that "we may at some stage be considering somewhat similar methods in the event that peace should break out . . . at that time this might serve as a good laboratory study."[90] In late January 1940, the chairman of the Federal Reserve, Marriner Eccles, agreed to wording that kept the IAB as an intergovernmental institution but left open the question of how each government would appoint its director. Reflecting this agreement, the final wording of the IAB's by-laws stated that each government appointed its director "in a manner to be determined by it."[91] The subsequent US implementing legislation, discussed in early 1941 by a Senate subcommittee, allowed for the US director to be chosen by a committee made up of the treasury secretary, the chair of the Federal Reserve Board, and the Federal Loan Administrator. The endorsement of the intergovernmental nature of the IAB set an important precedent for the creation of the IMF and IBRD—both of which were government-owned and controlled.

Another aspect of the governance of the IAB also acted as precursor to that of the Bretton Woods institutions: its system of weighted voting in which the United States would have an effective veto over important decisions. The bank was to be governed by a board of directors with one director for each country. Each government received twenty minimum votes and then one additional vote for each additional share it held, with minimum share levels set according to the importance of their foreign trade in 1938 (White's initial January 11 draft had used population as a determinant). Voting on the board would take place according to a simple majority-voting rule, but with important decisions requiring a four-fifths majority. Along with Brazil and Argentina, the United States would be required to subscribe to a minimum of fifty shares of $100,000 each, while other

89. MD, book 237, 259.
90. MD, book 237, 266.
91. Department of State 1940, 523. Eccles to Berle, January 29, 1940, CSF, 301.23-9. This final wording was not in fact very different from White's draft of January 11 which had noted that "each government shall have complete freedom in the method selected by it in appointing its director and alternate" ("Draft of By-Laws," p. 2).

countries faced lower minimum subscriptions. With this weighted voting system, US officials anticipated that they could quite easily acquire more than 20 percent of the vote and thus have an effective veto over important decisions.[92]

The board, which was to meet four times per year, was also empowered to appoint, and delegate its powers to, an executive committee. Gardner had argued in December 1939 that a body with all countries represented would be unworkable and he had suggested a small operating board made up of officials representing groups of countries.[93] This suggestion foreshadowed the constituency system of representation within the executive boards of the Bretton Woods institutions.

In other ways, however, the IAB represented a strange halfway station between the BIS governance model and that of the Bretton Woods institutions. While the bank was to be an intergovernmental one, it would be chartered as a corporation by an act of the US Congress (which promised not to change the act for twenty years without agreement) since the United States was to house its "principal office."[94] The bank was then to establish at least one branch or agency in the territory of every member country. Unlike the IMF and the IBRD, the IAB was also empowered to act like a regular private bank, accepting private deposits and dealing with private customers in other ways. Here is how one BIS official attempted to describe its unique nature: "Although an association of governments, the I.A.B. takes the form of a private corporation. Naturally it does not conform strictly to any known type but is sui generis. It may be described as a cross between a share company and a co-operative society."[95]

Some Missing Issues

There was one other way in which the IAB was distinctive vis-à-vis the Bretton Woods institutions. Unlike the IMF's articles of agreement, the IAB by-laws did not impose any obligations on members relating to exchange rates and currency convertibility. The IAB's formal purposes did mention that it would "assist in stabilizing the currencies of American Republics" and "encourage direct general exchanges of the currencies of American Republics." But members were not

---

92. For example, Welles to Lancaster, June 11, 1940. Argentina and Brazil might also have a veto. Indeed, this feature was deliberately included as a means of encouraging greater Argentine interest in the bank. If Argentina was to be granted a potential veto, US officials concluded that Brazil would need equal treatment. Hanson to White, January 5, 1940, TSF, Entry 67A1804, box 65.

93. Gardner to Board of Governors, "The Inter-American Bank Proposal."

94. Quote from Department of State 1940, 522. Some US officials, such as Cotton ("Inter-American Bank," p. 7), thought the IAB's headquarters should be in Latin America "with a view to securing the full-time service of a few qualified Latin Americans of reputation and of keeping the institution alive to the conditions where it must invest."

95. (Illegible author's name), "Inter-American Bank," p. 4.

required to maintain a currency peg or commit to current account convertibility. Initial discussion in the IFEAC about creating a new IAB regional currency unit also went nowhere and the IAB's capital and operations were expressed in dollars.[96]

Latin American governments made it quite clear that they were not interested in undertaking exchange rate obligations. In their answers to the IFEAC questionnaire, Hanson observed, Latin American governments had emphasized that "they believe their economies must be diversified and strengthened considerably before they are ready for such a step." United States policymakers were also sympathetic to this Latin American preference. As Hanson told White, "it would hardly do to press Latin America on currency stabilization now, in the absence of either theoretic or practical justification."[97]. In his testimony before the Senate subcommittee, Collado also reminded his audience that "the history of the currencies of colonial and raw-material-producing nations is that they are subject to extreme exchange pressure whenever there is a world depression." Instead of a "rigid pegging" of currencies as under the gold standard, what was needed was improvements in "the broader economic situation of the countries by diversifying their structures so that they are not dependent upon the exports of a few products."[98]

The IAB's provisions also steered clear of one other issue: debt restructuring. We have seen how past discussions—from Mexico's 1933 proposals to Hanson's mid-1939 ideas—suggested that an inter-American financial institution might play a useful role in this area. As we saw, the issue was raised again by White in his initial late November 1939 memo to Morgenthau. But debt restructuring was too controversial to be included in the IAB by-laws. When Peru's Larrañaga raised it at the first IFAEC subcommittee meeting in mid-November, Berle noted in his diary that everyone withheld comment on the issue, particularly because there were some debt-restructuring discussions going forward involving countries represented.[99]

The issue was also controversial within White's informal committee of US officials. In mid-December, White proposed that the IAB could not lend to a country in default unless that country had "made an offer of adjustment that the bank regards as reasonable." He would insert a very similar provision into his

---

96. Roosevelt had been keen on the idea of a new kind of inter-American currency that might be called "unitam" but most Latin American officials (Peru was an exception) preferred to use the dollar. US Senate 1941, 35, 38, 45, 62; "December 5, 1939," p. 2, BP, box 211; Delegate of Peru, "Memorandum." In White's early Bretton Woods plans a few years later, he discussed the idea of an international currency unit and gave it a very similar name: "unitas."

97. Hanson to White, March 27, 1940, p. 2, HDWP, box 5, folder 6.

98. US Senate 1941, 41.

99. Berle to Welles, November 17, 1939, pp. 1–2, BP, box 59.

first draft of the IBRD two years later. At this time, he was forced to acknowledge, however, there was no consensus in favor of the provision among US officials. All they could agree upon was that the bank might declare that it "was neither acting as an agency to force resumption of debt payments nor making it easy for them to borrow without regard to the status of their already acquired debts."[100] In early January 1940, Hanson urged White to clarify to Latin American governments in advance of the IAB's creation whether the United States would vote to block loans to countries because of past defaults or expropriations, but no such declaration was issued.[101]

The Fate of the IAB

Despite backing from various quarters, the IAB was never established. Some Latin American governments had concerns about specific aspects of the final IAB plans, such as the size and timing of initial stock subscriptions, the prospect of a US veto over key decisions, the absence of a US commitment to open its markets to their exports, and the insistence on government guarantees for loans to their citizens.[102] But eight Latin American governments joined the United States in signing the bank's convention in May 1940: Bolivia, Brazil, Colombia, Dominican Republic, Ecuador, Mexico, Nicaragua, and Paraguay.[103] Mexico also ratified the IAB convention, but the other Latin American governments waited for United States to act. US ratification never came. Roosevelt asked the Senate to approve the convention on July 5, 1940, but the Senate chose to delay hearings until April 1941 and then the issue was never even brought to the full Senate for a vote.

The failure of the United States to ratify the convention was surprising given how the dramatic German victories in continental Europe at this time had made Latin America even more strategically important for US policymakers. Collado noted that the ratification of the IAB was initially delayed because attention shifted to Roosevelt's request in July for a large increase in the Export-Import Bank's loans to Latin America. Once Congress approved that request in late September, Collado pushed for action on the IAB but it was delayed once again, despite many inquiries from Latin American IFEAC members and diplomats.[104]

---

100. White, "Outline of Tentatively Proposed Bank," p. 2.
101. Hanson to White, January 5, 1940, p. 2.
102. Green 1971, 64–65.
103. Department of State 1940, 517.
104. Collado to Duggan, Berle, and Welles, September 30, 1940, DSDF, 710.BANK/218; Green 1971, 66.

Berle reported that the official initially placed in charge of steering legislation through Congress, Jesse Jones, was waiting to act until after the election that fall, and there was also some speculation that the conservative Jones himself was not that keen on the whole proposal.[105]

It was also true, however, that the IAB proposal had attracted considerable controversy outside of the Roosevelt administration. Even before the final texts had been released publicly in mid-April 1940, the State Department had been inundated with letters of opposition to the proposal, many of them handwritten by senders in small towns across the country.[106] Some of the opponents feared that the organization would give more power to private international bankers. Others worried that the IAB would undermine US sovereignty. Still others saw the IAB proposal as a "Communist document."[107] The last description would have surprised the editorial writers for the Cuban Communist daily newspaper *Hoy* which had attacked the IAB proposal in February 1940 as an instrument of US imperialism through which American private banks could consolidate their control over the economic and political life of Latin America.[108]

Those editorial writers would also no doubt have been surprised by the fact the IAB was strongly opposed by New York banks. Their opposition was led by W. Randolph Burgess, vice president of the National City Bank of New York, the largest US bank operating in Latin America at the time. Burgess told Morgenthau in late May 1940 that one of his concerns was that "the set up of the proposed bank ties it too closely to politics."[109] He preferred to see central bankers take up the bank's stock and appoint its directors, as in the case of the BIS (whose creation he had been involved with). Burgess also worried that the IAB would be a competitor of US banks in Latin America because it would be making short-term loans and taking deposits.

To address the latter point, the State Department had already gone out of its way earlier in the month to emphasize that the IAB was meant "to complement existing financial institutions rather than to provide a substitute for them."[110] When Congressional attention finally began to focus on the IAB in early 1941, Roosevelt administration officials—led by Rockefeller, Joseph Rovensky, and Will Clayton—also negotiated with the bankers to scale back some of the bank's activities. Its by-laws were amended to restrict its activities involving financial instruments with less than two years maturity to those guaranteed by

---

105. Green 1971, 65–66.
106. See letters in Louis Ludlow to Hull, April 6, 1940, DSDF, 710.BANK/90.
107. Roy Caswell of Caswell's Store in Wilcox, Nebraska, April 11, 1940, DSDF, BANK/110.
108. Willard Beaulac to Hull, February 16, 1940, DSDF, 710.BANK/16.
109. Burgess to Morgenthau, May 9, 1940, p. 1, DSDF, 710.BANK/193.
110. Department of State 1940, 519. See also Welles to Lancaster, June 11, 1940.

governments and central banks. In return, the bankers agreed not to oppose the bill.[111] The Bankers Association for Foreign Trade even passed a resolution endorsing the bank in early 1941.[112] After hearing testimony from Berle, Collado, and Clayton, a subcommittee of the Senate Committee on Foreign Relations in May 1941 approved the IAB convention with no objections.[113]

But the powerful Democratic chair of the Senate Banking and Currency Committee from Virginia, Carter Glass, then insisted that his committee be permitted to examine the idea before it was presented to the Senate as a whole. Once this request was granted, the eighty-two-year old Glass simply delaying its examination.[114] An effort by some members of the Senate Foreign Relations Committee to bring the proposal to the Senate floor in January 1942 at the start of an important meeting of governments of the Americas in Rio was unsuccessful. So too were personal appeals to Glass from Eccles and even Roosevelt as late as mid-1942.[115]

Years later, Berle blamed Glass's opposition to the IAB on the influence of Burgess. He suggested that Burgess backed out of the administration's deal with the bankers, and told Glass to "kill" the bill. It is certainly true that Burgess continued to complain—including to Glass—that the IAB would compete with the business of commercial banks and would be run by governments rather than central bankers.[116] But the conservative Glass—who had strongly opposed the interventionist economic policies of the New Deal—also had his own reasons for disliking the IAB. In addition to complaining that Congress would have no control over the IAB, Glass objected to the fact that it would "be managed largely by South American Republics; whereas the Ex-Im Bank is now managed exclusively by American citizens."[117]

Although it never came into existence, the IAB was an important initiative in symbolizing what the US government called the "the economic implementation of the Good Neighbor policy."[118] It also left an important legacy. In early 1940, Berle had stressed that it was a "laboratory study" in how worldwide economic

---

111. US Senate 1941, 16, 25; Green 1971, 69–70; Collado to Secretary of State, September 7, 1943, TSF, 450/81/02/03, box 66.

112. "Inter-American Bank Convention," May 6, 1942, ISF, box 245; Nelson Rockefeller to Hull, January 13, 1941, DSDF, 710.BANK/223.

113. Green 1971, 70.

114. Green 1971, 60, 67–73, 314.

115. Green 1971, 70–73. See also "Inter-American Bank Chronology," January 27, 1942, ISF, box 245; Eccles to Glass, June 17, 1942, DSDF, 710.BANK/259; Southard, "Background on Senator Glass's Proposed Amendments on the Inter-American Bank," May 8, 1942, CFHDW, box 7, Chron 35.

116. Quote from Green 1971, 314. See also pp. 71–72; "Inter-American Bank Convention," May 6, 1942, ISF, box 245.

117. Quoted in Green 1971, 71.

118. Department of State 1940, 518.

relations would need to be rebuilt after the war, and that "this makes a nucleus around which things will grow."[119] When he saw White's initial Bretton Woods plans of early 1942, Berle applauded how they built on this Good Neighbor initiative in ways he had hoped for.[120] Collado later also pointed out that the IAB served as a "predecessor" to White's initial plans for Bretton Woods.[121] Indeed, it is striking how many of the US officials involved in the IAB's drafting went on to participate in various ways in the discussions surrounding the Bretton Woods agreements, including not just Berle and Collado but also Morgenthau, White, Bernstein, Clayton, Gardner, Goldenwesier, Riefler, Schmidt, and Viner. In their internal memos during the drafting process, US policymakers also drew explicitly on the IAB precedent.[122] As we shall see, when responding to the US plans, Latin American officials referred back to the IAB proposal too, and some of those involved in the IAB discussions played significant roles in the Bretton Woods negotiations, such as Mexico's Villaseñor and Monteros.

Like the IMF and IBRD, the IAB was to be a government-owned multilateral financial institution, with weighted voting, that lent for short-term balance of payments and long-term development purposes. The IAB's mandate to address capital flight also foreshadowed White's interest in this issue in his early drafts of the IMF (although he addressed it in a different way then, as we shall see). At more general level, the IAB combined a commitment to liberal multilateralism with support for new interventionist economic practices that had become popular during the 1930s—thus representing an important early expression of the embedded liberal vision of Bretton Woods. It was this innovative vision that led US banks, isolationists, and economic conservatives to oppose the IAB, just as they would later oppose the Bretton Woods agreements (although with less success). The rise and fall of the IAB proposal is thus properly seen as an early skirmish in the battle to shape the postwar international financial order.

In this skirmish, international development issues were front and center. Indeed, the negotiation of the IAB marked the first time in history that governments attempted to construct an international institution with a central mandate

---

119. Berle's "laboratory study" comment is cited earlier in this chapter from a January 23, 1940, conversation with Treasury officials (note 90). He made the same comment—along with the rest of the quotation here—in a conversation with Goldenweiser two days later: "Conversation between Dr. Goldenweiser and Mr. Berle," p. 8. See also Berle and Jacobs 1973, 284.

120. Schwartz 1987, 213.

121. McKinzie 1974, 5.

122. See for example "Bank for Reconstruction and Development: Points to be Discussed by American Technical Committee," April 11, 1944, p. 2, HDWP, box 8, folder 4; LC.A. and R.B., "Agreement to Form an International Stabilization Fund of the United and Associated Nations," October 18, 1943, pp. 28, 30–31, 34, 36, ALP, International Stabilization Fund, Memoranda, Correspondence, box 8/7.

to promote economic "development" in poorer countries. To be sure, article 22 of the 1919 League of Nations Covenant had declared that the "well-being and development" of peoples in mandate territories of the League formed "a sacred trust of civilization" that must be upheld. But this reference to "development" was very vague and the commitment was restricted geographically to the former colonies of Germany and territories of the Ottoman Empire that were judged—in the paternalistic and imperial language of the League's covenant—to be "inhabited by peoples not yet able to stand by themselves under the strenuous conditions of the modern world." Moreover, the League's involvement was also indirect since it had "entrusted" the administration and "tutelage" of the peoples of the mandate territories to what were called "advanced nations" such as Britain and France.[123] As noted in chapter 7, the one highly innovative proposal for the League to take on a more direct and significant international development mandate—a proposal that came from Sun Yat-sen in China—was rebuffed by Western powers at the time of the League's founding. After its founding, the League did begin to address issues such as agriculture, public health, education, and transportation in poorer parts of the world beyond the mandate territories, but these activities were very limited in scope, and they emerged in a rather ad hoc fashion rather than as part of a new comprehensive official international commitment to promote development goals.[124]

In contrast with the League experience, the promotion of international development was central to the purpose of the IAB (and this task was also associated by many of its supporters with rejection of past imperialist practices). This mandate was also to be fulfilled in much more ambitious ways than the League had attempted, including public international lending and the recycling of flight capital. The IAB's negotiation even inspired some innovative ideas about the role an international institution could play in debt restructuring. Each of these aspects of the IAB proposal would be drawn upon by White in his first drafts of the Bretton Woods institutions. Some scholars have made the important point that some of the IMF activities built upon the legacy of the financial activities of the League.[125] In the case of the international development provisions of Bretton Woods, however, the experience of the IAB and inter-American financial cooperation served as the key historical precedent.

In light of recent scholarship on the origins of international development, it is also worth noting that the IAB proposal was a product of both Northern and

---

123. Quotes from League Covenant in Rist 1997, 60. See also Murphy 1994, 210–11, Alcalde 1987, 12–14, 49–56.

124. Zanasi 2007; Murphy 1994, 211. See also Alcalde's (1987, 50–53) discussion of the League's 1922 report on economic development in Albania.

125. Pauly 1997.

Southern preferences. On the Northern side, US support for the IAB reflected the same complex mix of strategic concerns, New Deal values, and economic interests that drove the broader Good Neighbor financial partnership. But the original impetus for the IAB came from Latin America, not the United States. International development was not thrust upon Latin American governments; it was instead demanded by them as part of their new state-led developmental priorities that emerged out of the political and economic upheavals of the 1930s.

A NEW APPROACH TO MONEY DOCTORING

Cuba

Another policy innovation of the Good Neighbor financial partnership was the transformation of US financial advisory activities in Latin America. Between 1900 and 1930, American "money doctors" traveled across Latin America urging and assisting local authorities to tie local monetary systems to the gold standard.[1] In the early 1940s, a new wave of US advisory missions was launched, but with quite different advice that supported the new Latin American development priorities and embedded liberal ideological framework. These missions were explicitly designed to strengthen the development foundations of Bretton Woods.

The origins of this transformation came in a high-profile financial advisory mission to Cuba in 1941–42. The American Technical Mission to Cuba was also significant because it involved various US officials—including White as head of the mission—who went on to play a major role in developing the Bretton Woods agreements. Like the IAB, the mission provoked strong opposition from conservatives and New York bankers (led once again by Burgess) who felt that its advice departed too radically from pre-1930s thinking. Like the IAB debate, the political struggles around the Cuban mission foreshadowed broader domestic US debates surrounding the Bretton Woods negotiations.

Despite its significance, the Cuban mission has been even more neglected than the IAB by historians of the Bretton Woods negotiations. It has also received little attention in broader literatures on the Good Neighbor policy and international

---

1. Drake 1989, Rosenberg 2003.

money doctoring. Even historians of US-Cuban relations have overlooked the episode, perhaps because its impact on actual Cuban policy was delayed for many years. But like the IAB proposal, the 1941–42 mission played an important role in setting the scene for the development content of the Bretton Woods vision, in spite of the delayed implementation of its recommendations.

US-Cuban Monetary Relations before the Mission

At the time of the Cuban mission, Cuba was without a central bank and US dollars were used alongside the national currency, the peso. The dollar's role within the country dated back to the turn of the century when Cuba had first become a US protectorate and the dollar had become legal tender alongside a chaotic mix of French and Spanish gold and silver coinage. When the Cuban government created its own gold-based currency in 1914 and called in French and Spanish coins, the dollar retained its legal tender status and its use was reinforced by the fact that the new peso's value was tied to it. By the 1920s, dollars in fact became the dominant currency used in Cuba. United States officials and businesses at the time applauded how the dollar's role guaranteed monetary stability in Cuba and facilitated US-Cuban commerce.[2] Some also saw the currency's standing in the country as linked to the Platt Amendment, the codicil to Cuba's 1901 Constitution that allowed for US military intervention and restricted Cuba's autonomy in foreign policy.[3]

In the early 1920s, Cuban politicians became very interested in creating a central bank that would issue Cuban currency. One motivation was the terrible quality of the old US notes in circulation, but the key catalyst was the country's 1920–21 financial crisis. With no central bank to provide emergency help, the crisis had led to the collapse of three large Cuban-owned banks, leaving the banking system dominated by branches of US and Canadian banks that had been able to survive because of support from their head offices overseas.[4] In this context, proposals for a Cuban-owned central bank took on important nationalist tones.

Cuban proposals for a central bank were opposed by foreign banks in Cuba, US officials, and some conservative Cuban business interests. To head off the initiative, the US Federal Reserve Board—backed by the State Department— allowed the Federal Reserve Banks of Atlanta and Boston to open agencies in Cuba in 1923 that could perform central banking functions (the Boston agency

---

2. See for example F. Kellogg to Andrew Mellon, September 21, 1926, CSF, 301.12(6).
3. See for example Ward Albertson to Mr. McCord, May 9, 1919, CSF, 301.12(6).
4. Wallich 1950, 71–2.

withdrew in 1926). From the US standpoint, this move also preserved the dollar's role in the country, allowed US banks to hold fewer cash reserves and, in the words of the US ambassador, helped "add to the potential influence of the United States in Cuba."[5] Although the initiative temporarily quelled Cuban demands for monetary reform, Cuban dissatisfaction grew once again when the country was hit very hard by the collapse of world sugar prices in the late 1920s. Cuba's economic woes were compounded by the 1930 US Smoot-Hawley tariff which cut the country's sugar exports to the United States. Under its dollarized economy, depreciation was not an option. Instead, Cuba underwent a severe deflation that Collado later described as "probably the greatest currency contraction in history."[6]

The economic crisis generated serious political unrest that eventually caused the resignation of President Gerardo Machado in August 1933. A new government backed by the United States survived less than a month in power before it was ousted by an army revolt led by Fulgencio Batista. A newly installed nationalist government headed by Ramón Grau San Martín represented the first Cuban government since 1898 that had not been sanctioned officially by the United States. The Grau regime launched major reforms ranging from land reform to the suspension of external payments on public works loans. Facing opposition from the US government, foreign business, the Cuban elite, and eventually Batista, Grau resigned in mid-January and was replaced by Carlos Mendieta.[7] While more acceptable to the United States, Mendieta's government consolidated a number of Grau's goals, including the signing of a treaty with the new Roosevelt administration that ended the Platt Amendment.

In the monetary realm, Mendieta's government in fact went further than Grau's had in trying to create an independent currency system. Building on an initiative of the Grau government, the Mendieta administration expanded the issue of local silver coins and made them unlimited legal tender at par for all tax and private payments. When the government also introduced capital controls for the first time in early June 1934, it appeared to be moving toward the de-dollarization of the monetary system. In the face of strong domestic opposition, however, capital controls were quickly withdrawn and the government backed away from its ambitious plans.[8] But in the next few years, the Cuban government continued to

5. "Substance of undated telegram from the American Ambassador, Habana, Cuba, received May 5, 1923," pp. 3–4, CSF, 301.12(6). For this episode, see P. H. to E. H. Crowder, May 25, 1923, Harding to Crissinger, May 28, 1923, CSF, 301.12(6).

6. "Notes on Conference Concerning Cuba," p. 3, October 9, 1941, CSF, 501.2-15. See also Diaz-Alejandro 1988, 194.

7. Argote-Freyre 2006, ch.6–7; Pérez 1986, 322–33.

8. Wallich 1950, 75–87, 112; Diaz-Alejandro 1988, 196.

expand silver coin issue and also issued new Cuban currency notes in 1935 that were decorated with images of Cuban nationalist heroes.[9] As the issue of Cuban currency expanded, the peso began trading at a discount against the dollar, causing dollars to disappear from domestic circulation almost entirely in 1939 (until early 1941 when higher sugar exports strengthened the peso's value).[10]

In contrast to past US policy, the Roosevelt administration was quite supportive of these monetary initiatives. As part of its broader efforts to promote political stability in Cuba after Grau's departure, the administration asked the newly created US Export-Import Bank in April 1934 to arrange for the minting of new peso coins for Cuba.[11] By the end of 1936, the bank had helped Cuba coin almost $50 million pesos, generating seigniorage profits equivalent to about 15 percent of government revenue.[12] In 1938, the Federal Reserve Board also closed the agency of the Federal Reserve Bank of Atlanta on the island, despite opposition from the US business community.[13] At this time, officials from the Federal Reserve Board and the Treasury also quietly began discussing monetary and banking reforms with their Cuban counterparts, including confidential Cuban government plans for a new government-controlled central bank and a monetary law that would end the dollar's legal tender role.[14] Some of the ideas being discussed at this time envisaged a central bank with a very strong development focus. For example, the prominent US economist Irving Fisher, along with some colleagues, proposed a Cuban central bank whose ambitious mandate to "elevate the general average of the standard of living" of Cubans included giving "preference and encouragement to the development of industries and activities designed to produce for domestic consumption" as well as the "diversification of agriculture and industry which will tend to the economic independence of Cuba."[15]

The goal of encouraging a diversification of the Cuban economy had been backed by the US government at this time, particularly after a poor sugar crop in 1938 led to an economic downturn and the threat of new political unrest.[16] When a newly elected government led by Batista backed a settlement on defaulted debt in September 1940, the negotiations for US loans and broader economic cooperation accelerated, driven also by the US recognition of Cuba's importance

9. Museo Numismático del Banco Nacionale de Cuba 1980, 47–55.

10. Wallich 1950, chaps. 7–8.

11. Argote-Freyre 2006, 145.

12. Adams 1976, 139.

13. Morrill to Welles, August 11, 1938; J. C. Rovensky to Robert Parker, August 19, 1938; H. C. Fazer to Robert Parker, August 19, 1938, all in CSF, 301.12(6).

14. Glenn Goodman to Mr. Paulger, October 5, 1937, CSF 501.2-15; Gordon Murff to Mr. Paulger, March 4, 1938, CSF, 301.12(6); White to Taylor, December 17, 1938, CFHDW, box 2, Chron. 12.

15. Irving Fisher, Robert Hemphill, and Hans Cohrssen, "Outline For Proposed National Bank of the Republic of Cuba," p. 4 (undated but file date is April 16, 1938), CSF, 301.12(6).

16. Gellman 1973, 167, 184, 188, 232.

for defense cooperation after the outbreak of war. In the negotiations, Cuban authorities mentioned that they would welcome US assistance in undertaking monetary and banking reforms, including the creation of a central bank.[17] The new 1940 Cuban Constitution—whose drafting was presided over by Grau (after his party won the elections for the assembly developing the document)—had specified that a new central bank would be established and that "money and banking shall be subject to regulation and control by the Nation."[18]

When the Export-Import Bank approved a $25 million loan for agricultural diversification and public works in the spring of 1941, US officials told the Cuban government that $5 million had secretly been approved to help the establishment of a central bank pending the creation of detailed plan.[19] In August 1941, the Cuban government then issued a formal request for US technical experts to develop a plan for a central bank. The Cubans stated that they had originally hoped to develop a plan on their own to be submitted to US experts for advice. But they had had to ask for US help because of the urgency of the issue, its technical nature, and "the numerous problems which a legislation drafted after long drawn out consultations might involve."[20]

A New Kind of Financial Advisory Mission

The Cuban request attracted considerable attention in US financial policymaking circles. The expansion of US public lending to Latin America in the late 1930s had generated new interest in reviving financial advisory activities in Latin America. At this time, Cuba was the most important destination for US investment in the region as well as the sixth most important supplier of US imports and the eleventh largest market for US exports overall. According to US Ambassador George Messersmith, Cuba's cooperative attitude in defense matters was also "in many respects more important to us than with any of the American republics."[21] Not surprisingly, then, the State Department's Collado, who was "mainly responsible for arranging the mission," argued that the head of the mission had to be a well-known figure in order to "impress the Government with the importance that we have attached to their request."[22]

---

17. US State Department 1961, 790; 1962, 40, 146–47.
18. Quoted in Wallich 1950, 275.
19. US State Department 1961, 779; 1941, 158–59.
20. J. M. Cortina to US Ambassador, August 10, 1941, p. 1, CSF, 501.2-15.
21. Quote from US State Department 1962, 131. For Cuba's economic importance, see pp. 153–56.
22. First quotation from Gardner and Vest to Board of Governors, October 16, 1941, CSF, 501.2-15. Second quotation from Gardner, reporting Collado's views in Gardner to Goldenweiser, September 12, 1941, CSF, 501.2-15.

It was very soon apparent that this first high-profile US financial mission to Latin America in many years would be quite different from pre-1930 missions because of the new values and priorities of the Good Neighbor policy. To begin with, there was the issue of who would lead it. In the 1920s, the task of foreign monetary missions had often been left to prominent private US citizens such as Princeton economics professor Edwin Kemmerer, frequently backed informally by the State Department, the FRBNY, and/or private New York bankers.[23] But the Cuban mission was seen as one more properly to be led by public officials because of both the broader priorities of the Good Neighbor policy and the New Deal's efforts to bring monetary and financial issues under greater public control. But a key question needed to be answered: Which public officials?

Here, the bureaucratic rivalries of the New Deal came to the fore. Even before the Cuban request, Treasury officials had begun to signal their interest in foreign financial advising with their involvement in the discussions with Cuban officials in 1937–38 as well as in informal talks with Brazilian officials about the possible creation of a central bank in that country.[24] In late 1938, one Treasury official even proposed the placement of "Treasury Financial Counsellors" in major cities across the Americas who could offer financial advisory services to foreign governments.[25] Another suggested to White in May 1939 that the Treasury introduce a program under which Latin American officials would come to work at the Treasury for brief periods, a proposal that led White to suggest to Morgenthau the creation of a "training school."[26]

Interest in the relationship between financing advising and the new Good Neighbor financial partnership was also emerging in the Federal Reserve Board. In a May 1939 memo to Chairman Eccles, Gardner worried that efforts to cultivate goodwill of Latin America through loans might ultimately backfire if they led to defaults. Another way to gain Latin American support, he argued, might be by "lending American experts to those Latin American Governments who request their services in improving their operating effectiveness." Gardner also warned Eccles that the Federal Reserve Board needed to take the initiative in financial advising or else "the Treasury may take the whole field over." Gardner was also concerned that the FRBNY would try to get involved and thus challenge the principle that "the foreign activities and relations of the FRS are under the supervision and control of the Board of Governors of the FRS."[27] In the 1920s, the

---

23. Drake 1989; Rosenberg 2003.
24. Gellman 1979, 42; Blum 1959, 493; White to Taylor, February 6, 1939, CFHDW, box 2, Chron. 12.
25. Taylor to Morgenthau, November 1938, p. 2, TSF, 450/81/20/07, box 28.
26. Schmidt to White, May 5, 1939 and White to Morgenthau, May 10, 1939, CFHDW, box 3, Chron. 14.
27. Gardner to Eccles, May 29, 1939, p. 1, 3–4, ISF, box 236.

board's role in foreign missions had been passive, but the new financial advisory missions provided an opportunity to reinforce the new authority it had acquired under New Deal legislation.

These New Deal politics came to the surface in the selection of the personnel for the Cuban mission. The State Department apparently rejected the involvement of FRBNY officials in the mission outright, and vetoed a suggestion to include Louis Rosenthal, the vice president of Chase National Bank.[28] Instead, Collado approached both White in the Treasury and Gardner in the Federal Reserve Board for help. When White made it clear that he hoped to lead the mission, Gardner pushed the board to resist this outcome by recommending Goldenweiser on the grounds that Cuba should not be left with the impression that the creation of a central bank "was regarded as a province of the Treasury rather than of the Federal Reserve System."[29] When the board would not free Goldenweiser from his other responsibilities for the task, White was selected to lead the US government–financed mission.[30] But the membership included both Fed and Treasury officials: Gardner, George Vest (Fed), George Eddy (Treasury), Frank Southard (Treasury), and Harold Spiegel (Treasury). A representative of the Farm Credit Administration, A. T. Esgate, also joined the mission later. Although Gardner initially had some concerns that White was trying control the mission excessively, the board representatives successfully resisted this and were quickly satisfied with the degree of consultation and cordiality on the team. Indeed, in early November 1939 near the end of an initial four-week visit to Cuba by the mission (of which White was only able to participate in the latter half), Gardner reported to Goldenweiser that White was "on his best behavior" and that the mission seemed to be "in a small, but nevertheless significant, way improving our relations with the Treasury."[31]

The content of the mission's advice also signaled a new kind of American money doctoring. Kemmerer and other US money doctors in the pre-1930 years had been advocates of the gold standard and independent central banks, advice that stemmed from their neoclassical economic beliefs in a restricted state role in the economy, free trade, and the free flow of international investment. Historian Emily Rosenberg points out that they had seen their financial expertise as a kind of "universal and scientific product," and their advisory work as part of a civilizing mission bringing modern progress to poorer parts of the world. Most of the money doctors had in fact begun their careers in the US colonial

---

28. Bethea to Morrill, September 18, 1941, CSF, 501.2-15; US State Department 1962, 193–95.
29. Gardner to Goldenweiser, September 12, 1941. p. 1, CSF, 501.2-15.
30. Carpenter to Goldenweiser, September 17, 1941, CSF, 501.2-15.
31. Gardner to Goldenweiser, November 2, 1941, pp. 1, 3, CSF 501.2-15.

service (especially in the Philippines), and Rosenberg notes that they "considered U.S. imperialism to be a benevolent carrier of science and civilization that would uplift backward economies and people."[32]

It quickly became apparent that the members of the White mission held different views that were more in line with New Deal thinking. The mission's key recommendations came in a report released on April 22, 1942 that urged the Cuban government to create a publicly controlled central bank with goals quite different from those endorsed by Kemmerer across Latin America in the 1920s.[33] Instead of passively reflecting the country's balance of payments position, the central bank would take active responsibility "for the general level of business activity and employment" in the country and for "fostering economic development."[34] To fulfill this mandate, it would be empowered to conduct open market operations and to adjust private banks' reserve requirements, and its note issue was to be backed with reserves at a ratio of 25 percent rather than a rigid 100 percent (and some members of the mission had questioned whether a reserve rule was necessary at all).[35] The mission also backed legislation that allowed for the use of exchange rate adjustments and exchange controls in the event of a balance of payments crisis. In internal discussions, members of the mission had noted the potential need for these tools as an "adjusting device" because Cuban incomes were "subject to violent fluctuations—related to price of sugar."[36] They also pointed out that exchange controls could help address the "steady drain" of capital from the country.[37]

Another recommendation was that the central bank should "give reasonable assistance to the Central Government."[38] The mission acknowledged the controversial nature of this idea, but noted that the Cuban government "has faced almost insurmountable difficulties in borrowing money in Cuba," and argued that "domestic borrowing is frequently strongly preferable to incurring debts in a foreign currency." A "moderate amount" of central bank accommodation of

---

32. Rosenberg 2003, 194, 24.

33. American Technical Mission to Cuba 1942. The Cuban government was to appoint the governor of this central bank as well as a majority of its board of five directors (the two others would represent Cuban and foreign banks). An initial mission report in late November 1939 focused narrowly on short-term Cuban problems and recommended the creation of a central dollar or gold reserve. After issuing its main recommendations in April 1942, the mission released two supplementary reports in June and July commenting on Cuban draft legislation.

34. American Technical Mission to Cuba 1942, 783–84, 777.

35. Wallich to Knoke, August 22, 1942, ISF, box 110.

36. Quotes from Spiegel, "Factors relating to Cuban proposals," September 30, 1941, p. 2, CFHDW, box 5, Chron. 27.

37. Spiegel, "Factors relating to Cuban proposals," p. 2. In earlier discussions in late 1938, White had also supported Cuban proposals that included provisions for capital controls; White to Taylor, December 17, 1938, p. 3, CFHDW, box 2, Chron.12.

38. American Technical Mission to Cuba 1942, 784.

governments was "desirable under certain conditions," and "greater Central Bank assistance during periods of trade depression may be essential to the financial and economic welfare of the country."[39]

To enhance the central bank's control of the monetary system, the mission recommended eliminating the dollar's domestic legal tender status and centralizing the country's dollars as much as possible in a new stabilization fund that could help manage the external value of the Cuban currency and assist in "financing imports, repaying foreign indebtedness, and the like." In addition, the mission stated that the discouragement of the dollar's domestic role might help reduce capital flight linked to the Cuban tendency to keep savings in that currency.[40]

The mission also highlighted the developmental benefits of the lender of last resort role that the new central bank could perform. Echoing the arguments of Cuban nationalists in the early 1920s, the report stated that the absence of a central bank had been "one of the factors retarding the development of Cuban-owned banks."[41] In meetings with US officials, Cuban Cabinet members had emphasized this rationale for the central bank, noting that more Cuban-owned banking facilities were urgently needed to achieve their goal of economic diversification.[42] Messersmith had also emphasized that more Cuban-owned banking facilities were urgently needed to achieve this goal because foreign banks showed little interest in assisting domestic business.[43] To improve access to credit domestically, the Cuban government was also interested in emulating other Latin American governments that had begun to create public agricultural and industrial lending agencies during the 1930s. The White mission favored this goal, arguing that "the Cuban economy is in need of an official or semi-official agency to extend credit for agricultural purposes" and that consideration should be given to the creation of "agencies for industrial, public works and mortgage purposes." Furthermore, the central bank "should be authorized to give reasonable assistance to such agencies" and the central bank itself should be authorized

39. American Technical Mission to Cuba 1942, 777, 784.

40. American Technical Mission to Cuba 1942, 776. One further rationale for restricting the dollar's role was mentioned privately by Henry Wallich of the FRBNY at the time: "By eliminating the dollar from the Cuban circulation, we would greatly ease the problem resulting from the possibility that Axis dollars might be disposed of in Cuba." The State Department had already asked the Cuban government to strictly control the import of dollars for this reason, but there were concerns that Cuban measures were not targeting imports from other countries in the Americas; Wallich to Knoke, "Suggestions for Control of Dollars in Cuba," July 1, 1942, p. 2, ISF, box 110. For concerns about the dumping of Axis dollars in dollarized economies of Latin America at this time, see also Bernstein to White, March 11, 1942, "Meeting on the Control of American Currency Board," CFHDW, box 7, Chron. 33.

41. American Technical Mission to Cuba 1942, 775.

42. "Meeting of Mission with Certain Cabinet Members, October 8, 1941," CSF, 501.2-15.

43. Messersmith to Hull, November 8, 1941, p. 5, CSF, 501.2-15.

to lend directly to the public in "special emergencies of credit contraction when normal banking facilities are seriously disrupted and when banks against their wish are forced to call in old loans and to refuse new ones."[44]

Reactions

Very soon after the mission's April 1942 report was released, President Batista submitted legislation to the Cuban Congress that closely followed its advice, but the legislation and the US recommendations immediately produced controversy. The foreign banking community (which included both US and Canadian banks) was particularly opposed to the creation of a central bank. Their opposition had been anticipated by Messersmith who had told the mission in October 1941 that "the banks will not be pleased with the work of the Mission" and had advised Hull that their opposition should not influence any decisions of the US and Cuban governments.[45]

One objection from the foreign bankers was that the central bank could lend to the public, thereby creating competition for private banks.[46] They were also annoyed that their institutions would be required to deposit reserves with the bank and subscribe to its stock.[47] But the main objection of foreign bankers was that the central bank would be government-controlled and thus, in their view, likely to be mismanaged and exploited for political ends. In the words of one Federal Reserve official, US bankers criticized the White mission "for having failed to understand that the whole central bank project was simply due to the desire of some Cuban politicians to create a means of easy financing and an opportunity for graft."[48] Reporting on a meeting between the mission and foreign bankers, another US official recorded the view of Chase's Rosenthal that "a good credit system was impossible in Cuba because the Cubans are 'that sort of animal.'"[49]

---

44. American Technical Mission to Cuba, 784, 785. The mission prepared a report concerning the creation of an agricultural bank, but delayed its release because of a concern that the report "might lead to creation of a bank which might be used in risky war-time emergency financing, thereby endangering the long-run success of the institution." John DeBeers and L. Larry Leonard, "Cuba," January 1943, p. 6, CFHDW, box 9, Chron. 43.

45. "Conference of Mission with Ambassador Messersmith, October 8, 1941," p. 1, CSF, 501.2-15. See also Messersmith to Hull, November 8, 1941, pp. 6–7.

46. Wallich to Knoke, December 15, 1942, ISF, box 110; "Comments by American Technical Mission to Cuba on Memorandum Submitted by Mr. W. R. Burgess of the National City Bank of New York," CSF, 501.2-15.

47. "Conference of Cuba Mission with representatives of foreign banks in Cuba, April 2, 1942." April 7, 1942, ITM, box 20; "Interview Havana August 27, 1942," CSF, 501.2-15.

48. Wallich to Knoke, August 22, 1942, p. 2, ISF, box 110.

49. "Notes on Conference Concerning Cuba," p. 9.

While some foreign bankers saw the creation of a central bank as a political inevitability, one US official reported that there were others "who are so provoked with the Mission's report that they do not wish to have any dealings with any member of the Mission."[50] The highest-profile opponent engaged directly with the mission was Burgess, whose National City Bank was the largest bank in Cuba at the time. In early August, the mission felt compelled to write a formal response to his criticisms (approved by all members), in which it accepted some of Burgess's suggestions, such as the need for reserves to cover both the central bank's notes and its deposits, but did not budge on the core elements of the recommendations.[51]

The mission's report encountered resistance from some Cubans as well. The Cuban Chamber of Commerce opposed government control of the central bank and favored tighter restrictions on the bank's lending to the government, arguing that the latter would be tempted to misuse the bank to solve its financial difficulties.[52] While some newer Cuban banks favored a central bank (since it would help them handle runs), older and more conservative banks associated with the Havana Clearing House opposed the idea for similar reasons to those of their foreign counterparts.[53] Collado argued privately that they were afraid of a central bank "because it would strength the hand of the Cuban Government, and because the Cuban Government is no longer run by the first families."[54] If a central bank was to be created, the Clearing House wanted to see the institution's reserves set at a higher level and a prohibition on its lending to the public. The Clearing House also objected to the stabilization fund and wanted the dollar to remain legal tender.[55]

There were even members of the Cuban government who thought that the government would have too much influence over the central bank.[56] Some opposition politicians also shared this concern, including Joaquín Martínez Sáenz who had led the radical monetary reforms of 1934 as finance minister (until leaving Mendieta's government in June of that year) and who was now leader of the opposition ABC Party. According to one US official, Sáenz was pleased to see

50. "Interview Havana August 28, 1942," CSF, 501.2-15. For the sense of inevitability, see "Conference of Cuba Mission"; Southard to White, July 2, 1942, CSF, 501.2-15.

51. "Comments by American Technical Mission to Cuba on Memorandum Submitted by Mr. W. R. Burgess of the National City Bank of New York," CSF, 501.2-15.

52. R. W. Bean, "Analysis of the Cuban Chamber of Commerce Bank Proposal," December 16, 1942, ISF, box 110.

53. For this distinction between Cuban bankers, see for example Henry Wallich, "Monetary Reform in the Caribbean Area," December 28, 1945, ISF, box 221.

54. "Notes on Conference Concerning Cuba," p. 5.

55. "Memorandum Submitted by the Havana Clearing House to the Honorable Senate of the Republic," August 28, 1942, CSF, 501.2-15.

56. "Interview Havana August 28, 1942," CSF, 501.2-15.

that the mission had not set out to protect the interests of US banks but rather reflected "a liberal and independent viewpoint." But he was concerned about political control of the central bank because of his distrust of Batista (whom he had once challenged to a duel). Sáenz apparently identified two kinds of opponents of the central bank: "those who want to keep Cuba in a colonial position" and "those who do not trust Batista's economic leadership and will oppose a central bank which the Government can dominate."[57] Another member of the ABC Party, Luis Machado, reinforced this point, remarking that past initiatives to establish a central bank had failed "because of a widespread fear that any central bank would be a tool of politicians." For this reason, "he regarded it as important for the bank to look and be conservative in its early years in order to win popular support."[58]

One final source of opposition to the mission's report came from Spruille Braden, who became the new US ambassador to Cuba after Messersmith left in February 1942. As we have seen, Messersmith had been in favor of the creation of a central bank.[59] Although he was hardly a New Deal ideologue (many New Dealers disliked him), Messersmith was a reformer who accepted a greater role of the state in the economy because, in the words of his biographer, he believed that "the alternatives to protectionism and statism . . . would be more sweeping and far less palatable."[60] He was a strong supporter of US assistance to Cuba at this time because of its role in defense cooperation and the risk of domestic political unrest.

Braden brought quite a different perspective. In one historian's words, he was "a Republican to the core" who had "little use for the New Deal, home of intellectuals he considered soft and policies he considered softheaded." For him, "the Good Neighbor was a weak-kneed abdication of the virile [Theodore] Roosevelt's active commitment to the civilization of South America."[61] Before coming to Cuba, he had been ambassador to Colombia where he had opposed Colombian proposals for light industrialization, arguing that they "would nurture unsound nationalistic programs in commerce." He was also a notoriously strong personality; indeed, according to one scholar, "Dean Acheson once remarked that Braden was the only bull to carry around his own china shop."[62]

---

57. Quotes from US official describing Sáenz's views in "Interview, Habana, August 29, 1942," pp. 1, 2, CSF, 501.2-15. For his challenge to a duel, see Argote-Freyre 2006, 157.

58. Quotes from US official summarizing his views in "Interview Havana August 28, 1942," pp. 1, 2, CSF, 501.2-15.

59. See also Gardner to Board of Governors, November 14, 1941, CSF, 501.2-15; "Conference of Mission with Ambassador Messersmith, October 8, 1941," CSF, 501.2-15.

60. Stiller 1987, 271.

61. Stiller 1987, 231. See also Rivas 2002, 55.

62. Both quotes in Friedman 2003, 80.

In his memoirs, Braden describes how he read the mission report en route to Cuba and "was appalled." He concluded that "there was no time to lose," and urged Prime Minister Carlos Saladrigas to withdraw the legislation in their first meeting.[63] State Department officials in Washington felt that bankers were shaping Braden's perspective on this issue.[64] But Braden "resented being called a tool of the bankers" and insisted that he had come to his views before consulting with them, although he acknowledged that US bankers in Havana were "delighted" with his position.[65]

Braden outlined his views in a July 20, 1942 memo to Hull. He highlighted how the elimination of the dollar's legal tender role and the creation of the stabilization fund could undermine external currency stability and "prejudice trade with the United States," especially since these measures might lead to the establishment of exchange controls. He also noted the risk that the government might overborrow from the central bank, as had been the experience in other countries such as Chile (where his family's business was Braden Copper Company). His main point, however, was that "honest and competent administration in Government-controlled organizations has been and is a rarity in Cuba. . . . To launch a fundamentally important new system under these conditions is, to say the least, hazardous."[66]

In his memoirs, Braden writes that his letter to Hull "won the fight" and that "when Cordell Hull read it he hit the ceiling."[67] But the archival records tell a different story. Welles responded to Braden's memo several weeks later on August 15, stating simply that the State Department had already approved the mission's report and could not change its position now. He instructed Braden to back informally the mission's recommendations and stated that the State Department recognized that the Cuban desire for reform "represented the legitimate aspirations of an independent country."[68] A few days after Welles had written to Braden, Southard had a long meeting with the ambassador during which the latter reiterated his concerns about the establishment of a central bank. While Southard was convinced by the meeting that Braden's position "had not been influenced by the opposition of local bankers," he disagreed with it, arguing that Cubans "should be allowed to take their chances on a failure of the Central Bank due to political corruption and irresponsibility."[69]

---

63. Braden 1971, 305.
64. Frederick Livesey to White, July 16, 1942, ISF, box 110; Southard to Gardner, July 14, 1942, CSF, 501.2-15.
65. Braden 1971, 306.
66. US State Department 1963b, 298–99.
67. Braden 1971, 306.
68. US State Department 1963b, 307.
69. Southard to White and State Department Finance Division, August 19, 1942, p. 2, CSF, 501.2-15.

Defending the New Approach

In his response to Braden, Welles had also included a copy of much more detailed and strongly worded memo from the assistant chief of the Financial Division in the State Department, George F. Luthringer, which responded point by point to the issues that Braden had raised.[70] Luthringer's memo provided a much more blunt rationale for the shift in US policy toward Cuba's monetary situation than the mission's report had done. It is also noteworthy that Luthringer was no monetary radical. He had earlier worked with Kemmerer on his 1931 Princeton Ph.D. which focused on the Philippine gold exchange standard, concluding that it was "an economical, safe, and desirable monetary standard for the Philippines."[71]

To begin with, Luthringer noted that the mission recommended exchange controls be introduced only in a balance of payments crisis, under which circumstances he argued that "exchange control is a lesser evil than the extreme and uncontrolled deflation of the type experienced by Cuba during the depression." He also saw little practical point in limiting the central bank from lending to the government too restrictively since such limits were easily overridden or ignored. He went further to defend past Latin American practice in this area: ". . . in citing the experience of Chile in this regard or in citing experience of other Latin American countries one must always give consideration to the disastrous results that might have occurred in many instances had the central banks not taken action to counter extremely deflationary pressures. In many cases depreciation of the currency has doubtless provided a safety valve and means of adjustment for relieving intolerable social and economic pressure."[72]

Luthringer was also dismissive of Braden's main critique about political control of the central bank. The view that central banks should be independent of governments, he argued, "has been pretty well discredited during the 1930s both by monetary theorists and the march of political and economic events." Because of the absence of a strong Cuban banking sector, he pointed out, a Cuban central bank controlled by private bankers "would appear to perpetuate in Cuba a degree of control over the banking system by foreign bankers which the Cubans can hardly be expected to accept." In addition, while acknowledging that many Latin American central banks had made mistakes, he argued that "it would be very difficult to sustain the thesis that these countries would have been better off economically if they had been content to accept a dual monetary system or to use the

---

70. US State Department 1963b, 301–7.

71. Luthringer 1931, 299.

72. US State Department 1963b, 302, 306, 305.

dollar exclusively rather than make some attempt to control money and credit from the point of view of the particular social and economic needs of each."[73]

Luthringer finished up with a basic political argument about how US policy in this episode linked to broader US respect for Cuban sovereignty:

> . . . it is difficult to see why an exception should be made with respect to monetary and banking matters in the exercise of sovereignty by an American republic. The establishment of its own monetary system by Cuba is as much a prerogative of Cuban sovereignty as the establishment of its own army, police forces and courts. . . . I do not see how we could possibly object to the establishment by Cuba of its own independent monetary system without doing violence to our basic political policies toward Cuba.[74]

The State Department was not the only branch of the US government that favored the mission's recommendations. White had secured Morgenthau's approval for the report before its release.[75] The proposal that the Cuban central bank be what Gardner called an "arm of the Government" had also met no objection when it was discussed at the Federal Reserve Board.[76] Indeed, as far back as the 1938 informal discussions with Cuba, Goldenweiser had told the Cubans unofficially that he agreed with proposals for majority government ownership for the central bank.[77]

The lead role that officials from the Treasury and Federal Reserve Board played in challenging the traditional approaches to US money doctoring was fitting. Scholars who have examined the spread of Keynesian ideas to the United States in the late 1930s and 1940s have often identified both the Treasury and Federal Reserve Board as the most receptive government agencies to new economic ideas that challenged the predepression orthodoxy.[78] Many of the Keynesians in these government agencies were also linked to Harvard University's economics department which had emerged, in Galbraith's words, as "the principal avenue by which Keynes's ideas passed to the United States," despite the conservative leanings of many of its faculty.[79] The key figures associated with Latin American financial advising emerged from these Harvard-Treasury–Federal Reserve circles.

---

73. US State Department 1963b, 303–4, 305.
74. US State Department 1963b, 305.
75. White to Miss Chauncey, April 28, 1942, SMHDW, box 14, file: D1-No.3.
76. "Excerpt from the Minutes of the Meeting of the Board held on February 6, 1942," CSF, 501.2-15.
77. Goldenweiser to Eduardo Durrathy, January 13, 1938, CSF, 501.2-15.
78. Hirschman 1995, Salant 1989.
79. Galbraith 1972, 49.

More generally, it is worth noting that officials at the Federal Reserve Board had shown a much greater openness to new economic thinking than their colleagues at the FRBNY. The Board's chairman, Marriner Eccles, had been a banker from Utah, well outside New York circles, who had emerged as a prominent advocate of proto-Keynesian deficit spending during the Great Depression before Roosevelt had appointed him in late 1934. He had also been a strong backer of the 1935 Banking Act that restructured the Federal Reserve System to bring it under the more centralized control. As we have seen in the last chapter, key board officials such as Gardner and Goldenweiser were also supportive of some of the innovative proposals in the IAB project (despite their preference to see a central bank–controlled institution).

In a memo to Hull on September 9 that responded to Welles's letter, Braden stated that "the Department's instructions have been noted and will, of course, as always, be meticulously followed." He also clarified that his earlier ideas had been submitted "with a view to insuring the successful operation of the program which was recommended by the Mission."[80] He then responded to many of the points in Luthringer's memo and attached a document prepared by the Havana Clearing House that objected to Batista's legislation. The State Department's Laurence Duggan replied that the department now had a clear understanding of the position Braden had taken in his July 20 memo, and added: "I am sure you understand clearly the Department's position with regard to the monetary and banking legislation and, in the circumstances, I think you will agree that formal reply by the Department to your 961 [his September 9 memo] would not appear to be required."[81]

The Aftermath

In his 1971 memoirs, Braden saw the activities of Duggan and White in this episode as evidence of their role as Soviet spies, and he boasted that "the first thing I did in Cuba was to defeat a Communist plot involving both our State and Treasury Departments."[82] He argued as follows: "White had proceeded on the classic Leninist principle that one way to destroy the enemy is to corrupt his currency and bankrupt his economy. And in that case bankruptcy would have been a wedge driven between Cuba and the United States, with a good chance of

---

80. US State Department 1963b, 310, 311.
81. US State Department 1963b, 315.
82. Braden 1971, 304. For Duggan's involvement in espionage for the USSR, see Haynes, Kleher, and Vassiliev 2009, 220–45; Weinstein and Vassiliev 1999, chap. 1.

bringing about the Communist takeover years before (with plenty of help from Washington) Fidel Castro finally seized power. Duggan and White gambled for very high stakes indeed."[83] As noted above, however, support for the mission's recommendations extended far beyond White and Duggan. Moreover, as we shall see, the kind of advice given to Cuba then became standard fare for US financial advisory missions to many other Southern countries during the rest of the decade with the involvement of neither of them. Even FRBNY officials joined in the advocacy of this new approach.

Interestingly, US officials involved in later missions rarely made any mention of the precedent-setting nature of the Cuban mission. Instead, they usually highlighted the pioneering role of a 1943–44 Paraguayan mission led by the Federal Reserve Board's Robert Triffin. While Triffin's advice was immediately adopted by the Paraguayan government, the Cuban mission came to be seen as a failure because no central bank was established in its immediate wake. In explaining that failure, Triffin himself argued in 1944 that the Cuban mission may have had too much "publicity and fanfare," rather than working "more quietly in close contact with local people" to develop plans that the government would be fully committed to implement.[84] The main difficulty, however, was that the Cuban government faced ongoing domestic opposition to its central bank proposal after the Cuban Congress held inconclusive hearings in November and December 1942.

When Triffin visited the country briefly in August 1945 to provide further advice, Grau had become president (elected the previous year) but the country remained embroiled in domestic debate on the issue. Although the central bank proposal was now backed by the Cuban banking and business community and by opposition figures such as Sáenz, Triffin reported that "the central bank project is becoming a sort of political football, for which both the administration and the opposition want to get full credit."[85] Not until Grau's protégé Carlos Prío Socarrás was elected president was central bank legislation finally approved by the Cuban Congress in December 1948. The Banco Nacional de Cuba began operations in April 1950 with Felipe Pazos (who had represented Cuba at Bretton Woods) as president.[86]

---

83. Braden 1971, 311.
84. Triffin to Arthur Schlesinger, May 13, 1946, p. 6, ISF, box 156.
85. Triffin to Governor Szymczak, August 14, 1945, pp. 1–2, ISF, box 221. For Sáenz, see Triffin to Szymczak, August 21, 1945, ISF, box 221.
86. After Batista's coup d'état in March 1952, Pazos resigned and was replaced by Sáenz. When Castro came to power in 1959, Pazos was initially reinstalled but then resigned later in the year and was replaced with Ernesto "Che" Guevara. After visiting Cuba soon thereafter, two FRBNY officials recorded the following impressions of Guevara: "A lack of qualifications and pronounced leftist leanings also characterize the new National Bank president, a young (31) Argentine doctor who has never previously had any concern with financial matters but is apparently one of the Fidel Castro's closest

In its final form, the central bank legislation followed the basic ideas outlined by the American Technical Mission in 1942: the bank was government-controlled with a majority of the board appointed by the government and one representative each from the Cuban and foreign banking communities; it could lend to the government under strict conditions; exchange controls could be imposed in emergency conditions; it included an agricultural credit bank; notes and deposits were backed by a 25 percent reserve of gold and foreign exchange; a Monetary Stabilization Fund was created; private banks were subject to reserve requirements; and the peso became sole legal tender.[87] There were a few modifications; for example, the legislation allowed for multiple exchange rates and the provision that the central bank could lend to the public in emergency situations was dropped.[88] In the final stages of drafting, the Cuban government had been advised by Henry Wallich of the FRBNY (another Harvard Ph.D. graduate). As we shall see, Wallich had worked with Triffin on monetary reforms elsewhere in Latin America from the mid-1940s onward and been involved in US discussions about Cuba since the early 1940s. In a book published in 1950, he outlined the case for the central bank legislation in ways that echoed the thinking of the White mission and its supporters in its sympathy for Cuban industrialization and economic diversification, and the need for countercyclical monetary policies and exchange rate adjustments, as well as exchange control in the face of external shocks.[89]

The American Technical Mission of 1941–42 marked the culmination of a shift in US policy toward Cuban monetary affairs that had begun in the early days of the New Deal. This shift provided a pioneering example of the broader US initiatives to cultivate an active financial partnership with Latin America under the Good Neighbor policy that accelerated in the late 1930s.[90] The Cuban mission signaled that US officials were now willing to experiment with a new approach to financial advisory missions, a willingness that soon became even more apparent under Triffin's leadership as we shall see in subsequent chapters. These new missions

---

confidants (along with brother Raul Castro). Dr. Guevara impressed us as intelligent and earnest (despite his "revolutionary" costume and trappings of beret, beard, long hair, army fatigue uniform, and tommy guns) and he seemed, moreover, to have already been at work learning the elements of Cuban banking." Horace Sanford and Richard Dosik, "Report on the Visits to Central Banks of Argentina, Paraguay, Bolivia, Costa Rica, Nicaragua, and Cuba, November–December, 1959," pp. 19–20, January 1960, ISF, box 229.

87. E. P. Schlesinger to Knoke, "New Cuban Monetary and Banking Legislation," March 3, 1949, ISF, box 110.

88. Wallich 1950, 292.

89. Wallich 1950.

90. Benjamin (1977) notes that US policy toward Cuba more generally played a pioneering role in the birth of a more internationalist US foreign economic policy in the New Deal.

would be led by public officials and they would offer new kinds of advice favoring the new state-led development goals of Latin American governments that had become prominent in the wake of the Great Depression.

This advice was also in keeping with the embedded liberal ideology that informed US policymakers' thinking during the Bretton Woods negotiations. Two years before the Bretton Woods agreements were signed, the American Technical Mission endorsed in a bilateral context such policies as capital controls and adjustable exchange rates that were soon to be supported multilaterally under the IMF's articles of agreement. Not surprisingly, US opponents of the Cuban mission reemerged as critics of the Bretton Woods agreements. They were also joined by Kemmerer himself who vociferously criticized the agreements for departing too radically from the financial orthodoxy of the gold standard.[91]

When Triffin offered similar advice to that of the Cuban mission to Latin American countries from 1943 onward, he and other US officials often noted explicitly that their recommendations were designed to reinforce the goals of Bretton Woods. Latin American governments also recognized the link. This explicit connection between Bretton Woods and the new style of financial advising was missing from the White mission for the simple reason that the planning for Bretton Woods only in its infancy at the time. Interestingly, however, many of the officials involved in the mission would also be involved in the Bretton Woods negotiations, including not just White but also Bernstein, Collado, Gardner, Goldenweiser, Luthringer, and Southard. It is also noteworthy that White apparently drafted his first version of his plan for the IBRD during his visit to Cuba in late October and early November of 1941.[92] As we shall see in the next chapter, some of the provisions in White's early drafts of the Bretton Woods institutions reflected issues that he would have encountered in Cuba, such as the need for international commodity price stabilization, development lending, and the importance of containing capital flight for poorer countries.

---

91. "Comments of E. W. Kemmerer on Joint Statement by Experts on the Establishment of an International Monetary Fund," April 21, 1944, EKP, box 264, folder 2.

92. Horsefield 1969a, 11–12. White's wife reported this in a 1967 letter to a researcher (very likely Horsefield); see no author, "Twenty Year History," p. 13 n. 2, first draft, July 1967, JVP, box 50, folder 4. This version of the IBRD plan has apparently been lost to the historical record.

BUILDING FOUNDATIONS

US Postwar Planning

Serious US planning for the postwar international financial order began immediately after the United States entered World War II in December 1941. It is often
suggested that the US officials involved in this planning were largely disinterested
in development issues and the concerns of Southern governments. Contrary to
this conventional wisdom, the officials prioritized in their plans the kinds of
international development goals that had been pioneered in the context of the
Good Neighbor financial partnership with Latin America since the late 1930s.
Because of the centrality of the United States in the Bretton Woods negotiations,
these plans played a key role in building the development foundations of the
eventual agreements.

These international development goals were particularly prominent and ambitious in the initial US plans developed by White in consultation with other Treasury officials in early 1942. Because existing literature usually overlooks this point,
it is necessary to analyze in depth the development provisions of these early plans
and their direct relationship to White's previous experience in US–Latin American financial relations. Indeed, these provisions were aimed directly at Latin
American governments who were seen by US policymakers as important players
in the postwar planning process. Some of White's more ambitious development
ideas were subsequently watered down when the US plans were refined during
the lead-up to the Bretton Woods conference. But the commitment to promote
development in poorer countries remained central to US goals for the postwar international financial system. This commitment was strongly endorsed by
Roosevelt and others within his administration—as well as by many influential

Americans outside of the government—for the same kind of reasons as had been prominent in driving the Good Neighbor financial partnership.

The Development Content of White's Initial Plans

Although some US discussions about the postwar international financial system took place in the State Department in late 1939 and 1940, the most influential and important postwar planning began in the Treasury after the attack on Pearl Harbor on December 7, 1941.[1] On Sunday morning of December 14, 1941, Morgenthau telephoned White—whom he had just placed in charge of all foreign affairs for the Treasury—to ask him to prepare a plan for an "Inter-Allied Stabilization Fund."[2] White had apparently already been working, in his spare time, on postwar plans earlier in the year and had shown some of his colleagues one draft (likely of just the Fund) in the late summer or early fall.[3] These early drafts have not resurfaced for scholars to examine. What remains in the historical record are various drafts that White produced, often in consultation with other officials, after Morgenthau's initial request, culminating in one that Morgenthau presented to Roosevelt in mid-May 1942. White outlined two separate institutions in these plans—a fund and a bank—because he believed that their respective tasks were "sufficiently specialized to require different resources, different responsibilities, and different procedures and criteria for action."[4] Building on the IAB precedent, these were to be government-run institutions with provisions relating to international development that drew directly on the experience of US–Latin American financial partnership.

Was "Development" Overlooked in the Early Drafts of the Bank?

The development content of White's early proposal needs to be highlighted because it has been downplayed in much of the scholarly literature about White's role in the Bretton Woods negotiations. For example, the most recent detailed history of the World Bank asserts:

> HARRY WHITE'S first draft of a proposal for an international bank, written in early 1942, made no mention of development. This original proposal referred simply to a Bank for Reconstruction, designed "chiefly

---

1. For the State Department's discussions, see Young 1950.
2. "Note for the Secretary's Record," December 15, 1941, CFHDW, box 6, Chron. 30.
3. Oliver 1975, 110; 1985, 19 n. 1; Horsefield 1969a, 11–12.
4. White, "Suggested Plan for a United Nations Stabilization Fund and a United Nations Bank," January 1942, p. 4, BWA, box 44.

to supply the huge volume of capital . . . that will be needed for reconstruction, for relief, and for economic recovery." An April 1942 draft
called for a "Bank for Reconstruction of the United and Associated
Nations" and did include, at the end of a long list of other objectives,
a reference to development, stating that the Bank would also "raise the
productivity and hence the standard of living of the peoples of the member countries," but this draft failed to mention specifically the poorer
or less developed countries.[5]

This argument that White's early drafts had no development focus is difficult to accept when we look closer at the archival record. In order to back up
their claim about White's first draft, the historians of the Bank cite Richard
Gardner's analysis of the Bretton Woods negotiations that was first published
in 1956. In that work, Gardner stated the following in a footnote: "In the title of
the original Bank draft the word 'development' did not even appear." But Gardner then noted that "it was added in the later drafts of Mar. and Apr. 1942"—a
point that the Bank's historians cited above neglect to mention.[6] Gardner also
qualified his claim even about the absence of the word "development" in the
title of first draft. As he pointed out, his argument was based on a description of
one of three drafts he found in the White Papers held at Princeton University's
Seeley G. Mudd Manuscript Library. The draft—which is well over a hundred
pages—is titled "Suggested Plan for a United Nations Stabilization Fund and a
Bank for Reconstruction of the United and Associated Nations."[7] Gardner noted
that this draft was in fact undated and argued only tentatively that it "appears
to be the first."[8]

While this draft in the White Papers is undated on its cover, there are number
of inserted pages that do have dates of April 27, 28, 29, and 30.[9] The archives of
the Treasury for this period—which were not yet available when Gardner first
wrote his book—also contain a very similar document with the same title to the
one cited by Gardner with a date of April 29, 1942.[10] Given these dates, it seems

---

5. Kapur, Lewis, and Webb 1997, 57. For similar assessments, see Meier 1984a, 12; Eckes 1975, 46; Benjamin 2007, 12–13; Urquidi 1996, 38.

6. Gardner 1980, 85 n. 6.

7. White, "Suggested Plan for a United Nations Stabilization Fund and a Bank of Reconstruction of the United and Associated Nations" (undated), HDWP, box 6, folder 9. Pages are missing from
this draft and it ends abruptly in midsentence on p. 130.

8. Gardner 1980, 74 n. 1.

9. White, "Suggested Plan" (undated).

10. White, "Suggested Plan for a United Nations Stabilization Fund and a Bank for Reconstruction of the United and Associated Nations," April 29, 1942, BWA, box 44. Like the draft in the White
Papers, this draft has a number of page insertions (including ones dated April 28 and 30) and pencil
corrections.

quite clear that the draft Gardner was referring to was written in late April and thus was not White's first draft. As Gardner stated, there is a March 1942 draft that is also over 100 pages in length. And that draft does include "development" in its title: "Preliminary Draft: United Nations Stabilization Fund and A Bank for Reconstruction and Development of the United and Associated Nations."[11]

Even more important is the fact that there are earlier drafts from January 1942 in the Treasury archives that show how development goals were present in White's initial thinking. For example, one such draft is a short (seven page double-spaced) outline of a "Stabilization Fund of the United and Associated Nations" dated January 6, 1942. The plan was shared with Welles and Berle (for reasons outlined below) and had been discussed with Viner and Bernstein, but had not yet received Morgenthau's approval.[12] In a short cover note to this draft, White wrote that his proposed fund "is only one of the instrumentalities which will be needed in the field of international money and banking. Some form of international bank may also be needed to provide the capital necessary for post-war reconstruction and development."[13]

The Treasury archives also contain a much more detailed draft (forty-seven pages double-spaced) dated January 1942. Its cover page includes a handwritten statement that this is the "first mimeographed draft" and it describes in considerable detail White's plans for a "United Nations Stabilization Fund and a United Nations Bank."[14] The Bank's name in this first substantial draft did not include a reference to either development or reconstruction, but its purposes included the development goal that the Bank's historians quote: to "raise the productivity and hence the standard of living of the peoples of the United Nations."[15]

---

11. White, "'Preliminary Draft: United Nations Stabilization Fund and A Bank for Reconstruction and Development of the United and Associated Nations," March 1942, HDWP, box 6, folder 6. Van Dormael (1978, 45) argues that this draft was "obviously antedated" because it is "almost identical" to the polished "April 1942" draft in the White archives. He does not provide further evidence for this claim; even if it is accurate, it is not very significant for the core argument of this chapter since White's first drafts in January referred to the development role of the Bank, as noted below.

12. "Memorandum on a Projected Stabilization Fund of the United and Associated Nations," January 6, 1942, CFHDW, box 6, Chron. 31. See Black 1991, 36; Southard to Undersecretary Bell, January 15, 1942, JVP, box 49, folder 7; "Meeting of American Delegates to Rio, State Department—Mr. Welles' Office, January 7, 1942," BWCC, box 11/5; White to Welles, January 6, 1942, CFHDW, box 6, Chron. 31.

13. White, "Proposal for a Stabilization Fund of the United and Associated Nations," January 6, 1942, p. 2, CFHDW, box 6, Chron. 31.

14. White, "Suggested Plan" (January 1942). Although this document is quite detailed, it is missing the more in-depth justification of the Bank's provisions that appears in the March and later drafts.

15. White, "Suggested Plan" (January 1942), 17. There is also a two-and-a-half-page document by White from December 30, 1941 that calls for an "Inter-Allied Bank" and an "Inter-Allied Stabilization Fund." The former is meant to be "an agency with means and powers adequate to provide capital necessary (a) to aid in the economic reconstruction of the Allied countries; (b) to facilitate a rapid and smooth transition from a war-time economy to a peace-time economy in the Allied countries; (c) to supply short-term capital necessary to increase the volume of foreign trade—where such

As those scholars correctly observed, this latter phrase does not make a specific reference to poorer or less developed countries. But elsewhere in this January 1942 draft (as well as in the late April draft), White went out of his way to emphasize explicitly the dangers of ignoring the interests of "poorer" countries in postwar plans:

> It is true that rich and powerful countries can for long periods safely and easily ignore the interests of poorer or weaker neighbors or competitors, but by doing so they only imperil the future and reduce the potential of their own level of prosperity. The lesson that must be learned is that prosperous neighbors are the best neighbors; that a higher standard of living in one country begets higher standards in others, and that a high level of trade and business is most easily attained when generously and widely shared.[16]

The references to "neighbors"—and the broader content of this passage—invoke the Good Neighbor financial partnership. In this draft, White also discussed the importance of encouraging the movement of capital from "capital-rich to capital-poor countries."[17] As noted below, he also clearly had Latin American countries in mind as an audience for this draft, and he included a number of provisions that were of special interest to them that had arisen in the course of his Latin American work.

Why then did White briefly omit "development" from the name of the Bank in his late April draft? Interestingly, it was not uncommon for White to switch names throughout March and April. While the overall title of his March draft referred to the "Bank for Reconstruction and Development," one part of the table of contents (but not others) listed the Bank as simply the "Bank of Reconstruction" and the start of the subsection outlining the detailed provisions for the Bank was also simply titled "Bank of Reconstruction." In the introduction to the draft as a whole, White also shifted back and forth within several pages, referring to the Bank sometimes as the "Bank for Reconstruction" and elsewhere as the

---

capital is not available at reasonable rates from private sources" (p. 1). White, "A Suggested Program for Inter-Allied Monetary and Banking Action" December 30, 1941, ALP, box 8/8, file: "International Stabilization Fund, Preliminary Draft Outline." Because of the ambiguities surrounding the meaning of the term "economic reconstruction" discussed below, White's precise thinking around the Bank's role in "development" at the time of this memo is difficult to discern. But as noted above, the proposal he drafted a few days later on January 6 is clear about the development function of the Bank. The short December 30 memo was given only to several staff in White's Division of Monetary Research (Mikesell 1994, 6).

16. White, "Suggested Plan" (January 1942), p. 33.
17. White, "Suggested Plan" (January 1942), p. 26.

"Bank for Reconstruction and Development."[18] Similar inconsistencies appear in the April draft in the White Papers.[19]

These inconsistencies were even present in the material sent to Roosevelt in mid-May that is reproduced in the State Department's 1942 *Foreign Relations of the United States* volume. This material is the source from which the Bank's historians quote when suggesting that an April draft referred to a "Bank of Reconstruction." It does include a short (undated) summary of the proposal that in two places uses that name[20] But the Bank's historians neglect to mention that the same summary also refers to the "Bank of Reconstruction and Development" in its title as well as in the text.[21] Moreover, the April draft of the Fund and the Bank included in the material sent to Roosevelt used only the name "Bank for Reconstruction and Development" throughout.[22]

In some instances, White appears to have used the phrase "Bank for Reconstruction" simply as an easy shorthand for the longer name. It is also possible that his inconsistent switching of names reflected an ambiguity surrounding the meaning of the word "reconstruction" at this time. In his detailed history of US development policy, David Ekbladh points out that the word had a wider meaning before World War II that was inclusive of the concept of development. He notes, for example, that US initiatives before the war to promote rising living standards in countries such as the Philippines and Puerto Rico had been described as "reconstruction" initiatives. In the latter case, a new body created in 1935 with the goal of promoting economic modernization and higher incomes via planning was called the Puerto Rico Reconstruction Administration. As Ekbladh puts it, the term was widely used at this time to describe "diverse efforts to effect change within societies through reform based on 'scientific' and 'rational' methods."[23] This broader meaning of the phrase was common in policy circles in many other parts of the world too, including China and India.[24]

In advance of his early 1942 Bretton Woods drafts, White himself had used the term "reconstruction" in this wider sense that was inclusive of development

18. For inconsistencies, see White, "Preliminary Draft" (March 1942). pp. 5, 6, 10.

19. White, "Preliminary Draft: Proposal for United Nations Stabilization Fund and a Bank for Reconstruction and Development of the United and Associated Nations," April 1942, HDWP, box 6, folder 7.

20. US State Department 1963a, 175, 177.

21. The title is: "Suggested Plan for a United and Associated Nations Stabilization Fund and a Bank for Reconstruction and Development of the United and Associated Nations." US State Department 1942a, 172–77.

22. US State Department 1963a, 178–90.

23. Ekbladh 2010, 17. See also pp. 19, 22–25, and Alcalde 1987, 63.

24. See for example Anstey 1943, 339; Zanasi 2006, 15–17; Young 1963, 389–90. The British discussions (in government and think tanks) about postwar international economic plans going well beyond wartime recovery issues were also referred to as focusing on "reconstruction" (see chapter 8).

concerns. For example, he wrote a memo to Morgenthau in September 1941 that was titled "British Empire–American Cooperation on problems of post-war reconstruction," summarizing Australian proposals to raise living standards across the world.[25] White's staff members, such as Simon Hanson, had also talked of the need for the "economic reconstruction" of Latin America in the context of 1939 discussions to address "economic instability and low living standards" in the region.[26]

Ekbladh notes that it was during World War II that the term "reconstruction" became "increasingly confused with 'recovery.'"[27] In White's early drafts, however, the wider meaning was clearly present. For example, in the late April 1942 draft employing the narrower title of "Bank of Reconstruction," the Bank still had the wider development goal that its historians quote: to "raise the productivity and hence the standard of living of the peoples of the United Nations."[28] The same provisions of special interest to poorer countries that were in the January draft—outlined below—were also in this draft.[29] The absence of the word "development" from the title, in other words, did not reflect missing "development" content.

There is one further piece of evidence to support the view that White had a wider understanding of the meaning of reconstruction at this time. When sending White's plan to Roosevelt in May 1942, Morgenthau included a document proposing a conference to discuss the proposed Fund and Bank, and even a draft agenda, program, and invitations. White had in fact developed incredibly detailed plans for this proposed conference that was to take place over twenty-two days (ironically, the exact length of eventual Bretton Woods conference two years later).[30] He prepared drafts of the agendas for many subcommittees and even speeches for Morgenthau as well as for British, Mexican, and Brazilian officials. For our purposes, the content of the anticipated Brazilian speech was particularly interesting. It was titled "Statement of the representative of the United States of Brazil on the need for a Bank for Post-war Reconstruction." The speech used the name "Bank for Post-war Reconstruction" throughout and yet its content was focused primarily on development issues. It referred, for example, to

25. White to Morgenthau, "British Empire–American Cooperation on problems of post-war reconstruction," September 2, 1941, SMHDW, box 14.

26. Hanson to White, June 5, 1939, p. 1, TSF, Entry 67A1804, box 65.

27. Ekbladh 2010, 75.

28. White, "Suggested Plan" (April 29), p. 100.

29. In its broader discussion, this draft also included the same line quoted above from the January draft about the need for richer countries to help poorer countries. White, "Suggested Plan" (April 29), p. 19.

30. The 1944 conference was initially scheduled for just nineteen days but was extended to allow completion of the negotiations (De Vries 1986, 10).

the "necessity for a steady flow of capital for developmental purposes" and to the role the Bank could play in helping Brazil realize its "extensive potentialities for industrial development."[31]

In sum, it seems clear that White's occasional use of the shorter name "Bank of Reconstruction" was not very significant in terms of the development focus of his plans. Indeed, White's assistant Bernstein later recalled that it was his idea— not White's—to insert "development" into the title of the Bank.[32] This decision appears to have contributed considerably to the narrowing of the meaning of the term "reconstruction" by the time of the Bretton Woods conference. As we shall see, delegates at the 1944 conference argued fiercely over whether "reconstruction" or "development" should be prioritized in the Bank's lending. But at this earlier moment, White did not seem to see the two terms as mutually exclusive. And from his first January draft onward, he anticipated the Bank having a development role regardless of its precise title.

The Latin American Audience

It is also worth noting that White and other US policymakers saw poorer countries—particularly those in Latin America—as an important part of the intended audience for their postwar plans from the very start. When Roosevelt had met Keynes in the summer of 1941 to discuss his initial postwar plans, one British official reported that Roosevelt "felt that the terms of reference are too exclusively European. He attaches great importance to the South American countries being remembered in any world statement."[33] When Keynes and White met in the late summer of 1942 to discuss the details of postwar planning for the first time, White also rejected Keynes's preference for bilateral British-American negotiations, arguing that it would create the impression of an Anglo-American "gang-up." He wanted more countries involved, including Latin American countries.[34] Indeed, in the draft conference schedule White had developed a few months before, he planned for many countries to attend and with keynote speeches in plenary sessions to be given by Mexico and Brazil alongside the United States, Britain, the USSR, China, and the Netherlands.[35]

---

31. "Statement of the representative of the United States of Brazil on the need for a Bank for Post-war Reconstruction," pp. 2, 1, in "Conference on Agencies for International Monetary and Financial Cooperation," BWA, box 47. This document is in a file ""Conference of Finance Ministries of United and Associated Nations, 1942" but otherwise undated; its content suggests approximately March–April 1942. Van Dormael (1978, 51) states that White presented a folder to Morgenthau on May 8, 1942 that was titled "Conference of Finance Ministries of the United and Associated Nations."
32. Eckes 1975, 292 n. 35. See also Meier 1984a, 12; Kapur, Lewis, and Webb 1997, 57.
33. Viscount Halifax to Mr. Eden, May 28, 1941, p. 1, UKT 247/85.
34. Quote from Penrose 1953, 48. See also Oliver 1975, 126; 1971, 44.
35. "Conference on Agencies."

It is also often forgotten that White intended his initial Fund plan to be presented first at an inter-American meeting of foreign ministers in Rio on January 15–28, 1942. The meeting was organized in the wake of the US entry into the war, and the United States intended to use the occasion to offer additional economic assistance to the region in return for security cooperation and the severing of diplomatic ties to the Axis powers. One of the motivations for Morgenthau to ask White in December to begin to develop plans was very likely this upcoming meeting that White was to attend along with Welles (as head of the US delegation).[36] As part of the preparations for the Rio meeting, White showed his initial draft for the Fund to Welles and Berle on January 6, a draft that included a call for a conference to be held to discuss the creation of such a fund. White suggested that the draft could be presented at Rio and shared simultaneously with other allies.[37]

Welles and Berle liked the draft, but both wondered if it might be better to discuss the idea orally with Latin American governments rather than to present the formal document. If Latin American officials were in favor, a resolution could then be drafted in general terms to be adopted at the conference.[38] White liked this idea since he preferred to have more time to develop the proposal. At the conference itself, a resolution was indeed drafted and approved that called on finance ministers (or their representatives) of the American republics to attend a "special conference" to be held "for the purpose of considering the establishment of an international stabilization fund."[39] Morgenthau insisted that the resolution make no mention of the United Nations because of the absence of prior consultation with key UN members such as Britain, the Soviet Union, and China.[40] But at the conference, White clarified for the delegates that it was not meant to be "exclusively an inter-American fund" but rather one that would have "a much broader scope than the American currencies."[41]

The preamble to the resolution stated that the fund would "contribute to the realization of the economic objectives set forth at the First and Second Meetings of the Ministers of Foreign Affairs of the American Republics at Panama and Habana."[42] This wording provided a very clear confirmation to Latin American

---

36. Horsefield 1969a, 12; Mikesell 1994, 6.

37. White to Welles, January 6, 1942.

38. "Meeting of American Delegates to Rio, State Department—Mr. Welles' Office, January 7, 1942," BWCC, box 11/5; White to Morgenthau, January 14, 1942, JVP, box 49, folder 7.

39. Director General of the Pan American Union 1942, 44.

40. Southard, "Further consideration of the resolution on exchange stabilization for the Rio Conference," January 19, 1942, TSF, 450/81/20/07, box 29.

41. "Observations Made by Mr. H. D. White at the V Subcommittee of II Commission—Meeting Held Jan. 21, 1942," p. 1, TSF, 450/81/20/07, box 29.

42. Director General of the Pan American Union 1942, 43–44.

delegates of the link between postwar planning and the Good Neighbor financial partnership. The goals of the latter were also obvious in other resolutions passed at Rio that backed various initiatives to support economic development and bolster standards of living in the region. The conference also passed a resolution urging governments to study the IAB proposal if they had not yet ratified it. Indeed, at this time, White clearly saw the IAB working alongside his newly proposed Fund and Bank in Latin America, supplementing both of their activities in the region.[43] Supporters of the IAB within the United States also made a renewed (unsuccessful) effort at this time to convince Senator Glass to allow the proposal to be voted upon in the Senate as a whole.[44]

White had a Latin American audience in mind when developing not just the Fund draft but also the Bank proposal. As noted above, he chose a Brazilian official to deliver an imaginary speech on the virtues of the Bank at his proposed 1942 conference. When the Bank proposal began to be refined internally in September 1943 (it was not released publicly until November of that year), White and his colleagues also made special reference to "our neighbors in Latin America" in describing the Bank's development function in a memo to Roosevelt.[45]

The importance of the Latin American audience for the early US Bretton Woods drafts was also apparent in the frequent references to the "United and Associated Nations" in the proposals. The United Nations were the twenty-six countries that had initially signed the Declaration of the United Nations on January 1, 1942.[46] But the phrase "Associated Nations" was included to refer to countries that were neutral in the war but had broken diplomatic relations with the Axis powers. As Berle explained to a puzzled Canadian official, the phrase had been developed with Latin American countries in mind: "a number of South American countries are in this category and it is desired that these should be included in the scheme."[47]

---

43. See for example "Observations," p. 1; "Meeting on Proposal for an International Stabilization Fund and a World Bank," May 26, 1942, p. 2, ITM, box 20; White, "Preliminary Draft" (March 1942), II-36.

44. Green 1971, 70–73.

45. "Proposal for a United Nations Bank for Reconstruction and Development," p. 1 (undated but context suggests September 1943), HDWP, box 8, folder 3.

46. The signatories included nine Latin American countries (Costa Rica, Cuba, the Dominican Republic, El Salvador, Guatemala, Haiti, Honduras, Nicaragua, Panama) as well as Australia, Belgium, Canada, China, Czechoslovakia, Greece, India, Luxembourg, the Netherlands, New Zealand, Norway, Poland, South Africa, the United Kingdom, the United States, the USSR, and Yugoslavia. Later in 1942, Brazil and Mexico joined the United Nations as did Ethiopia and the Philippines. In 1943, Bolivia and Colombia joined as did Iran and Iraq. By the time of the Bretton Woods conference, the following Latin American countries had not joined: Argentina, Chile, Ecuador, Paraguay, Peru, Uruguay, and Venezuela.

47. (No author), "Canada–United States Discussion of Stabilization Fund Proposals, US Treasury April 21–26, 1943," p. 2. NAC, RG19, v. 3981.

Specific Development Provisions

The final piece of evidence that White had Latin American countries in mind when developing his early Fund and Bank drafts comes from the fact that they contain a number of specific provisions designed to serve the needs of poorer countries, provisions that drew directly on his experience in US–Latin American relations in the previous few years. The first such "development" provision has already been mentioned: the Bank's role in mobilizing international development finance. White stated in his first detailed January 1942 draft that the chief operations of the Bank were to involve the "provision of long-term capital for desirable productive projects" that served "directly or indirectly to permanently raise the standard of living of the borrowing country."[48] In a draft memorandum for Roosevelt prepared in May, White also stressed that one of the purposes of his plans was "to supply the huge volume of capital that will be needed abroad for relief, for reconstruction, and economic development essential for the attainment of world prosperity and higher standards of living."[49]

According to White's initial detailed draft of January 1942, the Bank was empowered to make direct loans to governments as well as to political subdivisions and private businesses (provided that the loan's servicing was guaranteed by the national government). It could also guarantee private loans, although subject to certain conditions: (1) the interest rate of such loans could not be excessive; (2) no more than 80 percent of principal and 50 percent of the interest could be guaranteed; and (3) a loan could not be "for the purpose of repayment of an old loan." White prioritized the Bank's guaranteeing role over its direct lending role, noting that "wherever possible the Bank should guarantee loans made by private investors, instead of making the loans directly." Perhaps with the memory of the opposition of US banks to the IAB proposal in mind, White also went out of his way to note that the Bank's direct loans could be made "only when it is reasonably certain that the funds cannot be borrowed from private investors except at high rates of interest."[50]

The second provision of relevance to poorer countries was the proposed Fund's capacity to provide short-term loans to support a country's balance of payments. In providing a rationale for this kind of compensatory balance of payments finance in his first plans, White did not explicitly mention the needs of Southern countries. But years later, Bernstein emphasized that White had built directly on his Latin American experience in developing his first draft of the

---

48. White, "Suggested Plan" (January 1942), p. 22, 23.
49. "Memorandum for the President," May 14, 1942, SMHDW, box 14. The same wording was in the cover letter Morgenthau wrote to Roosevelt (US State Department 1963a, 172).
50. White, "Suggested Plan" (January 1942), pp. 23, 22.

Fund; the IMF simply multilateralized the bilateral stabilization loans of the US Exchange Stabilization Fund that White had pioneered in the region.[51] The Latin American precedent was also highlighted later by the IMF's key legal expert Joseph Gold, who noted that the IMF's initial lending after the war used the US ESF line of credit to Mexico in November 1941 as a model.[52] When White's initial drafts began to circulate in US policymaking circles in early 1942, other US officials who had worked on Latin American issues also emphasized that the Fund's lending would be particularly useful for commodity exporting countries. In a March 1942 memo discussing White's initial drafts, Henry Wallich of the FRBNY remarked that "owing to the seasonal nature of many Latin American exports, there are regular fluctuations in the exchange reserves of some countries which the Fund could smooth out. Even somewhat larger disturbances might perhaps be taken care of in this manner."[53]

Third, as he had done during the IAB discussions and the Cuban mission, White called attention to the need to curtail capital flight from poorer countries. After discussing the disruptive nature of speculative financial flows in his March 1942 draft, White highlighted the special problems faced by these countries: "Less hectic and less dramatic yet in the case of some countries during some stages of their development capable in the long run of even greater harm, is the steady drain of capital from a country that needs the capital but is unable for one reason or another to offer sufficient monetary return to keep its capital at home."[54] The wording here was remarkably similar to a memo one of White's staff had sent him a few months earlier during the Cuban mission describing how exchange controls could help curtail the "steady drain" of capital from Cuba.[55]

Neither White's proposed Bank nor the Fund was designed to recycle flight capital by accepting private deposits as the IAB had been intended to do. Instead, White proposed to address capital flight in the same way that the American Technical Mission to Cuba did in its April 1942 report: with controls at the border on international financial flows. White's January 1942 plan included a provision that all member countries of the Fund would be required "to abandon, not later

---

51. Black 1991, 35. Two weeks before the start of the Bretton Woods conference, Bernstein made a similar point in an internal memo designed to help Morgenthau draft an opening speech for the meeting (in which he also invoked the history of the 1936 Tripartite Accord with France and Britain): E. M. Bernstein to Mr. Smith, June 12, 1944, MD, book 748, p. 170.
52. Gold 1988. See also Bordo and Schwartz 2001; Schwartz 1997, 152. Boughton (2004, 189–90) argues that the ESF lending to Mexico in 1936 was an earlier precedent than the 1941 agreement.
53. Wallich to Knoke, March 10, 1942, p. 6, ISF, box 247.
54. White, "Preliminary Draft" (March 1942), p. II-49. See also Horsefield 1969b, 67.
55. Spiegel, "Factors relating to Cuban proposals," September 30, 1941, p. 2, CFHDW, box 5, Chron. 27.

than 6 months after joining the Fund, all restrictions and controls over foreign exchange transactions with member countries, except with the approval of the Fund." But in his detailed explanation of this provision, he made clear that the Fund was expected to approve many such controls, including capital controls, and he went out of his way to argue that critics of such controls held views that were "both unrealistic and unsound."[56]

To highlight his support for capital controls, White went even further to propose a new kind of international cooperation that would help reinforce their effectiveness. He proposed that all members of the Fund would have to agree "(a) not to accept or permit deposits or investments from any member country except with the permission of that country, and (b) to make available to the government of any member country at its request all property in form of deposits, investments, securities, safety deposit vault contents, of the nationals of member countries."[57] This provision introduced a new kind of international obligation to enforce the national capital controls of other countries. In the case of capital flight, poorer countries having difficulty tracking illegal financial outflows could now request assistance from the countries receiving the funds. As White put it later in mid-1943, the Fund "provides for control of capital movements from both ends. Perhaps this double control will do the job."[58]

Fourth, White empowered both the Fund and the Bank to facilitate international debt restructuring. In his detailed January 1942 draft, one of the purposes of the Fund was "to facilitate the settlement and servicing of international debts— both public and private." Its role in settling debts stemmed from a provision that member countries were "not to permit any defaults on foreign obligations of the government, Central Bank or government agency without the approval of the Fund." White argued that this provision would allow more orderly and fair resolution of debt crises than that experienced in the 1930s. As he put it, "it can hardly be expected that objective decisions on defaults can be made by the defaulting country or by the country gaining most by continued servicing of a debt. To make approval a feasible instrument, the approval must be that of a large group of nations, the majority of whom are not directly and immediately affected by the decision. Approval of the Fund would seem to promise that kind of objectivity or fairness."[59] This provision remained in the subsequent drafts in early 1942,

---

56. White, "Suggested Plan" (January 1942), pp. 10, 34.

57. White, "Suggested Plan" (January 1942), p. 10. Very similar wording appears in subsequent early drafts, e.g. White, 'Preliminary Plan' (March 1942), p. II-48.

58. John Deutsch, "International Stabilization of Currencies—Informal expert discussions, US Treasury, June 15–17, 1943," p. 10, NAC, RG19, v. 3981. White had advocated restrictions on speculative capital inflows to the United States in the late 1930s (e.g. Acksay 200, 126).

59. White, "Suggested Plan" (January 1942), p. 9, 11, 45.

including in his March 1942 draft where he referred the Fund's ability to conduct "compulsory arbitration in debt adjustment."[60]

In the same January 1942 draft, White also prohibited the Bank from lending to countries whose national government had defaulted on a foreign loan unless "the defaulted government has agreed to renew service of the defaulted debt on a basis worked out by a special committee appointed by the Bank for that purpose."[61] This provision was very similar to the one White had discussed in December 1939 during the IAB discussions. In justifying this provision in his March 1942 draft, he highlighted how the Bank-appointed committee could do a "a splendid job" in "facilitating debt adjustments" because it "could approach the problem with a great deal more objectivity than could be true of a bondholders' committee representing the creditors and working with a committee representing the debtors." As he put it, the committee could "take a broader point of view and one that might well leave both the debtor and creditor nations better off than would be the case if a debt adjustment were to be obtained either as result of political pressure of one kind or another, or because of an inducement offered to the defaulted government in the shape of a new loan to be made, in effect, only if the bondholders give their approval to the terms of adjustment."[62]

These provisions revived the Latin American proposals of 1933 as well as Hanson's 1939 ideas, and they revealed how White was willing to go further on this issue than he had when drafting the IAB. Indeed, in defending the Bank provisions in his March draft, White even openly aired his frustrations with the fact that US bondholders had often blocked initiatives to boost public lending to Latin America in the late 1930s. After emphasizing that Bank loans would be made if the defaulting country accepted the recommendations of the Bank-appointed committee "irrespective of whether the bondholders did or did not," he stated: "As it is now the bondholders are in a position frequently to prevent the government from extending any credits on the grounds that they are not satisfied with the terms of adjustment offered by the defaulting government."[63]

White also mentioned two other nonfinancial issues that had arisen prominently in the US–Latin American discussions of the late 1930s and early 1940s. The first was international commodity price stabilization. In an echo of Roosevelt's plans of mid-1940, White's March 1942 draft stated that the Bank would "organize and finance an International Commodity Stabilization Corporation

---

60. White, "Preliminary Draft" {March 1942), p. II-59. See also Horsefield 1969, 71.
61. White, "Suggested Plan" (January 1942), p. 23. Two other exceptions were if "the defaulted loan was made between two Allies in a common war" and if "ninety percent of member votes approve the loan" (p. 23).
62. White, "Preliminary Draft" (March 1942), pp. III-12–13. See also Oliver 1975, 303.
63. White, "Preliminary Draft" (March 1942), p. III-13. See also Oliver 1975, 303.

for the purpose of stabilizing the price of important commodities."[64] In his detailed Fund proposal from January 1942, White also included a discussion of trade policy that included a very strong defense of infant industry tariff protection in poorer countries. The belief that trade liberalization will yield a higher standard of living, he argued, assumed "that a country chiefly agricultural in its economy has as many economic, political and social advantages as a country whose economy is chiefly industrial, or a country which has a balanced economy." He added: "It assumes that there are no gains to be achieved by diversification of output. It grossly underestimates the extent to which a country can virtually lift itself by its bootstraps in one generation if it is willing to pay the price. The view further overlooks the very important fact that political relationships among countries being what they are vital considerations exist in the shaping of the economic structure of a country other than that of producing goods with the least labor."[65] White's March 1942 draft reiterated the point, adding that the assumptions that underlie free trade theory were "not valid" and "unreal and unsound."[66]

In a letter to Vice President Henry Wallace in early December 1941, White had made clear that this perspective on trade policy had been shaped by the Latin American context. Commenting on a draft article that Wallace had written, White wrote: "I agree with the general objective of increasing industrialization and the necessity of doing so if the standard of living of many countries is to be increased." He then foreshadowed the case he would make the next month in his Fund draft:

> Any attempt to expand the industrial element in the economies of the least industrialized countries would be very difficult without the aid of a tariff schedule which would protect such industries during their infancy. It is hard to see how any of the Latin American countries, for example, could have any significant expansion of most industries unless they pursue a policy of protection for those industries. Most of them, I believe, are already pursuing such a policy. The industrialized countries, England, United States, Germany, Japan, etc., have so great an advantage in the production of numerous industrial commodities that it would be very difficulty for non-industrialized countries to build up competing industries without tariff protection or subsidy.[67]

---

64. White, "Preliminary Draft" (March 1942), p. I-15.
65. White, "Suggested Plan" (January 1942), pp. 43–44.
66. White, "Preliminary Draft" (March 1942), p. II-56. See also Horsefield 1969b, 70.
67. White, "Memorandum for Vice-President Wallace," December 1, 1941, pp. 3–4. SMHDW, box 14.

Toward the Bretton Woods Conference

In these ways, we can see how White's initial drafts reflected commitments to development issues that had already emerged in the context of the Good Neighbor financial partnership. After initially circulating just among Treasury colleagues, White's plans began to be discussed from May 1942 onward by an interdepartmental "technical committee," chaired by White. Its membership changed over time, but active members included—among others—a number of figures who had been involved in US–Latin American financial relations such as Berle, Bernstein, Collado, Clayton, Gardner, Goldenweiser, and John Parke Young.[68]

White initially focused the attention of the technical committee on the Fund proposal. It is important to note that this choice did not reflect a sentiment that the Bank was unimportant (as is sometimes suggested by scholars). When asked by an interviewer for the World Bank oral history project why US officials had devoted more attention to the Fund than the Bank, Ansel Luxford—a Treasury lawyer who was closely involved with the US technical committee and delegation at Bretton Woods—explained the decision this way: "The Fund, as a technical problem, was obviously a far more challenging problem than the Bank. . . . And we were satisfied in our own hearts that we would have no problem selling the Bank internationally." Later in the interview, he emphasized the point (using words that directly contradict Richard Peet's argument mentioned in the introduction): "The Bank was not an afterthought. It was started from the word go, the first White document . . . they were always treated as one package. But the complexities of the Bank were not the same as those of the Fund."[69] In one meeting in early April 1944, White himself told his colleagues that he was not worried about the slower progress on the Bank proposal because "the technical difficulties were comparatively small" and "could be easily ironed out."[70]

The decision to focus work initially on the Fund may also have been a tactical decision. If US officials presented the Bank proposal to the British too early, the British could have offered to accept it in return for US backing of Keynes's International Clearing Union proposal. Since White and other US officials had serious concerns about the latter, this was a scenario to avoid.[71] Luxford also noted later that US officials were very aware that the Bank would be more popular with the British and other countries than the Fund's exchange rate commitments.

---

68. Young 1950, 779 n. 2; Mikesell 1994, 7.
69. Oliver 1961a, 6, 8. See also Mikesell (2000, 25) who also worked closely with White at the time.
70. E. M. Bernstein, "Memorandum of Meeting at State Department, April 1, 1944," p. 1, BWCC, box 6/9.
71. Oliver 1957, 388; Harrod 1951, 541.

He recalls how US officials insisted that membership in the Bank be conditional on membership in the Fund for this reason: "basically we wanted to force countries to agree to standards in the monetary field as a condition to get the benefits of the Bank."[72] Given this strategy, the ordering of the negotiations of the two proposals also made sense.

After detailed discussions in the US technical committee, White's proposed "international stabilization fund" was released publicly in April 1943 at the same time as Keynes's International Clearing Union proposal. Only after White had completed extensive consultations on this draft with foreign governments in the summer of 1943 did US officials announce that they were ready to begin to refine the Bank proposal.[73] Beginning with a meeting of the US technical committee on August 31, internal US discussions on the Bank then proceeded very quickly because the committee was in general agreement on the need for the institution and on its main features.[74] In November 1943, a US draft of the Bank was released publicly.

Evolution of the US Plans

In the process of refining White's initial plans, some of his specific development provisions did not survive. One was the discussion of infant industry protection, which fell out of the plans for the simple reason that it pertained more to postwar international trade rules that were to be negotiated separately.[75] Another provision that disappeared was White's idea that the Bank could assist an international body mandated to stabilize commodity prices. In an early June 1943 meeting of the technical committee, White acknowledged that his proposal for a Commodity Stabilization Corporation was "controversial" and that he was anxious to give it "only an incidental place" in the future conference he planned.[76] When US officials began to discuss White's Bank draft in detail in the fall of 1943, Will Clayton also argued that the Bank's role in financing an international commodity corporation was not "politically feasible" and the provision was dropped.[77] After the gains made by the Republicans in the fall 1942 election, it was also clear that some of White's ambitions would need to be scaled back to gain Congressional approval.[78]

---

72. Oliver 1961a, 7. See also Collado's comments in McKinzie 1974, 13–14.
73. Oliver 1957, 397.
74. White to Morgenthau, September 22, 1943, SMHDW, box 14.
75. For the State Department's objection to the discussion of commodity price stabilization on this ground, see Oliver 1975, 158.
76. "Minutes of Meeting Held in Mr. White's Office," June 3, 1942, p. 3, ITM, box 20.
77. "Meeting in Mr. White's Office, Aug 31, 1943," p. 2, ITM, box 21. See also "Minutes of Meeting Held in Mr. White's Office," May 28, 1942, p. 4, ITM, box 20.
78. See for example Oliver 1961a, 4. A number of other aspects of his plans—such as the Bank's issuing of notes, extending of gold loans, and short-term financing of international trade—were also dropped for this reason (Oliver, 1975, 157–8).

White's proposals for an international debt-restructuring role for the Fund and Bank were also eliminated. The Fund's role in this area disappeared some time between a November 25, 1942 draft and one written on December 11.[79] I have found no explanation in US archives for the change at this specific time, but the documents reveal that the issue had already been controversial earlier in the year. When the proposal to create an international stabilization fund had first been put forward at the inter-American meeting in Rio in January 1942, the preamble of the original draft resolution had suggested that the fund could "facilitate the settlement of public and private international debts."[80] Morgenthau had insisted, however, that White remove this clause before the resolution was presented to the conference. Morgenthau's reasoning was the same as that of US officials at Montevideo in 1933. According to Southard, the treasury secretary stated that "he did not wish to be a party to any debt-collecting arrangement smacking as clearly of dollar diplomacy."[81] Although White had complied with this instruction at Rio, he had then reinserted the provision in his first drafts of the IMF, but appears to have been forced to withdraw it again later in the year.

When discussions of White's Bank proposal began in earnest in the fall of 1943, US officials also quickly deleted both the clause that prohibited the Bank from lending to countries in default and the provision that the Bank could help settle defaulted debt as a precondition for lending.[82] Both Luxford and the State Department's John Parke Young worried that countries in default, particularly in Latin America, would be less keen to support the Bank if they could not borrow without first reaching a debt settlement.[83] Somewhat differently, Collado argued that the Bank's role in fostering debt restructuring might encourage countries to default because the Bank would then assist in the adjustment of their debts.[84]

White's provisions relating to capital controls were both weakened and strengthened. On the weakening side, the proposal for mandatory international cooperation to control flight capital was eventually dropped (although countries

---

79. "Bretton Woods Institutions, IMF, Plans, US Treasury (White), 1942," ISF, box 55.

80. "Resolution on the Stabilization Fund of the United and Associated Nations," TSF, 450/81/20/07, box 29. This phrase was also in White's initial January 6, 1942 outline of the Fund that he presented to Welles (White, "Proposal for a United Nations Bank," p. 1).

81. Southard, "Further Consideration of the resolution on exchange stabilization for the Rio Conference," January 19, 1942, p. 2, CFHDW, box 6, Chron. 31.

82. The latter was deleted first between the September 3 and September 8 drafts, while the former disappeared by the draft of September 24. See ISF, box 55. In December, Walter Louchheim, assistant director of the Securities and Exchange Commission (and member of the technical committee), lobbied White unsuccessfully to reinsert into the purposes of the Bank that it could further the settlement of international debts; Louchheim to White, p. 1, December 8, 1943, HDWP, box 8, folder 3.

83. Luxford to White, September 4, 1943, HDWP, box 8, folder 3; J. P. Young, "Some Points of Possible Difficulty in Proposal for a United Nations Bank for Reconstruction and Development, Sept. 14, 1943," p. 1, ISF, box 55.

84. "Meeting in Mr. White's Office, Sept 22, 1943," p. 2, ITM, box 21.

were still *permitted* to cooperate in making their exchange control regulations more effective). The New York financial community strongly objected to the idea that the United States, as a country receiving flight capital, would be required to help foreign governments' efforts to curtail these capital flows. At the same time, the right of every member country to control capital flows on its own was strengthened. White's initial drafts had required IMF approval for such controls, but later drafts and the final Fund charter permitted all members the unambiguous right to control all capital movements without needing Fund approval. Many US bankers objected to this provision, but they were unable to dilute it.[85]

US policymakers also remained committed to the IBRD's role in mobilizing international development finance. As White put it in a September 1943 draft of the Bank, "large investment sums will be needed to help raise the very low productive level of countries in the Far East, South America, in the Balkans, and the Near East."[86] The priority of the Bank's development role is also clear from Morgenthau's statement when the Bank proposal was first released publicly in November 1943. He observed that "one great contribution that the United Nations can make to sustained peace and world-wide prosperity is to make certain that adequate capital is available on reasonable terms for productive uses in capital-poor countries." He had also gone out of his way to emphasize the importance to wealthy countries of international development finance: "It is imperative that we recognize that the investment of productive capital in undeveloped and capital-needy countries means not only that those countries will be able to supply at lower costs more of the goods the world needs but that they will at the same time become better markets for the world's goods."[87] In his September 1943 draft of the Bank, White had made very similar arguments and had added that rising standards of living worldwide would help generate future "political stability and friendly international collaboration."[88]

A US Treasury summary of the Bank proposal provided in June 1944 to delegates and journalists attending the upcoming Bretton Woods meeting also highlighted the importance of development lending. The document noted the urgent requirement in the postwar world for capital "for the development of economically backward regions." It also signaled the ongoing US support for loans that promoted economic diversification in commodity exporting countries: "One of the most difficult problems of some debtor countries has been the great fluctuation

---

85. Helleiner 1994, chap. 2. The exemption from needing IMF approval for using capital controls was included already in the public White Plan of the spring of 1943 (Horsefield 1969b, 95).

86. White, "Proposal for a Bank for Reconstruction and Development of the United and Associated Nations," September 3, 1943, p. 1, ISF, box 55.

87. US State Department 1948, 1618.

88. White, "Proposal" (September 3, 1943), pp. 4–5.

of foreign exchange receipts resulting from excessive dependence on one crop. Loans which would diversify their output and their exports would clearly be helpful in maintaining a greater equilibrium in their balance of payments."[89]

When invitations were issued in May 1944 to the Bretton Woods conference, it is true that the US government stated that the meeting was "for the purpose of formulating definite proposals for an International Monetary Fund, and possibly a Bank for Reconstruction and Development." The word "possibly" has raised some questions about the degree of US commitment to the Bank. But it was included simply because US officials were uncertain at the time of the invitation whether international negotiations on the Bank's content were sufficiently far along to reach agreement at the conference.[90] It did not reflect any lack of interest in the Bank.

The smaller amount of time devoted to the Bank at the conference also did not reflect an absence of enthusiasm for the institution. As Collado (who played a lead role in final drafting of the Bank's content at the conference) later put it, US officials "saw a great need" for the Bank despite the limited time spent on it.[91] After interviewing a number of attendees of the conference in 1957, one Bank staff summarized their collective reminiscences as follows: "The emphasis on the Fund did not mean that the Bank was considered less important. It was rather that the role for which the Fund was designed, to police the world's monetary systems, gave it the quality of spinach in the international diet, while the Bank had rather more the character of dessert. The drafters at Bretton Woods firmly believed in first things first, and as everyone knows, spinach comes before dessert."[92] Halfway through the conference, White also explained to his US colleagues why he had encouraged the conference to focus initially on the Fund: "the Fund was the thing to get out of the way first; it was more complicated, involved more work, and there were more differences of opinion."[93]

If US officials were very supportive of international development lending, why was a role specifically for a public institution seen as necessary in this sector? It was partly because White and other US officials anticipated that private investors were likely to be deterred by currency instability, foreign exchange controls, political uncertainty, "anti-foreign-capital" sentiments, and the risk of defaults.[94]

---

89. Schuler and Schuler 2013, 8, 26.
90. See for example Bernstein's comments in Black 1991, 42. See also Mason and Asher 1973, 19; Fuchs 1974b, 17.
91. McKinzie 1974, 17.
92. Boskey 1957, 2.
93. MD, book 753, p. 150. See also comments of a Belgian delegate in Kapur, Lewis, and Webb 1997, 59 n. 9.
94. White, "Proposal" (September 3, 1943), pp. 4–5. Quote from Viner in Norman Wait Harris Memorial Foundation 1941, 95.

The Bank's ability to guarantee loans was designed to help encourage a revival of private lending. Even if private investors were willing to lend, however, US officials still saw an important role for the Bank in direct lending because of their distrust of the ability of private markets to finance development goals adequately. For example, Harvard economics professor Alvin Hansen (a member of the technical committee and subsequent participant at Bretton Woods) noted that the Bank could fund projects that might not provide a good return but "without which private investment, industrialization and agricultural diversification would be impossible, and without which there could not be the increase in productivity and standard of living which these basic development projects make possible."[95] Federal Reserve Board official Arthur Bloomfield also argued that private lenders often showed little interest in "many necessary socio-economic developmental projects, such as public sanitation, conservation of natural resources, eradication of diseases, etc" whereas the Bank could be "guided by much broader considerations than the strict profit and market calculations."[96]

This still left the question of why it was necessary for the public role to be channeled through an international institution. The arguments for this arrangement were similar to those advanced at the time of the IAB proposal. For example, Gardner argued that "such an agency would not serve the political ambitions of any country. It could not be accused of dollar diplomacy."[97] Hansen suggested that "an International Bank would promote self-discipline among the members and would relieve the United States from alone carrying the onus of securing enforcement of contract."[98] In addition, Bloomfield argued that "by extending long-term loans through an impersonal international organization, the dangers of political clashes between debtor and creditor countries, or between creditor countries themselves would be greatly narrowed."[99]

Roosevelt and New Deal Values

The breadth of the US official interest in promoting economic development in poorer countries at this time also deserves to be underlined. Roosevelt himself

---

95. Alvin Hansen, "International Development and Investment Bank," p. 2, November 13, 1943, CFR, box 300, folder 3.

96. Arthur Bloomfield, "The Proposed United Nations Bank for Reconstruction and Development," p. 4, ISF, box 57.

97. Walter Gardner to Szymczak, "The International Investment Bank Proposed by the Treasury, Feb 15, 1944," p. 3, ISF, box 56. See also Division of Economic Studies, State Department, "Proposal for an International Investment Agency," September 28, 1943, p. 4, ISF, box 55.

98. Hansen 1944, 33–34. See also Bernstein's comments reported in Wallich to Knoke, January 20, 1944, ISF, box 56.

99. Arthur Bloomfield, "The Proposed United Nations Bank," pp. 5–6.

had prioritized development goals for the postwar world even before the United States entered the war. One of the "Four Freedoms" that Roosevelt proclaimed in his January 1941 State of the Union address after winning his third term in office was "freedom from want—which translated into world terms, means economic understandings which will secure to every nation a healthy peacetime life for its inhabitants—everywhere in the world."[100]

This ambitious goal was reiterated in the Atlantic Charter that Roosevelt and Churchill issued in August 14, 1941 and which historians recognize as the "first official statement . . . outlining the war's aims and the shape of the postwar world to come" (and whose purposes and principles were then affirmed in the January 1942 Declaration of the United Nations).[101] One of the charter's eight principles committed to the assurance "that all the men in all the lands may live out their lives in freedom from fear and want." Historian Elizabeth Borgwardt has pointed out how Roosevelt's commitment to the principle of "freedom from want" at this time was part of his bold attempt to "internationalize the New Deal." New Dealers had already linked the provision of economic security for individuals to the broader stability of the American polity. Roosevelt now saw the bolstering of standards of living throughout the world as a crucial foundation for postwar global political stability. He saw this and the other principles of the Atlantic Charter in very ambitious terms. As Borgwardt remarks, "in several of his press conferences, FDR compared the aspirations articulated in the Atlantic Charter to those of the US Constitution, the British Magna Carta, and even the Ten Commandments."[102]

After Roosevelt dictated his "Four Freedoms" speech (which he wrote entirely himself), one of his officials asked whether he really wanted "freedom from want" to apply "everywhere," since Americans might not be interested in the people of Java. Roosevelt apparently responded: "I'm afraid they'll have to be some day. . . . The world is getting so small that even the people in Java are getting to be our neighbors now."[103] The invocation of "neighbors" was not accidental. Kimball notes that Roosevelt "believed that his Good Neighbor Policy provided a paradigm for the postwar world."[104] As we have seen, Roosevelt's important 1936 speech in Buenos Aires had already highlighted the link between living standards and international political stability in the context of cultivating an inter-American antifascist alliance.[105]

---

100. Quoted in http://docs.fdrlibrary.marist.edu/od4frees.html.

101. Borgwardt 2005, 33.

102. Borgwardt 2005, 3, 5. For the Atlantic Charter quote, see p. 304.

103. Quoted in Rosenman 1952, 264.

104. Kimball 1991, 107. See also Pike 1995, 22–23, 223, 226.

105. Roosevelt's concept of "freedom from want" may also have been influenced by discussions in the British press in the fall of 1940 about the need to defeat Hitlerism with commitments to minimum standards for housing, food, education, and medical care (Rosenman 1952, 265). White was

Gerald Meier has argued that the Bretton Woods negotiations "remained largely immune" from the aspirations of Roosevelt's "Four Freedoms" speech, the Atlantic Charter, and the UN Charter.[106] This view is very difficult to accept. White made clear reference to these loftier goals in initial drafts of the Fund and the Bank. His January 6 1942 memo stated explicitly that his proposed Stabilization Fund was designed to facilitate "the attainment of the economic objectives of the Atlantic charter," and that membership would be open only to countries that subscribed to the objectives of the charter.[107] In his more detailed January 1942 draft, White also stated that members of the Bank would be required to "subscribe publicly to the "Magna Carta of the United Nations."[108] The same provision existed in his March draft where he explained that this Magna Carta would constitute "a bill of rights of the peoples of the United Nations" that set forth "the ideal of freedom for which most of the peoples are fighting the aggressor nations and hope they will be able to attain and believe they are defending."[109] White even went so far as to append a draft of such a Magna Carta to his proposals (although this appears to have been lost to the historical record). White justified this requirement of Bank members in the following way: "The inclusion of that provision would make clear to the peoples everywhere that these new instrumentalities which are being developed go far beyond usual commercial considerations and considerations of economic self-interest. They would be evidence of the beginning of a truly new order in the realm where it has hitherto been most lacking—international finance."[110]

The link between the early White drafts and Roosevelt's broader thinking was also highlighted by Morgenthau, who described White's plans to Roosevelt in May 1942 as a "New Deal in international economics."[111] One of the New Deal values Morgenthau had in mind was apparent in his final speech at Bretton Woods when he applauded how the new international institutions being proposed by the conference would "limit the control which certain private bankers have in the past exercised over international finance."[112] Morgenthau's desire to also curtail

---

also closely following British political developments at this time; see White to Morgenthau, "Recent Social Changes in England—Summary," December 11, 1940, CFHDW, box 4, Chron.18.

106. Meier 1984a, 11.

107. White, "Proposal" (January 6, 1942), p. 1.

108. White, "Suggested Plan" (January 1942), p. 20.

109. Quotes from White, "Preliminary Draft" (March 1942), pp. III-4, III-40. See also Oliver 1975, 319.

110. White, "Preliminary Draft" (March 1942), p. III-41. See also Oliver 1975, 319.

111. US State Department 1963a, 172. White had in fact penned these words: "Memorandum for the President," May 14, 1942, SMHDW, box 14, file: D1-No. 3.

112. Morgenthau continued: "It would by no means restrict the investment sphere in which bankers could engage. On the contrary, it would greatly expand this sphere by enlarging the volume of international investment and would act as an enormously effective stabilizer and guarantor of

the influence of central bankers—so apparent in the IAB discussions—was also clear in his advocacy of a Norwegian resolution at Bretton Woods calling for the abolition of the BIS "at the earliest possible moment."[113] But an equally important New Deal value was the commitment to address poverty. In his opening statement to the 1944 conference, he spoke of the goal of establishing "a satisfactory standard of living for all the people of all the countries on this earth."[114] He also argued that "Prosperity, like peace, is indivisible. We cannot afford to have it scattered here or there among the fortunate or to enjoy it at the expense of others. Poverty, wherever it exists, is menacing to us all and undermines the well-being of each of us."[115]

That last sentence of Morgenthau's was quite similar to a statement endorsed at an important conference of the International Labour Organization two months earlier: "poverty anywhere constitutes a danger to prosperity everywhere."[116] When Roosevelt received the ILO delegates to the White House at the end of the conference, he went out of his way to quote this line approvingly and added:

> This principle is a guide to all of our international economic deliberations . . . it is perfectly true that poverty anywhere constitutes a danger to prosperity everywhere. I think of a little colony, a little piece of the earth's surface, Gambia, where I happened to have landed from Brazil. Nice, peaceful people, and as the saying goes, poor as church mice. . . . Well, when I was there, I wasn't thinking in terms of who should do it, but if they had a little less poverty, that would bring prosperity to a lot more people outside of Gambia. They are kept down because of exploitation. I think that is going to be a new word in the next meeting

---

loans which they might make. The chief purpose of the Bank for International Reconstruction and Development is to guarantee private loans made through the usual investment channels. It would make loans only when these could not be floated through the normal channels at reasonable rates. The effect would be to provide capital for those who need it at lower interest rates than in the past and to drive only the usurious money lenders from the temple of international finance" (US State Department 1948, 1118–19). The last line seemed to invoke Roosevelt's first inauguration address from 1933 when the president had noted that "the money changers have fled from their high seats in the temple of our civilization. We may now restore that temple to the ancient truths. The measure of the restoration lies in the extent to which we apply social values more noble than mere monetary profit" (Roosevelt 1933). In one of the drafts of Morgenthau's speech that can be found in the Morgenthau Diaries (MD, book 757, p. 97), it is interesting to see that someone (presumably Morgenthau himself) had initially strengthened the phrase "to drive only the usurious money lenders from the temple of international finance" by crossing out the word "only." But the word was then reinserted in pencil and it appeared in the final speech.

113. See especially MD, book 755, pp. 174–86, 211–13; book 756, pp. 119–22, 134–36.

114. US State Department 1948, 82.

115. US State Department 1948, 81. The phrase "prosperity, like peace, is indivisible" was also included in a short summary of White's plan sent to Roosevelt in mid-May 1942 (US State Department 1963a, 174).

116. Quoted in Alcalde 1987, 141.

of the I.L.O., something that I have had in the back of my head a long time, something that says something against exploitation of the poor by the rich—by Governments, as well as individuals. I think we can get somewhere if we keep that idea of being "agin"—as we say in Irish-American—against exploitation everywhere. It will be an awfully good thing for all of us.[117]

Roosevelt's interest in promoting higher living standards in poorer parts of the world was apparent in other contexts as well.[118] Before the Bretton Woods conference was held, he invited countries to attend another meeting—the first of the United Nations—in Hot Springs, Virginia between May and June 1943 to address what one official called "freedom from want of food."[119] There was much discussion of the nutritional needs and the standards of living of people in poor countries at the meeting, which created an Interim Commission on Food and Agriculture (that commission then drafted the constitution for the Food and Agriculture Organization, which met for the first time in October 1945). In the spring of 1943, Roosevelt also asked an interdepartmental committee to develop a memo showing "that helping others raise their living standards is 'good for our own pocket-book and our own security.'"[120] The Latin American situation was clearly central in his mind. In a note to Rockefeller in June 1943, he wrote "I do want to get across the idea. . .that the economy and social welfare of Jesus Fernandez in Brazil does affect the economy and social welfare of Johnny Jones in Terre Haute, Indiana."[121] The resulting "living standards abroad" report—written by an interdepartmental committee that included Acheson, Clayton, Collado, and Rockefeller—argued that less industrialized countries could use an influx of between $3 and $3.5 billion in foreign funds over the following ten years, a considerable portion of which would need to come in the form of public loans with low interest rates and long amortization periods.

Wider US Interest in International Development

Roosevelt's vice president, Henry Wallace, was also keen to assist international development. After a 1940 trip to Mexico, he had become particularly supportive of Latin American industrialization, agrarian reform, the development of small

---

117. Roosevelt 1944, 1.
118. See also Pruessen 2009.
119. This phrase comes from Frank L. McDougall, "Draft Memorandum on a United Nations Program for Freedom From Want of Food," February 11, 1943, RIIACR, Economic Group Paper 75, Group Papers 9/22d.
120. Roosevelt's words quoted in Rivas 2002, 58. See also Green 1971, 123–29.
121. Quoted in Green 1971, 129.

farms, and improved literacy and nutrition in the region.[122] During the war, Wallace thought freedom from want was the most important of Roosevelt's "Four Freedoms," and he urged that postwar plans improve "conditions of life among the common people of the world."[123] In his view, higher living standards in poorer parts of the world would provide new markets for US exports, stave off fascism and communism, and provide a foundation for postwar peace and democracy. To assist development in poorer regions, he called for "an international bank and an international TVA" as well as an international agency to stabilize commodity prices.[124]

Wallace chaired the Board of Economic Warfare, which was represented on White's technical committee and which had initially been created (under the name Economic Defense Board) in July 1941 to strengthen ties with Latin America. Soon after its creation, the board began to discuss the need for an international institution that could promote development. Building on these discussions, Winfield Riefler—who had been involved in the IAB discussions—had written up a seventy-page plan for an "International Development Authority" in October 1941. The goal of his plan was "to demonstrate, concretely, a means by which the democracies can implement now the Peace Aim, 'Freedom from Want.'" His proposed institution was to be created by the United States and the United Kingdom in order to "provide particularly for the economic development of underdeveloped regions, e.g., the Caribbean, the Danube Valley, China, the Dutch East Indies, Latin America."[125] It would grant charters to international enterprises (public, private, or mixed) pursuing development projects approved by local governments. Private investors in the enterprises would be reassured by the fact that they could trade their shares for bonds of the International Development Authority, which would be backed by capital from the US and British governments.

Riefler's proposal immediately attracted the attention of Jacob Viner, who was a special assistant to Morgenthau and who would advise White on his Bretton Woods drafts just a few months later in early January 1942. In October 1941, Viner also recommended the proposal to Alvin Hansen who had been discussing with Viner his own latest plans for Anglo-American financial cooperation.[126] Since late 1939, Hansen had co-chaired with Viner a study group (of which Riefler

122. Walker 1976; Gellman 1979, 167–71; Woods 1979, 66–67; Cullather 2010, chap. 2; Rivas 2002, 54–57.

123. Quoted in Walker 1976, 83.

124. Wallace quoted in Ekbladh 2010, 85. See also Walker 1976, chap. 7; Rivas 2002, 56.

125. Winfield Riefler, "A Program to Stimulate International Investment," p. 1, October 4, 1941, JVP, box 109, folder 4. See also Oliver 1975, 360–61 n. 21. Riefler noted that he was not discussing publicly financed investment in his paper, but was working on that idea.

126. Viner to Hansen, October 24, 1941 and Hansen to Viner, October 28, 1941, JVP, box 13, folder 9.

was also a member) of the influential Council on Foreign Relations (CFR) that focused on "economic and financial problems" of postwar planning.[127] In May 1941, Hansen proposed an "international RFC" that would support not just the "rehabilitation and reconstruction of England and the Continent" but also "investment in Latin America and China."[128] His ideas likely informed a July 1941 CFR memo that recommended the creation of worldwide financial institutions for "stabilizing currencies and facilitating programs of capital investment for constructive undertakings in backward and underdeveloped regions."[129]

In September 1941, Hansen traveled to Britain where he discussed his ideas in numerous conferences with Keynes, other British economists and government officials, and even British Cabinet ministers.[130] He even drafted a one-page "Joint Declaration by the Governments of the United States and Great Britain" in which the two governments would—among other things—contribute capital to an "International Finance Corporation" that would invest in "development projects throughout the world."[131] It is noteworthy that Viner, when commenting on Hansen's ideas (which he liked and thought were similar to Riefler's) in early November 1941, stressed the importance of including small countries in the management of international lending institutions in order to avoid the appearance of what he called an Anglo-American "financial monopoly." As he put it in, "to be successful the proposed body must avoid the odium of two-power imperialism."[132] In January 1942, Hansen returned to London accompanied by Luther Gulick, a US expert on the TVA, on a trip sponsored by the State Department. They advanced a number of proposals that were presented to the British War Cabinet in late January, including an idea for an "international development corporation" whose stock would be held by governments.[133] Keynes drew directly on these ideas when developing his own plans.

Throughout the Bretton Woods negotiations, Hansen continued to see the promotion of international development as a key priority, backing White's Bank

---

127. For the influence of this group, see Nerozzi 2009; Shoup and Minter 1977, chap. 4; Ikenberry 1992, 201–4.

128. Quoted in Mehrling 1997, 122.

129. Quoted in Shoup and Minter 1977, 166. See also Nerozzi 2009, 29–30.

130. Hansen to Viner, p. 1, October 20, 1941, JVP, box 13, folder 9. See also Mehrling 1997, 122.

131. Quote from "Tentative Draft of Joint Declaration by the Governments of the United States and Great Britain," p. 1 (undated, but initially drafted when Hansen was in London and revised some time before October 20, 1941), JVP, box 13, folder 9.

132. Quoted in Nerozzi 2009, 59 n. 46 from a November 1, 1941 CFR document. See also Viner to Hansen, October 24, 1941, JVP, box 13, folder 9. In an April 1942 memo for the Council on Foreign Relations, Viner called for an international financial institution that could channel capital to "foster the development of backward areas." Like White, he was also interested in whether the institution could help settle international debts (Oliver 1975, 106–7). See also Shoup and Minter 1977, 167.

133. Horsefield 1969a, 13.

proposal (as well as commodity price stabilization schemes) even though the institution was weaker than he favored.[134] As he put it in an article co-written with Charles Kindleberger (who was working at the Federal Reserve Board) and published in *Foreign Affairs* in April 1942, "increases in the productivity of the Balkan peasant, of the Hindu and Moslem in India, of the Chinese may seem of remote interest to many Americans; but they will contribute in the long run to both the economic and the political security of the United States."[135] After Kindleberger moved to become chief economist of the Office of Strategic Services later in 1942, he too continued to promote "large-scale intergovernmental development loans" to boost living standards in "underdeveloped countries."[136] He was particularly keen to assist industrialization in poorer countries because of the vulnerability of primary producers and because the terms of trade were moving against those producers over time given the low income elasticity of demand for their products.[137] In a September 1942 paper that attracted the attention of White and Bernstein, Kindleberger was also more explicit than many other US officials about some of the political imperatives driving the new interest in international development:

> It may be doubted, however, whether wide inequalities in incomes received by like factors of production can endure for long today without some conscious effort to narrow them. While the physical mobility of the overwhelming majority of the world remains limited, there is great mobility of ideas, including the idea of what constitutes an adequate standard of living. Ease of communication of thought is a twentieth-century commonplace; but the consequence that like factors of production are beginning to insist upon a greater approach to equality of real income in spite of lack of mobility is barely beginning to be realized. The desire for greater equality in standards of living and its continued frustration lie close to the basis of the international disequilibrium of the twentieth century.[138]

This political point was made even more sharply by Peter Drucker in a 1943 article discussing the Keynes and White plans in *Harper's Magazine*. He argued

---

134. Mehrling 1997, 123; Nerozzi 2009, 47. For his support of commodity price stabilization, see "Minutes of Meeting Held in Mr. White's Office," May 28, 1942, ITM, box 20; Hansen, "International Monetary and Financial Programs," December 11, 1943, JVP, box 45, folder 5.

135. Hansen and Kindleberger 1942, 474. See also Mehrling 1997, 121–22.

136. Kindleberger 1943a, 353–54. See also Kindleberger 1943b; "C. P. Kindleberger's Proposed International Development Authority," September 16, 1942, BWA, box 27.

137. Kindleberger 1943a. Love (1996, 118, 136) points out that his ideas were an important precursor to the Prebisch-Singer hypothesis and that Prebisch was citing Kindleberger's work in 1944.

138. Kindleberger, "International Monetary Stabilization," September 4, 1942, p. 15, EBP, box 3/1, file: Miscellaneous Loose Materials. See Bernstein to White, October 3, 1942, in same location.

that "the spread of the will to industrialize is perhaps the most important recent event in international economics." He noted that "every raw-material-producing country is firmly convinced that in this present world only industrial countries enjoy full citizenship. And it is equally convinced that in a world of tanks and planes a country is lost unless it can produce its own basic mechanized equipment." Drucker argued that, in the absence of inflows of foreign capital, these countries would "be forced to obtain it by cutting down on the standard of living of their own—pitifully poor—populations, and they could do this only by setting up a totalitarian economic system similar to a war economy." To prevent growing economic nationalism of this kind, he urged White and other US officials to support industrialization in poorer countries through international development lending.[139]

Another prominent US supporter of international development in this period was the economist Eugene Staley, who was also a member of Viner's and Hansen's study group. As early as 1939, he had published a CFR book calling for an "international long-term investment bank" to support an "international development" program around the world.[140] His support for international development stemmed from a combination of humanitarian motives and the desire to offset the communist and fascist ideological challenges to liberal values worldwide.[141] Heinz Arndt argues that Staley was "the man who more than any other brought the theme of economic development into the American discussion."[142] But Staley himself acknowledged in 1939 that his ideas simply built on initiatives that US officials were already "getting under way in the Americas."[143]

One other member of the CFR's economic and financial group, Benjamin Cohen, deserves mention because he participated in White's technical committee as a representative of the White House and was a legal adviser to the US delegation at Bretton Woods.[144] At a CFR meeting in late January 1942 that Hansen also attended, Cohen (who was then with the Federal Power Commission) called for a "World Reconstruction Finance and Development Agency." He pointed out that there was a "growing consensus of opinion that one of the most important and promising functions of international co-operation after the war lies in the direction of investment into developmental projects in the relatively underdeveloped regions of the world such as Latin America, China and southeastern Europe."[145]

---

139. Quotes from Drucker 1943, 179, 180.
140. Staley 1939, 278, 282.
141. Ekbladh 2010.
142. Arndt 1972, 26. See also Ekbladh 2010; Alcalde 1987, 66–70.
143. Staley 1939, 283.
144. Given the prominence of CFR members among those advocating international development initiatives, it is worth mentioning that White was not a member.
145. "Second Special Meeting of the Economic and Financial Group, Council on Foreign Relations, January 24, 1942," p. 17, RIIACR, Economic Group Paper 46.

He also thought that an international body to stabilize commodity prices might be needed after the war.

A number of other individuals who had helped develop the Good Neighbor financial partnership favored the role of international development in US post-war plans in this period. In the State Department, Welles helped write the wording of the Atlantic Charter, and between July 1942 and June 1943 he chaired a committee that drafted an influential blueprint for the postwar United Nations that included proposals for an economic commission to promote international commodity price stabilization, global investment, and economic development.[146] Berle also backed White's plans from the start and was very involved in discussions of them in 1942 and throughout much of 1943.[147] He particularly approved the Bank's development role; indeed, Morgenthau told Keynes in September 1943 that Berle "deserved the credit for pushing this Bank."[148] As noted above, Collado also played a key role in the final drafting of the IBRD.[149] In mid-1944, he also wrote a detailed memo for an interdepartmental committee on the importance of assisting postwar Latin American development and industrialization more generally.[150] And as we shall see in the next chapter, the Federal Reserve Board's interest in development issues was also well demonstrated through its advisory missions to Latin American countries from 1943 onward.

Some of White's development ideas even found favor with John Williams, the Harvard economics professor and vice president of the FRBNY who became known as a leading critic of White's Bretton Woods plans and ally of the conservative New York banking community. It is sometimes forgotten that his "key currency" plan—developed as an alternative to the Keynes and White plans—was explicitly designed to emphasize the importance of recognizing the distinct needs of countries at different stages of development.[151] In the 1930s, he had emerged as a supporter of more flexible exchange rates for poorer countries as tools to help them insulate their domestic economies from external influences.[152] By mid-1944, he had come to the conclusion that exchange controls might be even more useful than exchange rate adjustments for these countries.[153] In a speech to a

---

146. O'Sullivan 2008, 68–72. For Welles's broader support for the Four Freedoms, see also 75–78.

147. Schwartz 1987, 213; Black 1991, 38; Keynes 1980b, 344; Harrod 1951, 340.

148. MD, book 664, p. 30. For his support for a development-oriented Bank in October 1942, see Berle and Jacobs 1973, 422.

149. McKinzie 1974, 12–13, 15–17.

150. US State Department 1967a, 45.

151. Asso and Fiorito 2009.

152. See for example Williams 1947 (1943). See also Asso and Fiorito (2009). Some of his analysis of core-periphery dynamics and criticisms of classical trade theory and the gold standard were similar to Prebisch's.

153. Williams 1947 (1944), xlvii–xlviii.

largely Latin American audience in May 1944 (where he shared the platform with Burgess), Williams even combined his advocacy of exchange controls with a strong critique of the theory of free trade which he argued was "designed to maintain the status quo—that is, to keep the raw material countries producing raw materials and nothing else. It gave them a colonial status. . . . In order to industrialize, protection was needed against the established enterprises of the big industrial countries. The modern and most comprehensive form of protection was exchange control." After Williams's comments, Gardner reported that "an electric wave of sympathy ran through the room. Delegates turned in their seats and nodded approvingly to one another." Villaseñor, who had been one of the lead Mexican advocates of the IAB, even stood up and complimented him.[154]

Some prominent members of the US business community had also become believers in international efforts to assist Southern industrialization. For example, the president of the US Chamber of Commerce, Eric Johnston, explained in May 1944 how Brazilian industrialization would generate larger markets for US products because "you can increase the purchasing power of a people better through industrialization than through any other means."[155] Important policy groups associated with large US manufacturing firms also backed efforts to promote Latin American industrialization during the war.[156] It is worth noting that White highlighted how the IMF's articles of agreement would benefit US businesses seeking to establish branch plants in Latin America and elsewhere because the withdrawal of dividends from earnings would be treated as a current account transaction (which could not be restricted by exchange controls). Here is the case he made to US delegates in a private meeting on the second day of the Bretton Woods conference: "Let's say the General Motors Company establishes a plant in Brazil. As it has been in the past, they have earned local currency. Now, they weren't at all certain that they could withdraw those currencies. . . . But under the Fund arrangement, these current earnings on investments must be treated just like payment for exports and imports, and are not subject to exchange controls. . . . That would mean that you would have a considerable stimulus for the kind of investment which is best for the country and best for us."[157]

Not everyone in the United States was entirely enthusiastic about supporting Southern industrialization. After the United States published its IBRD plan in November 1943, the American International Labor Conference on International

---

154. Gardner summarizing Williams's comments in Gardner to Goldenweiser, May 15, 1944, p. 1, ISF, box 247, pp. 1, 1–2. See also the defense of Latin American exchange controls by Hansen, "Latin America and Exchange Control," May 27, 1944, p. 1, ISF, box 156.

155. Quoted in Green 1971, 129–30.

156. Maxfield and Nolt 1990, 56.

157. MD, book 749, p. 181.

Affairs published a commentary by Albert Halasi that advocated "the industrial-ization of young and backward countries" but noted that attention would need to be given "to the adverse effects it may have on particular industries in the old industrial countries and to seek to facilitate the adjustment of these difficul-ties."[158] This concern was also remarked on by one of the members of the US delegation at the Bretton Woods conference, Jesse Wolcott, a Republican member of the House of Representatives from Michigan. After participating in some of the conference sessions developing the IBRD's articles of agreement, he told his US colleagues: "I sense in our conversations with all of these countries that they have a vision of their country being just covered with smokestacks. They are all going to want to industrialize." He noted that there was debate about "whether we should encourage with American capital the other countries to become man-ufacturing countries to the possible prejudice of the American market." White acknowledged the opposition but argued that it could be answered. When Wol-cott asked "What is going to happen when the Arabian desert is covered with factories?" White responded with his own quip: "some of us are going to be dead a long time."[159]

From the very start of the Bretton Woods planning process, US officials set out to design a postwar international financial order that gave prominence to the kinds of development issues that had already arisen in the context of US–Latin Ameri-can financial relations. Far from being an afterthought, development concerns were prioritized. White's initial plans were particularly ambitious in this respect, covering commodity price stabilization, infant industry trade protection, debt restructuring, capital flight, compensatory balance of payments financing, and long-term international development finance. This agenda for international eco-nomic reform anticipated many of the demands made by Southern countries in the New International Economic Order discussions of the 1970s.

It is also worth noting White's commitment to wide consultation on post-war plans with all United and Associated Nations, of which we will see more evidence in subsequent chapters. This commitment gave Southern countries an opportunity for considerable voice in international financial policymaking, and it contrasted with British policymakers' preference for an exclusively bilat-eral Anglo-American process. Other US officials also placed a high value on this inclusive process. As Berle noted in his diary after opening a Washington consul-tation session in mid-June 1943 involving eighteen countries, "the significance of

---

158. Albert Halasi, "The United Nations Bank for Reconstruction and Development: Comments on the Guiding Principles," pp. 11, 13, EBP, box 3/1, file: Miscellaneous Loose Materials.
    159. MD, book 756, pp. 20–21.

the meeting was not what it said, but that it was the first more or less democratic procedure for dealing with this sort of thing."[160] While Keynes initially proposed an international financial institution run by the United States and Britain, White had favored a multilateral institution from the start, in which both small and large countries were represented. Indeed, in his initial short draft of the Fund on January 6, 1942, White had even gone out of his way to state that although voting would be roughly in line with contributions, "the distribution of votes among the members might well be modified by giving the smaller countries a share of voting power greatly in excess of their share of subscription to the assets of the Fund."[161]

As the US plans evolved, some of White's initial "development" proposals fell off the agenda, and later we shall see how Southern countries sought unsuccessfully to bring some of them back. But in the final agreements, the core US commitment to international development remained. The support for it by US officials reflected a similar mix of strategic, economic, and ideational motivations that had been prominent in driving the Good Neighbor financial partnership. In a strategic sense, the promise to improve living standards helped to solidify wartime alliances, accommodate rising development aspirations, and invest in peace for the future. Economically, international development was seen to create new investment opportunities, to generate lower-cost imports by improving productivity abroad, and especially to boost markets for US products. Alongside these strategic and economic interests, New Deal values were also significant, such as a concern for social justice and the poor, sympathy for a more active state role in the economy, antipathy toward the New York financial elite and dollar diplomacy, and an association between economic security and political stability.

It was not just US officials who carried the experience of the Good Neighbor financial partnership into the Bretton Woods negotiations. United States opponents of that earlier policy did so too. Despite the watering down of the ambitious features of White's initial drafts in many areas, the final Bretton Woods Agreements were still opposed by various economic conservatives and isolationists, as well as by New York bankers.[162] The latter were led once again by Burgess in his role as president of the American Bankers Association. Congressional opponents of Bretton Woods also included figures such as Robert Taft and Arthur Vandenberg who had been strong opponents of the IAB and lending to Latin America before the US entry into the war. In the eyes of many opponents, the Fund's provisions represented too radical a break from the market-based

---

160. Berle and Jacobs 1943, 437. For this consultation, see chapter 7.
161. White, "Memorandum" (January 6, 1942), pp. 5–6.
162. See for example Gardner 1980, 129–43; Eckes 1975, chap. 7; Van Dormael 1978, chaps. 18–19; Blum 1967, 427–36.

principles and discipline of the international gold standard. Burgess and other critics also complained that the United States would end up being "soaked," as foreign countries, such as Russia, China and some Latin American countries, borrowed from the Fund.[163] Critics also questioned the need for public long-term international lending, while others preferred to see such lending channeled through the US-controlled Export-Import Bank, a suggestion that had also been raised by opponents of the IAB.[164]

Despite these various criticisms, the United States became the first country to ratify the Bretton Woods agreements after they were approved in both houses of Congress with very healthy majorities in June and July of 1945—a striking contrast with the IAB experience. This outcome was fostered by a Treasury-organized public relations campaign that resonated with wider domestic support for internationalism as the war wound down. It is worth noting that the development mandate of Bretton Woods was featured in this campaign. In one cartoon booklet produced for the public in May 1945, Bretton Woods delegates told representatives from poor countries: "If we help you to become prosperous, *you will be able to buy more things from us!*"[165] In a *Foreign Affairs* article in early 1945, Morgenthau also stressed that "the Bretton Woods approach is based on the realization that it is to the economic and political advantage of countries such as India and China, and also of countries such as England and the United States, that the industrialization and betterment of living conditions in the former be achieved with the aid and encouragement of the latter." Investment in poor countries would, he argued, not just boost US exports but also raise labor standards abroad and discourage those countries from industrializing on their own by "ruthlessly exploiting their own cheap labor, and undercutting countries with higher labor standards in the process." Prophetically, Morgenthau also noted the political need to accommodate Southern development goals in order to minimize future conflict between rich and poor countries: "Unless some framework which will make the desires of both sets of countries mutually compatible is established, economic and monetary conflicts between the less and more developed countries will almost certainly ensue. Nothing would be more menacing to world security than to have the less developed countries, comprising more than half the population of the world, ranged in economic battle against the less populous but industrially more advanced nations of the west."[166]

---

163. Burgess quoted in meeting with British officials; untitled and unauthored document from October 23, 1944 in UKT 247/63.

164. Washington to FO, Viscount Halifax, No. 441 REMAC, June 9, 1944, UKT 247/29; Oliver 1975, 213–14, 218–19; Casey 2001, 46; Patterson 1972, 292–93; Kemmerer 1944.

165. "The Story of Bretton Woods" (undated, but May 1945), p. 15–16, MP, container 293. Emphasis in the original.

166. Morgenthau 1945, 188, 190.

STRENGTHENING THE FOUNDATIONS
Paraguay

An additional way in which US officials supported international development goals during the Bretton Woods negotiations—one that has been quite overlooked in histories of Bretton Woods—was the 1943–44 financial advisory mission of Robert Triffin of the Federal Reserve Board, to Paraguay whose advice echoed that of the White mission to Cuba in 1941–42. This time, however, the US advice was implemented immediately, and the Paraguayan reforms quickly came to be seen as a model to be followed by Southern policymakers with development aspirations elsewhere. United States officials saw the Triffin mission as helping to prepare the country for membership in the new IMF, and the Fund's provisions for adjustable exchange rates and capital controls were written into Paraguay's new monetary legislation. As in Cuba, US officials also recommended domestic reforms to strengthen the government's capacity to further development, including the creation of a new central bank, a national currency, and mechanisms for providing domestic development finance.

While the Bretton Woods negotiations created a multilateral framework that favored Southern governments' development priorities, the Triffin mission strengthened the domestic institutional arrangements that allowed those priorities to be met. As we shall see in later chapters, Triffin and other US advisers then dispensed similar advice across Latin America and elsewhere to countries that had signed up to the Bretton Woods agreements. Triffin's Paraguayan mission also deserves attention because it teaches us more about political sources of the US backing for international development in this period. While US economic interests were negligible in Paraguay, strategic concerns were significant in driving

US policy toward the country, as they were elsewhere. The Paraguayan mission was also influenced by New Deal values, particularly the willingness of US officials to learn from, and partner with, Latin American policymakers who were pioneering new development-oriented financial polices at this time. As we shall see, the most significant of these policymakers was Raúl Prebisch, with whom Triffin worked closely in Paraguay.

The Emergence of the Mission

The Federal Reserve Board's participation in the Cuban mission represented its first extensive involvement in Latin American financial advisory work. It became much more involved after the arrival of the thirty-year-old Triffin in mid-August 1942 to organize and lead the Board's Latin American section of its research division. Triffin was a Belgian-born economist whose political sympathies there had been with center-left reformers.[1] He came to the United States in 1935 to study at Harvard, receiving his Ph.D. in 1938 working with Schumpeter, Leontief, and Chamberlin (and he spent a summer at the University of Chicago were he was turned off by the free-market Chicago School).[2] After returning briefly to Belgium, he took a three-year teaching appointment at Harvard between 1939 and 1942. In some ways, Triffin was an unlikely hire for the Federal Reserve role. His Ph.D. thesis (which, like White's, had won the prestigious Wells Prize for best thesis) was very theoretical, examining monopolistic competition and general equilibrium theory.[3] At the time, he had also never traveled to Latin America. But economists were in short supply during the war and Triffin's academic credentials were impressive, as were his Spanish language skills.

The Fed's Walter Gardner played the major role in training Triffin.[4] As we have seen, Gardner had been deeply involved with the IAB initiative and the Cuban mission, and he was a member of White's technical committee developing the Bretton Woods plans. He had also urged the Federal Reserve Board to assume a lead role in US financial missions to Latin America as far back as May 1939. Gardner found a very sympathetic colleague in Triffin. In a memo written just one month after his hiring, Triffin made clear that he supported the Good Neighbor financial initiatives that Gardner and others had pioneered. The memo advocated a program of large foreign lending to assist Latin American industrial development and economic diversification not just in the short term but also in

---

1. Triffin 1990.
2. Triffin 1981.
3. Triffin 1940.
4. Triffin to Gardner, August 28, 1945, p. 4, ISF, box 227.

the postwar period. Triffin argued that this program would reduce Latin American countries' dependence on commodity exports and also provide new markets for US exporters of capital equipment after the war.[5]

Because the Federal Reserve Board did not have access to good information on Latin American financial and monetary issues, Triffin immediately set to work on developing a major set of research studies that would compile statistics on money and banking issues for each Latin American country as well as analyses of their central bank operations and monetary and banking legislation. The goal was to have a set of country studies that, after receiving comments from each Latin American central bank, could be published in a single volume titled "Central Banking and Money Markets in Latin America." Gardner noted that the information would be particularly useful if the IAB was created. Even if wasn't, however, the work "will fill a long-felt want and will give the Board intimate contacts in Latin America and an influence on central banking philosophy in that area which could not otherwise possibly be achieved."[6]

Just as Triffin completed a draft of a first study of Colombia in mid-1943, he had his first opportunity to travel to the region as a member of a Treasury-led mission to Honduras that had been arranged by White. In addition to being struck by the poverty of the country, Triffin reported back to his superiors that he was impressed by the "enthusiastic response to our good neighbor policy" and by the fact that the policy "is certainly bringing fruit here and appears indispensable for any successful attack on the problem of Honduran progress and economic development."[7] The Honduran government had asked White for help in establishing a central bank. Like Cuba, the country had no central bank at the time and US currency was often used there, particularly on the north coast where two US fruit companies (Standard Fruit and United Fruit) grew bananas that made up a large portion of the country's exports.[8] The mission recommended the creation of a new public central bank that would have a monopoly of note issue backed with 30 percent reserves and that would be empowered to impose reserve requirements on banks as well as exchange controls. Within the central bank, the mission also recommended the creation of a credit department to help address the shortage of agricultural credit that placed farmers, in Triffin's words, "at the mercy of the local merchants who seem to exploit the situation to the full."[9]

5. Triffin, "Notes on an Investment Program for Latin America" September 25, 1942, ISF, box 152.
6. Gardner to Goldenweiser, July 24, 1943, p. 3, ISF, box 148. For the board's lack of good information on Latin America, see "Latin American Field," May 23, 1943, ISF, box 264.
7. Triffin to Szymczak, June 16, 1943, p. 3, ISF, box 227.
8. See, for example, Vinelli 1950.
9. Triffin to Szymczak, June 16, 1943, p. 1. For the mission's recommendations, see Julia Wooster to J. Burke Knapp, September 6, 1943, ISF, box 139.

The recommendations of the Honduran mission met the same fate as those of White's Cuban mission. It was not until 1950 that they were finally implemented. Years later, Triffin suggested that the powerful United Fruit Company had been one force working against them.[10] But as we will see below, he also felt that the mission's lack of success reflected the way that White had approached the Honduran government. By this time, Triffin had already found an opportunity to do things differently in another country: Paraguay.

Cultivating the Paraguayan Request

As far back as 1938, officials in Paraguay had sought US credit and technical expertise to help achieve their goal of stabilizing the Paraguayan currency.[11] The State Department had strongly supported the idea because of the country's strategic location in the region and out of fear that the Nazis were cultivating support among the large German population in the country. The first Nazi group overseas had been established in Paraguay in 1929 and the US ambassador estimated in 1941 that there were just twenty US citizens compared to twenty-six thousand Germans living in the country.[12] American fears about Axis influence only intensified when reports surfaced in 1939 that the Paraguayan government was negotiating a major economic deal with Germany and Bolivia, involving the building of an oil refinery in Paraguay to transport Bolivian oil to Buenos Aires for shipment to Europe.[13] Quickly thereafter, the United States approved an Export-Import Bank loan to the country for public works and to help stabilize the peso.[14] At the insistence of the Export-Import Bank, Paraguay's state bank—the Banco de la República del Paraguay—hired Eric Lamb, who had been a statistician at the FRBNY and had Latin American experience, to serve as financial adviser during the period of the loan.[15]

During Lamb's time, Paraguayan politics underwent a major transformation. The Liberal Party, which had dominated the country since the late nineteenth century, faced growing challenges to its rule in the late 1930s from groups who favored greater state intervention in the economy to bolster the nation's power and independence from foreign domination.[16] After several changes of government

---

10. Triffin 1990, 25.
11. Grow 1981, 53.
12. Friedman 2003, 21; Frost to Hull, April 7, 1944, WFP. More generally, see Grow 1981, Mora 1998.
13. See for example O. E. Moore to Mr. Knoke, August 4, 1939, ISF, box 101.
14. Grow 1981, 53; US State Department 1957, 759–61.
15. Adams 1976, 216–17; US State Department 1957, 764.
16. Grow 1981, 44–51.

and growing political instability, General Higinio Morínigo became president in September 1940 committed to these more nationalist goals. Dominating Paraguayan politics until 1948, he pushed for "a program of authoritarian modernization and reform" involving the creation of new public works programs, public monopolies, social security programs, and state assistance for industrialization and agriculture. In a speech in December 1940, he laid out his goals: "we believe that the true and direct object of the State is the development of all the faculties of the nation and the perfecting of its life. Hence we reject Liberalism, the product of the 19th century, which does not admit the intervention of the State positively in satisfying human needs and considerably reduces its mission."[17]

Many in Morínigo's government and the armed forces were sympathetic to the Axis cause. As part of broader efforts to improve relations with Paraguay, the US government replaced the existing ambassador, who had been hostile to the new regime, with Wesley Frost who was more supportive of its reforms and industrialization goals.[18] By mid-1941, Morínigo had decided to accept US military aid and his government subsequently, at the important inter-American conference in Rio in January 1942, agreed to break diplomatic ties with the Axis powers.[19] After this, a key goal of US policy was to reduce the country's economic dependence on Argentina, an objective that dovetailed with the preferences of Morínigo and other Paraguayan nationalists who were very wary of the influence of their powerful southern neighbor, especially since Argentina had instigated revolutions in Paraguay in the past.[20]

Just before he left the country in mid-1941, Lamb outlined a plan to improve the Banco's internal organization since its operations were growing dramatically. The bank was now involved not just in new financing of crop purchases but also in administering exchange controls that the government had put in place in February 1941. Lamb's plan was well received by the bank, but Lamb noted that the staff lacked confidence in their ability to carry it out. To address this situation, he suggested that the US government provide help to some members of the Banco to visit the United States on a training mission. The proposal was approved by the Banco and funded by the Office of the Coordinator of Inter-American Affairs.[21]

---

17. Quoted in Grow 1981, 62.

18. Grow 1981, 67–68, 101, 135–36. For Frost's support of industrialization goals, see for example Frost to Allan Dawson, January 3, 1944, WFP.

19. Grow 1981, 66–76. Paraguay did not declare war on the Axis until February 1945.

20. Frost to Hull, January 11, 1943, April 8, 1944, and Frost to Allan Dawson, February 1, 1944, all in WFP. See also "Summary Statement of United States Policy Toward Paraguay," December 12, 1944, DSDF, 250/44/7/7, box 58.

21. Eric Lamb, "Memorandum for Mr. Duggan," September 9, 1941 and Duggan to Compton, September 12, 1941, DSDF, 834.516/104; Rockefeller to Lawrence Clayton, March 25, 1942, ISF, box 264.

The Paraguayan Bankers Mission arrived in Washington in July 1942 with three officials, including the Banco's manager Harmodio Gonzales, just as Triffin was about to join the Federal Reserve Board. Although Treasury officials initially developed a plan for the Paraguayans to study the Federal Reserve and US monetary system, they did not show much interest in the Paraguayans' training.[22] Indeed, despite his usual enthusiasm for Latin American loans, White had been very skeptical of the Export-Import Bank loan to Paraguay in mid-1939, arguing that it would not yield "political benefits" because the country was firmly "in the economic orbit of Argentina."[23] Filling the vacuum, Triffin quickly assumed the major role in supervising Gonzales. When Gonzales indicated that he favored monetary, banking, and central bank reform in his country, Triffin steered the training toward the study of concrete monetary and banking experiences of Latin American countries as well as those of the agricultural exporting countries of the British dominions. Between October and December, Triffin in fact devoted most of his time to studying the Paraguayan situation and helping Gonzales. Gardner pointed out that "the association of the two men has proved to be particularly happy."[24]

Triffin's willingness to devote enormous time to the task of working with Gonzales stemmed from his view that Lamb's failure to convince the Banco to adopt his reform ideas was "due in part to the attempt to present Paraguay with a kind of 'fait accompli' in the form of projects drawn without their cooperation and which remained completely foreign to them."[25] He drew a similar lesson from the experience of the Treasury-led Cuban and Honduran missions. Although those missions had consulted with the local governments and various local interests, they had developed their proposals unilaterally and then presented them publicly to the local governments. Triffin felt that this had also been the approach of Kemmerer in the 1920s and that it should be rejected in favor of a more "flexible procedure designed to ensure full participation and responsibility of the Latin American countries themselves in the plans ultimately worked out."[26]

Triffin's work with Gonzales paid off. By December, Gonzales asked Gardner if he would to come to Paraguay to help oversee a major reform of the country's monetary and banking system.[27] Gardner was too busy and Triffin was chosen to head the mission which was formally approved in May 1943 by the Federal

---

22. Triffin 1990, 26. For the study plan, see DeBeers to Glasser, August 11, 1942 and Debeers to White, August 14, 1942, TSF, Entry 66A0155, box 54.

23. White to Morgenthau, "Paraguay," May 4, 1939, p. 1, CFHDW, box 3, file 14.

24. Gardner to Goldenweiser, December 19, 1942, p. 1, ISF, box 231. See also Triffin to Gardner, December 3, 1942 and Triffin ""Suggested Outline of Study for Dr. Gonzales," December 12, 1942, ISF, box 259.

25. Triffin, "Suggested Outline," p. 2. See also Triffin to Gardner, December 3, 1942.

26. Triffin, "The New York Federal Reserve Bank and the Latin America Work," n.d. (but January 1944), p. 1, ISF, box 229. See also Triffin to Arthur Schlesinger, May 13, 1946, p. 6, ISF, box 156.

27. Gardner to Goldenweiser, December 19, 1942, p. 1, ISF, box 231.

Reserve Board. It was to be the first foreign financial advisory mission led by the board and Gardner highlighted (as he had at earlier moments) how missions of this kind would help boost the Fed's influence in the region as well as at home.[28] Treasury officials noted how the mission had arisen because the Fed had "culti-vated assiduously" the contact with Gonzales, but they seemed content simply to be involved in discussions about potential reforms.[29] Indeed, some Treasury officials thought the mission was "a mistake" because "the political situation in Paraguay is very bad . . . and will probably block adaptation of any recommen-dations."[30] The Treasury's position was not helped by the fact that Paraguay's minister of finance, Rogelio Espinoza, apparently hated Morgenthau because of a perceived snub during a previous Washington visit.[31]

Triffin's Two Visits: Monetary and Central Bank Reforms

Triffin first visited Paraguay between August and October of 1943, accompa-nied by Bray Hammond of the Federal Reserve Board. On the trip to Asunción, they stopped in Bolivia, Colombia, Ecuador, and Peru, making contacts with local central bankers, other officials, and businessmen in order to assist Triffin's broader Latin American research project. Triffin and Hammond were particu-larly impressed by their Colombian visit where they received helpful comments on Triffin's draft study of the country and were hosted by Enrique Dávila, assis-tant secretary to the Bank of Colombia.[32] Indeed, they were so impressed with Dávila that they negotiated with the Colombian authorities for him to join them in Paraguay for five or six weeks to help with the mission.[33]

In the discussions with officials in various countries, Hammond reported to Fed Governor Mat Szymczak that Triffin's background proved particularly useful:

> I have observed that he is singularly well suited for the work, apart from the fluency with which he can talk with these people in their own

---

28. Gardner, "Latin American Field," May 25, 1943, and Gardner to Szymczak, November 11, 1943, ISF, box 231.

29. Quote from deBeers to White, "United States Economic Advice to Latin America," January 22, 1943, p. 1, TSF, 450/81/20/07, box 28. See also deBeers to White, December 2, 1942, TSF, Entry 66A0155, box 54.

30. DeBeers to White, "United States Economic Advice to Latin America," p. 1.

31. Hammond to Governor, September 21, 1943, ISF, box 231. Espinoza had studied economics at the London School of Economics and was described in general by Frost as "a staunch friend of the United States"; Frost to Hull, March 9, 1942, DSDF, 834.516/107.

32. Hammond to Szymczak, August 28, 1943, ISF, box 231; Hammond to Morrill, Goldenweiser, and Thurston, November 24, 1943, ISF, box 148.

33. Edmund Montgomery to Hull, October 21, 1943, DSDF, 834.51A/118.

language. You will remember that many or rather *most* of these bankers, officials, and business men we meet have been educated in Europe. To find an American representative with the background of European culture which they know and value surprises and delights them. I have noticed time after time how an official's face softens and lights up when he finds himself addressed easily in Spanish and when finds further he can switch to French.[34]

After arriving in Asunción as "physical wrecks" after ten days of travel, Triffin and Hammond set to work at the Banco in a shared office which Hammond contrasted sharply with the opulent central banks they had visited in Colombia and Peru: "There is no collection of gold treasure here, nor paintings, nor ceramics. It is the rattiest, dirtiest, messiest business office I have ever had anything to do with."[35] Triffin met for long hours with local officials to develop a new monetary law that was designed to consolidate a new currency. Because the Paraguayan currency had been so unstable for many years, Argentine currency acted as the dominant medium of exchange and many large-scale transactions were even denominated in an abstract "gold peso" based on an obsolete Argentine monetary unit. The new proposed law would consolidate the note issue with the Banco and replace with gold peso with a new currency, the guaraní. As a temporary measure until international monetary stability was restored, the value of the unit would be tied to a basket of currencies made up of the Argentine, Brazilian, British, and the US currencies.

The monetary reform was adopted very quickly in early October 1943. At the time, the Banco's president, Carlos Pedretti, stressed that the reform would contribute to economic development by providing greater stability and convenience, and would allow for "the recuperation of our monetary independence and sovereignty." He also pointed out that the new currency's name gave "homage to the indomitable race which impressed its characteristic stamp upon our nation."[36] Triffin was impressed with both Pedretti and Espinoza, and he noted that Pedretti "especially is now a very good friend," a friendship to which he later attributed the success of his mission.[37] Of the government more generally, he was critical of its constraints on the press, but he added that "it is generally conceded, however,

---

34. Hammond to Szymczak, September 9, 1943, p. 7, ISF, box 231.
35. Hammond to Szymczak, September 9, 1943, p. 7, and September 21, 1943, p. 3, ISF, box 231.
36. Quotes from Pedretti, "The Monetary Reform" (address to the Asunción Chamber of Commerce on October 13, 1943), pp. 16, 5, ISF, box 162. For the details of the reform, see Triffin 1946.
37. Quote from Triffin to Captain Marion Allen Leonard, November 18, 1943, p. 6, ISF, box 231. See also Triffin 1990, 27.

even by the liberals, that Morínigo has done much more for the country in two years than the liberal governments have done in the course of their thirty years in power."[38]

On their way back from Paraguay, Triffin and Hammond made stops in Uruguay, Argentina, Chile, Peru, and Panama to support the broader Latin American research project. Soon after their return, the Paraguayan government asked if Triffin could come again to Paraguay. He went back for a second visit between April and December 1944, accompanied initially by an official from the Federal Bank of Cleveland and then by David Grove from the Federal Reserve Board (and another Harvard graduate). On this second trip, Triffin helped draft new central bank legislation working closely with Espinoza.[39] The legislation was approved unanimously by the Paraguayan legislature in September 1944, along with new banking and exchange control laws.[40]

The overall goals of these legislative measures were similar to those put forward by White's earlier Cuban mission. But Triffin's recommendations went further in some areas and he justified the overall approach in much more detail than the White mission had. In his 170-page report on the Paraguayan mission and in other publications at this time, Triffin argued forcefully that the interwar experience had demonstrated that Latin American monetary management should no longer be guided by the automatic adjustment mechanism of the gold standard. In his words, "the domestic disruptions implicit in this mechanism ... were especially drastic in undeveloped economies, dependent to an extreme degree on international trade and capital movements."[41] For example, in the late 1920s, enormous capital inflows into Latin America generated "a perfectly orthodox inflation, based on the piling up of gold and dollar assets in the central bank." Then, between 1929 and 1931, orthodox policy had reinforced the contractionary effect of the collapse of international lending, commodity prices, and external markets, resulting in "the near collapse of the economic and social structure of these countries."[42]

Even if these domestic disruptions were economically and socially tolerable, Triffin questioned whether they were as self-equilibrating as the gold standard

---

38. Triffin to Captain Marion Allen Leonard, p. 5.

39. Triffin 1946, 113.

40. The legislation had been delayed during the summer by opposition from the minister of agriculture, Dos Santos, who personally disliked Pedretti. Triffin became quite involved in mediating between Dos Santos and Pendretti, and eventually played a role in convincing the former to drop his opposition; Grove to Gardner and Hammond, August 25, 1944, ISF, box 230; Triffin to Board of Governors, "Second Mission to Paraguay," January 10, 1945, ISF, box 162.

41. Triffin 1946, 22.

42. Robert Triffin, "Address to the Pan American Society on Recent Monetary and Exchange Developments in Latin America," April 11, 1945, p. 3, ISF, box 156.

theory assumed. He noted that balance of payments movements "were often due to erratic fluctuations in crop yields or to cyclical movements in the buying countries, rather than to basic disparities in the international price and cost structure." In cases such as these, "the internal adaptions forced upon the country by adherence to the gold standard were fundamentally disruptive rather than re-equilibrating." He concluded: "in monoculture countries characterized by an extreme dependence vis-à-vis the fluctuations of international trade and of capital movements, it [the gold standard] subjects the economy to unbearable and often unnecessary disruptions."[43]

Policy Autonomy and Bretton Woods

What was needed, Triffin argued, was a new form of monetary management that was focused on "the internal needs of the economy."[44] In describing his proposals to the Federal Reserve Board, he pointed out that "the rigid monetary automatism of the gold standard has been avoided in favor of a bold attempt at autonomous monetary management. The new approach follows the very general trend in monetary and banking organization and its necessity is ten times greater in the case of Latin American countries." He continued: "The most novel aspect of the Paraguay legislation resides in the thoroughness with which these new trends have been integrated into a unified and logically systemized structure."[45]

This " structure" included equipping the central bank with strong domestic powers to conduct activist monetary management. Triffin observed that open-market operations and discount rate changes were often ineffective in Latin America because domestic financial markets were underdeveloped and the banking system was dominated by foreign banks responding primarily to monetary developments in their home countries. For this reason, the central bank's monetary department was authorized to impose flexible reserve requirements on private banks and to issue and retire its own bonds "to take the place of open market operations."[46]

But Triffin went further to argue that the central bank had to become an active banker to the public. He had much more in mind than the limited emergency lending that had provoked so much controversy in the Cuban debate. Triffin proposed that the central bank include two departments that would engage in regular banking activities: a banking department and a savings and mortgage

---

43. Triffin 1946, 22, 74.
44. Triffin 1946, 79.
45. Robert Triffin to Board of Governors, "Second Mission," January 10, 1945, p. 6.
46. Triffin 1946, 21.

department. As in the Honduran case, these banking activities would be useful partly in addressing "the inadequacy of credit facilities for production and developmental loans" caused by the fact that the foreign banks dominating the banking system were focused mainly on the foreign trade sector.[47] But Triffin also noted that the activities of the two central bank departments would provide a direct mechanism for it to influence monetary conditions. He argued that this kind of direct intervention in the market had "been found indispensable for monetary management in new countries, characterized by monoculture, a high degree of dependence on foreign trade, and the absence of a developed financial market."[48] The two departments would be supervised by the monetary department in order to ensure that their lending activities served the goals of monetary policy. Grove, for his part, also sought to strengthen the research and statistical capacity of the central bank and link this to its policy work.[49]

Alongside these measures to strengthen the central bank's domestic powers, new provisions were developed to protect national monetary policy from external influences. To begin with, the strict link between reserve levels and domestic monetary conditions was loosened by allowing the monetary issue to be guided by two "warning signals": the rate of expansion of the medium of circulation and the ratio of net international reserves to normal exchange requirements. Triffin also went out of his way to state that monetary reserves should be used "to moderate the harmful effects of fluctuations in the balance of payments on the money supply, on credit, and on economic activities in general."[50]

The domestic economy could also be buffered from external forces by exchange rate adjustments and capital controls. The former required legislative approval, while the central bank was empowered to control cross-border capital flows at its discretion. In his defense of capital controls, Triffin also endorsed the country's exchange controls, while drafting legislation that modified them "in a liberal direction" by allocating foreign exchange for nonessential transactions via an auction.[51] The new exchange control legislation also ensured that these restrictions would serve monetary policy more directly by placing responsibility for their management with the monetary department of the central bank. Triffin made sure to run his draft proposals for exchange controls by an interdepartment

47. Triffin 1946, 19.
48. Triffin to Board of Governors, "Second Mission," p. 5.
49. Grove to Board of Governors, January 11, 1945, ISF, box 230. This work of Grove provides a good example of what Mitchell (2002, 8) calls the broader "politics of calculation" emerging across the world at this time. According to Grove, among Latin American central banks, only the Argentine one had organized its statistical and research department in a manner that would help it effectively address core economic problems of the country.
50. Triffin 1946, 22, 78.
51. Triffin to Board of Governors, January 11, 1945, p. 3.

group that met at the State Department and the proposals met no objections.[52] In a later draft memo, Triffin developed arguments for US acceptance of exchange controls abroad that made explicit reference to US policymakers' need to recognize the distinctiveness of the Latin American economic context:

> We often lose sight of the fact that the general attitude taken in this country with respect to exchange control may be related to the peculiar circumstances of our own economy and does not take into consideration the fundamentally different characteristics of other economies, more dependent on international transactions and subject to violent disruptions associated with quasi monoculture. In other words, we tend to generalize and give universal validity to rigid principles derived from familiarity with conditions specific to the United States or at least to highly developed and well balanced economies.[53]

In developing Paraguay's legislation relating to external controls and exchange rates, Triffin was careful to ensure that they conformed with the Bretton Woods plans.[54] The Paraguayan government was one of the first to respond to a US invitation in early 1943 extended to thirty-seven countries to send technical experts to Washington to consult on the White plan.[55] Since Gonzales was already in Washington, he assumed the role of conferring bilaterally with White, and he also attended a mid-June multilateral consultation session that White hosted with eighteen countries.[56] At the time that the Paraguayan monetary law of October 1943 was approved, Pedretti also expressed interest in pegging the new Paraguayan currency to the international standard of "bancor" or "unitas" that the Keynes and White plans proposed.[57]

United States officials had also seen their Paraguayan work as linked to the Bretton Woods plans from very early on. On the first trip to Paraguay, Hammond remarked in an October 1943 letter to the Fed Board that he and Triffin saw their mission as complementary to the drafting of the White's proposed Fund. As he put it, "the extent that you do establish and maintain monetary stability within any country, you ease the difficulty of stabilization through the Fund. In Paraguay, if we succeed in our banking program, we shall have checked instability at

---

52. Triffin to Szymczak, "The Development of Exchange Control Policy for the International Monetary Fund," Draft 3/1/45, RTP, box 7.
53. Triffin to Szymczak, "The Development of Exchange Control Policy," pp. 1–2.
54. Triffin 1946, 17.
55. White to Morgenthau, May 3, 1943, CFHDW, box 9, Chron. 47.
56. For his bilateral consultation with White, see Ness to White and Mikesell, June 4, 1943 and Gonzales to White, June 10, 1943, HDWP, box 8, folder 2.
57. Pedretti, "The Monetary Reform," p. 9.

one of its sources at least and shall have made the task of international stability to some degree less difficult."[58] Two months later, Gardner also highlighted how the work of the Board's Latin American group would be of great value "to the international financial agencies now being discussed in Washington"[59]

During his second trip, Triffin wrote to Hammond (just as the Bretton Woods conference was ending) that he hoped his Latin American work would "contribute significantly to the stabilization mission of the monetary fund, as far as Latin America is concerned."[60] After his return from Paraguay, he explained the link in more detail to the Fed Board:

> I view our present work in Latin America as part of a general program of monetary stabilization in that area. It need not be emphasized that the progress of the International Monetary Fund will depend very largely on the development of better monetary and central banking management in each individual country. Failing that, it is to be feared that the resources of the International Fund will be uselessly sacrificed in a never-ending process. There is, however, at present a very deep and widespread interest throughout Latin America in improvements in monetary and banking institutions. The Fund constitutes no direct help in this respect, since its operations affect only the level of international reserves of each country. In order to stabilize the internal monetary situation, action on the national scale is required. . . . Finally, it is painfully obvious that the Fund will be unable to intelligently examine the monetary situation of the Latin American countries and to give them the advice which it will be called upon to offer under various circumstances, if only the information and data presently available in Washington is at their disposal. Our missions to Latin America are progressively developing excellent personal contacts and a broad basis for statistical and economic studies of Latin America.[61]

Just after the Bretton Woods conference ended, Gardner stressed this last point to the Fed Board in discussing Triffin's activities in Paraguay.[62] In an earlier June 1944 letter to Gardner from Paraguay, Triffin had also noted that he anticipated that some staff involved in the Fed missions to Latin America would soon move

58. Hammond to Governor, October 18, 1943, p. 4, ISF, box 231.

59. Gardner to Szymczak, "Tentative program of the Latin American group for the year 1944," December 1, 1943, p. 2, ISF, box 148.

60. Triffin to Hammond, July 21, 1944, p. 1, ISF, box 109.

61. Triffin to Board, "Questions on which Board decisions or guidance are needed," January 11, 1945, pp. 3–4, ISF, box 230.

62. Gardner to Triffin, August 24, 1944, ISF, box 230.

on to the Fund and Bank.[63] Triffin himself moved to the Fund in 1946, taking charge of the Fund's exchange control division. On the Paraguayan mission, Triffin had taken a particular interest in harmonizing Paraguay's exchange control legislation with the new Fund's rules, allowing permanent controls only for the purpose of controlling capital movements.[64] In correspondence in March 1945, he expressed a hope that the type of exchange controls introduced in Paraguay "may be of interest to the IMF and provide some sort of pattern for the future policy of the Fund."[65] When his draft proposals had been discussed by the interdepartmental group at the State Department, the suggestion had also been made that a general international convention on exchange controls might be developed along the lines of the Paraguayan example—a suggestion that Triffin had greatly appreciated.[66]

United States Politics and the Paraguayan Mission

The Paraguayan reforms were much less controversial within the United States than the Cuban ones. Few American private businesses had any direct stake in the results since US economic ties to the country were minimal and no US banks operated in the country. Opposition may also have been lessened because prominent members of the New York financial community had been impressed with the quality and usefulness of Triffin's Colombia study which was published in mid-1944 (with five hundred copies sent across Latin America). Even Burgess had made a point of writing to Hammond in August 1944 to say that people in his bank thought the study was excellent.[67] The praise was impressive since the report had been implicitly critical of Kemmerer's work in establishing the country's central bank in 1923, a criticism that Fed officials had deliberately toned down in order to avoid giving offense.[68]

Still, there were a few grumblings about the Paraguay reforms in the banking community. Triffin reported in mid-1945 that "one of the most intelligent, practical bankers in the United States recently commented to me that while the

---

63. Triffin to Gardner, June 23, 1944, ISF, box 231.
64. Triffin to Board of Governors, January 11, 1945; Triffin to Szymczak, "The Development of Exchange," p. 24.
65. Quoted in Dosman 2008, 204.
66. Triffin to Szymczak, "The Development of Exchange," p. 2.
67. W. Randolph Burgess to Hammond, August 18, 1944 and Gerald Beal to Hammond, November 28, 1944, ISF, box 109.
68. Hammond to Triffin, July 4, 1944, ISF, box 231.

Kemmerer legislation was admittedly completely inadequate and did not pay any attention to the peculiar needs and circumstances of Latin American countries, the Paraguayan legislation ran the risk of being also unrealistic in that it did not take sufficiently into account the administrative backwardness of the country." Triffin dismissed the criticism, arguing that the "comment is probably very much exaggerated and that you can find more honesty and competence in Paraguay than he would have thought from New York." He also argued that the only alternative to his "some flexible system" was the more rigid Kemmerer approach that he thought unrealistic: "Flexibility may be abused but rigidity will be swept away in practice."[69]

Triffin later recalled that some of his work in Paraguay had attracted very strong criticism from the Treasury, against which Eccles had defended him.[70] He did not explain the nature of the criticism and I have found no archival documents to fill in the story. It seems very unlikely that the Treasury objected to the content of Triffin's advice since it was similar to that of the earlier Treasury-led Cuban and Honduran missions. Instead, jurisdictional jealousies were the likely cause, particularly given the success of Triffin's work. Indeed, Triffin reports that White even tried to recruit him to the Treasury at one point, an offer Triffin had refused because of his "concern for independence" which he thought would have been compromised in White's "regimented staff." White did not take the rejection well; Triffin reports that White had been "scornful of my stupidity" given that the Treasury's held greater power than the Fed within the government.[71] In advance of his second trip to Paraguay, Triffin made a point of involving the Treasury's Latin American point person, Norman Ness, in the Fed's discussions about the content of his recommendations and Ness approved all the legislative drafts that Triffin took to the country.[72]

The success of Triffin's first visit also appeared to annoy some FRBNY officials who asked to be notified in advance of future board missions and to participate in them. Gardner reminded Eccles that the board had in fact asked the FRBNY whether any of their people were available for the Paraguayan mission but had been told no one was available for such an unimportant country. As Gardner put it, "they failed at that time to appreciate the fact that the Paraguayan job would have a significance far beyond Paraguay itself."[73] Gardner also told Eccles that he and Triffin would be happy to involve the FRBNY in future advisory work, but

69. Triffin to Prebisch, July 23, 1945, pp. 1–2, ISF, box 162.
70. Triffin 1990, 27.
71. Triffin 1981, 243.
72. Triffin 1946, 113; Hammond to Triffin, May 24, 1944, ISF, box 231.
73. Gardner to Eccles, "Relations with FRBNY," January 23, 1944, p. 2, ISF, box 148.

only "so long as it is clear that the Board is taking the lead and it is also under-stood that the method we have developed for working with the Latin Americans is not going to be blocked."[74] In advance of his second trip, Triffin sent all the material relating to the mission to Henry Wallich in the FRBNY and invited his comments (which were largely approving).[75] Wallich was not, however, included in the formal "technical commission" that commented on the Paraguayan rec-ommendations in Washington during January and February of 1944; that body included Ness and five Federal Reserve Board officials (Triffin, Gardner, Ham-mond, George Bach, Julia Wooster).[76]

While Triffin's work generated some annoyance in the Treasury and FRBNY, the Federal Reserve Board was particularly happy with his accomplishments. After his second trip, one Fed official declared that the new central bank law was "one of the most advanced and far-reaching legislations, both from the theo-retical and practical point of view, ever adopted in a Latin American country."[77] The Fed even approved a large print run of one thousand copies of the formal report on the Paraguayan reforms, an expense that one Fed official justified by pointing out that the reforms had "attracted considerable attention throughout Latin America" and "should be considered as a pathbreaking innovation in this field." The official also mentioned that "the Board itself showed a great interest in this matter and at the time expressed the hope that this new adventure might influence thinking in the field of central banking both at home and abroad."[78] In a statement to the board in January 1945, Triffin also highlighted the particular benefits that accrued to the board itself from the Paraguayan mission: "the Board has acquired a great deal of goodwill and prestige throughout Latin America and it is emphasized everywhere that our work constitutes a most welcome evidence of our general good-neighbor policy."[79]

It is clear, then, that the Fed's own bureaucratic interests vis-à-vis the Treasury and FRBNY played a role in encouraging the Paraguayan mission. But Fed offi-cials themselves were also very aware that their work was tied to US foreign policy objectives. As Hammond observed in one letter from Paraguay in October 1943, "if we are doing a good job in Paraguay, it means that our country's foreign policy is being strengthened."[80] One British official in Asunción also told his superiors that Triffin's explanations of his proposed reforms to Paraguayans often included

---

74. Gardner to Eccles, "Relations with FRBNY," 1–2.
75. Wallich, "Comments on Draft of Paraguayan Central Bank Law," June 7, 1944, ISF, box 162.
76. Triffin 1946, 113.
77. Eduardo Montealegre to Mr. Hammond, August 2, 1944, p. 1, ISF, box 162. For the board's support of Triffin's work, see Triffin 1990, 26; Triffin 1981, 242.
78. Woodlief Thomas to Board of Governors, January 16, 1946, p. 1, ISF, box 162. See also Gard-ner to Thomas, July 24, 1945, ISF, box 162.
79. Triffin to Board, "Questions on which Board decisions or guidance are needed," p. 4.
80. Hammond to Governor, October 18, 1943, p. 3.

"the playing up of Paraguayan nationalist sentiment directed to detaching them from the Argentine."[81] The State Department also praised Triffin's work as a "practical implementation of the Good Neighbor Policy."[82] As the war wound down and fears of German power in the region diminished, this strategic motivation fell away and more general US national interests were emphasized. In a March 1945 document, the board explained how missions such as that in Paraguay "may reduce the disturbances to our domestic credit situation that originate in foreign economies" and "will also work to the enhancement of American prestige and the cultivation of friendly and mutually helpful international relations."[83]

In addition to bureaucratic and foreign policy goals, the Paraguayan mission was also informed by New Deal values. Near the end of his time in Paraguay, Hammond expressed the humanitarian case for why the United States should be helping the country: "They are not so well off as we, they are victims of a lot of hard luck, their situation is disadvantageous, and it won't hurt us to give them some help."[84] In true New Deal fashion, Triffin also appeared to enjoy challenging the old liberal orthodoxy in international monetary thought. He went out of his way to trumpet the unorthodox nature of Paraguay's new monetary and central banking laws, describing them as "wholly unorthodox" and "revolutionary."[85] In an address to the Pan American Society a few months after returning from Paraguay, Triffin also emphasized that "the success or failure of our efforts at international economic monetary stability will depend largely on our willingness to give up ready-made, dogmatic, formulas of supposedly universal applicability."[86] This view was very different from that of Kemmerer and his colleagues who held the view that the financial advice they gave was a universal and scientific product.[87] While Kemmerer offered very similar recommendations to each country he advised, Triffin went out of his way to tailor his advice to the distinct circumstances of each country.[88]

Learning from Latin America

This aspect of Triffin's approach to financial advising stemmed from one further New Deal value: a willingness to learn from Latin American experience and

81. F. F. J. Powell, September 22, 1944, p. 1, BOE, OV 167/1.

82. Stettinius to Eccles, January 31, 1944, p. 1, DSDF, 834.51A/119. See also Willard Beaulac to Secretary of State, October 3, 1944, ISF, box 230.

83. (No author), "Foreign Missions of the Federal Reserve System," March 29, 1945, ISF, box 218.

84. Hammond to Governor, October 18, 1943, p. 2. See also Hammond to Szymczak, September 9, 1943, ISF, box 231.

85. Triffin 1946, 23, 25.

86. Triffin, "Address," p. 6.

87. Rosenberg 2003, 194.

88. For Kemmerer's similar advice everywhere, see Drake 1989, 25.

ideas. Triffin was keen to differentiate his approach from that of Kemmerer in the 1920s when, as he put it, "orthodox, but thoroughly alien, central banking reform attempted to transplant bodily in La Paz or Quito the monetary and banking mechanisms of older financial centers"[89] By contrast, Triffin extensively studied, and drew inspiration from, the experience of Latin American central banks that had experimented with unorthodox policies during the 1930s such as exchange controls, activist monetary policies, and central bank financing of agricultural and industrial projects.

The Paraguayan recommendations also emerged from discussions with leading monetary thinkers across Latin America. Particularly important were Triffin's consultations with Raúl Prebisch. At this time, Prebisch was one of the best known central bankers in Latin America. He had played a central role in the creation of Argentina's central bank in 1935, a bank that had been assigned far-reaching powers to regulate banks, administer exchange controls, pursue activist monetary management through open-market operations, and adjust the country's exchange rate. Prebisch became the bank's first head and remained in that position until October 1943 when he was fired in the wake of a military coup in June. He then delivered a series of high-profile lectures at the Bank of Mexico between late January and the end of March 1944 that further bolstered his stature as one of the most foremost monetary thinkers in Latin America. The lectures had been given to a small group of the Bank of Mexico's staff, including its head Villaseñor (who had promoted the IAB proposal), but portions of his text were also published in the daily press.[90] One of the officials involved, Victor Urquidi, later described the seminars as "an outstanding occasion."[91]

At this time, Prebisch was consolidating some of the broader economic ideas for which he would soon become well-known beyond the region, notably his case for state-supported industrialization to help poorer countries escape from their vulnerability to external shocks and declining terms of trade associated with commodity exporting. At the core of Prebisch's thought at this time was a commitment to greater national policy autonomy. This commitment echoed that of Keynes except that Prebisch was critical of the fact that Keynes had ignored the distinct circumstances and difficulties facing poorer agricultural exporting countries. In Prebisch's view, these countries needed to insulate themselves from powerful shocks emanating from the industrialized countries and to carve out policy space to promote state-supported industrialization and economic development.[92]

---

89. Triffin, "Address," p. 2.
90. Dosman 2008, 188–93.
91. Urquidi 1996, 34.
92. Dosman 2001; 2008, 218–19; Love 1996, 126–27.

Triffin first met Prebisch during the latter's early 1944 Mexican visit. Even before they had met, Triffin had decided that the Argentine central bank legislation of 1935 was "the best starting point for the preparation of a Paraguayan banking law" because it was "concise and flexible" and embodied "most of the important features of other modern banking reforms" as well as because the two countries were very close "in economic and legal background."[93] After their meeting in Mexico, Triffin and Prebisch quickly struck up a close personal friendship characterized by mutual intellectual respect.[94] Triffin frequently cited his debt to Prebisch's "pioneering work" in his publications.[95] Triffin drew not just on Prebisch's general monetary ideas but also on some specific policy innovations Prebisch had developed in Argentina. For example, Paraguay's exchange controls drew directly on Argentina's experience of allocating foreign exchange for nonessential transactions by an auction system.

After the Paraguayan reforms had been approved, Triffin arranged for Prebisch to spend three months in Paraguay, starting in early December 1944, to help implement them.[96] Triffin told the Fed's Board that "we could have no better guarantee for the ultimate success of our mission" than to involve Prebisch since both of them were "thoroughly in agreement upon the essential problems of monetary, banking, and exchange organization in Paraguay."[97] Given the broader US suspicions of Argentina at the time, Prebisch's role might have been expected to raise some questions. But he had been a high-profile advocate of closer Argentine links to the United States after the outbreak of World War II. Indeed, his strong US links were one of the reasons he had been fired from his central bank post.[98] Prebisch was also very well regarded within the Fed where Goldenweiser described him as "without any doubt, the most outstanding man in his field in Latin America and one of the outstanding ones in the world."[99] He also had an excellent reputation with many New York bankers as well as with Berle who had described him as "brilliant" after they met during a trip Prebisch made to the United States in late 1940.[100]

In light of later postwar US criticisms of Prebisch's views, it is also worth noting that much of his thinking about development was similar not just to Triffin's

93. Triffin to Gardner, April 9, 1943, p. 1, ISF, box 162.
94. See for example Triffin to Prebisch, July 23, 1945, p. 4.
95. Triffin 1966 (1947), 141 n. 2.
96. Triffin to Board of Governors, "Second Mission"; Dosman 2008, 197–202.
97. Triffin to Board of Governors, "Second Mission," p. 4.
98. Dosman 2008, chaps. 6–8. Still, J. Edgar Hoover and some other US officials had raised questions about his loyalties (Dosman 2008, 151–52).
99. Goldenweiser to Roger Evans, February 23, 1945, ISF, box 156. See also Dosman 2008, 132, 233; Gardner to Federal Reserve Board, August 18, 1944, p. 1, ISF, box 230.
100. For Berle, see Berle and Jacoby 1973, 353. For bankers, see their interest in sponsoring his visit to Harvard in 1945; Szymczak to Nelson Rockefeller, February 5, 1945, ISF, box 156.

but also to that of other prominent US economists discussed in the previous chapter. For example, his arguments about the need for industrialization in the face of declining terms of trade echoed Kindleberger's ideas (which Prebisch had read at the time).[101] Much of his thinking was also reminiscent of John Williams's work, including Prebisch's arguments about the destabilizing impact of the gold standard on the periphery, his advocacy of exchange controls, his criticism of classical trade theory, and his broader emphasis on the distinctive economic needs of poorer countries.[102] Again, Prebisch was very familiar with Williams's work, having translated the latter's 1920 book on Argentina's prewar trade and having met with him in subsequent years.[103]

Prebisch welcomed Triffin's offer to help implement the Paraguayan reforms in late 1944 not just because of the difficult political situation in Argentina. Earlier in the year in Mexico, Prebisch had told his audience how encouraged he had been by White's 1942 Cuban mission report which he felt had shown that the US government now recognized the usefulness of exchange controls for countries experiencing large balance of payments fluctuations.[104] At the time, he expressed his desire to discuss the issue more with US officials, an opportunity that arose right away when he met Triffin. His appreciation for Triffin's ideas was clear. For example, he wrote to Triffin in June 1945 after reading the latter's summary of the Paraguayan work:

> You have developed monetary principles in your projects which are most suitable to countries like ours. I deliberately include Argentina: if I had to prepare a new project for my country I would adopt a great part of what you have proposed. Paraguay now has an efficient instrument for the stabilization of its economy. If managed with good judgment and prudence, the reform will be the beginning of a new monetary orthodoxy in our countries, under the auspices of the big shots of the Federal Reserve. We shall be freed, my dear friend, of the exorcisms by which foreign advisors would have wished to purify the exchange policy of these countries in not too remote periods.[105]

Triffin replied, thanking Prebisch "for the nicest letter I have received in a very long time" and for his "extraordinary contribution to the success of those

---

101. Prebisch (1991 [1944], 197–98) cited Kindleberger's work in his Mexico seminar in early 1944.

102. For these ideas in Williams's work, see Asso and Fiorito 2009.

103. Dosman 2008, 36, 122, 131.

104. Prebisch (1991 [1944]), 200–201. Prebisch had met White during his late 1940 trip to the United States.

105. Prebisch to Triffin, June 17, 1945, p. 2, ISF, box 162.

reforms in Paraguay." He observed: "If the reform is successful I think the credit should always go to you. Yours was really the hard work while mine remained perforce confined to more or less academic theorizing."[106]

Prebisch was not the only Latin American thinker that Triffin drew upon. Triffin was also initially interested in the ideas of Herman Max, a Chilean professor at the University of Santiago and adviser to the Chilean central bank who had also served as adviser for monetary reforms in Costa Rica in 1936, Venezuela in 1939, and Nicaragua in the fall of 1940. Drawing on the experience of the depression, Max had become a strong critic of the gold standard, arguing that countries needed to be able to adjust exchange rates in response to external or internal developments in order to preserve domestic stability. He was also an advocate of activist monetary management and suggested that central banks should be able to lend directly to the public, in part because this might help make their interest rates effective vis-à-vis commercial banks.[107]

During the Paraguayan Bankers Mission to the United States, Triffin had encouraged Gonzales to read the ideas of Max.[108] When returning from his first trip to Paraguay, Triffin also made a point of meeting with Max in Santiago. On his return trip in April 1944, he again stopped in Chile to discuss with Max the draft legislation he was going to propose to the Paraguayans.[109] Triffin thought the Max-led reforms were "better adapted to the basic economy and financial characteristics of the countries involved" than those of Kemmerer had been. He ultimately concluded, however, that the detailed nature of Max's legislation was not appropriate for Paraguay "which up to now has not had even the most rudimentary of banking laws and in which the machinery of banking supervision can be built up only slowly and progressively."[110]

Triffin's proposal that Paraguay's central bank create monetary, banking, and savings and mortgage departments also drew directly on the experience of the Costa Rican central bank.[111] In mid-1943, Triffin had met several times in Washington with the general manager of that bank, Julio Peña, and then had asked in early 1944 for Peña's comments on his draft recommendations for the Paraguayan central bank.[112] After Triffin stopped in Costa Rica on his way to

---

106. Triffin to Prebisch, July 23, 1945, pp. 1, 2.

107. See for example O. E. Moore to Sproul, "Dr. Herman Max," October 29, 1940, and Jack Corbett to Sproul, "Monetary Views of Dr. Herman Max," November 4, 1940, ISF, box 180.

108. See for example Triffin, ""Suggested Outline of Study for Dr. Gonzales," December 12, 1942, ISF, box 259.

109. Triffin 1946, 113.

110. Triffin to Gardner, April 9, 1943, p. 1.

111. Triffin 1946, 74–75; Triffin to Gardner, March 15, 1944, ISF, box 231; Triffin to Board of Governors, January 11, 1945.

112. Peña to Triffin, March 3, 1944, ISF, box 231.

Paraguay in May 1944, Hammond also suggested that Paraguayan officials be sent, at US expense, to Costa Rica to study the administration of that country's central bank.[113] Indeed, both Triffin and Hammond were very keen more generally to encourage these kinds of intra–Latin American exchanges of financial expertise, building on the model they had used with Dávila and Prebisch in Paraguay. Their rationale was that Latin American officials could learn much more from each other than they could from US officials and practices.[114] As Triffin put it, "experience shows that a Paraguayan or any other banking employee of a small and primitive country is bewildered rather than effectively trained by a sojourn in the United States."[115]

Triffin's mission to Paraguay was an important episode in the Good Neighbor financial partnership. It attracted much attention across Latin America for pioneering a new approach to financial advising that was supportive of development goals of governments in the region. Since White's Cuban mission had been the actual pioneer, this reputation was not entirely deserved, but in contrast to the Cuban experience, the recommendations of the Paraguayan mission were immediately adopted. The Paraguayan mission's higher political profile in the region also reflected the fact that Triffin devoted much more time and effort to publicly explaining and justifying the new approach. In addition, he went out of his way to consult with, and involve, leading Latin American authorities in the process of the developing the Paraguayan reforms.

Despite its importance, Triffin's Paraguayan financial advisory mission has received very little attention from historians of US foreign economic policy.[116] This is striking given that the mission served as the model for subsequent Fed missions to Latin America that were one of the more prominent and popular aspects of the Good Neighbor policy in this period. After the entry of the United States into World War II in December 1941, Latin American officials had become frustrated by the fact that US financial assistance to the region increasingly focused on initiatives that served US defense needs directly rather than broader regional development goals.[117] In this context, the Paraguayan missions—and its development content—served as an important sign of the enduring US

---

113. Hammond to Gardner, May 19, 1944, ISF, box 264.

114. Triffin to Board, January 11, 1945; Triffin and Hammond to Board of Governors, January 11, 1945 and Hammond to Morrill, October 9, 1944, ISF, box 22; Hammond, "Exchange of Personnel for Foreign Study," August 7, 1946, CSF 001.411.

115. Triffin to Szymczak, "The Mexican Invitation to an Inter-American Conference of Central Banks," p. 3, January 11, 1945, RTP, box 3.

116. It is even overlooked in Michael Grow's (1981) fascinating history of US-Paraguayan relations in this period and Mora's (1998) important survey of those relations.

117. Green 1971, chap. 4.

commitment to the Good Neighbor financial partnership that had begun in the late 1930s.

The neglect of the Paraguayan mission also by historians of Bretton Woods is unfortunate because the mission revealed a further dimension of the development content of the Bretton Woods goals. As we have seen, U.S. and Paraguayan officials explicitly drafted Paraguayan legislation to be consistent with the Fund's endorsement of adjustable exchange rate pegs and capital controls. In keeping with embedded liberal ideology, these provisions were seen as crucial for protecting Paraguayan policy autonomy. Instead of supporting the welfare state and Keynesian full employment policies (as in Northern countries), adjustable exchange rate pegs and capital controls were designed to defend the Paraguayan government's ability to pursue the kinds of state-led development objectives that had become popular across Latin America in the 1930s. To reinforce this point, US financial advisers went much further than the IMF could in supporting domestic institutional reforms that strengthened the capacity of the Paraguayan state to pursue these goals, including the creation of a national currency, central bank reforms, and new credit facilities to serve the local economy more effectively. In this way, the Paraguayan mission linked the new Bretton Woods framework very directly to Latin American development aspirations.

The initial Fed backing for the Paraguayan mission stemmed from both bureaucratic rivalries and the same strategic motivations of countering Axis influence as other aspects of the Good Neighbor financial partnership. In addition, the content of the US advice to Paraguay was influenced by New Deal values such as the desire to help the poor and challenge liberal economic orthodoxy as well as by a willingness to learn from Latin American experience and work with reformers in the region. The fact that these New Deal values were so prominent among US central bankers deserves underlining. At this time, central bankers were often portrayed as conservative thinkers attached to the liberal orthodoxy of the 1920s and skeptical of the new interventionist ideals embodied in the Bretton Woods framework. But as we have seen, the Federal Reserve Board was a rather distinct intellectual environment. In Latin America, too, central bankers such as Prebisch had taken a lead role—often through force of circumstances—in challenging orthodox policy and thought. This alliance of central bankers committed to development-oriented embedded liberal ideas would soon be strengthened further.

LATIN AMERICAN BACKING FOR BRETTON WOODS

In their plans for the postwar international financial order, US policymakers built directly on the Good Neighbor financial partnership with Latin America and its development goals. The perspectives of officials and analysts from Latin America also helped shaped the outcomes of Bretton Woods negotiations more directly. Most accounts of the Bretton Woods negotiations focus on the US consultations with Britain and there is no question that the Anglo-American negotiations were critical in determining the final outcomes. But the United States and Britain also consulted with a wider group of countries, including many poorer countries. Latin American countries (excepting Argentina) were the most numerous of this latter group.

Latin Americans saw the Bretton Woods negotiations as an opportunity to strengthen international assistance for their development goals. They were particularly interested in the Bank's role in mobilizing long-term development lending, a role that they helped to protect and strengthen at the Bretton Woods conference. They also helped insert a provision allowing greater IMF short-term financing of countries coping with fluctuations in their balances of payments caused by their dependence on commodity exports. In addition, Latin American officials backed provisions of the IMF's articles of agreement allowing exchange rate adjustments and capital controls, provisions that would provide some protection of their policy autonomy. And they pushed successfully for a conference resolution calling for a future international agreement relating to commodity marketing and pricing, an initiative that held out the promise of a possible resurrection of the commodity price stabilization proposals of White's early drafts.

Alongside their contributions to the formal negotiations, Latin American governments expressed their support for the development content of Bretton Woods in another way. In the wake of the Bretton Woods conference, Triffin received a number of requests from governments in the region to repeat in their countries the work he had done for Paraguay. Like the Paraguayan government, these governments saw the content of Triffin's advice as furthering their development aspirations and linked to their participation in the Bretton Woods system. Even Latin American governments that did not seek out Triffin's advice expressed their interest in, and support for, his work in the region.

Latin America and the Bretton Woods Negotiations

Most general histories of the negotiations do not devote a great deal of attention to the role of Latin American governments. As we have seen, however, US officials made clear to Keynes as early as 1941 that they considered Latin American countries to be important partners in the development of postwar plans. This point was reinforced by the fact that they chose an inter-American conference—the Rio Conference of January 1942—to announce their interest in planning for the postwar international financial order. When US officials decided in July 1942 to begin informal consultations on White's initial plans with a small group of countries, they included Brazil and Mexico in this inner clique, along with Britain, Russia, China, Canada, and Australia.[1]

Latin American countries then made up nineteen of the thirty-seven countries initially invited by Morgenthau in April 1943 to send technical experts to Washington to discuss White's first public draft of his Stabilization Fund (Argentina was the only Latin American republic not included).[2] Many of those Latin American countries sent representatives to Washington at that time for bilateral discussions with US officials. A few (Brazil, Ecuador, Paraguay, and Venezuela) also participated in a three-day multilateral consultation session that White

---

1. White to Morgenthau, July 21, 1942, CFHDW, box 8, Chron. 8.
2. US State Department 1948, 1574. The list provided there does not include six countries that did receive subsequent invitations, many of which participated in the 1943 consultations: Egypt, France, Iceland, Iran, Liberia, and the Philippines. For their invitations and participation, see White to Morgenthau, May 3, 1943, CFHDW, box 9, Chron. 47; J. Deutsch, "International Stabilization of Currencies—Informal expert discussions, US. Treasury, June 15–17, 1943," NAC, RG19 v. 3981. The full forty-three countries eventually invited by the United States to the 1943 consultations were the same countries that were invited to Bretton Woods the following year.

chaired between June 15 and 17 involving eighteen countries in total.[3] Some of the Latin American governments who did not send representatives to Washington in this period submitted written comments on White's plans.[4]

The British government also recognized the importance of Latin American countries at this time. After the Keynes plan for an International Clearing Union had been released publically in the spring of 1943, the British Embassy in Washington made sure that a copy was sent to all Latin American officials traveling to White's consultations.[5] British officials also went out of their way to travel across Latin America promoting the ICU proposal at the time.[6] Keynes was particularly pleased to hear from British officials that Prebisch preferred his plan over White's, declaring that the news was "exceptionally important" and that "it is the greatest pity we have to cold-shoulder Argentina."[7] According to one British official, Prebisch felt the White plan "bore the stamp of something designed in effect to give United States a wholly dominating direction of post war monetary affairs."[8] We have seen how Prebisch formed a much more positive impression of US goals, after being removed from his post as head of Argentina's central bank in October 1943, through his work with Triffin. At this earlier moment, however, he was more skeptical and was also clearly irritated more generally with the US refusal to invite Argentina to its Washington consultations. He apparently told the British that it was "somewhat paradoxical that Argentina with its unbroken debt record and its organised Central Bank should be the one South American country left out of a discussion which so vitally affects interests of all."[9]

American and British officials continued in the months leading up to the Bretton Woods conference to recognize the importance of Latin American countries. When the United States and Britain published their Joint Statement of Experts on draft plans for the Fund on April 22, 1944, they made sure that it was published simultaneously not just in Washington, London, Moscow, Chungking, and Ottawa but also in Rio, Mexico City, and Havana. Brazil, Mexico, Cuba, and Chile were also included among the sixteen countries invited to the pre–Bretton Woods

---

3. The other US officials in attendance were Bernstein, Gardner, Goldenweiser, Hansen, and Viner. Berle also opened the meeting.

4. See HDWP, box 8, folders 1–2.

5. Skidelsky 2000, 249.

6. E. W. Playfair to E. Ashton, May 4, 1943, UKT 247/36.

7. Keynes to Catto and Eady, "The Argentine and the Clearing Union," May 26, 1943, p. 1, UKT 247/36.

8. Meynell, "From Buenos Aires to Foreign Office," No. 320, May 8, 1943, p. 1, UKT 247/36.

9. Meynell, "From Buenos Aires to Foreign Office," 1. At the Bretton Woods conference, the one US banker on the US delegation (Edward Brown) also noted privately at one point that Argentina was probably the soundest country financially in South America (MD, book 755, p. 220).

drafting conference at Atlantic City in late June.[10] White chaired that meeting and he appointed a veteran of the IAB negotiations, Mexico's Antonio Espinosa de los Monteros, to be one of his four deputy chairs (alongside Keynes as well as officials from the USSR and China).[11]

At the Bretton Woods conference itself, Mexico's finance minister Eduardo Suárez was given the role of nominating Morgenthau as "permanent president of the conference" and was chosen to chair one of the three commissions around which the conference was organized (White and Keynes chaired the other two).[12] In addition, Suárez and Brazil's finance minister, Artur de Souza Costa, were invited to give formal addresses to the inaugural plenary session on the first day of the conference (along with Morgenthau and the chairs of delegations from Canada, China, Czechoslovakia, and the USSR).[13] In a US planning meeting on June 30 1944, White had insisted on this prominent role for these two officials, noting that "we need the support of the South Americans."[14] In a private meeting giving instructions to the US delegates on the first day of the conference, White reiterated that "it is the South American countries who in this are going to be important to us."[15]

The importance of the Latin American countries came from the fact that they made up nineteen of the forty-four delegations attending the conference.[16] This numerical dominance worried British officials who anticipated that Latin American countries would side with the United States on many issues. Indeed, the British even hoped to avoid formal votes at the conference for this reason. As one British official wrote to his superiors in the middle of the meeting, "if the issue comes to the vote every country will count for one with the result that Latin America is almost sufficient to settle any issue in a way the United States wishes."[17] White recognized the British fears, noting privately at one point that British efforts to delay a decision on the location of the Fund's headquarters reflected Keynes's frustration with the fact that "the vote of Costa Rica is the same

---

10. The other twelve represented were Australia, Belgium, Canada, China, Czechoslovakia, France, India, the Netherlands, the Philippines, the United Kingdom, the United States, and the USSR. About seventy-five people were present at the meeting (MD, book 740, p. 95; book 749, p. 2)

11. General Meeting, June 24, 1944, BWCC, box 1/12.

12. White and Keynes chaired the commissions drafting the IMF and the IBRD respectively, and Suárez chaired the one examining "other means of international financial cooperation."

13. US State Department 1948, 8.

14. MD, book 748, pp. 226.

15. MD, box 749, p. 3.

16. These included Bolivia, Brazil, Chile, Colombia, Costa Rica, Cuba, the Dominican Republic, Ecuador, El Salvador, Guatemala, Haiti, Honduras, Mexico, Nicaragua, Panama, Paraguay, Peru, Uruguay, and Venezuela.

17. "From Bretton Woods British Delegation (Monetary Conference) to Foreign Office," p. 12, No. 50 REMAC, July 10, 1944. UKT 247/29.

as the vote of the United Kingdom."[18] Latin American delegates at the conference also did not hesitate to remind other delegates that they represented "practically one-half of the nations here assembled."[19] Their influence was boosted by the fact that they felt a sense of solidarity and tried to work together as a group at the conference.[20] As one US official pointed out halfway through the conference, "the Latin American countries are really operating as a unit.... They have a pretty definite machine."[21]

Latin American countries thus had many opportunities to provide input into the Bretton Woods negotiations. What perspectives did they offer? Existing histories often mention how some Latin American governments led by Mexico secured a vague statement that further study should be undertaken of silver's role within the international monetary system. They also usually cite Latin American demands for larger quota sizes (which helped determine voting shares and access to borrowing) and representation within the Fund, particularly after it appeared that their combined quota size might leave them with no more than one seat on the Fund's executive board.[22] These demands produced the result that Latin America was guaranteed two of the twelve seats on the Fund's board (a Cuban proposal backed by the United States). No other region received this kind of guaranteed representation.[23] Indeed, a similar proposal from Egypt, Iran, and Iraq for the Middle East to receive one guaranteed seat was voted down.[24]

Beyond these specific issues, Latin American governments were generally very supportive of the US plans throughout the process. For example, during the Washington consultations of mid-1943, many Latin American officials told White that they liked his Fund proposal.[25] This backing even came from governments that were not sure that the Fund would be of much use to them, such as the Panamanian government which stated that it faced no problem of monetary stabilization because of the country's dollarized monetary system.[26] At the Bretton

---

18. MD, book 753, p. 160.

19. Luis Machado from Cuba quoted in "Informal Minutes: Commission 1, United Nations Monetary and Financial Conference at Bretton Woods, July 1944," p. 121, BWCC, box 13/1.

20. Suárez 1977, 277.

21. Luxford in MD, book 752, p. 5.

22. See for example Van Dormael 1978, 166, 178–81.

23. MD, book 750, p. 131, 263; book 751, pp. 293–97; book 752, p. 5. Latin America was not guaranteed a seat on the board of the Bank.

24. When the Cuban proposal as voted upon, it received some dissenting votes. Schuler and Rosenberg 2012, 102–5, 229–31, 235, 239, 276–80.

25. See HDWP, box 8, folders 1–2, 4 as well as various memos of bilateral meetings in ITM (especially boxes 20 and 21); and CFHDW. El Salvador was one Latin American country that announced it was not in a fiscal position to contribute to White's proposed Fund; R. Samayoa, "Re: Stabilization Fund of the United and Associated Nations," May 31, 1943, HDWP, box 8, folder 2.

26. Oscar Muller, "Memorandum on the Proposal for a Stabilization Fund of the United and Associated Nations," (undated but US translation of June 28, 1943), HDWP, box 8, folder 2.

Woods conference itself, leading figures in the Latin American coalition, such as Cuba's Luis Machado and Mexico's Antonio Espinosa de los Monteros, worked closely with US officials.[27] At one point on July 10, Luxford told his US colleagues that Machado had "assured me we could get a vote on any issue we wanted to."[28] At the end of the conference, White also noted privately that Cuba "has given us more help than all the others combined," and insisted that the country be given a speaking role in the final ceremonies.[29] More generally, Luxford recalled later that White was "popular" with the Latin American delegates because "having dealt with the man for years in various problems" they "had confidence that here is the man who will understand our problem and who, if he sees our problem, will fight, and he's not afraid to fight."[30] In the case of Monteros, this confidence may also have been reinforced by his experience working closely with White in the small IFEAC subcommittee that developed the IAB proposal in 1939–40, as well as by long-standing personal ties. He and White had been classmates at Harvard; indeed, White referred to him as "Tony" at the Bretton Woods conference.[31]

The key problem that many Latin American delegates hoped White could help them address during the Bretton Woods negotiations was the low living standards of their countries. Suárez highlighted this in his opening statement at the conference where he emphasized his hope that the conference would help raise "the standard of living of humanity as a whole."[32] He reiterated this in an interview for a special radio show that CBS broadcast about the conference on July 18: "My country, Mexico, has been poor for centuries. . . . We would like to make our people healthy, strong and happy. So would the representatives of all the United Nations. That will be another result of this conference. It will make people well all over the world."[33] Suárez and other Latin American officials had appreciated US initiatives to help promote higher living standards in their region since the late 1930s. By 1944, however, many Latin American policymakers were becoming concerned that the US interest in assisting the region's development was waning

---

27. Eckes 1975, 154. Goldenweiser, who attended the conference, also identified Monteros and Machado as key leaders of the Latin American officials (E. Goldenweiser, "Bretton Woods," p. 2, CSF, 001.411). Luxford also identified Machado as the leader (MD, book 752, p. 5). For the tendency of Latin America to support the United States at the conference, see also Mikesell 2000, 43.

28. MD, book 752, p. 5. According to a later account from a Soviet source, White apparently also joked with Soviet officials privately that he could mobilize the support of Latin American votes to secure decisions (Steil 2013, 249), but the credibility of this source is questionable since it claims White talked of mobilizing "the votes of the 22 Latin American Republics" when there were only 19 Latin American countries represented at the conference.

29. MD, book 756, p. 273. The other invited speakers were from Brazil, Britain, Canada, France, Norway, and the Soviet Union.

30. Oliver 1961a, 18–19.

31. Urquidi 1996, 50 n. 5.

32. US State Department 1948, 76.

33. MD, book 755, p. 263.

as the security threat of the Axis powers diminished and as supportive figures such as Sumner Welles left office.[34] The Bretton Woods negotiations provided a mechanism that might help sustain the US backing for rising standards of living in Latin America.[35] This thinking was encouraged by the fact that White and other US officials had explicitly linked US postwar plans to the goals of Good Neighbor financial partnership at Rio in January 1942.

Promoting the Bank's Development-Lending Role

Latin American countries were particularly interested in the potential of the IBRD to mobilize development loans. Mexican officials played a lead role on this issue. During the early bilateral consultations with White in May 1943, Monteros and the Bank of Mexico's Rodrigo Gómez urged that White's Fund proposal be accompanied by "other agencies for long-term capital."[36] Mexican officials had been long frustrated by the failure of their 1939 IAB initiative and they saw the postwar planning process as a way to help bring to fruition some of its goals. One of the chief IAB advocates, the Bank of Mexico's head Eduardo Villaseñor, was also deeply involved in the discussion of the postwar plans. Mexican interest in this issue had been reinforced by studies showing that Mexico would need foreign financial assistance for its ambitious postwar development goals, which included plans relating to infrastructure, roads, electricity, irrigation, and broader agricultural and industrial growth.[37] Prebisch's high-profile seminar at the Bank of Mexico in early 1944 also reinforced the interest of top Mexican officials in development-oriented perspectives on the Bretton Woods plans.

In the lead-up to the Bretton Woods conference, Mexican officials carefully studied the American IBRD proposals of November 1943 and compared them to the early IAB plans.[38] They found the US draft encouraging but wanted to be sure that the Bank would provide adequate support for development goals. As one Mexican delegate to Bretton Woods, Victor Urquidi, put it later, the Mexican delegation "arrived at Bretton Woods ready to inject some interest in economic development issues into the debate."[39] In addition to Urquidi, the delegation included Monteros, Gómez, Suárez, and the head of the Bank of Mexico's economic research department, Daniel Cosío Villegas (who had also been part of the

---

34. Whitaker 1944, 44; Rivas 2002, 63; Gellman 1979, 179. Welles resigned in September 1943.

35. Inman 1944, 3.

36. "Memorandum of a Meeting on the International Stabilization Fund in Mr. White's Office, May 25, 1943," p. 1, ITM, box 20.

37. Urquidi 1994; 1996, 40, 50 n. 24.

38. Urquidi 1996, 35.

39. Urquidi 1996, 40.

Mexican delegation to the 1933 Montevideo conference when Puig had advanced his controversial debt proposals).[40] Although Urquidi was just the technical secretary to the delegation and the youngest delegate at the conference, he played a significant role for the Mexican delegation because of his fluency in English (he had received his B.A. from the London School of Economics).[41]

Later in life, Urquidi reproduced the text of a graduate seminar he gave at Harvard on his way home from the Bretton Woods conference that well expressed the "development" mindset of Mexican officials at the time. In the seminar, he argued that Latin American development was long overdue, citing statistics from Colin Clark's work that showed the region (with the exception of Argentina and Uruguay) to have relatively low productivity and income per capita. To address this situation, Urquidi told the seminar that planning and "investment for development purposes" were needed to raise agricultural productivity and enlarge the domestic market as a basis for industrialization. In his view, this program required foreign public—rather than private—assistance because private investors "will be after profits, or lower corporation taxes" and will not interested in "our organic development or industrialization as a whole."[42]

At the Bretton Woods conference itself, Urquidi and other Mexican officials suggested a change to the wording of the purposes of the Bank in order to make sure that it would provide this kind of support. An initial Anglo-American draft emerging from the discussions at Atlantic City had outlined purposes such as assisting "in the reconstruction and development of member countries" and "encouraging international investment for the development of the productive resources of member countries." The Mexican delegates suggested a blunter statement as the very first purpose of the Bank: "to encourage permanently the economic development of member countries." In the end, Mexico accepted wording that made explicit reference to the development of "less developed countries" in the first formal purpose of the Bank: "To assist in the reconstruction and development of territories of members by facilitating the investment of capital for productive purposes, including the restoration of economies destroyed or disrupted by war, the reconversion of productive facilities to peacetime needs and the encouragement of the development of productive facilities and resources in less developed countries."[43]

The Mexican delegation also pushed for stronger development wording in the Bank's general loan provisions. After a sentence that read "the resources and

40. For Cosío Villegas, see Babb 2001, 30; Urquidi 1996, 50 n. 6.
41. Meier (1984a, 13) notes that Urquidi was the youngest delegate.
42. Quotes from his original notes in Urquidi 1996, 43.
43. US State Department 1948, 366–67, 485, 1049–50.

facilities of the Bank shall be used exclusively for the benefit of members," Mexico proposed adding the following line: "The Bank shall give equal consideration to projects for development and to projects for reconstruction, and its resources and facilities shall always be made available to the same extent for either kind of project."[44] In an accompanying statement prepared and presented by Urquidi, the Mexican government stated that it did not want "to impose on the Bank a rigid fifty-fifty rule," but felt that the new sentence was important to guarantee that the Bank would focus on development issues. As Urquidi put it, "in the very short run, perhaps reconstruction will be more urgent for the world as a whole, but in the long run, Mr. Chairman—before we are all *too* dead, if I may say so—development must prevail if we are to sustain and increase real income everywhere." Urquidi also noted that Mexico and other countries "have resources which are still untapped" and "a large part of our population has not yet attained an adequate standard of living." He continued: "If we tackle these—and for that we require sums of capital we do not dispose of at home—we will undoubtedly benefit not only ourselves but the world as a whole, and particularly the industrial nations, in that we shall provide better markets for them and better customers."[45]

Urquidi also highlighted one further point that spoke directly to Latin American support for the Bank. He noted that Mexico and many other Latin American countries were being asked to contribute funds to the Bank that could otherwise be used for "the import of capital goods for our development." For this reason, they needed to be assured that their "requests for capital for development purposes" would be given equal consideration as those for reconstruction.[46] This issue had in fact become quite politicized among the Latin American delegations at the conference. If IBRD's resources were going to flow largely to Europe for reconstruction purposes, some Latin American officials began to talk openly about refusing to contribute to the Bank. Brazil's Souza Costa worked hard to prevent this outcome, arguing that the IBRD would increasingly shift its lending away from Europe over time to serve development goals, and that Latin America would also benefit directly from European reconstruction in terms of enhanced exports.[47] Latin American concerns were partially addressed by an offer from the Canadian and Chinese delegations to increase their quotas in the Bank in order

---

44. US State Department 1948, 373–74. See also Urquidi 1996, 41.
45. US State Department 1948, 1177, 1176, 1176–77. See also Urquidi 1996, 42.
46. US State Department 1948, 1177.
47. Otávio Gouvêa de Bulhões, "A Conferencia de Bretton Woods ante os problemas da estabilidade das moedas no câmbio, a concessao de recursos a prazo curto e os investimentos a prazo longo," August 19, 1944, pp. 47–49, FGV, SC mf/dG 1944.05.08 II-10. See also Souza Costa 1944.

to allow Latin American countries to reduce their contributions.[48] Brazil, Mexico, Cuba, Peru, and Colombia also all agreed to contribute a little more to offset the lower commitments of other Latin American countries.[49]

Particularly helpful in shoring up Latin American support for the Bank, however, was the reception of Mexico's proposed amendment. After Cuba endorsed Mexico's proposal, a Dutch delegate pointed out that if the conference adopted the Mexican wording, development lending would in fact have to decline as reconstruction needs diminished (because the Bank's resources had be used equally for development and reconstruction).[50] While approving the "spirit" of the Mexican proposal, Keynes then quickly suggested slightly alternative wording that Mexico immediately welcomed and that was refined by a drafting committee as follows: "The resources and the facilities of the Bank shall be used exclusively for the benefit of members with equitable consideration to projects for development and projects for reconstruction alike."[51] Two days later, Poland attempted to prioritize reconstruction lending by suggesting one further clause at the end of the sentence: "with due regard to the extreme urgency of immediate post-war reconstruction of war-torn areas."[52] But Keynes and the lead US official involved, Dean Acheson, favored equal treatment of reconstruction and development loans and Acheson later reported that "the solid weight of the Latin American delegations threw the decision our way."[53] The drafting committee's formulation was then endorsed formally.[54] In these ways, Mexico and other Latin American countries helped to defend and strengthen the development focus of the Bank, although Urquidi himself worried after the conference that the Bank would still put "too little emphasis on development" and its activities "would be mostly to supplement private investors . . . instead of lending its own money."[55]

---

48. Mikesell 1994, 41; Bittermann 1971, 74.
49. MD, book 756, pp. 4, 8.
50. Howson and Moggridge 1990, 180.
51. Quote from US State Department 1948, 496. See also Schuler and Rosenberg 2012, 528–30.
52. US State Department 1948, 581. Before the conference, Czechoslovakian officials had also pressed for priority to be given to reconstruction lending; "Meeting on the Bank in Room 218, April 29, 1944," HDWP, box 8, folder 4.
53. Acheson 1969, 84. For the broader Latin American support, see also Oliver 1961b, 3. Acheson states that White disagreed with his and Keynes's view but he provides no details. Perhaps he is referring to a subsequent dispute he had with White had over a proposal (designed to satisfy the Soviet Union) to allow the Bank to give special regard to lightening the terms of loans to countries that suffered devastation from enemy occupation or hostilities. Acheson strongly opposed the proposal on the grounds that Latin America might think it undermined the "Keynes compromise" (MD, book 755, pp. 208), but White thought these fears were overblown. The proposal was subsequently approved (MD, book 755, pp. 203–9; US State Department 1948, 827–28, 923–24, 988).
54. US State Department 1948, 593–94.
55. Quotes from his original notes in Urquidi 1996, 43.

Compensatory Balance of Payments Finance: The Waiver Clause

Many Latin American officials were also keen on the IMF's capacity to offer short-term loans to help compensate for sudden balance of payments difficulties. Brazilian officials particularly favored this aspect of the Fund during the mid-1943 consultations with the United States. Brazil was represented at the consultations by the finance ministry official Otávio Gouvêa de Bulhões who had been a student of Harry Dexter White at American University in the late 1930s and whose presence had been explicitly requested by White.[56] Bulhões would also become the Brazilian representative at the Atlantic City conference and a member of the Brazilian delegation to Bretton Woods. At the mid-1943 consultations, Bulhões argued that the Fund might need to be more flexible in lending for countries that experienced seasonal fluctuations in their balances of payments.[57]

After the meeting, Bulhões prepared a forty-eight-page report on the Keynes and White plans which argued that White's proposed Fund would be useful in helping Brazil and other agricultural exporting countries offset short-term fluctuations in their balances of payments.[58] Bulhões noted that countries dependent on raw materials and agricultural exports such as Brazil were subject to much greater short-term seasonal and cyclical fluctuations in their balances of payments than exporters of manufactured products. In contrast to the gold standard, White's proposed Fund would offer credits that permitted countries to "avoid deflation" when they were "experiencing a temporary shortage of exchange in a period of seasonal or cyclical export depression." Although governments could protect the domestic economy with large gold reserves, Bulhões remarked, "the conservation of such reserves has been onerous, since it may be likened to an insurance maintained exclusively by the insured." The White plan would allow Brazil and other countries to reduce the costs of such self-insurance. Bulhões also liked the fact that the White plan was much more explicit than the Keynes plan in identifying *fluctuations* in the balance of payments as the basis for external finance from the Fund.[59]

---

56. Bulhões 1990, 46. White's teaching of him is mentioned in: (illegible name) to Keynes, September 13, 1943, UKT 247/36.

57. "Memorandum of a meeting on the International Stabilization Fund in Room 394, June 17, 1943," p. 5, BWCC, box 11/15.

58. "Relatorio Octavio Bulhões Sobre Os Planos Keynes e White e Seus Debates," FGV, EUG/Bulhões, G.pi0000.00.00/2. For an English translation, see Bulhões, "Report on the Keynes and White Plans and Discussion Thereon," n.d (but August 1943), Rio de Janeiro: Ministério da Fazenda, Gabinete do Ministro, Seccão de estudos econômicos e financieros, HDWP, box 8, folder 2.

59. Bulhões, "Report," 10, 3, 13–14. See also D. H. Robertson to Octavio Bulhões, May 25, 1943, UKT 247/36. At the same time, he liked the fact that the Keynes plan had more to say about the adjustment responsibility of surplus countries.

The less specific focus on balance of payments fluctuations in the Keynes plan in fact led Bulhões to worry that Keynes's clearing union might offer excessive short-term loans to deficit countries, thereby preventing necessary domestic adjustments. As Bulhões told the Washington consultation meeting in mid-June 1943, "South American countries must always have effective brakes against inflation."[60] This concern was shared by Eugênio Gudin, a neoclassical economist acting as an adviser to the government (and subsequently a member of Brazil's Bretton Woods delegation).[61] Chile's Herman Max (who would also attend the Bretton Woods conference) similarly told British officials in May 1943 that he thought the penalties against debtors in the Keynes plan began too late and were too soft.[62] These kinds of worries about a potential lack of discipline had also been expressed by officials such as Villaseñor during the IAB discussions.[63] Indeed, it is noteworthy that the IAB often came up in White's 1943 consultations with Latin American officials on the Fund proposal. For example, when White met in May 1943 with Bulhões and Eurico Penteado (who had also been involved in the IAB negotiations as Brazil's representative on the IFEAC), comparisons were made between the two institutions.[64] In a meeting between White and Cuban officials, it was also noted that the Fund could take on many of the tasks that the IAB had been assigned, although it was also agreed "that there may still be a place for a special bank for specifically American problems."[65]

During the lead up to the Bretton Woods conference, Brazilian officials continued to stress the risks of excessive Fund lending while lauding its role in offsetting the kinds of seasonal and cyclical balance of payments fluctuations that commodity exporting countries experienced. In a May 1944 speech, Souza Costa warned that the Fund should not aid countries "which do not subject themselves to a healthy internal policy," but stressed that countries exporting raw materials and agricultural products were especially interested in assistance to meet seasonal and cyclical fluctuations. Like Bulhões, he likened the Fund to an "insurance system" that would allow Brazil and other commodity exporters both to access credit "without the necessity of resorting to onerous loans as in the past"

---

60. Quoted in Deutsch, "International Stabilization," p. 48. See also Robertson to Bulhões, May 25, 1943.

61. Gudin, "Reflexões Que Me Ocorreram ao Ler o Relatorio Bulhões Sobre os Planos Keynes e White" (n.d.), FGV, EUG/Bulhões, G.pi0000.00.00/2. For Gudin's reputation as a neoclassical economist, see Love 1996, 149–50.

62. G. M. Watson to Frederick Philipps, May 2, 1943, UKT 247/36.

63. Villaseñor 1941, 170–71.

64. "Memorandum of a Meeting on the International Stabilization Fund in Mr. White's Office, May 14, 1943," BWCC, box 4/7.

65. "Memorandum of meeting on the International Stabilization Fund in Mr. White's office, Aug. 23, 1943," BWCC, box 5/1.

as well as to free up hard currency reserves that they could use for development projects.[66] Officials from other Latin American countries such as Mexico and Cuba also favored the Fund's potential lending role for these same reasons.[67]

At the Bretton Woods conference, delegates discussed at some length the special balance of payments problems faced by countries that were dependent on commodity exports. The Australian delegation proposed that the issue be addressed by allowing countries to borrow a higher percentage of their quotas from the Fund. Brazilian officials were sympathetic to the proposal, but reluctant to see access to borrowing increased too much and also aware of US and British opposition to the idea. As an alternative, Brazil became a leading proponent of a "waiver clause" that would allow the Fund to overrule its regular lending limits as a way to differentiate between different countries' needs.[68] This proposal built on the fact that the Anglo-American Joint Statement of April 1944 already included a very general sentence that empowered the Fund to waive at its discretion regular conditions on borrowing.

An ad hoc committee set up to resolve the issue—which included Mexico and Brazil—sided with the waiver idea but suggested additional wording that instructed the Fund to "take into consideration periodic or exceptional requirements" of member countries and also prioritized waivers for "members with a record of avoiding large or continuous use of the Fund's resources."[69] United States officials saw the waiver proposal as "rather innocuous" and they backed it as a way to deal with pressure from Australia, Brazil, and others (such as France and New Zealand) for action on this issue.[70] As White put it, "I think it is a happy solution to a difficult problem, although we would have liked the whole thing out if we had our choice."[71] The committee's suggestions were subsequently endorsed by the conference, a result that the Brazilian government trumpeted as a victory for its proposal to better protect the interests of agricultural exporting countries. The government also declared that agricultural countries such as Brazil and other Latin American countries deserved large quotas in the Fund because of the fluctuations they experienced in their balance of payments.[72]

---

66. Souza Costa, "Translation: The Currency Problem in the International Field," p. 8, 9 (speech from May 8, 1944), HDWP, box 8, folder 1. See also Souza Costa 1944, 13–15.

67. Urquidi 1994; McKinzie 1974, 13; US State Department 1948, 429–30.

68. Pinho Barreiros 2009; MD, book 752, p. 25; Bulhões, "A Conferencia de Bretton," pp. 44–46.

69. The committee also accepted a subsequent suggestion from Monteros that "the Fund shall also take into account a member's willingness to pledge as collateral gold, silver, securities, or other acceptable assets." US State Department 1948, 487.

70. Quote from Walter Gardner in MD, book 752, p. 25. For the various country positions, see US State Department 1948, 30, 120; Schuler and Rosenberg 2012, 364–71.

71. MD, book 752, p. 26.

72. Press release, July 16, 1944, pp. 2–3, FGV, SC mf/dg1944.05.08 I-54; Pinho Barreiros 2009. For the conference endorsement, see US State Department 1948, 949.

Commodity Prices, Trade Protection, and Policy Autonomy

In the midst of this discussion, the Cuban delegation made a formal statement declaring its sympathy with the goal of providing more flexible use of the Fund's resources "to meet the special needs of raw materials producing countries." Although the Cuban delegation backed Brazil's proposal, it also argued that the Fund's resources were unlikely to be sufficient to compensate fully for balance of payments problems experienced by Cuba and other commodity exporters.[73] Instead of trying to boost the size of the Fund, the Cuban delegates argued, it would be better to work toward "an international price stabilization scheme" for commodities. They argued firmly that "if prices of staple commodities are not stabilized the purposes of monetary stabilization cannot be attained," and they called for the convening of "an international conference" to establish an "international agency" for this purpose.[74]

Earlier in 1943, both Urquidi and Max had also argued firmly that Latin American countries would be unlikely to maintain stable exchange rates unless international commodity prices were regulated more effectively.[75] At the Bretton Woods conference, the Brazilian delegation also echoed the Cuban call, putting forward a formal proposal for a "Conference to Promote Stability in the Prices of Primary International Commodities." Pointing out that both the US and the British government had expressed support for international commodity price stabilization in their postwar plans, Brazilian officials argued that the proposed conference could discuss the creation of a new international organization to serve this purpose.[76] Other proposals addressing this issue were advanced by Bolivia, Chile, Cuba, and Peru. Bolivia's was the most detailed, calling for the countries at the Bretton Woods conference to organize international commodity agreements, arrange for more orderly termination of commodity contracts to protect suppliers, and favor natural products over synthetic and substitute ones. These measures, Bolivia argued, would boost the domestic productivity, purchasing power, and development of commodity-exporting countries.[77] After some discussion, these proposals were eventually consolidated into a resolution approved by the conference that recommended governments to seek agreement

---

73. Quotes from US State Department 1948, 429–30. Cuba had made the same point at Atlantic City; "General meeting, June 26, 1944," BWCC, box 1/12.

74. US State Department 1948, 430. Cuban officials had asked about international commodity initiatives earlier in 1944 as well; "Meeting in Mr. Bernstein's Office, February 24, 1944," HDWP, box 8, folder 4.

75. Eckes 1975, 91–92; Watson to Philipps, May 2, 1943. For general Latin American pressure on this issue before the conference, see also Bernstein 1996, 91.

76. US State Department 1948, 482–84.

77. US State Department 1948, 431–32; Schuler and Rosenberg 2012, 573–74.

on ways and means to "bring about the orderly marketing of staple commodities at prices fair to the producer and consumer alike."[78] The resolution spoke to Latin American concerns, although Bolivia and Peru hoped for more specific recommendations and Bulhões wished Brazil's idea had received more attention at the conference.[79]

Commodity price stabilization was not the only part of White's original "development" agenda that Latin American countries attempted to resurrect at the conference. Colombian delegate Carlos Lleras Restrepo called for future commercial agreements to allow "the necessary protection which must be given in the new countries to their infant industries, as was given at one time by today's industrial countries to their own industries during their first steps in industrial development." Echoing this sentiment, Peru's Juan Chávez called for "the diversification of the economies of new countries, so that they also become industrialized" and he emphasized how the IBRD "may do a great deal of good in this field, but the young industries will be in need of a certain amount of protection from the sort of unfair competition that large manufactures in the great industrial centers can carry on to prevent them from developing from the very start." Chávez also lamented more generally that "the basic difference between the economies of large industrial countries and of the new raw material producing nations is not always given due attention."[80]

One final preference of many Latin American governments that deserves mention was their desire to preserve policy autonomy through the use of the kinds of exchange rate adjustments and external controls that they had employed in the 1930s. During the IAB negotiations, Latin American governments had made clear their desire to avoid assuming any obligations regarding their exchange rate policies and their use of external controls. Because White's Fund plan was predicated on the idea that countries would accept constraints on their behavior in these areas, Latin American governments now tried to minimize these constraints.

In the realm of exchange rate policy, a number of Latin American policymakers pressed for flexibility in rules during the mid-1943 consultations. As Chile's Max told British officials, "it is much easier for the industrial nations to agree to maintain stability of exchange rates than for the South American primary producers with their wide swings."[81] Latin American preferences for adjustable

---

78. US State Department 1948, 1098.
79. Bulhões, "A Conferencia de Bretton Woods," pp. 54–55. For Bolivia and Peru, see US State Department 1948, 731.
80. US State Department 1948, 1186, 746.
81. Watson to Philipps, May 2, 1943, p. 2. Mexican and Costa Rica also stressed in their mid-1943 consultations with White that they would want to continue to adjust their exchange rate after

exchange rates were accommodated to some extent by the Anglo-American Joint Statement which allowed adjustments of exchange rates up to 10 percent in value without requiring Fund approval. At the Bretton Woods conference itself, countries such as Peru continued to stress that the Fund would need to allow exchange rate adjustments in order to prevent "small, raw material exporting countries" from suffering from the deflationary policies that some had experienced during the depression when they had failed to devalue.[82] Mexico even pushed for an amendment allowing smaller countries (defined as those with less than 10 percent of the aggregate quotas) to adjust their exchange rates up to 20 percent, although the proposal did not receive sufficient backing.[83]

During their mid-1943 consultations with White, some Latin American policymakers also wanted to know whether they would be able to retain their exchange control regimes if they joined the Fund. Even countries such as Mexico that did not employ exchange controls had strongly favored White's initial proposals for international cooperative initiatives to control capital flows.[84] Again, Latin American preferences were partially accommodated in this area. Although White's proposals for mandatory cooperative controls disappeared, IMF members were given an unconditional right to employ national capital controls. As White explained to Latin American countries in 1943, exchange controls were also allowed as along as they were aimed only at controlling capital movements and did not restrict current account transactions.[85]

United States officials were also quite accommodating of Latin American preferences to use multiple exchange rates. In 1943, when Latin American governments had first raised the question of whether these practices would be allowed, Keynes had told British officials that they were contrary to the spirit of both his and White's plans and should be resisted.[86] White's early January 1942 draft

---

becoming members of the Fund. Deutsch, "International Stabilization," p. 7; Mexican Government, "Memorandum on Changes in Rates," May 28, 1943, HDWP, box 8, folder 2; "Memorandum of a Meeting" (May 25, 1943); "Memorandum of a Meeting on the International Stabilization Fund in Mr. White's Office, July 20, 1943," ITM, box 21.

82. US State Department 1948, 744.

83. US State Department 1948, 95–96, 225. Brazil also favored exchange rate flexibility; Pinho Barreiros 2009.

84. "Memorandum of a Meeting" (July 25, 1943). For other Latin American support for capital controls, see for example Eckes 1975, 92; Pinho Barreiros 2009; "Memorandum of a Meeting" (July 20, 1943).

85. See for example "Memorandum of a Meeting on the International Stabilization Fund in Mr. White's Office, July 8, 1943, 1943," and "Memorandum of a Meeting" (July 20, 1943); "Memorandum of a Meeting on the International Stabilization Fund in Mr. White's Office, May 17, 1943," BP, box 69.

86. Keynes to Waley and Eady, May 11, 1943, Keynes to Playfair, "The Currency Arrangements of Latin America" May 21, 1943, Keynes to Playfair and Waley, "South America and C.U.," June 2, 1943, UKT 247/36.

had also explicitly stated that a goal of the Fund was "to eliminate multiple currency practices."[87] By the time of the Bretton Woods conference, their views had softened, as countries such as Venezuela pressed for flexibility on this issue.[88] Immediately after the conference, US officials predicted that the Fund was likely to approve such practices if they were "not discriminatory and do not interfere with trade," and the IMF did indeed subsequently accept these practices.[89]

Although the Bretton Woods results thus went some way to accommodate Latin American (and other countries') preferences in these areas, Fund membership did still impose greater constraints on Latin American policy than had the IAB charter. One State Department official, William Brown, told a British delegate at the conference that the whole scheme would have been suspect in the eyes of Congress if it did not impose some obligations on Latin American policymaking.[90] US officials who had been involved in the IAB discussions, such as Collado, worried that Latin American countries might balk at the constraints. He supported White's provision that Bank membership was conditional on Fund membership, on the grounds that the prospect of IBRD loans might encourage Latin American governments to accept the Fund obligations.[91] In the end, however, concerns about Latin American participation proved to be overblown. All Latin American countries joined the Bretton Woods institutions by the end of 1946 with the single exception of Haiti (which joined in 1953).

The Appeal of the Paraguayan Model

Triffin's Paraguayan mission of 1943–44 was also particularly helpful in signaling to Latin American officials that US postwar plans were not intended to place excessive constraints on their national policy autonomy. Not only did Triffin endorse the use of adjustable exchange rates and exchange controls, but he also recommended ways for the Paraguayan government actually to strengthen its capacity to intervene in the domestic monetary and financial system. These specific recommendations were also accompanied by detailed justifications from Triffin that endorsed many of the development aspirations that had arisen across the region during the 1930s. Triffin's Paraguayan mission, in other words,

---

87. White, "Suggested Plan for a United Nations Stabilization Fund and a United Nations Bank," January 1942, p. 9, BWA, box 44.

88. Maffry and Mikesell to White, July 7, 1944, ALP, box 7/6, file: "Fund—Bretton Woods Conference, Discussions by other nations."

89. E. Arnold to Mr. Luxford, August 25, 1944, p. 4, ALP, box 9/5, file: "John Laytin Material (Drafts)." For subsequent IMF acceptance of multiple exchange rates, see De Vries 1986, chap. 3.

90. Howson and Moggridge 1990, 176.

91. McKinzie 1974, 13–14.

reassured Latin American officials that the Bretton Woods order was not just compatible with their new development goals but actively supportive of them.

The importance of the Paraguayan mission in this respect was apparent from the interest it generated across the region. Requests from other Latin American governments quickly began to arrive on Triffin's desk, asking him to help reshape their countries' monetary and financial legislation along the lines of the Paraguayan model as part of their entry into the Bretton Woods system. The first request came from Julio Peña of the Costa Rican central bank in March 1944, even before Triffin had completed his Paraguayan work. Peña sought Triffin's help in strengthening tools for monetary and credit control, and in bringing the country's existing monetary and exchange control legislation in harmony with the new Bretton Woods agreements.[92]

During a brief visit on his way home from Paraguay in December 1944, Triffin prepared drafts for new Costa Rican exchange control and monetary legislation that were consistent with the Bretton Woods agreements. The exchange control measures followed the Paraguayan model, while the monetary legislation relinked the Costa Rican currency to gold but allowed the central bank to adjust its parity in certain circumstances that conformed to the IMF's language of "fundamental disequilibrium." In an effort to define and tailor the latter phrase for the local context, the Costa Rican legislation allowed exchange rate adjustments in order to cope with major fluctuations in prices that most affected its economy (such as export crops) or to correct a fundamental and durable disequilibrium in the balance of payments relating to disparities between internal and external prices and production costs.[93] In a December 1944 letter to Eccles thanking him for Triffin's work, Peña noted that the reforms prepared "the internal aspect of the monetary legislations in just accordance with the Bretton Woods agreements."[94]

In January 1945, the Bolivian government also asked the Federal Reserve Board for Triffin to help reform its central bank and monetary laws. Because of his other commitments, Triffin told the Board that he preferred not to accept this invitation.[95] His preference may have been influenced by the negative impression of the country and its central bank he had gained during a brief four-day stop that he and Hammond had made en route to Paraguay in September 1943. At the time, he had told a friend that he had "never met anywhere such an extreme

92. Peña to Triffin, March 3, 1944, ISF, box 231; Triffin to Gardner, November 15, 1944, ISF, box 109.

93. Triffin, "Preliminary Project of Monetary Law and of Regulation of International Transfers: Prepared for the National Bank of Costa Rica," December 1944, EBP, box 3/1: "Miscellaneous Loose Materials"; Triffin to Szymczak, "The development of exchange control policy for the International Monetary Fund," Draft 3/1/45, RTP, box 7.

94. Peña to Eccles, December 15, 1944, ISF, box 230.

95. Triffin to Board, January 11, 1945, ISF, box 230.

contrast between wealth and destitution" and where the government seemed "to be in the hands of the foreign mining companies and graft is open and insolent."[96] But Triffin subsequently sent the central bank's manager Franklin Antezana Paz, whom he had met on that earlier trip, a copy of the Paraguayan reforms.[97] In early 1946, Paz wrote to Triffin to inform him that a recent Bolivian reorganization of the central bank—the first major reform since its founding with Kemmerer's help in 1929—had been "motivated to a large extent" by the Paraguayan example.[98]

Triffin did, however, accept another invitation in May 1945 from the Trujillo dictatorship in the Dominican Republic that asked—in Gardner's words— whether "Mr. Triffin do somewhat the same sort of job for them as he did for Paraguay." According to Gardner, the motivation of the Dominican officials was that they "wished to get into a position to play their part in the Bretton Woods arrangement and that until they had a banking and currency set-up of their own they could hardly function effectively."[99] At the time, the Dominican Republic had a monetary system based largely on US currency and a banking system dominated by two branches of Canadian banks and one government-owned bank. The government wanted to create a new national currency and transform its bank into more of a central bank.[100] Indeed, when White had requested comments on his draft Fund proposal in 1943, Dominican officials had already made this preference clear, arguing that each member of the proposed Fund should have its own monetary system to serve its interests and avoid "bias" that might result from the use of a foreign currency.[101]

The Dominican mission was important in marking the first time that the Federal Reserve Board involved a member of the FRBNY staff—Henry Wallich—on a mission. Much to the frustration of FRBNY president Allan Sproul, the Board insisted that Triffin be in a supervisory role vis-à-vis Wallich, in keeping with its March 1945 decision that "the foreign activities of the System should be unified under the Board's direction."[102] The tussles between the Board and the FRBNY

---

96. Triffin to Captain Marion Allen Leonard, November 18, 1943, ISF, box 231. See also Triffin to Gardner, September 10, 1943, and Hammond to Szymczak, September 9, 1943, ISF, box 231.

97. Triffin to Antezana Paz, April 13, 1945, ISF, box 101.

98. Antezana Paz to Triffin, February 1, 1946, ISF, box 101.

99. Gardner to Governor Szymczak, May 12, 1945, p. 1, ISF, box 221.

100. Dominican Government, "Memorandum on Banking Reorganization in the Dominican Republic" n.d. (but sent on May 23, 1945), ISF, box 221.

101. Office of the Secretary of State of the Treasury and Commerce, Dominican Republic, "Memorandum in Regard to the Plan for the Establishment of a Monetary Stabilization Fund by the United Nations and Associates," April 4, 1943, p. 2, HDWP, box 8, folder 1.

102. (No author), "Foreign Missions of the Federal Reserve System" March 29, 1945, pp. 2, 1, ISF, box 218. For the debates on this issue, see for example Hammond to Szymczak, June 29, 1945, p. 1, ISF, box 221; Eccles to Sproul, November 25, 1945, and Sproul to Hammond, November 26, 1945, ISF, box 218; Szymczak to Board, February 26, 1945, and (no author), "Memorandum of Conference on Foreign Missions, May 4, 1945," ISF, box 230; Eccles to Secretary Snyder, April 9, 1948, ISF, box 273.

on this issue reflected not just ongoing bureaucratic turf battles over the control of the Federal Reserve System but also ideological disagreements. More conservative FRBNY officials such as Sproul warned—in a similar manner as Braden had in Cuba—that the Board staff should not encourage Latin American reforms that were "beyond the administrative competence and integrity of its [i.e. the Latin American country's] people."[103] On the other side, Triffin and others in the Board were wary of the FRBNY's closeness to the New York banking community and also angry at how Sproul and Williams had publicly criticized the government's Bretton Woods plans during the lead-up to the 1944 conference (despite the Board's efforts to silence them).[104]

Triffin and Wallich traveled to the Dominican Republic in late July, where Triffin stayed for two weeks and Wallich remained longer to help with the detailed legislative drafting. Of Wallich, Triffin reported to the Board that "his philosophy is, of course, different from ours, but we came easily to an agreement upon our basic recommendations."[105] They proposed a new national currency, an end to the dollar's legal tender status, and the creation of a central bank—recommendations that were soon implemented in 1947.[106] The proposals largely followed the pattern established in Paraguay and Costa Rica, but the country's strong balance of payments position meant that exchange controls were not needed to defend the new currency (although the possibility for controls was left open). Because of the conservative political climate in the country and the need to cultivate public confidence in the new currency, Triffin and Wallich also recommended that the central bank not lend directly to the public and that existing foreign banks' lending activities not be subject to stringent regulation.[107] In explaining to a Dominican official why his advice for the country differed from that he had given elsewhere, Triffin noted the different circumstances in the Dominican Republic and then summed up his general philosophy well: "You know that I do not believe that the same legislation can serve as a passkey for every country in Latin America."[108] As in Paraguay, Triffin also invited Prebisch to participate in the development of the reforms, and Prebisch visited the country for several weeks in September 1946.[109]

---

103. Sproul to Szymcak, July 13, 1945, p. 1, ISF, box 221.

104. For Triffin's views, "The New York Federal Reserve Bank and the Latin America Work" (no date, but 1945), ISF, box 229. For the latter, see Asso and Fiorito 2009, 210–11, and Eccles to Sproul, November 25, 1945.

105. Triffin to Szymczak, August 21, 1945, p. 3, ISF, box 221.

106. Wallich, ""Preliminary Report on Mission to the Dominican Republic," December 28, 1945, ISF, box 221.

107. Wallich to Sproul, October 22, 1947, ISF, box 221; Triffin to Gardner, May 17, 1946, ISF, box 113. Triffin to Board of Governors, October 2, 1945, ISF, box 221.

108. Triffin to Alfonso Rochac, January 7, 1946, p. 1, ISF, box 221.

109. Triffin to Prebisch, September 25, 1945, ISF, box 138; Dosman 2008, 204, 215.

Guatemala and Ecuador

Triffin was much more interested in a request for his services that came a few months later from Guatemala. In the Dominican Republic, Triffin was forced to work with a regime that he described as "extremely oppressive, scornful of personal life or property" and where "the President's gang absorbs a substantial part of the very low national income of the country."[110] The Guatemalan mission offered an entirely different political environment. In late 1944, a prodemocratic uprising had deposed the dictator Jorge Ubico y Castañeda who had been in power since 1931. A subsequent election—the first genuinely democratic one in the country's history—was won decisively by Juan José Arévalo, a philosophy professor who had been in exile. In the face of much resistance from the country's elite, the new government launched various reforms ranging from labor law changes and improved social security to the extension of the electoral franchise to all adults. The new government was also committed to monetary and banking reforms, and it invited Triffin to provide advice.

Triffin traveled to Guatemala from the Dominican Republic for a month between August 20 and September 18, 1945, stopping on the way for a five-day visit in Cuba where he provided advice on the implementation of the 1942 White mission report. As in Paraguay, he was accompanied by his colleague David Grove (who would soon succeed him as head of the Board's Latin American division when he left to work at the IMF in September 1946). Triffin had tremendous enthusiasm for the mission, telling Prebisch in advance that the job "interests me immensely in view of the composition of the present Guatemalan Government."[111] After his first visit, he wrote again to Prebisch (while urging him to come help with the reforms) that "of all the countries in which I have worked so far Guatemala is really the one in which I have been most deeply interested," and that the "country is now engaged in an extraordinary effort of national progress and reconstruction in a magnificent spirit of social and economic betterment and along completely democratic lines."[112]

After arriving, Triffin visited many parts of the country, held daily consultation hours for the public, and spoke to many audiences ranging from a special session of Congress to a university public forum.[113] He was proud that, unlike in Paraguay, he had been able to discuss the reforms "with people in every walk of life."[114] Triffin was also enthusiastic about the Guatemalan work because of the

110. Triffin to Thomas, Knapp, and Gardner, July 23, 1946, p. 2, ISF, box 221.
111. Triffin to Prebisch, July 23, 1945, ISF, box 162.
112. Triffin to Prebisch, September 25, 1945, pp. 1, 3.
113. Triffin to Board of Governors, October 2, 1945, ISF, box 221.
114. Triffin to Prebisch, September 25, 1945, p. 1.

quality of the local experts, particularly the economy minister, Manuel Noriega Morales, who had been a student at Harvard and had attended Bretton Woods as the sole Guatemalan delegate.[115] Because its banking system had been almost completely wiped out by the Ubico regime, Triffin also remarked that "never have I encountered such an opportunity for a complete and integrated program of monetary and banking reconstruction."[116] The prospects for successful reform were improved by the fact that the country had no internal or external debt and a currency backed by large foreign exchange reserves.

As in Paraguay and Costa Rica, Triffin developed legislation for an adjustable peg exchange rate and provisions for capital and exchange controls that were, in his words, "entirely geared to the Bretton Woods agreement."[117] These provisions marked a potential change for Guatemala which had been one of the very few Latin American countries to have had a completely stable exchange rate against the dollar over the previous two decades and to have never introduced exchange controls. As Triffin declared to the IMF Executive Board, "this stability was achieved at a very high cost. Economic development and social progress were retarded by severe deflationary policies, and the country was left undefended against external shocks arising from cyclical fluctuations in foreign markets." At the same time, given the country's distinctive history, Triffin stressed the benefits of exchange rate stability in the future:

> Confidence in the currency is an immense and rare asset in Latin America. It is one of the main prerequisites for the stimulation of domestic savings and of their investment at home in the development of the economy. It is also a necessary condition for the creation of effective instruments of monetary policy designed to shelter the economy, as far as possible, from the tremendous inflationary and deflationary pressures arising from cyclical fluctuations in the major industrial countries.[118]

Triffin went out of his way to stress how Guatemala's situation was distinct from that of other countries in other respects as well. Before Triffin went with Grove to Guatemala, the government had developed draft monetary and banking legislation modeled almost entirely on his earlier Paraguayan and Costa Rican reforms. But Triffin warned Noriega that "many of the provisions of the

---

115. At the conference, Morales had said very little, particularly after he had been scolded by a British delegate for suggesting the conference should deal with the issue of sterling balances (Urquidi 1994). For Triffin's impressions of local experts, see Triffin to Grove, November 29, 1945, p. 2, ISF, box 138.

116. Triffin to Prebisch, September 25, 1945, p. 1.

117. Triffin to Board of Governors, October 2, 1945, p. 6.

118. Triffin, "Initial Par Values—Guatemala," November 16, 1946, p. 1, RTP, box 6, file: "Latin America—Guatemala."

Paraguayan laws are derived from special problems of Paraguay and would not be applicable to Guatemala."[119] For example, given Guatemala's enormous foreign exchange reserves, the introduction of exchange controls was less necessary for the country. Because of the government's healthier financial position, Triffin also believed it was possible to create a government bond market quickly and he thus gave greater emphasis to the possibility of open-market operations in the central bank law. Because of paucity of banking facilities, Triffin observed, "plans for developmental credit were as urgent as plans for monetary stabilization," and he expressed interest "in studying the possibility of financing the many Indian communities, which are run in part on a semi-communal basis."[120] Discussions with local officials prompted Triffin to recommend the creation of a separate public commercial and mortgage bank (although still supervised by the central bank) to lend to the public rather than providing for the central bank itself to take on this task as in Paraguay. In addition, Triffin was encouraged to outline a clearer set of guidelines for monetary policy whenever the central bank faced balance of payments problems and inflationary or deflationary tendencies.[121]

After his return to the United States, Triffin discussed his proposals with various government agencies and all were in favor.[122] The Guatemalan Congress subsequently approved monetary and central banking legislation that followed Triffin's recommendations closely in most respects (although the government refused to accept that exchange controls could not be used for discriminatory purposes).[123] Noriega became the first head of the central bank, a post he retained until he was dismissed following the 1954 coup. In that position, he emerged as what one Federal Reserve official later called one of the "intellectual leaders" of ambitious development goals for the country.[124]

Triffin was also particularly proud of a mission he led to Ecuador in 1947.[125] By this time, he had joined the IMF in order to set up its exchange control department.[126] The Ecuadorean government had requested IMF assistance because of a serious foreign exchange crisis and the Triffin mission recommended the immediate introduction of controls. The controls allowed for multiple exchange rates

---

119. Triffin to Noriega, April 14, 1945, p. 3, ISF, box 138. See also Triffin to Noriega, October 30, 1945, ISF, box 138.

120. Quotes from Triffin to Prebisch, September 25, 1945, p. 1; Triffin to Szymczak, August 28, 1945, p. 3, ISF, box 227.

121. Triffin to Prebisch, September 25, 1945.

122. Triffin to Noriega, October 30, 1945; Triffin to Szymczak, Morrill, Carpenter, Hammond, Thomas, Gardner, October 29, 1945, ISF, box 221.

123. David Grove to Triffin, November 24, 1945, ISF, box 138.

124. Quote from Adler to Moore, July 23, 1949, p. 1, ISF, box 226.

125. Triffin 1990, 30. For details, see RTP box 4.

126. Triffin 1981, 243.

and were established in conformity with a decision of the Fund's executive board in early 1947 to allow multiple exchange rates under the transitional provisions of the IMF's charter.[127]

Triffin's mission also recommended reforms to the country's monetary law and central bank. The recommendations followed the general pattern of the Paraguayan and Guatemala missions, but were differentiated in some ways to fit the Ecuadorean context. For example, because of the "disorderly history of Ecuadorean public finance," the monetary board of the central bank was given more autonomy from government control than in Guatemala and Paraguay, with only three of the nine members being government appointees.[128] Unlike in Guatemala, the central bank was also given the ability to lend directly to the public because an already existing government mortgage and development bank was judged not well suited for the role. This lending was tightly restricted only to situations where deflationary conditions needed to be counteracted. In addition, the central bank was given a unique set of indicators that helped warn of the need for a change in policy. The Ecuadorean government implemented the mission's advice in March 1948.[129]

Broader Interest across Latin America

Officials in other Latin American countries also expressed interest in Triffin's reform ideas in this period. For example, during his second Paraguayan trip, Triffin traveled to Rio where he met with the Brazilian minister of finance; the minister was impressed with his Paraguayan work and favored a central bank for Brazil but noted the ongoing opposition of the Bank of Brazil to the idea.[130] Triffin also visited Uruguay in late 1944 where he reported that local officials showed "an extraordinary interest in the Paraguayan reform" and asked for his help in transforming the Banco de la República del Uruguay into a fully fledged central bank.[131] By 1946, however, the manager of the Banco had decided that Uruguay

127. Grove to Board of Governors, "Report on Mission to Ecuador," August 21, 1947, ISF, box 113. Harry Dexter White—who had become US executive director of the IMF in May 1946—was also involved in an initial IMF trip to Ecuador to discuss the mission but he suffered a heart attack there in late February 1947 and subsequently resigned from his IMF role in March 1947 because of his health (Boughton 2009, 7, 19 n. 2; Craig 2004, 368 n. 31; Triffin to Bernstein, February 26, 1947, RTP, box 4). Another figure involved was Felipe Pazos who had represented Cuba at Bretton Woods and was now working as chief of the IMF's Latin American division.

128. Quoted from M. Kybal, "Ecuador's New Monetary and Central Bank Legislation," July 1, 1948, p. 12, ISF, box 113.

129. Kybal, "Ecuador's New Monetary and Central Bank Legislation"; Grove to Knapp, June 16, 1947, ISF, box 222.

130. Triffin to Gardner and Hammond, November 8, 1944, ISF, box 230.

131. Triffin to Board of Governors, January 10, 1945, p. 1, ISF, box 178.

was not yet ready for a modern central bank, and he apparently told FRBNY officials that "the Triffin banks were too good for the environment in which they were to operate."[132]

In Colombia, the banking superintendent Hector José Vargas drew attention to the new advice of Federal Reserve experts and wrote in his annual report in early 1945 that "it is urgent to face boldly the problem of reorganization of our Central Bank, adapting it to the new ideas about money and credit and pulling it out of the morass of the Kemmererian ideas in which it is still enmeshed in spite of the abandonment of the gold standard." He also emphasized his interest in securing the Fed's assistance: "I am very much in favor of a decided position toward a managed currency directed to industrial development and the progress of the country. . . . These ideas are neither revolutionary nor original; all I need to say is that my desire would be that the technicians of the Federal Reserve be our advisers in this reorganization of our Central Bank and that these trends are now being sanctioned in the reorganization of various central banks of Latin America."[133]

Finally, it is worth mentioning the Mexican interest in working closely with Triffin in this period. The Mexicans did not seek his help with domestic reforms but rather with an initiative to foster closer central bank cooperation across the region. After Prebisch's visit to Mexico City in early 1944 and the Latin American solidarity witnessed at Bretton Woods, Mexican officials began to plan for a conference involving central bankers from across the Americas. They hoped the event would encourage informal discussion and reciprocal visits of research staff as well as perhaps lead to the creation of an inter-American institute of central banking. The key enthusiastic on the Mexican side was Urquidi, who asked Triffin to speak about the Paraguayan reforms at the conference.[134]

Triffin was very supportive of Urquidi's conference proposal, seeing it as an initiative that could "focus the interest of all and provide the necessary strength and support for the elaboration of new theories and practices and for their actual carrying out."[135] During a visit to the Fed just after the Bretton Woods conference, Urquidi had already made a good impression on Fed staff such as Gardner, who told Triffin that "we were all much impressed by the readiness with which

132. Quote from Milic Kybal of FRBNY; M. Kybal to Mr. Sproul, August 26, 1948, p. 4, ISF, box 178.
133. Quoted in Triffin to Szymczak, February 24, 1945, p. 1, ISF, box 109.
134. Grove to Triffin, October 17, 1944, Hammond to Triffin, August 22, 1944, ISF, box 230; Triffin, "Federal Reserve Participation in a Conference of Central Banks in Mexico City," January 11, 1945, ISF, box 230; Hammond to Morrill, October 9, 1944, ISF, box 22. Triffin notes that the original Mexican plan was for a purely Latin American meeting without the United States and Canada involved; Triffin to Szymczak, "The Mexican Invitation to an Inter-American Conference of Central Banks," January 11, 1945, RTP, box 3.
135. Triffin to Hammond, October 30, 1944, p. 1, ISF, box 22.

Urquidi talked our language in economics."[136] After returning from Paraguay, Triffin sought out the advice of Urquidi and other Bank of Mexico officials on his work on Paraguay, Costa Rica, Colombia, and Guatemala, and he and Urquidi soon worked together to draft the agenda of the conference that eventually took place in Mexico City in August 1946.[137]

The meeting was attended by experts from almost all countries in the Americas and included key figures such as Prebisch (who had been very supportive of the initiative), Bulhões, Max, and Villaseñor.[138] It agreed provisionally to create a permanent committee of central banks in the region that would share information and facilitate interchange and training of technical personnel. This initiative eventually led to the creation in 1952 of the Center for Latin American Monetary Studies, a body that became a very prestigious club for central banks in the region during the 1950s and 1960s.[139]

Prebisch was a key figure at the 1946 conference, highlighting how "periphery" countries were deeply affected by the "core," a point that apparently found widespread agreement among the Latin American delegates.[140] There were also some interesting disagreements among the luminaries at the meeting. While Triffin and Prebisch advocated exchange controls to handle balance of payments problems, Max preferred exchange rate flexibility.[141] In earlier correspondence with Triffin, Urquidi had also raised the question of whether a more flexible exchange rate might be preferable for Latin American countries to fixed rates defended by exchange controls, given how difficult the latter were to administer.[142] These disagreements did not question the new Bretton Woods embedded liberal paradigm for Latin America, but rather concerned the most appropriate mechanisms for adjusting to balance of payments disequilibria in a manner that would not involve too much of a sacrifice of national policy autonomy. There were no calls for a return to the gold standard. Even FRBNY economists acknowledged that adjustments to balance of payments deficits "probably cannot

---

136. Gardner to Triffin, August 24, 1944, p. 4, ISF, box 230.

137. Triffin to Urquidi, January 26, 1945, and Banco de Mexico to Board of Governors of FRS, December 17, 1945, ISF, box 22; Triffin to Board of Governors, "Mexico," October 2, 1945, RTP, box 3.

138. Representatives of every country in the Americas (including Canada) attended except Cuba, Haiti, Honduras, and Panama. For Prebisch's support, see Triffin to Hammond, October 30, 1944, ISF, box 22.

139. Coates 2009.

140. Grove, "Report on Mexico City Conference of Central Bank experts," September 25, 1946, ISF, box 21.

141. Grove, "Report on Mexico City Conference."

142. Urquidi to Triffin, February 17, 1945, p. 2, ISF, box 148. For similar critiques, see Triffin to Haberler, May 20 and June 27, 1946, CSF, 500.721; James Nelson to Triffin, March 10, 1945, ISF, box 101; William Neiswanger to Triffin, May 28, 1945, ISF, box 109. For Triffin's critique of flexible exchange rates, see Triffin to Szymczak, "The Development of Exchange Control Policy for the International Monetary Fund," p. 8, Draft 3/1/45, RTP, box 7.

be done by deflation" any more.[143] In this way, the Mexican central bank meeting symbolized the triumph of the new intellectual framework. While the European-dominated BIS remained a bastion of liberal orthodoxy in this period, this new Pan-American gathering included central bankers who were a vanguard of the Southern dimension of the new embedded liberal ideology that underlay the Bretton Woods agreements.

Latin American policymakers played an important role in the creation of the Bretton Woods system. Besides their initiatives associated with the Good Neighbor financial partnership before the formal Bretton Woods negotiations began, they were also actively involved in the negotiations themselves, showing a particular interest in the question of how postwar plans could help achieve their development aspirations.

They played an important role in protecting and bolstering the development lending role of the IBRD that many saw as a successor to the earlier IAB proposal. They also helped to strengthen the IMF's "waiver clause," which offered the possibility of greater short-term compensatory balance of payments financing for commodity exporting countries. In addition, in their public comments at the conference, they called attention to two "development" issues on the international trade agenda that had been mentioned in White's original plans: the need for infant industry trade provision for poor countries and for commodity price stabilization. In the case of the latter, they secured the passage of a conference resolution that recommended governments reach an international agreement to address commodity marketing and prices. Latin American governments also favored the provisions in the Bretton Woods proposals that protected their policy autonomy via exchange rates adjustments and capital controls.

United States officials, for their part, saw the relevance of these provisions for Latin America. Their support was apparent not just in the Bretton Woods negotiations but also in the extension of Triffin's popular financial advisory activities across the region in the immediate wake of the Bretton Woods conference. These missions helped secure Latin American backing for the Bretton Woods order by reinforcing the view that the latter was compatible with, and even actively helpful to their desire for policy autonomy to pursue state-led development policies.

When lobbying for each of these items on the Bretton Woods agenda, Latin American officials emphasized the distinctiveness of their needs as "less developed countries" (to use the words of the IBRD's charter). United States

---

143. L. W. Knoke and H. Wallich, "Final Report on Tour of Six South American Central Banks, April 3 to May 24, 1947," August 8, 1947, p. 9, ISF, box 229.

policymakers also recognized and emphasized the point. The support of both US and Latin American officials for the development content of Bretton Woods built directly on the Good Neighbor financial partnership. Although this support served various interests of both the US and the Latin American governments, it also grew out of an emerging transnational community of experts with shared values, many of whom were present at the Mexico City conference in 1946. This community has received much less attention in histories of Bretton Woods than the Anglo-American expert axis led by Keynes and White, perhaps because two of its key leaders—Triffin and Prebisch—were absent from the Bretton Woods meeting itself. In July 1944, Triffin was buried deep in the legislative details of the Paraguay reforms in Asunción. Without any official position and coming from a country not even represented at the conference, Prebisch also watched it from afar, envying officials such as Urquidi who were at the center of the action.[144] Despite being marginal to the conference, both Triffin and Prebisch deserve recognition for their role in helping to create a transnational expert alliance that backed the development foundations of the Bretton Woods order.

---

144. Dosman 2008, 197.

DEVELOPMENT ASPIRATIONS IN EAST ASIA

The international development provisions of the Bretton Woods agreements enjoyed backing that extended well beyond the US–Latin American partnership, including from two countries in East Asia that attended the Bretton Woods conference: China and the Philippines. These two countries were in fact the only representatives of the East Asian region at Bretton Woods. A few weeks before the start of the conference, Chinese officials had asked whether Korea could be represented or at least attend as an observer. White liked the suggestion but had to check with the State Department, after which the idea appears to have been dropped.[1]

The role of the Dutch East Indies (Indonesia) also became the subject of an interesting discussion within the US delegation at the conference itself after the Dutch invoked their colony's trade to justify their request for a larger quota in the Fund.[2] To prevent any perception of endorsing Dutch colonial rule, one US delegate—New York Democratic senator Robert Wagner—wondered whether separate quotas should be created for the Dutch and their colony. Others argued, however, that this idea—which was relevant to other colonial powers too—would

---

1. "Meeting in Mr. White's Office, June 9, 1944," ITM, box 21; T. L. Soong and Hsi Te-mou to Kung, June 9, 1944, AYP, box 78.
2. In justifying the need for the Dutch to be invited to the Atlantic City conference, Keynes had also talked of the importance of "Holland and her Empire"; Keynes, "The Monetary Conference," p. 3, to Sir D. Waley and Sir W. Eady, May 30, 1944, UKT 247/28. One of the delegates of the Dutch delegation at Bretton Woods, was Daniel Crena de Iongh who was President of the Board for the Netherlands Indies, Surinam, and Curaçao in the United States.

result in a major political row, and Collado noted that the United States had already set the scene by inviting the Netherlands and not its colony. To address the fact that the quota size of countries such as the Netherlands and Belgium was completely unjustifiable without their colonies, another proposal was then discussed to create an explicit provision for members' quotas to be broken up in the event of loss of colonies.[3] Even this idea raised political concerns, however, and Acheson suggested that the whole issue be ignored because "nobody will bother about it at all unless we raise it."[4] In the end, Morgenthau insisted the delegation keep quiet about the discussion and they agreed to explore the second idea further, but it was soon abandoned.

In spite of being the only East Asian representatives at the negotiations, China and the Philippines demonstrated well two distinct ways in which Southern policymakers backed the development content of Bretton Woods, each of which we have already witnessed in the Latin American context. In China's case, this support was expressed vocally during the negotiations themselves by the Kuomintang (KMT) government that represented China. China's role in the creation of the Bretton Woods system has received little attention in existing academic literature.[5] Indeed, China does not even appear in the index of Gardner's classic account of the Bretton Woods negotiations.[6] This neglect is strange since Chinese representatives were actively involved in the negotiations. It was even one of the few countries to prepare a formal alternative to the Keynes and White plans in 1943 (the others were Canada, France, and Norway), and it brought the second largest delegation after that of the United States to the Bretton Woods conference itself.[7] For the purposes of this book, China's role in the Bretton Woods

---

3. Luxford made this proposal and White and Morgenthau liked it. Edward Brown thought the whole issue was overstated because it applied primarily just to the Dutch and Belgians. He argued that it was less relevant to Britain's quota size because that was already small and because its African colonies were unlikely to become independent. He applied a similar logic in the French case, arguing that Algeria "hasn't the slightest chance of independence" (although he thought Morocco and Tunisia might). Acheson agreed with this analysis and thought that even in the Belgian case, the chance of the Belgian Congo's independence was "pretty slight." In addition to noting that this analysis overlooked French Indochina, White argued that these ideas missed the point that some provision needed to be made for the future. Luxford agreed and noted that no one would be able to prevent the Dutch from simply keeping their existing quota when the Dutch East Indies became independent. For this entire discussion, see MD, book 751, pp. 280–90. Brown and Acheson quotes on pp. 286, 287.

4. MD, box 75, p. 289.

5. The most detailed discussions I have found are Young 1963, 377–81; 1965, 310–12. While the discussion here draws on various archival sources, its major limitation is its reliance on English-language literature and the absence of Chinese archival sources. My discussion thus represents only a first step to filling this gap in existing literature.

6. Gardner 1980.

7. The delegation included nine formal delegates, a secretary general, four advisers, seven technical experts, two technical consultants, and nine secretaries. For the Canadian and French proposals, see Horsefield 1969b. For Norway's proposal, see HDWP, box 8, folder 2.

negotiations was particularly significant because of its advocacy of international development goals.

The support of Philippine policymakers for the development content of Bretton Woods took a different form. They played little role in the actual negotiations. After the conference, however, Philippine officials made clear their enthusiasm for the kind of development-oriented monetary reforms that Triffin had advocated in Latin America as part of building the new Bretton Woods order. Like many of their Latin American counterparts, Philippine policymakers saw these reforms as conducive to their state-led development and industrialization goals. As in Latin America, officials from the US Federal Reserve also backed the reforms and associated them with the broader Bretton Woods framework.

China and Bretton Woods

The scholarly neglect of China's role in the Bretton Woods negotiations is no doubt largely a product of the fact that mainland China ceased to be part of the Bretton Woods system after the communist revolution of 1949, and did not resume membership in the Bretton Woods institutions until 1980. At the time of the negotiations, however, China was seen as a significant player in the construction of the postwar international financial order because Roosevelt viewed the country as one of four great powers, along with Britain and the USSR, that would help to govern the postwar world.[8] As a result, when US officials in July 1942 chose an inner circle of countries that would be consulted on early drafts of White's proposals, China was included in it.[9] Archival records also suggest that US officials initially hoped that China and the USSR would be signatories of the April 1944 Joint Statement, although it appears as though there was not enough time for consultations with the two countries to take place.[10] At the Bretton Woods conference itself, China also received the fourth largest quota and voting share in the Bretton Woods institutions (behind the United States,

---

8. See for example Bagby 1992. The British were much less keen on the American cultivation of China, not least because of Chiang's support for Indian independence (O'Sullivan 2008). At the Bretton Woods conference, the British delegate Lionel Robbins noted in his diary that "the Chinese position at the conference is, of course, largely bogus, and the high place they are assigned to generally by American diplomacy rests on illusion—at any rate as regards our day, whatever may be the case in fifty years' time." At the same time, he noted: "Nevertheless, the fundamental fact remains that they are civilised and tough . . . and you can talk to them with the frankness and familiarity which you would adopt with a fellow Englishman. What a contrast in relations with our poor Indian fellow citizens." (Howson and Moggridge 1990, 171).

9. See chapter 6.

10. See for example "Meeting in Mr. White's office, March 13, 1944," "Meeting in Mr. White's office, April 5, 1944," BWCC, box 11/5. Acksay (2000, 280–82) notes that the USSR did respond late.

Britain, and the USSR), thereby guaranteeing it a seat on the executive boards of these bodies.

The Chinese government was far from a passive participant in the Bretton Woods negotiations. Its officials expressed strong views about the content of the postwar international financial order. Particularly prominent was their desire to see a commitment to international development incorporated within it. We have seen how Latin American proposals for development-oriented international financial institutions predated the Bretton Woods negotiations. In their contributions to the Bretton Woods discussions, Chinese policymakers drew on even earlier ideas put forward by the famous Chinese political leader Sun Yat-sen.

Sun Yat-sen's Thought

More than two decades before the inter-American negotiations for the IAB began, Sun had written *International Development of China*, which outlined in some detail the need for an "International Development Organization" to increase the standard of living of the Chinese people through the provision of foreign capital, technology, and expertise.[11] Sun's proposal deserves attention because it highlights how the inter-American system was not the only incubator of the idea of international development institution. Indeed, because of the early timing of his ideas, Sun deserves the title of pioneer of the concept of "international development" more than any other figure examined in this book. His views are also important because they formed the basis of Chinese official engagement with the Bretton Woods negotiations.

Sun Yat-sen had emerged as a major figure in Chinese politics through his efforts to overthrow the emperor during the years leading up to the 1911 Revolution and his subsequent brief role as provisional president. In the ensuing political upheavals and creation of rival governments in different parts of the country, he had fled into exile, but then reemerged as a significant politician after returning to China in 1917 and resurrecting his political party, the Kuomintang. Sun Yat-sen published *International Development of China* in 1918 at the end of World War I when he was in Shanghai.[12]

Sun had long been deeply committed to the economic modernization and strengthening of China as part of his broader philosophy of supporting the "people's livelihood." The latter concept drew on classical Chinese economic ideas and Sun associated it with government responsibility to help provide the "Four

---

11. Sun 1922, 219.
12. Wilbur 1976.

Great Necessities of the People—food, clothing, shelter and means of travel."[13] In historian Margherita Zanasi's words, the "people's livelihood" principle was "ultimately a socialist goal which implied state intervention, restriction of private capital, and the building of state capital."[14]

But Sun felt that the modernization of China could not be achieved without international assistance because of the magnitude of the challenge involved. While China had not even entered the first industrial revolution, he noted that the United States and Europe had already reached the second. As Sun put it, "so China has to begin the two stages of industrial evolution at once." In order to leapfrog into the modern age, he argued that China needed foreign capital, expertise and machinery to help with the development of railways, roads, canals, ports, modern cities with public utilities, water power, irrigation, reforestation, iron and steel works, cement plants, mining, agriculture, and the "colonization in Manchuria, Mongolia, Sinkiang, Kokonor, and Thibet."[15]

In specific terms, Sun proposed that "the various Governments of the Capital-supplying Powers must agree to joint action and a unified policy to form an International Organization" that would formulate plans and then negotiate a formal contract with the Chinese government for investing in the development work. The contract would specify how foreign loans would be repaid, but it would also outline that "the property thus created will be state owned and will be managed for the benefit of the whole nation." Because he was critical of how foreign bankers in the past had often "entirely disregarded the will of the Chinese people," he argued that the "enthusiastic support" of the people had to be secured before negotiations even took place between the international organization and the Chinese government. As he put it, "in my International Development Scheme, I intend to make all the national industries of China into a Great Trust owned by the Chinese people, and financed with international capital for mutual benefit."[16]

Sun stated that his proposal built on his experience of negotiating a contract in 1913 with the Pauling Company of London for the construction of a railway. By channeling foreign support through an intergovernmental organization, Sun argued, the kinds of imperialist rivalries and spheres of influence that had

---

13. Quoted in Zanasi 2006, 38.
14. Zanasi 2006, 34.
15. Sun 1922, 5, 8. In discussing "colonization," he invoked the examples of the United States, Canada, Argentina, and Australia, and wrote about applying foreign machinery to agricultural production on land that was divided into homesteads for Chinese labor. In one example, he wrote of the movement of "ten millions of the people, from the congested provinces of China, to the Northwestern territory" (Sun 1922, 24).
16. Sun 1922, 9–10, 11, 236.

afflicted China in the past could be avoided. Indeed, by preventing a future war from breaking out over China, Sun suggested, his proposed "international development scheme" would promote world peace and become "the keystone in the arch of the League of Nations."[17] Sun argued that China's development would also benefit rich countries by serving as an outlet for their surplus capital and providing a growing Chinese market for their products as their war industries converted to peacetime purposes.

Several scholars have commented on the innovative nature of Sun's ideas. In his history of development thinking, Arndt argues that Sun Yat-sen was the first to advocate "economic development" in the modern sense of term.[18] C. Martin Wilbur also observes regarding Sun's plans that "there is a far-sighted and modern quality to the thought which underlay them: the modernization of an underdeveloped country through cooperative foreign efforts."[19] In some ways, Sun's proposal for an "International Development Organization" can be seen as a kind of forerunner to the IAB and IBRD initiatives. He seemed, however, to imagine an intergovernmental organization with only the "capital-supplying powers" as members. In this sense, the plan was in fact closer to Riefler's 1941 proposal for the United States and Britain to create an organization that could grant charters to enterprises undertaking development projects (see chapter 4).

Although Sun's ideas were pioneering, they were also ahead of their time. The help that he sought from the League was not forthcoming despite his efforts to send his plans to the 1919 Paris Peace Conference as well as to US, British, and Italian officials.[20] The refusal of the US government to back Sun was particularly important because of America's position as the world's major creditor after the war. When Sun first approached American officials, the latter did not take him seriously because he had no government position at the time. When he became head of a military government in South China (based in Canton) in May 1921, relations became worse rather than better because US government officials considered him a rebel against the existing Chinese government in Beijing that they recognized. United States policymakers even actively thwarted Sun's efforts to secure private economic assistance in the United States. When Sun failed to secure financial support from other Western powers as well, he turned in 1922 for help to the Soviet Union despite his lack of enthusiasm for Marxist ideas.[21]

Although Sun failed to attract official Western support for his plan before his death in 1925, his ideas garnered attention abroad and help to inspire interest in

---

17. Sun 1922, 231, 9.
18. Arndt 1987, 16.
19. Wilbur 1976, 100.
20. Sun 1922, 233, appendices 2–5; Wilbur 1976.
21. Wilbur 1976, 102–8, chaps. 4, 5.

international development. The prominent US advocate of international development, Eugene Staley, declared that Sun's book was a template for his own ideas about the need for a UN Development Authority.[22] Sun's ideas also likely encouraged League of Nations technical assistance missions to China in the 1930s that focused on various issues such as agricultural development, public health, education, and transportation.[23] These missions emerged from a 1931 agreement that the League signed with the KMT government that had come to reunify much of the country by the late 1920s under the leadership of Sun's successor, Chiang Kai-shek.[24] Indeed, Sun's ideas about economic development were very popular with Chiang and his government. As Zanasi points out, his concept of the four great necessities of the people became "one of the tropes of political legitimacy favored by the Nationalists" during the 1930s.[25]

When the KMT government developed plans during World War II for the country's postwar economy, it also drew directly on Sun's plans for state-led economic development backed by foreign capital, technology, and expertise. At an important September 1943 meeting of the KMT's Central Executive Committee, resolutions were passed that committed the government to international collaboration to realize Sun's economic program.[26] As one British observer noted in 1945, Sun's 1918 book was "frequently quoted by Chinese economists and officials" at the time.[27] Like their counterparts in other poor regions of the world, Chinese analysts and officials saw industrialization as a particular imperative. As economics professor (and subsequent member of China's delegation to Bretton Woods) Choh-Ming Li put it in 1943, "only by industrializing the country will the living standard of the people be appreciably raised and the economic strength of the nation rapidly developed." Like Sun, Li also emphasized that "all post-war foreign investments in the country must be purged of 'imperialistic' motives. Foreign lending as a means of economic or political exploitation will no longer find any place in China—or, for that matter, let us hope, anywhere else in the world."[28]

The Chinese at Bretton Woods

Sun's ideas heavily informed the Chinese government's policy toward the Bretton Woods negotiations. This policy was shaped by a small circle of the KMT elite that

---

22. Ekbladh 2010, 74.
23. Zanasi 2007.
24. In this chapter, I have used English forms of Chinese names and places that are in keeping with the historical documents I have consulted and the practices of the time.
25. Zanasi 2006, 38.
26. Li 1943, 221; MD, book 663, pp. 200–201. See also Wu 1943.
27. "The Future Economic Development of China, Record of a Private meeting held at Chatham House on 31st October 1945," p. 1, RIIA, file 8/1167.
28. Li 1943, 218–20.

was attempting to govern China in the early 1940s in the face of the Communist challenge to its rule and the Japanese invasion of the country. After retreating in the face of the Japanese, the government had established a provisional capital at Chungking in 1937. By the time of the Bretton Woods conference itself, Japan's Ichigo Offensive, launched in April of 1944, had weakened Chiang enormously as the invaders conquered large swaths of territory and threatened to take Chungking itself.

China's need for US support in this situation may help to explain the large size of its delegation at Bretton Woods. The United States had been providing financial assistance to the Chinese government since late 1938 because of the security situation in Asia, including an unconditional loan of $500 million that was extended after the United States entered the war. By 1944, however, the confidence of US policymakers in Chiang's government was waning in the face of the gravity of the military situation and growing concerns about government waste and corruption associated with US loans and payments for the costs of US forces in China.[29] White, who had been a strong backer of financial assistance to China since the late 1930s, was among those with growing concerns.[30]

The leader of the Chinese delegation to the Bretton Woods conference, Hsiang-Hsi Kung, was very conscious of the need to be cultivating US goodwill. At this time, Kung was in the powerful position of being both minister of finance and head of the central bank. Educated in the United States at Oberlin and Yale, Kung had long been Chiang's close colleague as well as his brother-in-law (as well as of Sun Yat-sen, because all three had married daughters of Charlie Soong). Kung and his family were widely considered in China at the time to be quite corrupt and US officials observed that he was under considerable pressure at the conference to perform well because of his various enemies.[31] During the Atlantic City and Bretton Woods conferences, Kung instructed his officials not to offend White or other US policymakers by pressing too hard on specific issues because of China's need for US support.[32] Indeed, in the middle of the Bretton Woods meeting, he even held discussions with US officials on the contentious topic of payments for US military spending in China.[33]

Near the start of the Bretton Woods meeting, Kung made a point of emphasizing China's development goals and their links to the broader goals of the conference. In a formal statement to the press, he declared: "China is looking forward to a period of great economic development and expansion after the war. This includes

---

29. See for example US State Department 1967b, 1060; Bagby 1992, 65; White and Jacoby 1946, 115.
30. Craig 2004, chap. 8. White's concerns about unconditional lending to Chiang's government dated back to early 1940 (Boughton 2004, 187).
31. MD, book 755, p. 103. See also Pakula 2009, 505–6. In November 1944, Kung resigned as finance minister in the face of opposition within the KMT.
32. Fuchs 1974a, 109–10, 114.
33. MD, book 755, pp. 13–64.

a large-scale program of industrialization, besides the development and modernization of agriculture. It is my firm conviction that an economically strong China is an indispensible condition to the maintenance of peace and the improvement of well-being of the world." Kung then reminded his audience of Sun Yat-sen's proposal: "After the first World War, Dr. Sun Yat-sen proposed a plan for what he termed 'the international development of China.' He emphasized the principle of cooperation with friendly nations and utilization of foreign capital for the development of China's resources. Dr. Sun's teaching constituted the basis of China's national policy. America and others of the United Nations, I hope, will take an active part in aiding the post-war development of China."[34] In a speech a few days later at the conference, he also assured his audience that China's ambitious development plans were designed not "to compete with other industrial countries of the world but for the purpose of raising the standard of living of our people." Like Sun, he noted that China's development would contribute to "world prosperity through the opening of new opportunities for trade" as well as help China "play an important part in helping to stabilize conditions in the Far East and the world."[35]

Given these goals, it was not surprising that Chinese officials had been strong supporters of the Bretton Woods negotiations from the start. When the Chinese government received the initial 1943 White and Keynes plans, the initiatives had been welcomed as a potential source of financial assistance.[36] But the Chinese ministry of finance had also pointed out in April 1943 that "neither plan gives sufficient consideration to the development of industrially weak nations," and other Chinese analysts had concurred.[37] At a meeting discussing the international monetary plans on May 21, Tsu-yee Pei of the Bank of China (who would be a member of China's Bretton Woods delegation) suggested that China should present its views and those of the weaker countries before the United States and Britain finalized their plans. He argued that it might be difficult for China to present its case unless it could rally the support of weaker countries and surmised that perhaps "it may be necessary for China, as one of the four great powers, to be the leader of the undeveloped countries." Kung agreed that China "should speak for the weaker powers" and that any propositions it had to make should be made before the final agreement was reached.[38] Support quickly emerged for the idea

34. US State Department 1948, 1156.
35. US State Department 1948, 1165–66.
36. Young 1963, 377.
37. Quote from "Summary of Comments on International Monetary Plans," Chungking, May 25, 1943, p. 7, AYP, box 78, summarizing "Memorandum from the Ministry of Finance, April 21, 1943." For similar comments, see also p. 2 of the latter document.
38. "Summary of Conference, Chungking, May 21, 1943," pp. 2, 10, AYP, box 78. Others supported the idea of allying with poorer countries at the meeting, such as vice minister of finance Y. C. Koo (p. 5).

of presenting an alternative Chinese plan that could both highlight the country's distinctive concerns and help to contribute to a reconciliation of the Keynes and White plans.

The Chinese Plan for an International Fund

Interestingly, the lead role in drafting this plan fell to an American, Arthur Young, who had been a student of Kemmerer's and had been employed as a financial adviser to the Chinese government since 1929. He had been asked to study the Keynes and White plans and make recommendations, and had submitted some draft proposals on international monetary arrangements on May 18.[39] Because of his earlier involvement with the League's stabilization loans to Austria and Hungary after World War I, Young's initial reaction to the White plan in early May had been that it was "all wrong in suggesting that fixed exchange is the starting point, rather than the reform of individual situations largely by internal action but with external aid."[40] He now worked closely with Kung and various Chinese experts to produce on June 9 a formal plan for an international fund that incorporated various ideas that had been raised in the Chinese internal discussions.[41] On June 15, Kung asked for the plan to be transmitted to the State Department, although an accompanying memo warned that the Chinese Government was "not necessarily committed" to it.[42] The plan and memo also formed the basis of the instructions Kung gave to four Chinese officials—Te-mou Hsi, Ping-Wen Kuo, Kuo-Ching Li, and Ts-Liang Soong—who attended White's consultations in Washington in mid-June (and who would all become Chinese delegates to Bretton Woods).[43]

These Chinese documents highlighted well the link that Chinese officials drew between their development goals and plans for the postwar international financial system. To begin with, the memo noted approvingly that both the White and the Keynes plans had referred to the need for international development loans. While recognizing that the "medium and long term provision of capital may well be discussed separately from monetary arrangements," the

---

39. Fuchs 1974a, 107; Young to Kung, May 18, 1943, AYP, box 78.

40. Young (1963, 378) quoting his diary entry of May 4, 1943. See also Fuchs 1974a, 72–73, 107–10.

41. For the various Chinese discussions and proposals, see AYP, box 78.

42. "Preliminary Draft of a Proposal for a United and Associated Nations Fund for Monetary Rehabilitation and Stabilization," and "Memorandum As Submitted by Chinese Experts Giving General Observations on American and British Plans for International Monetary Organization," June 9, 1943, HDWP, box 8, folder 1. For Kung's request for the transmittal, see Kung to Wei Tao-ming (Chinese ambassador in Washington), June 15, 1943, AYP, box 78.

43. H. H. Kung, "To the Chinese representatives appointed to confer at Washington regarding international monetary arrangements," June 15, 1943, AYP, box 78.

Chinese government stated that it "would stress the very great importance to China of provision of capital and its close bearing upon the satisfactory working of any plan for monetary rehabilitation and stabilization."[44] When they met for a bilateral meeting with White on June 18, 1943, Chinese officials also noted that "Dr Kung felt that discussions on the International Bank and the International Fund should be held simultaneously. This would give some assurance that the matter of long-term capital needs were being taken care of as well as short-term needs for current account."[45] Other Chinese officials were even developing ideas of their own at this time for the creation of international development lending institutions. For example, at the May 21 meeting in China where Chinese officials and experts had discussed international monetary plans, the vice minister of finance, Yee-Chun Koo (who would also join China's Bretton Woods delegation), had proposed the creation of an "International Reconstruction Finance Corporation" which (among other things) would encourage investments in "various relatively undeveloped countries" as well as hold commodities "to prevent wide fluctuation of prices of commodities of the world."[46]

In their specific proposal for a monetary fund, the Chinese also stressed their distinctive needs for external financial assistance. They outlined a formal draft of a "United and Associated Nations Fund for Monetary Rehabilitation and Stabilization."[47] While the "stabilization" role of the Fund was similar to that of Keynes's ICU and White's Stabilization Fund, the "rehabilitation" function was more distinctive, reflecting China's urgent need for foreign help to help stabilize its currency. Young had in fact warned the Chinese government that it might be unable to become a full member of the proposed multilateral Fund because it was unlikely to be able to maintain a gold parity immediately after the war. In his view, China's immediate priority should be to contain its acute inflationary pressures rather than draw up ambitious development plans. Chinese officials were unwilling to abandon their development ambitions, but they agreed with Young that the Anglo-American plans should be modified to address the problem of monetary rehabilitation.[48] Under the Chinese plan, countries whose monetary systems had been "seriously disrupted by the war" could take advantage—subject

44. "Memorandum As Submitted," p. 3.

45. "Conference in Mr. White's Office, June 18, 1943," BP, box 69.

46. "Summary of Conference," p. 5. A four-page proposal dated May 11, 1943 for an institution with this name can be found in AYP, box 78, developed by a Chinese individual from the Farmers Bank of China.

47. "Preliminary Draft."

48. Young 1963, 377–81, 385, 391–94, 446–47; Fuchs 1974a, 72–73, 107–9.

to the agreement of the Board—of a "transitional period" in which they could request credits from the Fund but did not need to commit to currency convertibility at a fixed exchange rate.[49]

Many other aspects of the plan drew upon or modified slightly key components of the Keynes and White plans, as the Chinese freely acknowledged.[50] For example, similar to White's proposal, currency values were to be defined in terms of gold (thereby committing China to define its currency in gold for the first time) and exchange rates could not be changed without the agreement of the Fund's board (although countries could unilaterally undertake a one-off devaluation if they had a large net debit balance over two years).[51] Chinese experts linked their advocacy of stable exchange rates to their development goals, pointing out that China would need a stable currency to attract foreign capital.[52] Echoing Keynes's proposals, the Chinese plan also ensured that adjustment burdens were imposed not just on deficit countries but also on creditor countries such as the United States. Countries that had large debit balances in the Fund would be forced to pay a charge and accept its recommendations for restoring equilibrium, but countries with net credit balances would also face a (lesser) charge and have to undertake discussions with the Fund about measures to reduce their surpluses, including increasing "international lending."[53]

Chinese officials also favored the US and British plans concerning capital controls, particularly the provisions for cooperation which they hoped might help China to control outgoing flight capital. Under the Chinese proposal, each member of the Fund would be required "upon request, to cooperate with any other member nation that may regulate international capital movements." Echoing the White plan, each member country could be asked "(1) to prohibit in its jurisdiction acquisition of deposits or other assets by nationals of any member nation imposing restrictions of capital transfers except upon authorization of the latter nation; (2) to furnish the Government of any member nation on request full information regarding such deposits and other assets; and (3) to consider such other measures as the Board may recommend."[54] Although provisions for

---

49. "Preliminary Draft," p. 2.
50. "Memorandum As Submitted," p. 6.
51. "Preliminary Draft," p. 5.
52. Dr. S. Y. Liu, "Memorandum," May 15, 1943, p. 1, AYP, box 78. Liu was one of the officials consulted by Young in preparing the plan.
53. "Preliminary Draft," p. 6. The board could also chose to waive the charges on credit countries and increase those on debit countries "if in its judgment unduly expansionist conditions are impending in the world economy."
54. "Preliminary Draft," p. 9. See also "Memorandum as Submitted," p. 4, and Kung, "To the Chinese," p. 3.

cooperative controls subsequently disappeared from US proposals, Chinese interest in the idea remained, particularly as public concern grew in the country about those who had sent money abroad during the war. This concern culminated in a resolution being passed at the May 1945 Sixth KMT Congress that requested the US government to provide the names of Chinese citizens holding capital in the United States and the amounts involved. The request was refused.[55]

Further Chinese Input

Although Kung asked for the plan to be sent officially to the United States in mid-June, it was not delivered to the State Department and White until early September because of wartime transportation difficulties.[56] On reading it, one US official told White that the main new point was the provision for international monetary rehabilitation, and that he thought the idea of special treatment in the postwar transitional period might have some value, as long as it was not a cover to use the Fund for reconstruction lending.[57] Morgenthau subsequently wrote to Kung on September 14, noting that US technical experts "have indicated considerable interest in the views expressed in these proposals, particularly with regard to the desirability of giving special consideration to the needs of China and countries in a similar position."[58]

In subsequent meetings with White in the fall of 1943, Hsi and T.-L. Soong showed great interest in the progress of the proposal for the IBRD. After receiving the first public US draft in late November, they suggested that the Bank should be able to receive deposits in order to increase its available funds, a suggestion that White had endorsed in his earlier IAB proposal but now rejected.[59] Commentators in the Chinese press also called for more to be done to foster postwar long-term international development lending. Here, for example, are the comments of economist Chun-fan Ku published in a Chungking newspaper on September 5, 1943: "The lofty ideals of the Atlantic Charter should be the goal of mankind in post-war reconstruction and the development of world resources. Full economic cooperation requires that the investor countries should give whatever is in their

55. Young 1963, 387–88.

56. Hsi Te-mou to White, p. 1, September 2, 1943, HDWP, box 8, folder 1. A copy was sent to the British and Soviet financial representatives in Washington in mid-October; Hsi Te-mou to Kung, October 22, 1943, AYP, box 78. Young also sent informally a memo outlining his views to the US State Department (where his brother John Parke Young was involved in postwar planning) in July 1943 (Fuchs 1974a, 110; Young 1965, 311, 375–77).

57. Friedman to White, p. 1, September 10, 1943, HDWP, box 8, folder 1.

58. Morgenthau to Kung, p. 1, September 14, 1943, HDWP, box 8, folder 1.

59. A. Lipsman, "Meeting in Mr. White's Office, October 29, 1943" and "Meeting in Mr. White's Office, December 3, 1943," HDWP, box 8, folder 4.

power to give and the countries receiving the investments should have whatever they are in need of."[60]

When the Joint Statement on the Fund was published in Chungking in April 1944, T.-L. Soong expressed satisfaction that China's proposal for a transition period—a provision that the UK and others had also pushed for—had been accepted.[61] In his public comments, Koo also linked the proposed Fund to development goals, arguing that its ultimate aim was to link up currencies and "to elevate the living standard of all peoples." He pointed out that the Fund's establishment "will necessitate the inflow of foreign capital into China to be utilized in opening up her natural resources and developing her foreign trade which will naturally raise the living standard of the Chinese people."[62] But questions continued to be asked in the Chinese press about why more was not being done to address long-term development lending.[63] When Kung received a draft of the Joint Statement on the Fund, he also asked when a statement would be released about the Bank.[64]

At a meeting a few weeks later, Hsi presented Bernstein with a memo from Chungking declaring that the IBRD proposal was "of very great importance to China" and asking whether the Bank could be authorized to engage in lending for "monetary rehabilitation" since the Fund was "not intended to adequately provide for this."[65] White's early drafts of the Bank had allowed this kind of lending, but the provision had been removed in internal US discussions because of domestic opposition.[66] Although Bernstein told Hsi that the Bank could lend only for specific projects, a clause was subsequently inserted in the Bank's charter at the Bretton Woods conference that stated that "loans made or guaranteed by the Bank shall, *except in special circumstances*, be for the purpose of specific projects of reconstruction or development."[67] The phrase "except in special

---

60. Ku Chun-fan, "International Post-war monetary planning," *Ta Kung Pao* (Independent), Sept. 5, 1943, translation in NAC, RG19, v. 3982, M-1-7-3.

61. "Establishment of International Monetary Fund Favourably Commented on by Chinese Experts," *Central Daily News,* Chungking, April 26, 1944, HDWP, box 8, folder 1. For UK pressure for a transitional period, see for example Mikesell 1996, 27–28, Moggridge 1992, 743. Not all delegates favored a transition period. Indian officials, for example, worried that Britain would take advantage of it to maintain the sterling area and its exchange controls, and even to devalue the pound, thereby undermining the value of India's sterling balances (e.g. Mukherjee 2002, 167).

62. Central News Agency, "Y. C. Koo Comments on International Monetary Fund," April 28, 1944, p. 1, AYP, box 78.

63. See for example "The International Monetary Fund" (Editorial from the *Sin Ming Pao*, Chungking, April 24, 1944), pp. 1–2, HDWP, box 8, folder 1

64. A. Lipsman, "Meeting in Mr. Friedman's Office, April 20, 1944," BWCC, box 11/5.

65. "Memorandum, Proposal for a United Nations Bank, April 17, 1944," p. 1, BWCC, box 11/5 (presented to Bernstein on May 8); "Meeting in Mr. Bernstein's Office, May 8, 1944," BWCC, box 11/5.

66. Oliver 1957, 370, 439; Mikesell 1994, 31; Mason and Asher 1973, 25.

67. Quoted in Mikesell 1994, 40. Emphasis in original. A number of countries pushed at the June Atlantic City conference for the Bank to be able to make gold loans for currency reserves, but the United States had remained opposed there (Mason and Asher 1973, 20).

circumstances" created a loophole that allowed the Bank's board in March 1946 to agree that the IBRD could lend in special circumstances for reconstruction of monetary systems, including stabilization loans.[68]

With the approval of the IBRD at the Bretton Woods conference, the Chinese delegation achieved one of their key objectives. Some foreign analysts also echoed their Chinese counterparts in seeing this as the realization of Sun's 1918 proposal. As Austin Grey, writing in the United States–based *Far Eastern Survey,* put it just after the conference:

> It is interesting to note that the Bank's purposes, objectives, and methods of operation closely correspond with the pattern of foreign lending by economically more advanced countries, and of borrowing by those less advanced, proposed by the late Dr. Sun Yat-sen in "International Development of China." The promotion of foreign investment and international trade, the development of productive resources and the raising of standards of living, as enunciated in Article I of the Articles of Agreement of the International Bank, admirably fit in with the goal of the third of the Three People's Principles, the Principle of the People's Livelihood. It will be a particular source of pride to foreign admirers of Dr. Sun Yat-sen, as well as to all Chinese, that a concrete scheme born out of the world's exigencies at the "beginning of the end" of World War II should follow the lines laid down by the Father of the Chinese Republic in his brilliant diagnosis both of the world economic situation as it unfolded toward the end of World War 1 and of the respective needs of China and of the industrial countries of the West.[69]

An influential American internationalist lobby group, the Commission to Study the Organization of Peace, described the Bretton Woods institutions more generally—along with the Hot Springs conference on food and agriculture issues and the United Nations Relief and Rehabilitation Administration—as "international mechanisms that will be needed to achieve what the great Chinese leader Sun Yat-sen once described as 'the principle of livelihood'—what we now call 'freedom from want.'"[70]

The Fund's final articles of agreement also included provisions that accorded with Chinese preferences such as the acceptance of capital controls and stable but

---

68. Mason and Asher 1973, 24–25.
69. Grey 1944, 167.
70. Quoted in Borgwardt 2005, 133–34.

adjustable exchange rates.[71] At the Bretton Woods conference, Young (who served as a "technical consultant" to China's delegation) and Pei even succeeded in securing a provision that gave enemy-occupied countries some flexibility in determining initial par values.[72] Chinese policymakers were also particularly pleased that their country received the fourth largest quota in the Bretton Woods institutions, a goal they had sought from the very start. Because this standing was difficult to justify on economic grounds, US officials produced this outcome only through some very arbitrary adjustments of the quotas behind closed doors, a move that left countries such as France extremely annoyed.[73] Morgenthau noted privately to his US colleagues that China's quota was "the most difficult to explain, and we did that for the magnificent fight they made for the last seven years!"[74]

Although Chinese officials achieved many of their objectives at Bretton Woods, how much impact did they actually have on the outcomes? There is no doubt that they were actively involved in the negotiations. As Austin Grey declared at the time, "the peoples of the Far East are becoming more and more the subjects and less and less the objects of the historical process. This trend was recognized and reinforced at Bretton Woods."[75] Their precise impact is difficult to judge in many instances because the provisions they backed also found support among other delegations. However, we can certainly conclude that China reinforced the case for including development issues within the Bretton Woods negotiations. At a deeper level, it is also important to recognize that Sun's ideas helped build the intellectual case for international development. Although the Good Neighbor financial partnership played the critical role in generating many of the Bretton Woods development initiatives, Sun's thinking and activism established a foundation for these initiatives two decades earlier.

As a final point, it is worth noting that the political commitment within China to the kind of international development project outlined by Sun was not restricted to the KMT leadership. US officials discovered just after the Bretton Woods conference that it was even shared by Chiang's rival in China's civil war, Mao Tse-tung. The Chinese Communist Party had its first official contact with the US government through a group of US military advisers who traveled to

---

71. China also contributed to discussions clarifying that remittances would be considered current account transactions, a clarification supported by other Southern countries such as Greece, India, Egypt, and El Salvador (but opposed by some such as Bolivia, which was a host to migrants) (Schuler and Rosenberg 2012, 253–56, 284–87).

72. Young 1963, 380.

73. Mikesell 1994, 22–23, 36–37. For China's appreciation of this result, see Young 1963, 381.

74. MD, book 755, p. 8.

75. Grey 1944, 166.

its headquarters in Yenan in July 1944, the very month of the Bretton Woods conference. At the time, Mao recognized that the United States would play a major postwar role in the region and he hoped to cultivate its trust in ways that might help check the KMT's power.[76] According to a State Department official who spoke with him on August 23 1944, Mao expressed his strong support for postwar economic cooperation with the United States centered around the goal of Chinese economic development: "China *must* industrialize. This can be done—in China—only by free enterprise and with the aid of foreign capital. Chinese and American interests are correlated and similar. . . . We can and must work together."[77]

On November 14, 1944, a US Treasury official in China, Irving Friedman, received an invitation from another top Communist official, Chou En-lai, who was visiting Chungking secretly under US protection and who wished to convey a similar message to Morgenthau. According to Friedman, Chou noted that "with regard to China's post-war position, her greatest economic need would be for foreign capital. . . . Moreover, China had to participate in international economic and financial organizations if she was to overcome her present backward state."[78] Chou's statement appeared to be confirmation of the Communist Party's support for the development role of the Bretton Woods institutions and China's participation in them. Along with Mao's views, it highlighted the breadth of the support across the Chinese political spectrum at this time for the kind of vision that Sun had outlined in 1918.

Monetary Reformers in the Philippines

There is no question that Philippine officials had very little influence on the Bretton Woods negotiations. At the time of the Bretton Woods conference, the Philippines was under Japanese occupation, as it had been since May 1942. It was represented at the conference by officials from its Washington-based government-in-exile headed by President Quezón. After annexing the islands at the turn of the century, the United States had in 1934 transformed the Philippines into a self-governing commonwealth with full independence scheduled for 1946. The Japanese occupation had then encouraged the United States to promise immediate independence after liberation and to treat its government-in-exile in the same way as any independent government.[79]

---

76. Jian 2001, 23–24.
77. Service summarizing Mao's comments in MD, book 796, p. 253.
78. MD, book 801, p. 272.
79. O'Sullivan 2008, 141.

The Philippine government was initially overlooked, however, when Morgenthau first extended invitations to thirty-seven foreign governments to its mid-1943 consultations in Washington. When President Quezón read about the invitations in the newspaper from his room in the Shoreham Hotel in Washington, he wrote an irritated memo to Morgenthau reminding him that the Philippines was "a full-fledged member of the United Nations" and that the future Philippine Republic would "have full control on matters affecting its currency."[80] Morgenthau quickly apologized for the oversight and sent an invitation to the Philippine minister of finance, Andrés Soriano.[81]

Soriano was a member of the Philippine elite and a leading businessman with interests that ranged from the San Miguel Brewery to Philippine Airlines. He had also been a prominent supporter of the pro-Franco Falange movement, a fact that concerned many US officials.[82] Given White's and Morgenthau's strong antifascist views, it is difficult to imagine that they had much interest in hearing his opinions. In his initial consultations with White and other US officials in May 1943, Soriano indicated that the Philippine government was very much in favor of the US Fund proposal even though the Philippines was unlikely to require financial assistance because of the strength of its currency.[83] Soriano also participated in White's mid-June 1943 consultation session with representatives of eighteen countries. The Philippines was then invited to participate in the Atlantic City conference, although the invitation came once again only after all the other attendees had been invited and Quezón had asked if extra countries could attend.[84] At the Bretton Woods conference itself, the small Philippine delegation led by Soriano made very little contribution to the discussions.

The Philippine Push for Monetary Reform

The commitment of Philippine officials to the Bretton Woods development vision became more apparent after independence and the election of Manuel Roxas as president in May 1946. Roxas was strongly committed to rapid import substitution industrialization and his administration saw domestic monetary reform as an important tool in achieving this goal. After annexation by the United States, the Philippines' monetary system had been a gold exchange

---

80. Manuel Quezon to Morgenthau, April 7, 1943, p. 1, TSF, Entry 67A245, box 26.
81. Morgenthau to Quezon, April 10, TSF, Entry 67A245, box 26.
82. Cullather 1994, 12, 25, 93, 203 n. 11.
83. "Memorandum of a Meeting on the International Stabilization Fund in Mr. White's Office, May 12, 1943," May 19, 1943, TSF, Entry 67A245, box 26. See also Soriano to Morgenthau, May 15, 1943, BWCC, box 5/3.
84. D. W. Bell to Quezon, June 14, 1944, TSF, Entry 67A245, box 26.

standard (that Kemmerer helped create in 1903) and then a dollar exchange standard after the United States left gold in 1933.[85] Now that the Philippines was independent, key officials in the Roxas administration—particularly the finance minister Miguel Cuaderno—wanted a central bank to more actively manage the country's currency and credit to serve domestic needs as well as to make better use of the country's foreign exchange reserves, including for deficit financing.[86]

Cuaderno had in fact been interested in creating a central bank since the early 1930s to foster the Philippines' economic growth and industrialization. After researching central banks around the world for many years, he had concluded that the Guatemalan central bank—established with Triffin's help—should be the model for the Philippines because of the similar social and economic conditions of the two countries.[87] Cuaderno's interest in a Philippine central bank in the 1930s had not been unique. The Philippine National Assembly had approved a proposal to establish a central bank in June 1939, only to withdraw the proposal when it became clear that the Roosevelt would not approve it. During the Japanese occupation in February 1944, another proposal for a powerful government-owned central bank had been passed by the Philippine legislature but without any follow-up.[88]

In 1946–47, Cuaderno used his role as co-chair of a prominent US-Philippine Finance Commission to push once again for the creation of a central bank.[89] The commission had been set up to discuss the government's growing fiscal deficits (which had become larger than US aid could cover) and options for monetary reform.[90] It included three Philippine members and three US members. Like Cuaderno, the other two Philippine members—Pio Pedrosa and Vicente Carmona—favored the creation of a central bank. President Roxas also urged the commission to recommend such an institution.[91]

Two of the American members were also very supportive: Arthur Stuart from the Treasury and John Exter from the Federal Reserve.[92] Exter (another Harvard economics graduate) was particularly keen, and his arguments echoed those made by his Federal Reserve colleagues regarding Latin America. In his view, the most important role the central bank could perform was "to cushion the economy against unusual and extreme fluctuations in the balance of international

---

85. Nagano 2010.
86. Cullather 1994, 63; Cullather 1992, 81.
87. Fajardo et al. 1987, 7
88. Exter to Board of Governors, September 2, 1947, ISF, box 232.
89. Cullather 1994, 63–67.
90. Knapp to Governor Ransom, September 6, 1946, ISF, box 232.
91. Exter to Board of Governors, September 2, 1947, Knapp to Goldenweiser, August 6, 1947, ISF, box 232; Arthur Stuart to Orvis Schmidt, January 31, 1947, TSF, Entry 67A245, box 30.
92. Arthur Stuart to Harold Glasser, April 1, 1947, TSF, Entry 67A245, box 30.

payments."[93] He thought the Philippine government should loosen the 100 percent reserve backing for the currency and be given the power to adjust the exchange rate and even impose exchange controls (the latter had apparently not been initially considered by Philippine officials).[94]

Exter spent much of his time on the commission trying to persuade the more conservative US co-chair, Edgar Crossman, to support reform. Representing the State Department, Crossman was a New York lawyer who had served as legal adviser to a US governor general in the Philippines in the late 1920s. His views had been influenced by discussions with Randolph Burgess in New York and, after he arrived in the country, with the manager of the National City Bank's local Philippine branch who had been an old friend. From these discussions, he had become concerned that any tampering with the monetary system, particularly at a time when the local government was experiencing fiscal deficits, might deter US investment in the Philippines and provoke capital flight.[95]

At the last moment, however, Crossman relented and the commission recommended in its June 1947 report the appointment of a "central bank council" to prepare for the establishment of a central bank. Many of the commission's specific recommendations were modeled on the Fed's advice in Latin America. Indeed, Exter had requested in March 1947 that a copy of the Guatemalan law be sent to him.[96] The commission suggested that the central bank be government-owned and empowered to lend to the government and to direct credit to specific sectors to foster industrial growth. It also urged that the central bank be assigned wide discretionary power to manage the monetary system in order to serve domestic needs, and that the currency be backed by flexible foreign exchange reserve requirements. In keeping with the Bretton Woods rules, the commission also recommended that the country's exchange rate could be adjusted and that the central bank should have the power to introduce exchange controls to contain capital flight.[97]

United States Support for Reforms

The commission's recommendations provoked some strong reactions. Burgess and representatives of other US banking interests opposed the recommendations

---

93. Exter to Edgar Crossman, November 7, 1947, p. 3, ISF box 232.
94. Exter to Knapp, January 31, 1947, ISF, box 232.
95. Exter to Board of Governors, September 2, 1947. For Burgess's views, see Burgess to Snyder, March 26, 1947, TSF, Entry 67A245, box 30; Exter to Knapp, February 27, 1947, ISF, box 232.
96. Knapp to Exter, March 18, 1947, ISF, box 232.
97. Exter to Knapp, January 31, 1947.

vigorously.[98] Even years later, US business critics of the report argued that it had been "the work, on the one hand, of 'New Deal' planners and bureaucrats from the United States, and, on the other, of Filipino officials fascinated by the governmental financial and economic manipulations encouraged by the Keynesian school of economics."[99] In the State Department, some officials were also concerned about the possibility of exchange controls, devaluation, and inappropriate political tampering with the currency.[100]

But Federal Reserve Chairman Eccles was very much in favor of the commission's recommendations. In a letter to Treasury Secretary John Snyder in April 1947 (copied to Burgess), he stated that he was in "thorough disagreement with some of the implications and assumptions" of Burgess's views. In his view, US businesses would not be deterred from investing in the country by a flexible currency system, given the many profitable opportunities that existed there. He also emphasized the politics involved: "We may have to recognize that our grant to the Philippines of political independence would be virtually nullified if we placed further barriers in the path of their economic self-administration. We must remember that such action might well appear in the Philippines—and elsewhere, especially in Asiatic countries—as an attempt to maintain a system of colonial imperialism which we publicly disavow." More generally, Eccles highlighted the economic case for the changes:

> My basic position is that usually it is inordinately expensive—I would say extravagant—for any foreign country to administer its currency system on a straight U.S. dollar basis, whether it uses U.S. dollars as its sole medium of circulation or issues its own currency backed 100 per cent by a U.S. dollar reserve. Not only does such a system involve locking up highly valuable foreign exchange assets which might be used productively to finance imports for development purposes. In addition it deprives the country concerned of any freedom of action in managing its domestic monetary affairs. It forces a rigid pattern of monetary policy, completely at the mercy of the flow of funds in the balance of payments, and in time of depression leaves the country concerned without effective defense against stagnation and waste of resources. Furthermore, in the specific case of the Philippines which is suffering a budgetary deficit imposed by reconstruction difficulties, it forces the country to assume

98. Knapp to Goldenweiser, August 6, 1947, ISF, box 232.
99. Hartendorp 1958, 255.
100. Cullather 1994, 66, 77.

burdensome external liabilities to meet purely domestic expenditure requirements.[101]

Some Fed board staff members, such as J. Burke Knapp, thought that Eccles had "a somewhat excessive enthusiasm for the proposal, being less than fully conscious of the limitations upon Central Bank action (and the possibilities of abuse) in an underdeveloped economy such as the Philippines."[102] But he and others on the Fed staff and board were still supportive of the commission's recommendations. Exter too remained deeply committed to the commission's goals, writing to Crossman in November 1947 that the approach to Philippine monetary problems of Burgess and other US bankers "strikes me as ostrich-like."[103] He reported that many local banks were also very much in favor of the central bank proposal since it would offer them protection and "an opportunity to expand their loans."[104]

In the end, President Truman threw his support behind the commission's recommendations, as did Treasury Secretary Snyder. A key reason was that the central bank's creation and the lowering of reserve backing of the currency could provide immediate revenue for the Philippine government at a time when US Congress was increasingly reluctant to approve new aid. In historian Nick Cullather's words, the proposal promised to give "the Philippine government desperately-needed short-term financing at no cost to the United States."[105] US officials were also encouraged to accommodate Philippine preferences because of strategic concerns: the country provided an important base for the US military, particularly given the growing uncertainties in China. Political scientists Sylvia Maxfield and James Nolt also highlight divisions within the US business community at this time, with internationally oriented US manufacturing firms emerging as quite supportive of US initiatives to promote Philippine import-substitution industrialization. As in Latin America, these firms saw ISI policies as a way of boosting overseas markets for their products and providing opportunities to establish protected subsidiaries behind tariff walls.[106]

When Cuaderno requested the Fed's help with the creation of the central bank, Exter and Grove were quickly dispatched to the Philippines to help refine his

---

101. Eccles to Snyder, April 11, 1947, pp. 1, 3, ISF, box 232.
102. Knapp to Goldenweiser, August 6, 1947.
103. Exter to Crossman, November 7, 1947, p. 1, ISF, box 232.
104. Exter to Knapp, February 27, 1947, p. 1.
105. Cullather 1992, 80. This rationale had already been prominent in US policymaking circles at the time the commission was established; e.g. Knapp to Governor Ransom, September 6, 1946, ISF, box 232.
106. Maxfield and Nolt 1990, 62–68.

initial draft legislation. Cuaderno reported that his draft had been patterned after the model that Triffin and Grove had developed for Latin American countries, because he "was greatly impressed by the realistic view which these two gentlemen took of conditions obtaining in smaller and less economically developed countries such as those of South America."[107] The final legislation, completed by March 1948, also followed the Paraguayan and Guatemalan models in many ways, although it replaced specific minimum reserve requirements for the central bank with some broad guidelines for credit policy relating to trends in the money supply or cost of living.[108]

As in the case of the Latin American reforms, the provisions in the Philippine legislation for exchange rate adjustments and capital controls conformed to what was allowed under the Bretton Woods agreements. In their final report, Grove and Exter also justified the reforms in language that reflected well the embedded liberal orientation of Bretton Woods: ". . . it could hardly be expected that the Philippine Government would retain a monetary system whose excessive rigidity might delay its program of reconstruction and development or might deprive it of any effective defense against the domestic consequences of world economic fluctuations."[109] They also launched a broader development-oriented attack on the deflationary consequences of the old monetary regime: "When a system requiring a 100 per cent reserve against the note issue is applied to a growing economy, it may logically be expected to impart to it a consistently deflationary bias. In order to create the larger money supply required for an increasing population and an ever-expanding domestic trade, it would be necessary for the country to have a persistently active balance of payments, which in itself would be a costly luxury for an under-developed economy."[110]

Triffin no doubt appreciated these lines of argument. So did Philippine politicians, who approved the central bank law very soon after Grove and Exter had submitted their draft legislation. After legislative approval in June 1948, the central bank opened in January 1949. Cuaderno was named its first governor.

The governments of the two East Asian countries represented at Bretton Woods emerged as strong supporters of the development content of Bretton Woods. Like many Latin American policymakers, Chinese officials saw the negotiations as an opportunity to secure international backing for their development ambitions, ambitions that were focused particularly on industrialization as a means

---

107. Cuaderno to Eccles, December 9, 1947, p. 1, ISF, box 232.
108. Knapp to Board of Governors, March 10, 1948, ISF, box 232.
109. Grove and Exter 1948, 939.
110. Grove and Exter 1948, 939.

to achieve higher living standards. While Latin American expectations had been shaped in part by the Good Neighbor financial partnership, Chinese interest in international development drew on the deeper legacy of Sun Yat-sen's ideas. Sun had failed to find international support for his pioneering proposals at the time of the establishment of the League of Nations. By the early 1940s, however, Chinese officials found the United States and other foreign partners much more willing to back their goal of constructing an international financial order that was conducive to development goals. Just after the Bretton Woods meeting ended, US officials discovered that these goals were even supported by the leadership of the KMT's rival, the Chinese Communist Party.

The Philippines was a much less active participant in the Bretton Woods negotiations. But after the country's independence and the election of Roxas, policymakers in the Philippines made clear their desire to introduce monetary reforms based on the model that Triffin had developed in Latin America in order to realize their ambitious development plans. As in Latin America, US policymakers—led by Federal Reserve officials—then helped craft and implement these reforms, seeing them as part of the new Bretton Woods framework. Fed officials soon did the same in other Asian countries that were not present at Bretton Woods, such as Ceylon in 1950 (where Exter played the lead role) and South Korea that same year (where the key figure was Arthur Bloomfield, whose support for development was noted earlier).[111] As we shall shortly see, Harry Dexter White and other US officials also assisted with developed-oriented monetary reforms in Ethiopia around the time of the Bretton Woods conference. These various episodes revealed another way in which the innovations of the Good Neighbor financial partnership were globalized beyond the US–Latin American context in the process of construction of the development foundations of Bretton Woods.

---

111. Alacevich and Asso 2009, Karunatilake 1973.

LUKEWARM AND INCONSISTENT BRITAIN

Development issues also played a role in British plans for the postwar international financial system, though not so prominently or consistently as in the case of the United States. Conventional histories of the Bretton Woods negotiations suggest that Keynes and other British officials were largely uninterested in international development. Even their support for the IBRD is said by some analysts to have emerged only a few months before the conference and largely because the British hoped it would help fund their own country's reconstruction.[1] However, these arguments understate the British commitment to international development during negotiations. Keynes himself included a commitment to international development lending in his very early thinking about the postwar international financial order, and his interest in the issue endured throughout the negotiations leading up to Bretton Woods. His support for international development was also shared more widely in British official circles.

At the same time, the interest of many British officials in these issues was much more lukewarm and inconsistent than that of the US policymakers involved in the Bretton Woods negotiations. Although British officials were interested in international development lending, they deliberately took a back seat to US officials in the initial planning of the IBRD and they ultimately contributed to watering down its public lending role. British officials also showed little interest

1. See for example Kapur, Lewis, and Webb 1997, 58, who cite Oliver 1961a, 7. For Keynes's alleged belated interest, see also Meier 1984a, 12.

in some of the other development issues that White addressed in his initial plans and they were much less keen on involving Southern countries in the Bretton Woods planning process than US officials. The British also thwarted the efforts of countries such as Ethiopia to pursue the kinds of development-oriented monetary reforms that Latin American countries were undertaking at this time. In addition, Southern countries holding large sterling balances resented the stance that the British adopted toward these debts at Bretton Woods, seeing it as an antidevelopment one.

Keynes's Initial Plans

In analyzing Britain's role in Bretton Woods planning, it is necessary first to recognize the dominance of Keynes. Although he was officially just an unpaid, part-time adviser to the British chancellor of the exchequer, he was Britain's most famous economist at the time, with what Robert Skidelsky calls enormous "personal authority" within the UK Treasury.[2] Keynes first began developing his ideas for the postwar international financial order in late 1940 when he was asked to comment on British initiatives to counter German propaganda on this topic. In his first November 1940 draft of a proposed radio broadcast, he highlighted the need to internationalize new domestic commitments to social security: "Mr. Bevin said recently that social security must be the first object of our domestic policy after the war. And social security for the peoples of all the European countries will be our policy abroad not less than at home. Indeed the one is hardly possible without the other; for we are all members of one family."[3] As this remark makes clear, however, Keynes's focus at this point was on Europe rather than the wider world.

Keynes's reference to Bevin's ideas was interesting. Ernest Bevin had been one of the most prominent trade union leaders in Britain before becoming Minister of Labour and National Service as part of Churchill's new coalition government in May 1940. By October, as the risk of a German invasion intensified, he had been invited to join the inner War Cabinet and he played a key role in managing labor relations in Britain's industries whose production was key for the war effort. Like Roosevelt, Bevin believed that the masses had turned to dictatorships before the war because of the absence of "social security." In October and

---

2. Skidelsky 2000, 135.

3. Keynes to Wilson, November 25, 1940, p. 1, UKT 247/85. See also Keynes, "Proposals to counter the German "New Order," December 1, 1940, p. 3, UKT 247/85. For others in Britain thinking along these lines, see Carr 1939, 238–39.

November, he began making speeches about how peace in the postwar world would thus need to rest on international commitments to provide citizens with this kind of security.[4]

For this, Bevin argued, a new approach to international relations was needed that gave more focus to economic and social issues of interest to the common person, and that endorsed international economic planning. Unlike Keynes, he cast this vision from the start in a wider context than just the European one. Here is the case he made in a private memo to the foreign secretary, Lord Halifax, in the fall of 1940:

> It seems necessary to look for a binding form for peace not in the Customs Unions or economic groups, although these will emerge, but in those matters in which all human beings, irrespective of nationality, have a common interest. These are security against poverty, care in sickness and trouble, protection against injury, provision for old age, all of which tend to assist in the great impelling human desire to have a home, to rear a family in decent and independent circumstances and to have a life in which work and leisure are properly adjusted. In short, international policy should be based not on the increase and safeguarding of the total trade and income of individual countries, but on the provision by international cooperation of the needs of human individuals.... Britishers, Poles, Chileans, etc. being looked at together as human beings whose well-being is interdependent. . . . The above conception would lead to directed planning of the use of international resources and capital instead of national or international financier investments for profit, with human betterment a major objective and not merely an incidental result.[5]

In a high-profile speech in late May 1941, Foreign Secretary Anthony Eden repeated Keynes's idea that "social security will be our policy abroad no less than at home" and linked British goals to Roosevelt's commitment to "freedom from want" which the latter had laid out in his January 1941 speech.[6] This link was then formalized and universalized when the British government endorsed the Atlantic Charter in August 1941 that committed the Anglo-American powers to the assurance "that all the men in all the lands may live out their lives in freedom

---

4. Bullock 1967, 39–42.
5. Bullock 1967, 201–2.
6. Eden quote from Broad 1955, 154. As noted in chapter 4, Roosevelt's "Four Freedoms" speech in January 1941 may itself have been influenced by British debates on social security in the fall of 1940.

from fear and want."[7] In their initial draft of the Atlantic Charter, the British had called for "a fair and equitable distribution of essential produce . . . not only within their territorial boundaries but between the nations of the world."[8] That clause did not make it into the final version, but another one initially drafted (in slightly different form) by Bevin was included that called for "the fullest collaboration between all nations in the economic field, with the object of securing for all improved labor standards, economic advancement, and social security."[9] Bevin told an audience in April 1942 that this phrase "really means the end of exploitation as we knew it in the nineteenth century."[10] His biographer also describes how Bevin remained throughout the war just as interested in "the need to attack the poverty and low standard of living of the underdeveloped areas outside Europe and North America" as he was in domestic reforms.[11]

As historian Elizabeth Borgwardt notes, Churchill saw the charter as "for European ears only, intended to shore up Britain's sagging morale and the hopes of the invaded countries of Europe."[12] Roosevelt and Welles, however, insisted that its provisions applied to the whole world, as did Churchill's deputy prime minister, Clement Attlee, as well as Bevin.[13] Keynes also embraced a wider global perspective when he developed his more specific proposals for an International Clearing Union (ICU) in the fall of 1941 and early 1942. In one draft, Keynes noted that countries accumulating credits in the ICU would be encouraged to provide "international loans for the development of backward countries" as one of four potential means to restore equilibrium. He also pointed out that his plan could be used to further "general world purposes" including an "international TVA." He saw his ICU working alongside, and providing support for, the "International Investment or Development Corporation" that had been proposed by Alvin Hansen.[14] Drawing on his previous interest in commodity price stabilization (and his long experience in commodity speculation), Keynes also proposed that his scheme could help with "the finance of commodity agreements" by providing overdraft facilities to

---

7. Quoted in Borgwardt 2005, 304. Within Britain, this commitment was then reinforced further by the publication in late 1942 of the Beveridge Report which explicitly invoked the Atlantic Charter in recommending a domestic plan for social security.

8. Quoted in Borgwardt 2005, 23.

9. Quoted in Borgwardt 2005, 27. See also p. 23 and Bullock 1967, 69.

10. Quoted in Bullock 1967, 203.

11. Bullock 1967, 278.

12. Borgwardt 2005, 34. This was rather ironic since he was the likely source of the line "all the men in all the lands" (pp. 28–29).

13. Patrick 2009, 187; O'Sullivan 2008, 138; Borgwardt 2005, 34.

14. Keynes 1980b, 80, 94, 94, 91. See also pp. 47, 59, 91; Skidelsky 2000, 218; Harrod 1951, 527–28.

international bodies that could stabilize prices of key international commodities by controlling buffer stocks.[15]

The Broader Interest in International Development

Around the time that Keynes's proposals were presented to the British Cabinet in early April 1942, other British officials also expressed interested in international development lending. For example, the Cabinet Office's Alfred Hurst asked Keynes and Richard Hopkins on April 1 to develop ideas for the War Cabinet about "the development of backward countries by investment on such terms as to repayment as will not build up an unsupportable burden of indebtedness."[16] A few months later, Roy Harrod in the office of the War Cabinet was also lobbying for Keynes's ICU to be complemented by an international financial body that would encourage lending from surplus countries, including to poorer countries for the purpose of "raising standards of living." Like Berle and other US officials, Harrod argued in the summer of 1942 that private financial flows could not be relied on for this task since "investors may have scant regard for social welfare in undeveloped countries." He also asserted that "Imperialist 'exploitation' should be no part of the new system." But his conception of what international lending and technical assistance could do in promoting development was more restrictive that than of US New Dealers. Rather than supporting what he called "premature industrialization," Harrod argued that "the most natural way of proceeding is to teach people to do better what they are used to doing already. I understand that there is no lack of scope in backward regions for improving methods of extraction."[17]

The influential Royal Institute of International Affairs (RIIA) also expressed interest in incorporating international development goals into postwar plans at this time. The institute had established a Reconstruction Committee to discuss postwar economic plans in early 1941, and its Economic Group—which included many prominent economists in government and in Keynes's circle such as Denis Robertson, James Meade, and Hubert Henderson—was quickly engaged in some

---

15. Keynes 1980b, 94. See also Dimand and Dimand 1990; Moggridge 1992, 680–81; Skidelsky 2000, 234–49. As noted in chapter 4, further discussions of the commodity issue took place outside of the Bretton Woods negotiations. For Britain's involvement, see also Penrose 1953, chap. 4.

16. Alfred Hurst to R. Hopkins, April 1, 1942, p. 2, UKT 247/115.

17. Roy Harrod, "Foreign Lending, Industrialization and the Clearing Union," p. 13, 7, 13 (n.d. but around August 1942), UKT 247/33. See also Harrod, "Three Immediate Questions," pp. 1, 2, October 9, 1942, UKT 247/11.

quite detailed discussions about how to operationalize the commitments made by US and British policymakers to raise standards of living worldwide. In June 1941, the group concluded that the merits of various postwar international economic plans would be judged by how well they would release all peoples from poverty and its evil consequences, primarily through provision of economic security for everyone who desires it, and secondarily through the advancement of standards of living, conditioned as (it must be recognised) such progress will always be by realist popular insistence a) that military security shall be assured, and b) that prosperity shall begin at home."[18] When they discussed the goals in more detail in early 1943, they clarified that "the provision of minimum essential requirements postulated in the agreed objectives is called for on a world-wide basis," and they argued that a plan would be needed "in which the provision of the essential needs of food, clothing, shelter, education and health, should have the first claim on the world's productive resources, whether the recipients can afford to pay for what they receive or not."[19] As we will see in the next chapter, the group—with these ends in mind—was involved in the preparation in 1943–45 of very detailed plans for the development of central and eastern Europe.

Other prominent British officials who had been associated with colonial administration were taking up the cause of raising the standard of living specifically in British colonies. As far back as 1929, the British government had introduced a Colonial Development Act that established a small fund to help finance economic development in the colonies. The primary goal at that time had been to create British jobs by boosting overseas markets for British products. In the late 1930s, British officials became more interested in how colonial economic "development" might also improve the lives of the colonized, a shift symbolized by the Cabinet's approval (with more funding) in March 1940 of a new Colonial Development and Welfare Act. This changed British focus was supported strongly by many associated with the Labour Party and was driven primarily by the outbreak of serious political unrest in 1937–38 in several British colonies in the Caribbean, Africa, and Asia as well as by challenges to British colonial rule emanating from Germany and Japan.[20]

The lead advocate of the new British policy was Lord Hailey, who had held high office in India and was a member of the Permanent Mandates Commission of the League of Nations. Appointed to head a committee investigating postwar

---

18. June 1941 document quoted in A. A. Evans, "Objectives," February 4, 1943, p. 1.

19. A. A. Evans, "Objectives," February 4, 1943, pp. 6–7.

20. Havinden and Meredith 1993, chaps. 7, 9; Lee 1967; Alcalde 1987, 30–32, 45–49, 70–74, 117–19. The United States was also pressing the British to promote economic development in its Caribbean colonies, through a joint Anglo-American Caribbean Commission created in March 1942 (Howard 2003, Alcalde 1987, 131–34).

colonial policy that began meeting in April 1941, he made a speech in October of that year that was seen as a turning point, announcing as he did "a new philosophy of colonial rule" involving concern for standards of living of colonial subjects.[21] As he put it in early 1942, the key issue for British colonial administration was now "whether our policy has been such as to secure the maximum development possible, or development of the type most conducive to raising the standard of living of the colonial population." He argued that the new prioritization of development was driven partly by knowledge of conditions in the colonies but also by the growth of "the new conceptions regarding the function of the State as an agency for the promotion of social welfare which have forced their way from domestic into colonial policy." He acknowledged that colonial subjects were asking, "How far has our policy secured the fullest measure of economic advance which their natural resources permit to them? How far has it contributed to a substantial improvement in their standards of social life?"[22] Indeed, many protesters in the colonies in the late 1930s were demanding policies to promote industrialization in their territories.[23]

Hailey argued that new approaches to colonial economic policy were needed to serve these goals: "If our primary concern is to be the improvement of colonial standards of living, some of our older conceptions regarding the proper field for the exercise of State intervention in economic matters must be revised." Hailey also backed international initiatives to raise commodity prices on the grounds that they would help to improve the standard of living in the colonies. In addition, unlike Harrod, Hailey saw the need to encourage some forms of industrialization in the colonies. His reasoning was similar to that of US and Latin American officials: "The creation of secondary industries in the Colonies is essential if we are to secure a more balanced economy for them, and to protect them from the worst effects of those periods of price depression which have hitherto hampered their economic development." Hailey's next sentence, however, showed that his support for industrialization did not go too far: "Their chief reliance must always be on agriculture."[24]

There were other limits to the Colonial Office's embrace of new ideas. At the same time that British officials were attacking the racism of Nazi Germany, the Colonial Office refused to employ non-Europeans.[25] In 1941, however, Hailey had hired a young economist from the Caribbean colony of St. Lucia at the

---

21. Quoted in Lee 1967, 16–17. See also Alcalde 1987, 117–19; Havinden and Meredith 1993, 215.
22. Hailey 1942, 111. See also Cowen and Shenton, 1996, 294–95; Arndt 1987, 22–29.
23. Farrell 1980, Bose 1997.
24. Hailey 1942, 112–13.
25. Hypocrisy on race issues was not limited to the British. See, for example, Welles's views (O'Sullivan 2008, xviii, 138–39, 178).

London School of Economics, Arthur Lewis, to study economic issues. Lewis had been actively involved in a campaign of the League of Coloured Peoples to challenge the racist hiring policy of the Colonial Office. He subsequently assumed an important role with the Colonial Economic Advisory Board in 1943–44 studying postwar plans for the colonies. But Lewis's advocacy of industrialization and a greater state role encountered strong opposition from more conservative Colonial Office officials, leading to his resignation in late 1944. Lewis would go on to a prestigious academic career as one of the pioneers of the field of development economics and winner of the Nobel Prize in economics.[26]

Finally, it is worth mentioning that British business groups also indicated their interest in raising the standard of living of poorer regions of the world at this time. In the summer of 1942, five different organizations representing British business released reports on postwar planning and all favored initiatives to promote this goal as a means of generating demand for their products after the war. The London Chamber of Commerce, for example, advocated policies "to raise the standard of living of the backward nations." Similarly, the Federation of British Industries (FBI) called for initiatives to "to raise the purchasing power of the world," declaring that there were "vast tracts on the globe where a small rise in the individual standard of life would have a profound effect on the world economy." The FBI suggested that postwar international investment in poorer parts of the world should be directed not just to the provision of commodities but also toward encouraging "simpler types of local manufacture and services for the needs of the local population." Support for industrialization, however, was once again controversial. The National Union of Manufacturers, for example, expressed concern about whether industrialization abroad might hurt British exports, and the FBI stressed that international investments in local manufacturing abroad should ensure that undue injury was not afflicted on "established interests."[27]

Toward Bretton Woods

As negotiations with the United States about the Keynes and White plans got underway in the fall of 1942, British official interest in international development lending remained. Keynes, however, decided that it would be "better for the Americans to take the initiative" in the development of specific proposals

---

26. Tignor 2006, chap. 2. See also Farrell 1980.
27. All quotes in (no author), "British Business Men on Post-war Reconstruction," July 6, 1942, p. 3, RIIACR, Economic Group Paper 49.

concerning international investment because the United States would be the world's major creditor after the war.[28] Indeed, Keynes was very concerned at this time about Britain's ability to offer postwar financial assistance. When discussing a proposal in late 1942 for the UK to offer a large postwar loan to China, Keynes commented that it had been "written in what one can only describe as an almost lunatic ignorance of the post-war prospects."[29]

As White delayed US work on the topic of international investment, Keynes became increasingly anxious. In late 1942, he asked British officials "Is Harry White giving any sign of life here?"[30] In April 1943, he asked again: "Is there any news whatever about a possible American project on the subject of international investment?" In consultations with European allies, Keynes heard similar concerns. As he told a British colleague in April 1943, "some of the European Allies are taking very strongly the line that neither C.U. [Clearing Union] nor S.F. [Stabilization Fund] is complete without an international investment organization, and they are reluctant to pass finally on the currency proposals until they know a little more about what is intended on the investment field."[31]

At this time, Keynes even suggested to the Dutch that they should consider taking the initiative on the issue.[32] In a memo written in late December 1942 (and subsequently shared with Keynes), Johan Willem Beyen, financial adviser to the Dutch government in exile (and BIS president from 1937 to 1940), had argued for an international lending institution to foster the "development of backward countries," clarifying that "development means a rising standard of living."[33] Like others, he was also mindful of the importance to primary exporting countries of initiatives to regulate commodity prices and to provide international short-term credits. When the Dutch finance minister sent formal comments to White on the US and British plans in May 1943, he noted that "adjustment in the case of backward countries may be found in granting long term credits on conditions not hampering but fostering the development of such countries."[34]

---

28. Keynes 1980b, 200. See also p. 196 and Harrod 1951, 533.

29. Keynes, "Mr Harcourt Johnstone on Post-war Loans to China," December 17, 1942, p. 1, UKT 247/3.

30. Keynes 1980b, 200. White also reported that the British were asking about the IBRD plan in late 1942. "Interdepartmental Subcommittee meeting in Mr. White's office, December 1, 1942," in "Memoranda: Treasury Meetings, Fund and Bank 1942–44," BWCC, box 11/5.

31. Both quotes in Keynes 1980b, 243. As we shall see in the next chapter, Keynes was also very encouraging at this time of a Polish proposal for international TVA-like lending to east central Europe.

32. Keynes 1980b, 243.

33. J. W. Beyen, "Notes on Monetary Conditions After the War," December 30, 1942, p. 4 (but submitted to the US Treasury in April 24, 1943), HDWP, box 8, folder 2. See also Beyen 1949, 148; Bittermann 1971, 63 n. 9. Li (2007) also notes the growing interest of the Dutch in improving standards of living in their Dutch East Indies colony (Indonesia) in the first few decades of the twentieth century.

34. J. Van Den Broek, "Remarks Concerning the American and British Plans for International Stabilization of Currencies," May 20, 1943, p. 7, HDWP, box 8, folder 2.

Keynes may also have been aware of Canadian interest in the issue. His ex-student Robert Bryce was working in the Canadian Department of Finance and had made a strong case for development lending in a December 1941 memo: "During the tempestuous twenty years between the wars we all fell far short of achieving that freedom from want which we now recognized as one of the new rights of man. We must do better after this war—if our civilization is to survive. We must achieve freedom from want, as Roosevelt said, 'everywhere in the world.'"[35] Bryce was particularly optimistic about what long-term investment in China could achieve given the size of its population and territory, and he argued that "the challenge of developing China seems far more likely to appeal to the American imagination than the repair of Europe." He continued:

> This looks to be the opening for that New Imperialism which one hears about these days—a benevolent, liberal and far-sighted, if not actually socialist, imperialism—A TVA imperialism. The new imperialists would have as objectives not a high return on capital, but rather a flourishing trade built up on the basis that would be created by the rising standard of living in the capital importing country. More distant objectives would be the peace and strategic security for the lending country, achieved not so much through political influence as through the political stability that a prosperous trade and progressive economic and social development would ensure in the borrowing country.[36]

Unlike the Dutch, the Canadian government published a formal alternative to the Keynes and White monetary plans in mid-1943. The plan focused on bridging the gap between those plans rather than on Bryce's ideas about development lending, but it mentioned the need for "some continuing and stable arrangements regarding international long-term investment" and for action to address "the instability of primary product prices."[37] In the same year, Bryce also published his ideas in a prominent US book where he made the following argument: "If our wartime protestations of allied solidarity and of a desire to improve the standard of living of all those who live in want are to be carried out . . . then we must have substantial loans from the richer states to the poorer states of the United Nations. . . . Billions upon billions of dollars must be invested in Asia, Polynesia, South America, and Africa, if the great masses in these lands are to be

---

35. R. B. Bryce, "Basic Issues in Post-war International Economic Relations," December 1941, p. 2, NAC, RG19 vol. 3977 E-3-1-2.

36. Bryce, "Basic Issues," 5.

37. Horsefield 1969b, 104.

made productive and eventually brought up to minimum standards of health and decency, let alone comfort."[38]

The British were also being lobbied to prioritize development issues by the Australian high commissioner in London (and ex–prime minister) Stanley Melbourne Bruce and his close adviser Frank McDougall (who was also a member of the RIIA Economic Group). Both had emerged as high-profile advocates of improved nutrition and living standards within the League of Nations in the 1930s.[39] After the outbreak of World War II, they urged British officials to focus more on these issues in postwar planning discussions. In a speech to the RIIA in May 1940, Bruce put the case this way: "the greatest problem we have to face is the problem of poverty; the poverty of other peoples and, also, the poverty of some nations. We must have international cooperation in any attempt to raise the standard of living of the people . . . this is not merely, as some people seem to think, some humanitarian desire of a social reformer, it is the soundest economic commonsense. We must raise the standard of living of the people and the spending power of the general masses if we are to restore prosperity to the world." He also made the case in strategic terms, arguing "there is the necessity for providing economic equality of opportunity for all nations" because "is not the basis of the whole unrest that has led to the present war the fact that we have not faced up in the past to this problem of the inequality of opportunity of different nations?"[40]

In addition to their participation in British debates, Bruce and McDougall sought to influence US postwar planning. During a Washington visit in the summer of 1941, McDougall met with top US officials, urging them to prioritize Roosevelt's goal of "freedom from want," and especially the goal of providing abundant food for all. He argued that the latter would be an achievable and popular objective, and it would help the agricultural sector and stimulate international trade. But when McDougall sent Morgenthau a memo in August (co-written with Bruce) about Anglo-American cooperation to raise postwar standards of living, the treasury secretary told White that he did not want to

---

38. Bryce 1943, 364.

39. Lee 2010, 105, 112–13, 122–24; O'Brien 2000.

40. "'The League and Economic Reconstruction' by Rt Honourable S. M. Bruce, Record of Meeting Held at Chatham House on Thursday May 9th, 1940," pp. 8–9, RIIA, file 8/630. Bruce and McDougall were also aware that the international promotion of better nutrition and diets would benefit Australian agricultural exports (e.g. O'Brien 2000). Bruce's speech was in fact reporting on a special committee of the League of Nations he had chaired in the summer of 1939 that recommended strengthened international economic and social cooperation. Although the committee's final report did not explicitly refer to "development," it had called attention to the aspirations for higher living standards in poorer parts of the world (League of Nations 1939, 9). Bruce's arguments highlighted how the rationale for promoting development in League circles was shifting away from the paternalistic "civilizing mission" of the League's covenant (see chapter 2) to a focus on world prosperity and peace (see also Zanasi 2007, 148-50; Nurkse 1944, 203; Love 1996, 116–17).

discuss it: "I have met this fellow McDougall and he bores me to death, and I am not interested in post war at this time.... I have got too many things to do to win the war before we talk about what we are going to do afterward."[41] One year later, in September 1942, McDougall had more luck when he found an opportunity to lobby Roosevelt directly about the issue at a dinner that Eleanor Roosevelt had arranged. When Roosevelt announced in early 1943 that the first UN conference would focus on food and agriculture issues, McDougall was delighted, and he became deeply involved in the preparatory work for the May 1943 Hot Springs conference.[42]

Because of his focus on postwar monetary plans, Keynes himself was not much involved in the preparations for Hot Springs. Indeed, he was annoyed that Roosevelt had decided "to start with vitamins" rather than international monetary issues in the postwar UN plans.[43] But when Keynes published his ICU plan in April 1943, he pointed out in the preface that the postwar world would also need "investment aid, both medium and long term, for the countries whose economic development needs assistance from outside." As in earlier drafts, countries with large credit balances in the ICU were encouraged to reestablish equilibrium through measures that included "international development loans." The ICU was also designed to serve broader international purposes, including working with other agencies such as "a Board for International Investment" and an "International Investment or Development Corporation."[44]

When British officials unofficially received a draft of White's IBRD dated August 4, 1943, they were appreciative that the United States had finally addressed the issue but they were critical of details of the plan.[45] Because of their government's financial constraints, British policymakers were wary of White's idea of a bank to which governments would commit capital. They preferred initiatives that were designed to mobilize private international investment. For example, they discussed the need for an "International Development Commission" that could help initiate, coordinate, and supervise plans for international investment projects. Private investors would be encouraged to fund these projects and the IDC could also work closely with an International Investment Corporation that would raise private funds to lend on to the IDC, by issuing securities in creditor countries whose balances in the ICU were above their quotas.[46]

---

41. MD, book 437, pp. 35–36. See also White to Morgenthau, "British Empire–American Cooperation on problems of post-war reconstruction," September 2, 1941, SMHDW, box 14; Stirling 1974, 205, 258.
42. Lee 2010, 169–70; O'Brien 2000, 173–74.
43. Quoted in Skidelsky 2000, 300.
44. Horsefield 1969b, 19, 24, 34.
45. Keynes 1980b, 338–39.
46. J. E. M., "International Investment," September 9, 1943, UKT 247/76.

When the British government provided official comments on the US public IBRD plan of November 1943 in mid-April 1944, it continued to urge US officials to focus more on the Bank's role of guaranteeing private rather than direct lending, and they suggested that countries should not be forced to subscribe capital to the Bank unless they had the capacity to pay (namely by having surpluses in their balances of payments).[47] The efforts of British policymakers to resist making substantial commitments to the Bank's capital reflected their ongoing concerns about Britain's finances. In mid-May 1944, Keynes wrote a forceful internal memo highlighting these concerns. He argued that various proposals of British government departments for postwar foreign loans were entirely unrealistic given Britain's severe financial constraints and possible postwar drawing down of balances that been accumulated in London by members of the sterling area and frozen by Britain during the war. In his words, these proposals represented "the gracious activities of Lady Bountiful, all-oblivious of the bailiff's clutch, the universal and unthinking benevolence of a family which has always felt rich and for whom charity has become not so much a sacrifice as a convention."[48]

While Britain's financial situation led Keynes to resist expensive commitments to the Bank, it also provided an incentive for British officials to back the establishment of the IBRD as soon as possible. As Keynes put it, "failing this, there will be the strongest pressure on us to make advances far beyond what we can afford."[49] At the Atlantic City conference, Keynes made it clear that the British government was in favor of creating the Bank, and he made some further suggestions, included limiting the size of each country's initial capital subscription.[50] American policymakers largely accommodated the British preferences, setting the stage for the Bank's formal discussion at Bretton Woods.

At the conference itself, Keynes chaired the commission drafting the Bank's articles of agreement and he highlighted its development function in his opening comments. After noting that the Bank would initially focus on reconstruction, he added: "as soon as possible, and with increasing emphasis as time goes on, there is a second primary duty laid upon it, namely, to develop the resources and productive capacity of the world, with special attention to the less developed countries, to raising the standard of life and conditions of labour everywhere, to make the resources of the world more fully available to all mankind, and so to order its operations as to promote and maintain equilibrium in the international

---

47. "Comments on the United States Proposals," April 13, 1944, UKT 247/21.
48. Keynes, "Our Financial Problem in the Transition," May 16, 1944, p. 22, UKT 247/55. See also W. Eady to Richard Hopkins, April 3, 1944, p. 1, UKT 247/27.
49. Keynes, "The Bank for Reconstruction and Development," June 9, 1944, p. 1, UKT 231/354.
50. Mason and Asher 1973, 20; US State Department 1948, vi; Bernstein 1993, 196; Mikesell 1994, 40.

balances of payments of all member countries."[51] As we have seen, Keynes also made an important intervention in favor of Mexico's efforts to ensure that the Bank would give equal consideration to development and reconstruction projects. At the conference, it was also a British official—Lionel Robbins—who insisted on maintaining a reference in the purposes of the Bank to its role in "assisting in raising productivity, the standard of living, and conditions of labor in member countries." Robbins told the other delegates that Bevin would be "very unhappy" if this language was removed.[52]

While Keynes's support for the development role of the IBRD was appreciated by Southern officials, he encountered strong Southern concerns at Bretton Woods about British policy toward sterling balances held in London. Those holding such frozen balances wanted to be able to access the funds, and they also worried that Britain might devalue sterling or not repay these debts in full after the war.[53] At Bretton Woods, the two largest holders of sterling balances—India and Egypt—urged the conference delegates to allow the IMF to help liquidate them. They cast the issue in development terms. As one Indian delegate, Ardeshir Darabshaw Shroff, put it, "our country is pulsating with hopes and aspirations of large scale industrial development to raise the standard of living of four hundred millions of our population. We cannot, therefore, be asked to wait indefinitely till the United Kingdom has reached a stage where sterling would be freely convertible into other currencies."[54] A few days later, Shroff released a press statement that reinforced the point: "if you don't accept our position, you are placing us in a situation which I may compare to the position of a man with a million dollar balance in the bank but not sufficient cash to pay his taxi fare. . . . Mr Morgenthau in his very fine opening address said 'Poverty is a menace wherever it is found.' Do you expect to fulfill the main objectives of the Fund if you allow large countries to be festered with this sort of poverty?"[55]

British officials were very worried about the Indian and Egyptian initiative and they opposed it vigorously.[56] They were supported in this stance by the United States. Although White's early plans had included provisions for liquidating blocked balances, the size of sterling balances had grown enormously since then and US officials were now concerned, in Goldenweiser's words, that "the

51. Keynes 1980c, 73.

52. Robbins quoted in Urquidi 1996, 36.

53. The latter fears were well founded; see Penrose 1953, 55.

54. Shroff in US State Department 1948, 426.

55. US State Department 1948, 1173. For Egypt, see US State Department 1948, 128, 185.

56. See for example Howson and Moggridge 1990, 172–74, 179. Their fears about sterling balances also help to explain the British resistance to the Fund having jurisdiction over capital account transactions (James 1996, 40). The British had made sure that there was no mention of the sterling balance issue in the April 1944 Joint Statement (Mikesell 1994, 24).

amounts involved are so great that they far exceed the entire operation of the Fund."[57] In the end, India and Egypt withdrew their proposal after Keynes made the following public promise: "when the end is reached and we can see our way into the daylight, we will take it without any delay to settle honorably what was honorably and generously given."[58]

Keynes and International Development

Although Keynes supported the inclusion of development issues among the Bretton Woods goals, his interest in the issue did not seem to match that of many US officials. Kapur, Lewis, and Webb note perceptively that Keynes's opening speech to Commission II at Bretton Woods quoted above made "development appear to be a means for international stabilization, rather than its end."[59] As we have seen, this tendency had been apparent from his very early detailed plans in late 1941. Keynes's reference in his opening speech to making the resources of the world "more fully available to all mankind" also downplayed the needs of poor countries themselves and was reminiscent of earlier British justifications of colonialism according to which Britain was developing the resources of its colonies for the world as a whole.[60] To be sure, Keynes did also speak of giving special attention to "the less developed countries" and of raising the standard of living everywhere (and we shall see in the next chapter how he favored international development schemes drawn up in Britain during the war by East Europeans). But for a man of such eloquence, it is striking that he said relatively little about the cause of addressing poverty or raising standards of living in poorer countries, either at Bretton Woods or in his earlier work in postwar planning.

Beyond his early work on Indian currency and finance, Keynes rarely seemed very drawn to the study of economic development in poorer countries throughout his career.[61] Unlike US officials such as White, Welles, Triffin, or Berle, Keynes had traveled very little in developing countries, aside from a holiday in Tunisia and Egypt. Keynes's views of imperialism also seemed much less critical than

---

57. Schuler and Rosenberg 2012, 323. See also Steil 2013, 218; US State Department 1948, 1168–69. White told US delegates at the start of the conference that the United States needed to stay out of the India-UK dispute on this issue (MD, book 749, pp. 14, 19). At the conference, others also opposed the Indian and Egyptian initiative, such as China, France, Poland, and Brazil (Schuler and Rosenberg 2012, 325, 348–49; US State Department 1948, 1173–74).

58. Schuler and Rosenberg 2012, 72. Egypt also secured a British promise to invite Egypt to London "to arrive at a satisfactory solution of the problem" (Schuler and Rosenberg 2012, 572).

59. Kapur, Lewis, and Webb 1997, 62.

60. For the earlier British view, see for example Alcalde 1987, 29; Hodge 2007, 118.

61. Chandavarkar 1989, 146; Arndt 1972, 17; Johnson 1978; Alcalde 1987, 29.

those of many New Dealers. As Chandavarkar puts it, "Keynes's image of British rule in India was that of a paternalistic regime which protected the Indian peasant against the grasping middleman-moneylender and the urban businessman; gave India a sound monetary system; brought moral and material progress with law and order; and, in short, introduced good government." Chandavarkar also observes that Keynes, unlike White, was also "strangely impervious to the infant-industry argument" for tariff protection in developing countries and he was "sceptical of India's industrialisation, and argued with almost Physiocratic fervour that 'her future prosperity is to be sought almost entirely in the application of more skill and knowledge, and especially of more capital, to the methods of agriculture.'"[62]

Keynes has also been criticized by many scholars for dismissing the potential contribution of developing countries at the Bretton Woods conference itself. After learning the details of the planning for the conference in late May 1944, Keynes wrote to two Treasury colleagues: "Twenty one countries have been invited which clearly have nothing to contribute and will merely encumber the ground, namely, Columbia, Costa Rica, Dominica, Ecuador, Salvador, Guatemala, Haiti, Honduras, Liberia, Nicaragua, Panama, Paraguay, Philippines, Venezuela, Peru, Uruguay, Ethiopia, Iceland, Iran, Iraq, Luxemburg. The most monstrous monkey-house assembled for years. To these might be perhaps added: Egypt, Chile and (in present circumstances) Yugo-slavia." He then added some further comments about the membership of the drafting committee that would meet at Atlantic City before Bretton Woods. The United States had already nominated ten countries for the meeting—itself, the UK, Russia, China, Canada, Belgium, Czechoslovakia, France, Brazil, and Mexico—and Keynes noted that US officials had indicated that they would not object if Australia was added to the list. But he also wanted to add Greece and Holland, and US officials stated that they would only accept Holland if Belgium was dropped. When the United States also wanted Cuba included, Keynes was provoked to make the following comment: "Certainly it would seem quite outrageous and hopelessly unreal to put on to the Committee not only a pack of countries which know nothing of international finance but even Cuba whilst excluding Holland and her Empire. Of Dr. White's Drafting Committee, Russia, China, Brazil, Mexico and Cuba, know little or nothing of international finance."[63]

Keynes was clearly wrong to dismiss the international financial knowledge of officials from many of the countries he listed and their contribution to the

---

62. Chandavarkar 1989, 2, 182, 136, 135.
63. Keynes, "The Monetary Conference," to Sir D. Waley and Sir W. Eady, May 30, 1944, pp. 2, 3, UKT 247/28. The country spellings are in the original.

Bretton Woods process. But Keynes's comments also contradicted earlier statements he himself had made. For example, in November 1943, he had told a colleague that the Chinese commentary on the Keynes and White plans was "an excellent piece of work and shows that there are some people in Chungking who thoroughly understand what the whole thing is about."[64] Keynes had also corresponded with officials from countries such as Brazil and Mexico about the plans and was aware of their deep understanding of the issues. His comments at this time very likely reflected his long-standing broader frustration with the US approach to postwar planning. As early as 1941, Keynes had favored a planning process in which the postwar international financial order was designed through Anglo-American bilateral negotiations and in which other countries were invited to join only after the rules had been set.[65] As we have seen, US officials consistently rejected this idea, insisting on a process in which all the United and Associated Nations, large and small, would have an opportunity for input first through informal consultations and then through a multilateral conference.

Kapur, Lewis, and Webb suggest that Keynes's resistance to the US approach may have reflected "an imperial distaste for the democratic charade of an international agreement."[66] It is also worth noting that Keynes had a history of invoking the "monkey-house" metaphor to criticize large formal international meetings in general. As far back as World War I, he had used the phrase to describe the Inter-Ally Council he had attended starting in late 1917 whose core members included the UK, the United States, France, and Italy, and which involved other war allies as appropriate.[67] But there were also concrete national interests at stake in Keynes's opposition to the US preference for a large-scale formal international conference. From the perspective of British officials, this format risked undermining their influence. We have seen how British officials feared that the sheer number of Latin American delegates at the Bretton Woods conference would provide the United States with allies who would hold a dominant share of votes on key issues. On the list of countries Keynes dismissed, Latin American countries were very prominent (as were various other countries with close relations to the United States at the time). When he had first seen White's initial plans in July 1942, Keynes had also expressed deep concern that the voting scheme would allow Latin American countries to outvote Britain and Europe.[68]

---

64. Keynes to Mr. N. E. Young, November 11, 1943, p. 2, UKT 249/3.
65. Keynes 1980b, 45, 54.
66. Kapur, Lewis, and Webb 1997, 62.
67. Steil 2013, 69. He had also used the "monkey-house" image in 1942 with White when arguing against the idea of a large conference (Penrose 1953, 49). See Steil (2013, 164) for another use in February 1943.
68. Keynes 1980b, 162.

When invoking these passages of Keynes, contemporary analysts sometimes also cite a comment of White's at this time as evidence of the latter's equal insensitivity to the voices of Southern countries. One week before Keynes's comment, the British official Redvers Opie had been negotiating the membership of the Atlantic City drafting committee with US and Soviet officials (the Chinese were also involved but did not make the meeting). After one session, Opie reported to Keynes that he and White had discussed privately some further issues, one of which was the following: "He said that he hoped you would not object strongly if someone suggested Cuba. They would be silent members and their main function would be to bring cigars."[69] If we accept Opie's version of this conversation, White's comments were certainly insensitive. But to what extent was White simply playing to British prejudices as part of his effort at the time to enhance Latin American representation at the meeting to offset British influence? White was clearly very concerned at this time about how the British were trying to stack the Atlantic City meeting with their dominions and allies (he considered Greece "nothing but a British stooge" and the Dutch as "almost like Stooges") and he later told Morgenthau that he had addressed this through an agreement with Opie.[70] More generally, as we have seen, White had deep experience with the Cubans and would have known that they had strong views about international monetary and financial issues. Indeed, at the Bretton Woods conference itself, they were far from silent about expressing these views and they acted as a key leader of the Latin American bloc that was supportive of many US goals. As we saw, White even singled them out at the end of the meeting for particular praise for the important role they had played.

One final question needs to be addressed concerning Keynes's perspectives toward development: did he share the enthusiasm of White, Triffin, and other US officials for a new kind of development-oriented money doctoring in poorer countries? Keynes was indeed very critical in the mid-1940s of the British government's practice of establishing currency boards in many of its colonies that guaranteed convertibility of local currencies into sterling at a fixed rate and that were backed 100 percent with sterling reserves held in London. When he was asked to comment in 1945 on Burmese currency reform after the country's liberation from Japanese occupation, he argued that "the existing system of our Currency Boards is . . . so frantically out of date and, indeed, unreasonable from the point of view of anyone's interests but our own, that there is not the smallest chance of inducing any self-governing country to hold it. The notion that a country can

69. Opie to Treasury, Viscount Halifax, No. 391 REMAC, May 24, 1944, p. 2, UKT 247/29.

70. Quotes from MD, book 740, p. 84; book 749, p. 145. For his insistence on greater Latin American representation at Atlantic City to offset British allies, see also the discussion in the next chapter.

only expand its domestic purchasing power when it is in a position to cover the increase 100 per cent with foreign resources, belongs I am convinced, to an era of thought that can never return."[71] In another memo, he described the 100 percent requirement as a means of "cheating the Colonies," and declared, "whether we are justified in using our prerogative to go on taking money off the other Colonies in so indefensible a way is a question of conscience."[72] For Burma, he suggested that the 100 percent sterling cover be reduced to create a fiduciary note issue that would provide extra resources to the Burmese government, an arrangement that he argued might also reduce the need for British financial assistance.

Keynes's willingness to challenge colonial monetary orthodoxy had also emerged early in his career during his discussion of Indian currency and finance. In his first book in 1913, he advocated the creation of a state-owned central bank for India, an idea that was not popular in most British official circles at the time. He also argued that the framers of the new bank's constitution should "put far from their minds all thoughts of the Bank of England," and should look instead for a proper model in the "state banks of Europe, especially in that of Germany, or in those perhaps of Holland or Russia."[73] Those state-owned banks, he averred, were less inclined to follow the automatic strictures of the gold standard, which allowed them to give greater priority to domestic goals. Keynes also hoped India's central bank could be engaged in commercial banking and in encouraging the general development of banking in India. As Chandavarkar puts it, "Keynes was the first economist to present the economic rationale for a central bank as a developmental agency to promote financial intermediation and finance economic development in an emergent economy, instead of being merely a controller of the monetary system as in developed economies like England."[74] In these ways, Keynes's ideas were a precursor to those of US and Latin American officials in the early 1940s (although I have found no evidence that the latter drew on them).

This side of Keynes's thinking did not, however, find an outlet during the Bretton Woods negotiations. British officialdom remained committed to backing orthodox monetary policies in developing countries within its sphere of influence at this time. Policymaking in this area was dominated by more conservative officials from the Colonial Office, the Foreign Office, and the Bank of England rather than by Keynes's Treasury. A particularly clear example of the contrast between British and US views on this issue appeared in the case of one of the few African countries that was represented at the Bretton Woods conference: Ethiopia.

71. Keynes to Rowe-Dutton, "Burma Currency," July 10, 1945, p. 2, UKT 247/5.
72. Keynes to D. Waley, "Burma Currency," June 7, 1945, pp. 1–2, UKT 247/5.
73. Keynes 1980a, 168.
74. Chandavarkar 1989, 138.

British vs. American Money Doctoring in Ethiopia

Africa had few representatives at Bretton Woods for the simple reason that most of the continent was under colonial rule in 1944. Ethiopia, together with Egypt, Liberia, and South Africa, were the only African countries invited to the meeting. South Africa's conservative government led by Jan Smuts did not show much interest in development issues at the conference and Liberia's delegation contributed little to the discussion (and then did not even join the IMF until 1962). Egypt's delegation was more engaged with the development debates, joining India in demanding action on sterling balances and emphasizing the need to support Southern industrialization goals.[75]

The official records of the conference do not record many contributions of the small Ethiopian delegation, but its chairman Blatta Ephrem Tewelde Medhen (the Ethiopian minister to the United States) made such a good impression on some US officials that they pushed (unsuccessfully) for his inclusion among the speakers in the final ceremonies.[76] He was also one of only a few foreign delegates featured in a special CBS radio show about the Bretton Woods conference that was broadcast on July 18, 1944. There, he took the opportunity to tell the US audience about his country's aspirations to "raise our standard of living."[77] It was outside of the conference, however, in the Ethiopian government's discussions on monetary reform with U.S. and UK officials, that the clearest example of the link between development goals and Bretton Woods was brought out in the African context.

After Ethiopia had been liberated from a five-year Italian occupation in 1941, the British government recognized its independence in a January 1942 agreement but insisted—much to the frustration of Emperor Haile Selassie and other Ethiopians—on retaining final authority on some issues, including those relating to currency.[78] The question of currency reform quickly became a major source of friction between British and Ethiopian officials. At the time, the Ethiopian monetary system consisted of a chaotic mix of foreign currencies, including the silver Maria Theresa thaler that had long served as a key monetary instrument in the country. Under a plan presented to Ethiopian officials in April 1942, the British proposed the creation of a new national currency, the Ethiopian pound, whose management would be modeled on the currencies of British colonies in

---

75. For Egyptian support for Southern industrialization, see US State Department 1948, 1194. For India's support, see chapter 9.

76. MD, book 756, p. 273.

77. MD, book 755, p. 266.

78. Degefe 1995.

East and West Africa. The currency would be pegged to sterling, backed 100 percent by reserves, and managed by a London-based currency board run by two
British officials and one representative of the Ethiopian government.[79] Foreign
exchange earned from exports would continue to be surrendered to the British
exchange control board, even though Ethiopia had not been formally admitted
as a member of the sterling area.[80]

The Ethiopian government refused the British plan. If a currency board was to
be created, they wanted it under their full control in Addis Ababa.[81] But like their
Latin American counterparts, Ethiopian officials in fact favored the creation of
a central bank that would actively manage the money supply and credit creation
with domestic development goals in mind. They stated that a currency board
would simply generate procyclical episodes of deflation and inflation in the country according to the state of balance of payments. In addition, they argued that
100 percent backing of the currency would lock up precious foreign exchange
that could be used for developmental purposes such as importing capital goods.
They also objected to the constraints imposed by British exchange controls. More
generally, they viewed Britain's proposal for a sterling-based currency board as an
effort to turn the country into a protectorate or colony.[82]

In the face of British intransigence, the Ethiopian government chose unilaterally in August 1942 to reopen the Bank of Ethiopia that Selassie had established
before the Italian occupation.[83] Although its purposes were initially described
simply as offering industrial loans and acting as the government's fiscal agent,
the ultimate goal was to transform it into a modern central bank managing a
new Ethiopian currency.[84] To achieve that goal, the government's top financial
official, British-educated economist Yilma Deressa, decided to reach out to the
US government for backing.[85] On a trip representing Ethiopia at the Hot Springs
conference between May and August 1943, Deressa met with various US officials, making the case that international financial and technical assistance for
Ethiopia's development goals was "implied in the Atlantic Charter."[86] Ethiopia
had already been made eligible for Lend-Lease in late 1942 and US officials were

---

79. For the British plans, see Degefe 1995, 237, 242–23 and Deressa to White, July 21, 1943, TSF,
Entry 67A245, box 2.

80. William Cole, "The Current Banking and Exchange Situation in Ethiopia," February 28, 1944,
DSFS, Ethiopia, Classified and Unclassified General Records 1943–1955, box 3.

81. Deressa to White, July 21, 1943, TSF, Entry 67A245, box 2.

82. Degefe 1995.

83. Schaefer 1992.

84. For the bank's initial purpose, see Degefe 1995, 236–38; Mauri 2010.

85. His British education is mentioned in Norberg (1977, 83 n. 39) but I have found no other
details.

86. Deressa to US Secretary of State, June 24, 1943, p. 3, DSFS, Ethiopia, Classified and Unclassified General Records 1943–1955, box 1; MD, book 654, pp. 170ff.

now very much in favor of offering assistance, with Adolf Berle taking on the task of coordinating help.[87]

The United States had only some "minor" strategic and economic interests in the country at the time.[88] The primary US interest in supporting Ethiopia stemmed from the country's broader symbolic importance. As one prominent US adviser to the Ethiopian government later put it, "Ethiopia had become the first of the states opposing Axis aggression to be freed from its domination. The United States was anxious to embark upon a program of rehabilitation there to serve as encouragement to the peoples of countries still under enemy occupation."[89] Roosevelt was particularly concerned that British conditions at Ethiopia's expense in the 1942 agreement were inconsistent with the Atlantic Charter and he worried that Britain was trying to impose a protectorate on the "First to be Freed."[90] As an independent African country, Ethiopia had also long been important to many African Americans "as a symbol of Black power, pride, and possibilities."[91] African Americans had protested very actively against Italy's invasion of the country in the mid-1930s as well as against the US decision not to become involved in the conflict.[92] United States officials were quite conscious of the symbolic value of assisting Ethiopia in this situation; as one internal State Department memo put it in late 1942, US assistance would show "in a concrete way the interest of the United States in the stake which Negroes have in this war."[93]

As part of his requests for US assistance, Deressa met with Harry Dexter White and other Treasury officials to discuss the country's monetary problems. Included in some of the meetings was George Blowers, an American to whom Deressa had offered the governorship of the Bank of Ethiopia in June without notifying the British or even the incumbent governor (a Canadian with British citizenship

---

87. "Proposed Export-Import Bank Loan to Ethiopia," July 19 1943, DSDF, 884.51/7-2944. For Berle's role, see for example Berle to Mr. Pierson, August 4, 1943, and Morgenthau to Berle, August 6, 1943, DSDF, 884.51/66.

88. Quote from "Memorandum of Conversation: Monetary Problems involved in American Supplies to Ethiopia," June 6, 1944, pp. 6–7, DS, Lot File No. 56 D 418 Office of African Affairs, Subject File, 1943–55, file: Middle East-Financial Pool-1944 Ethiopia. The US war effort in Europe and the Middle East benefited from cereal purchased from Ethiopia as well as from machinery and radio communications facilities in the country. Some US firms were interested in oil concessions and civil aircraft rights in the country (Spencer 1984, 104, 113; Marcus 1983).

89. Spencer 1984, 103; see also Marcus 1983.

90. Spencer 1984, 104.

91. Gramby-Sobukwe 2005, 784.

92. Scott 1993.

93. Quoted in Spencer 1984, 103–4. When prominent financial officials from many countries attended a conference in Savannah, Georgia in 1946 to establish the IMF, local crowds showed almost as much interest in the arrival of the Ethiopian delegation as they did in that of the famous Keynes. The fact that the country was represented by George Blowers, a white American head of the Bank of Ethiopia, however, created what one US official called "a big letdown for everybody" (McKinzie 1972, 45).

named Charles Collier).[94] Blowers was a useful ally for Deressa, and he would represent Ethiopia at the Bretton Woods meetings along with Medhen and a secretary, Helen Willard. In addition to being "strongly anti-British,"[95] Blowers had previously worked for the Bank of Monrovia (Liberia's only bank) where he had helped the country's government in mid-1942 to lobby the US Treasury to back a Liberian plan to replace British coin with US currency.[96] At the time, White had concluded that it might be best to avoid offending Britain and simply allow the use of US currency to grow naturally as US army spending in Liberia expanded.[97] But when Deressa presented him with plans for the Ethiopian currency reform, White was more willing to challenge British influence.

At a July 1943 meeting with Deressa and Blowers (and after consulting with the State Department), White indicated his willingness to back Ethiopia's desire for a new currency.[98] He suggested that the currency use the decimal system (and Deressa reported at a meeting in August that Ethiopia would use the dollar as its unit[99]); that Ethiopia should create a fiduciary issue of the currency equal to approximately 50 percent of the East African currency presently in circulation (which would be retired); and that the rest of the issue should be backed 100 percent in foreign exchange and gold. He also suggested that the US Exchange Stabilization Fund might be able to lend funds to help Ethiopia acquire reserves for the new currency, although he added that nothing could be done before the 1942 UK-Ethiopia agreement ended.

In May 1944, two months before the Bretton Woods conference, the Ethiopian government gave notice that it would terminate the 1942 agreement and by

---

94. (Illegible name) to Secretary of State in Washington, December 28, 1943 and Caldwell to Secretary of State, October 22, 1943 and (Illegible name) to John K. Caldwell, December 6, 1943, DSFS, Ethiopia, Classified and Unclassified General Records 1943–1955, box 1. For the initial offer of employment, see also "Memorandum of Conservation: Governor of the State Bank of Ethiopia," June 22, 1943, DSDF, 884.516/15. Blowers formally assumed the position in mid-November.

95. Source 1067, "Anglo-Ethiopian Relations." August 20, 1945, p. 1, DSFS, Ethiopia, Classified and Unclassified General Records 1943–1955, box 6.

96. Before joining the Bank of Monrovia in 1937, Blowers had worked in Singapore and China for National City Bank (which perhaps not coincidently was printing the new Ethiopian notes). Source 1067, "American Advisers with the Ethiopian Government," August 20, 1945, DSFS, Ethiopia, Classified and Unclassified General Records 1943–1955, box 6. For National City Bank's printing of the notes, see W. Doll to Lord De La Warr, December 15, 1944, FO 921/358.

97. See for example Southard, "Liberian Currency Problem," July 13, 1942, CFHDW, box 8, Chron. 37; White to Bell, April 23, 1942, CFHDW, box 7, Chron. 34. For White's involvement in this Liberian episode, see also Boughton 2009, 15. The Liberian government did finally make the US dollar sole legal tender on January 1, 1944.

98. "Memorandum of a Meeting in Mr. White's Office, July 9, 1943," ITM, box 21; Glendinning to White, July 16, 1943, TSF, Entry 67A245, box 2. See also J. W. Gunter to Mr. White, "Meeting in Mr. White's Office with Representatives of Ethiopia on May 15, 1943," May 22, 1943, CFHDW, box 9, Chron. 47.

99. C. D. Glendinning, "Meeting in Mr. White's Office, August 12, 1943, with the Ethiopian Minister of Finance," ITM, box 21.

December a new treaty had been signed with Britain giving Ethiopia full sovereignty, thus clearing the way for the currency plan to be introduced. At the time of the May 1944 announcement, the country's new notes and coins had already begun to be produced secretly in the United States. Not until December 1944 were the British finally made aware of Deressa's and Blowers's plan for a new Ethiopian dollar, although Medhen had made no secret in his CBS radio interview at Bretton Woods of the fact "it is our hope that after this war we will have our own medium of exchange."[100] After the British learned of the detailed plan, British officials said they had "very little hope for the new currency" although they also acknowledged that "we cannot stop this scheme however crack brained we think it."[101] But when the Ethiopian dollar was finally introduced on the emperor's birthday in July 1945, British officials were forced to acknowledge that the new currency "was an immediate success."[102]

United States officials were much more welcoming of the new currency, stating that the new Ethiopian monetary legislation was "well adapted to the International Monetary Fund."[103] Federal Reserve officials called the 1945 monetary reform "a step toward the economic emancipation of Ethiopia." They also highlighted the broader connection between Ethiopia's development aspirations and its participation in the Bretton Woods institutions, noting that the IMF would help support its fragile balance of payments while the IBRD would provide crucial foreign capital to "carry through a program of long-term development."[104] Indeed, when the Ethiopian government requested US comment on the legislation it had introduced in July 1945, Treasury officials suggested modifications that might allow the monetary system to serve the country's development goals even better. Because of the need to build confidence in the new currency, the Ethiopian government had initially backed it with a reserve fund made up of a minimum of 75 percent of gold, silver, and foreign currencies and a maximum of 25 percent in Imperial Treasury debt.[105] One of White's staff prepared a memo that recommended lowering gold, silver, and foreign exchange share below 75 percent in order "to allow for an expansion in government financial operations or a higher level of domestic production." The memo also suggested that

---

100. MD, book 755, p. 266.

101. Quotes from W. Doll to De La Warr, December 15, 1944, p. 3, FO 921/358; and Miss Evans, December 22, 1944, p. 1, FO 921/358.

102. "Economic Report," p. 5, J2264/210/1, FO 371/53461. See also Spencer 1984, 166. Although the government had also hoped to eliminate the Maria Theresa thaler from circulation immediately, the thaler's use persisted for a number of years afterward (e.g. H. D. Jellinek to Knoke, February 11, 1947, ISF, box 114).

103. Wasserman 1946, 361.

104. H. D. Jellinek to Knoke, May 17, 1946, p. 1, 5, ISF, box 114.

105. Wasserman 1946, 360.

Ethiopia's legislation provide more detail about the ability of the government to sell its debt to the central bank, because deficit financing might be desirable "if the Ethiopian government intends to engage directly in the financing of the internal industrial development of the country." In addition, the absence of any provisions for exchange controls was noted and the memo encouraged this gap to be remedied.[106]

This advice was in keeping with the general tone of the recommendations that White had backed in Cuba and Honduras and that Triffin was promoting elsewhere in Latin America. White approved the ideas, but he was also very aware that they departed considerably from British views of appropriate Ethiopian currency policy. To avoid controversy with the British, he recommended that the memo be sent to Ethiopian authorities through unofficial channels.[107] The differing perspectives of American and British officials on Ethiopian reforms were indeed striking, and they reflected a deeper contrast between the two sets of policy-makers in their views toward monetary policy in Southern countries. While the Americans were keen to assist in the creation of central banks with developmental missions, the British worked actively against this in Southern countries within their sphere of influence, preferring to maintain sterling-backed currency board arrangements.

The British preferences partly reflected the financial conservatism of many of the country's officials as well as the fact that sterling-backed currency boards supported its fragile balance of payments. But British policy was also influenced by imperial attitudes. In Ethiopia, local British officials were very resentful of Blowers and other Americans who were seen, in the words of one British Foreign Office bureaucrat, to "pander to the worst Ethiopian instincts rather than advise in accordance with the British schoolmasterly tradition."[108] Local British policymakers also described the Ethiopians in charge of financial and economic affairs as "nothing more than unqualified, incompetent and greedy amateurs." By contrast, US officials often saw the British complaints about Ethiopian officials as "exaggerated" and simply "an attempt to disparage Ethiopia's efforts to handle her own political and economic affairs."[109] More generally, US officials also

---

106. REH, "Ethiopia's Plan for a new monetary system," October15, 1945, pp. 1, 2, TSF, Entry 67A245, box 2.

107. It is unclear whether the memo was ever sent. See Frank Coe to Glendinning, November 23, 1945; Coe to White, December 10, 1945, Coe to Gunter, December 13, 1945; TSF, Entry 67A245, box 2.

108. D. Riche, January 20, 1945, p. 1, FO 371/46049.

109. Glendinning to Glasser, July 9, 1946, p. 1, TSF, Entry 67A245, box 2. British quote from W. Doll to De La Warr, November 6, 1944, p. 1, FO 921/358. See also Scrivener, "Ethiopia," memorandum to Secretary of State, August 9, 1945, FO 371/46053.

complained that British advisers in Ethiopia were "dominated by crude concepts of Empire" and "no effort is made to help the country develop."[110]

There is no question that the British government backed commitments to international development during the Bretton Woods negotiations, but British officials certainly did not play any kind of leadership role in this area. Keynes's proposals for development lending in his first detailed drafts appeared largely derived from US ideas and he also deliberately left the development of the IBRD to the Americans. He was also reluctant about committing public money for development lending, thus contributing to the watering down of the IBRD's direct lending role in favor of its function of guaranteeing private investment. British officials also showed little interest in some of the other development issues that White addressed in his initial plans, such as regulation of capital flight and debt restructuring, and they were less inclined to support import-substitution industrialization and new US-backed approaches to money doctoring. In addition, the British government's stance toward frozen sterling balances was unpopular among important Southern countries, and British officials were much less keen than the Americans on involving Southern countries in the design of the postwar international financial order.

These British views on development were influenced by a variety of factors, such as the country's financial constraints, imperial and conservative attitudes, the desire to maximize British influence on postwar plans, and Keynes's own intellectual interests. To be sure, there were some British officials, particularly those on the left such as Bevin, whose enthusiasm for international development matched that of many US New Dealers. The same was true of officials from other parts of the world who sought to influence British policy, including not just Ethiopian policymakers but also individuals such as Lewis, Bryce, Bruce, and McDougall. As we shall see, the British also encountered strong backing for international development from their most important colony, India, as well as from a number of figures from eastern Europe who were living in London during the war.

---

110. James Landes, "American Policy in the Middle East," (n.d., but stamped October 11, 1944), Annex E, p. 1, DSFS, Ethiopia, Classified and Unclassified General Records 1943–1955, box 2.

ENTHUSIASM FROM EASTERN EUROPE AND INDIA

Although many British officials were not terribly passionate about the incorporation of international development goals in Bretton Woods, they were certainly aware of the enthusiasm for it elsewhere in the world. Two sources of this support were particularly close to home for the British. First, a number of analysts and policymakers with links to eastern Europe who were living in Britain during the war developed detailed plans for postwar international assistance for state-led industrialization policies designed to address the low standards of living within their region.[1] Their ideas were very similar to those that had arisen in the US–Latin American context; indeed, policy innovations in the latter were even cited by eastern Europeans. The ideas of these eastern Europeans contributed to both British and US debates on postwar plans as well as the Bretton Woods process directly through the official representation of eastern European countries in the negotiations.

Second, the British were also very conscious during the Bretton Woods negotiations of the demand for development coming from their colonies that British officials involved in colonial administration, such as Hailey, had highlighted in their discussions of postwar planning. But most British colonial subjects had no

---

1. I have used the term "eastern Europe" throughout the book because it was commonly used by the individuals most relevant to my analysis in this chapter, although the discussions also sometimes concerned "south eastern Europe," "eastern and south-eastern Europe," "central Europe," "central and south-east Europe," and "east-central Europe."

opportunity to comment directly on postwar plans (unless they were employed in the Colonial Office, as in Arthur Lewis's case). India, however, was an important exception. The British-run Government of India consulted Indian opinions on the postwar international financial plans and it was also represented at the Bretton Woods conference itself with a delegation that included Indians. Indian officials and analysts drew strong links between their development aspirations and the Bretton Woods negotiations, and they urged the inclusion of international development objectives within the postwar international financial order.

Eastern European Perspectives

Historian Joseph Love has demonstrated the importance of intellectuals from eastern Europe in the emergence of modern development economics.[2] As early as 1929, thinkers such as the Romanian Mihail Manoilescu began to develop theoretical justifications for import-substitution industrialization that built explicitly on Friedrich List's nineteenth-century ideas. Manoilescu discussed the disadvantages facing commodity-producing countries in international trade within a broader political discourse about the international struggle between "proletarian" and "plutocratic" nations and the need for a "socialism of nations."[3] As Love put it, "he thus anticipated demands by Third World governments in the 1970s for a New International Economic Order." Love also highlights how these ideas traveled to Latin America and were known by Prebisch and others who subsequently pioneered Latin American "structuralist" thought (although Prebisch denied that Manoilescu was an influence on his ideas).[4] It is also interesting that Harry Dexter White had read thoroughly Manoilescu's 1929 book on international trade in the early 1930s, although he was critical of it.[5]

In the late 1930s and early 1940s, eastern European countries found themselves in a very different international political situation from that of Latin America. While White and other New Deal policymakers increasingly supported Latin American development goals, eastern European countries faced a dominant regional power—Germany—with quite different views. Rather than sympathizing with their industrialization aspirations, the Nazis saw eastern European

---

2. Love 1996, 5.
3. Quoted in Love 1996, 84.
4. Love 1996, 84, 135. Bank of Mexico officials were also influenced by Manoilescu's ideas as well as by those of Rosenstein-Rodan (Gootenberg 2004, 247).
5. Rees 1973, 39.

countries playing a role as agricultural exporters within a German-controlled regional economy. When Manoilescu became involved in profascist politics during the late 1930s, even he endorsed this role for Romania, renouncing his earlier advocacy of import-substitution industrialization.[6]

When British officials signaled their interest in international development issues as part of postwar planning, a number of analysts and officials with links to eastern Europe, who had moved to Britain during the 1930s and wartime, saw an opportunity to finally build international support for the development aspirations of the region. They played a particularly significant role within the RIIA's Economic Group (see last chapter), which had stressed "the release of all peoples from poverty" and "the advancement of standards of living" as goals for postwar planning in its initial mid-1941 deliberations. From the very start, the Economic Group showed a particular interest in promoting the development of eastern Europe. In an early planning paper from May 1941, the group prioritized "International Public Works" and emphasized the need for further discussion of the "needs of eastern Europe" in terms of "capital investment."[7]

The key staff member of the Economic Group, a German émigré Heinz Wolfgang Arndt, later explained that the interest in this region partly reflected "the presence in London of several refugee governments and economists from Czechoslovakia, Poland, and Yugoslavia."[8] Indeed, in June 1941, the group solicited a presentation from the former governor of the Polish National Bank, Leon Baranski, on the problems of the region. Baranski's presentation demonstrated well the interest in international development among some eastern European policymakers. In the postwar period, he argued, the region would need "an influx of foreign capital in order to secure the economic development of those countries and their industrialisation."[9] Official foreign financial assistance could provide foreign exchange needed to import machines and equipment from Western powers that would, in turn, build up the production of mass-consumption goods for their own internal market. This program of foreign-assisted, import-substitution industrialization would, he argued, correct these countries' "economic lack of balance." He lamented how Germany had made the region into "the granary of the Reich," arguing that their future could not be based on agricultural exports since they could never compete with lower-cost producers in countries such as the United States, Canada, Argentina, and Australia. He also highlighted the

---

6. Love 1996, 78, 94–95.
7. "Draft Syllabus for Group Discussions, May 8, 1941," p. 4. RIIACR, Economic Group, Group Papers 9/22b.
8. Arndt 1987, 47. See also Rosenstein-Rodan 1984, 207.
9. "Discussion Meeting: Problems of the Economic Reconstruction of Poland and Central Europe," June 13, 1941, p. 2, RIIACR, Economic Group, Group Papers 9/22b.

strategic need for industrialization. His plan would "create strong economic units, capable of defending themselves" and thus would establish "a political balance of power in Europe" and "help ward off the danger of imperialistic conquest and of economic policies of exploitation and robbery."[10]

Baranski argued that Western powers would benefit from assisting eastern European industrialization not just for this strategic reason. Economically, they would also have new markets for the export of machinery. Echoing US New Deal officials, he argued that "the industrialisation of backward countries does not decrease, but rather increases, their foreign trade."[11] He linked this argument to a vision of a new postwar international division of labor: "some countries should produce the means of production for the whole world, while other countries should use these means of production to produce mass consumption goods for their own internal markets."[12] Interestingly, Baranski pointed to the US public lending to Latin America as a model for his plan: "I would like to mention here the scheme under which the Export-Import Bank took part in financing the industrialisation of South American countries. This and similar schemes applied to a large extent would be sufficient to solve the problem of industrialisation of Central Europe so far as it concerns foreign credit."[13]

Rosenstein-Rodan's RIIA Seminar

In October 1941, the RIIA hired Paul Rosenstein-Rodan as secretary to the Economic Group in order to direct research into postwar economic issues in the eastern European region. Born in Poland, Rosenstein-Rodan had lived in Vienna before coming to Britain where he became a citizen in 1930.[14] At the time he joined the RIIA, he was a member of the department of economics at University College London, and he would remain with the RIIA until early 1947. In August 1942, Rosenstein-Rodan remarked on the growing interest among the Allies in discussing postwar plans and he proposed the creation of a research group involving British and eastern European economists to prepare detailed material to support this planning.[15] In outlining the goals of the research group, he argued that it should explore the "causes of low standards of living in eastern Europe" and the problem of how "to reform the economic structure of South

10. "Problems of the Economic Reconstruction of Poland and Central Europe, Address by Dr. Leon Baranski"), June 10, 1941, pp. 7, 9, RIIACR, Economic Group Paper 6, Group Papers 9/22b.

11. "Discussion Meeting," p. 3.

12. "Problems of the Economic Reconstruction," p. 7

13. "Discussion Meeting," p. 3.

14. Meier and Seers 1984, 205.

15. Rosenstein-Rodan to Wilson, August 24, 1942, RIIACR, Group Papers 9/23a.

eastern Europe (considered as one example of an international depressed area) so as to fit into a World Economy designed to ensure maximization of output by international division of labour." In outlining possible forms of international investment in the region, he also mentioned the possibility of a "T.V.A. for the Danube Valley" and an "International Reconstruction Finance Corporation."[16]

The research group—called the "Economic and Statistical Seminar of British and Allied Economists"—was established by 1943, and it focused on developing statistics and plans for Greece, Yugoslavia, Albania, Bulgaria, Romania, Hungary, Czechoslovakia, and Poland.[17] The seminar included some British economists as well as British officials such as Hubert Henderson, E. Robinson, and Doreen Warriner. But the group was dominated by eastern Europeans, including a number associated with governments-in-exile or ex-officials such as Rudolf Bićanić (vice-governor of the Yugoslav National Bank), Ladislav Feierabend (minister of finance of the Czechslovak government in-exile), and Tadeusz Lychowski (from the Polish Ministry of Commerce and Trade).[18] The group even included a former Bulgarian minister, N. Momtchiloff, despite the fact that Bulgaria was an enemy country. For the eastern Europeans, Rosenstein-Rodan made clear the political importance of the seminar's work:

> More or less detailed investment plans had been prepared in the United States for China. When the problem of international developmental investment may arise, it will be of the utmost importance that comparable plans should exist for Eastern and S. E. Europe. Otherwise, it might happen that too great a proportion of investible funds would go to the only region for which detailed investment plans had been worked out. Such plans should be concrete enough to give the costing and the relative proportions of different industries to be developed.[19]

Rosenstein-Rodan suggested that eastern Europe was just one example of an international depressed area, but in a February 1944 paper titled "the International Development of Economically Underdeveloped Areas," he also went out of his way to argue that eastern Europe deserved priority as a region for international development assistance. He identified five "economically underdeveloped areas" or "international depressed areas": the Far East (India and China),

---

16. "Syllabus of Inter-Allied Economic Seminar, August 1942," pp. 2, 1. This is attached to Rosenstein-Rodan to Wilson, August 24, 1942.

17. "Notes of a Meeting held on Friday October 8th, 1943, at 3 p.m., Economic and Statistical Seminar, Technical Sub-committee," RIIACR, Group Papers 9/23c.

18. A list of the members of the seminar can be found in RIIACR, Group Papers 9/23a.

19. "Memorandum VI: The Problem of Financing Development in Central and South eastern Europe," May 25, 1944, p. 1, Economic Research Group, RIIACR, Group Papers 9/23a.

colonial empires (especially Africa), the Caribbean, the Middle East, and eastern and southeastern Europe. He argued that international investment in the Far East might not result in rising living standards because of rapid population growth in that region. The focus of international investment in colonized regions such as Africa and Caribbean, he predicted, would be focused mostly on increasing agricultural productivity. While the Middle East's prospects were promising, he argued that those of eastern Europe were even better because its standards of living were already the highest of the five areas.[20]

Between 1943 and 1945, the seminar produced an enormous amount of material, including detailed statistics and studies of development plans over a ten-year time frame for postwar eastern Europe. The original plan was that the seminar's work would form the basis for a report of the Economic Group. But in June 1943, Arndt proposed that the group produce its own volume with wider relevance that "would consist of an introductory chapter outlining the general principles of economic planning which should govern the economic reconstruction of an international 'depressed area' such as Eastern and South eastern Europe." He argued that "information on these questions should be of considerable value to all concerned with the economic problems of, for instance, the British Colonies, the Caribbean, and the Far East."[21]

Rosenstein-Rodan did compile such a volume, but it was never published. Instead, he published two articles in 1943–44 in the *Economic Journal* and *International Affairs* that summarized core ideas from the group.[22] The first focused on the "problems of industrialization in Eastern and South-eastern Europe," while the second examined "the international development of economically backward areas" more generally. The latter was based on a lecture that Arndt later described as "at once a manifesto calling on the developed countries to wake up to the needs and demands of the underdeveloped and an example of the application of techniques of economic analysis to the problems of underdevelopment."[23] Taken together, Arndt argues, these two publications "may well be regarded as the beginning of modern development economics," and he credits

---

20. "Chapter 1: The International Development of Economically Underdeveloped Areas," February 1944, in "Analysis and Method in the Study of Economic Development: Selected Papers Relating to eastern Europe, Compiled by Dr. P. N. Rosenstein-Rodan, edited and with an introduction by A. L. Minkes," RIIACCR, Group Papers 9/23qq. This chapter was very similar in content to Rosenstein-Rodan 1944.

21. Arndt to Miss Cleeve, June 15, 1943, p. 1, RIIACR, Group Papers 9/23a.

22. Rosenstein-Rodan 1943, 1944. For the unpublished volume, see "Analysis and Method in the Study of Economic Development." For further material generated by the RIIA seminar, see the two volumes titled "Material on Economic Development of Eastern and S.E. Europe," LSE, Charles Webster papers, COLL MISC 324.

23. Arndt 1972, 29.

Rosenstein-Rodan with being "the founder of the structuralist school of development economics" that called attention to the distinctive structural problems facing poorer countries.[24] As Rosenstein-Rodan himself later put it in discussing the formation of his RIIA research seminar, "I recognized that underdeveloped countries have special economic problems. It is obvious today but was considered somewhat heretic in 1942."[25]

The core recommendation in Rosenstein-Rodan's publications—and the seminar's larger unpublished volume—was that the industrialization of poorer regions should be assisted by large-scale international public investment. Industrialization was seen as crucial to generate rising living standards in these regions, but it was also viewed as serving a wider international political purpose. Rosenstein-Rodan pointed out that income distribution between nations had widened over the previous one hundred years to the point where 29 percent of the world's population now owned more than two-thirds of the world's total wealth. He argued that this inequality posed not just a moral problem but also a political one, "because we can assume that people will always prefer to die fighting rather than to see no prospect of a better life. If we want to ensure a stable and prosperous peace, we have to provide for some international action to improve the living conditions of those peoples who missed the industrialisation 'bus' in the nineteenth century."[26]

Echoing Stanley Bruce's emphasis on the need for an "equality of opportunity" among countries, Rosenstein-Rodan argued: "International action is required to redress the imbalance and to give the depressed areas of the world, I do not say an equal income, but equality of opportunity." He noted: "there was no counterpart in the international system to the State mechanism within the advanced countries, which could exercise a distributive function in regard to wealth."[27] But the promotion of industrialization of poorer areas was "*the* way of achieving a more equal distribution of income between different areas of the world by raising incomes in depressed areas at a higher rate than in the rich areas."[28] He summed up: "The development of the economically underdeveloped areas of the world is, therefore, the most important task facing us in the making of the peace."[29]

24. Arndt 1987, 47–48; 1996, 1.
25. Oliver 1961c, 1. Rosenstein-Rodan (1984, 207) later argued that the term "underdeveloped countries" appeared "for the first time" in his RIIA seminar, but this is not accurate given the other work we have examined in the inter-American context.
26. Rosenstein-Rodan 1944, 158.
27. Rosenstein-Rodan 1944, 158–59, 158.
28. Rosenstein-Rodan 1943, 202. Emphasis in original.
29. Rosenstein-Rodan 1944, 159.

Rosenstein-Rodan also argued that supporting industrialization in poorer countries was in the economic interest of the world. In the absence of international help, poorer regions might set out to industrialize on their own by relying on internal savings with the aim of achieving "self-sufficiency" (as the Soviet Union had). That strategy that would be slower and involve a sacrifice of living standards, and it would also be wasteful from a global economic standpoint "because each area should specialize on such products as are particularly suited to it." If countries received international help, they could "be fitted more easily into a world economy which would preserve the advantages of an international division of labour and would therefore, in the end, produce more wealth for everybody."[30] Like Baranski, he suggested that international investment could support the development of labor-intensive industry initially while richer countries supplied the necessary machinery.

Rosenstein-Rodan argued that public international investment was needed for this purpose because of the political risks in international lending and the scale of the task. He also pointed out that private investors had no incentive to take on "many investments which are profitable in terms of 'social marginal net product,' but do not appear profitable in terms of 'private marginal net product.'"[31] He proposed the creation of a government-run international trust, the Eastern European Industrial Trust, in which creditor and debtor countries would each acquire 50 percent of the shares. When the RIIA's Economic Group discussed the issue, they also agreed that public loans would be necessary because the private loans of the 1920s to eastern Europe had not been well coordinated and usually did not boost productive capacity of countries, leading to the defaults of 1930s. In order to avoid the problems of the past, the Economic Group argued that "it would be necessary to ensure that capital imports should be utilised and distributed according to a co-ordinated plan."[32]

Rosenstein-Rodan did not refer to the Bretton Woods plan for the IBRD, but later, in a 1961 interview, he argued that his proposal "was in a way a contribution towards it and it was intended as a contribution towards it." At that time, he stated that his first article had been published when the Bank "was not yet thought out" and that he had been in touch with Keynes who (along with Hubert Henderson) "at once took very much to this programming for underdeveloped countries approach" and "took up with great enthusiasm this idea." When asked by the interviewer whether his suggestion helped persuade Keynes that the Bank

---

30. Rosenstein-Rodan 1944, 161–62.
31. Rosenstein-Rodan 1943, 206.
32. "Memorandum VI," p. 8.

would be a good idea, he replied: "Well, he, undoubtedly, would have had it without it." He continued: "The historian, in the history of ideas, should look at what was in the air and who happened to crystallize it first is, in my opinion, almost a matter of accident. I happen to have formulated it relatively first. Several people were thinking it was the way in which modern economics was moving. I mean whoever happens to crystallize it on paper should not claim too much merit for it because he's a product of his epoch, of his environment, of his time, of its atmosphere."[33] Given the IAB proposal of 1939–40 and other US proposals for development lending before 1942 (including Hansen's proposal which influenced Keynes), Rosenstein-Rodan was right not to overstate his significance. But his ideas and those of his seminar were still important in reinforcing support for international development, particularly in British circles.

Figures associated with Rosenstein-Rodan's RIIA seminar also promoted international development goals through other institutions. One was the Oxford Institute of Statistics where a number of émigré economists were working under the leadership of the Polish economist Michał Kalecki (who was a member of Rosenstein-Rodan's seminar). Hired by the institute in 1940, Kalecki had Keynesian ideas and he had also supported Manoilescu's advocacy of trade protectionism in a 1938 review.[34] In a 1943 article, Kalecki and his German-born colleague E. F. Schumacher (who also participated in Rosenstein-Rodan's seminar) discussed Keynes's clearing union plan, giving particular focus to development issues. In their view, Keynes's clearing union was too focused on preventing advanced countries from accumulating export surpluses. Because these surpluses could be usefully recycled in the form of investment flows to poorer countries, they argued that "any discouragement of surpluses would only slow down the advancement of under-developed regions." In place of the system of penalties on creditor and debtor countries, they favored the idea of attaching an International Investment Board to the ICU that could encourage long-term "development loans" to "industrializing countries" such as Poland and China.[35]

Another economist in Kalecki's circle at the Oxford Institute working on development issues was the German émigré Kurt Mandelbaum (also a member of Rosenstein-Rodan's seminar). As part of its wider work on the postwar world

---

33. Quotes from Oliver 1961c, 51, 52, 53.
34. Love 1996, 92–93.
35. Quotes from Kalecki and Schumacher 1943, 31, 32, 31. Schumacher (1943, 160) had developed some similar ideas and Keynes had been given an early version of that paper in September 1941 just after he completed the first version of his ICU (Keynes 1980b, 21 n. 5). Schumacher's writings were also being read in the US Treasury in July 1942 and Goldenweiser also sent them to White in September 1942; see BWCC, box 14/6 and "United Nations Stab. Fund and Bank: Kindleberger Memo and Various Proposals" BWA, box 27.

economy, the Oxford Institute assigned Mandelbaum the task of working on the postwar reconstruction of southeastern Europe. Drawing on his past work on planning, Mandelbaum transformed his assignment into an ambitious project for transforming the region from an agrarian to an industrial economy with international help.[36] His work was published in 1945 as *The Industrialization of Backward Areas,* a book that became a classic in development economics. Mandelbaum saw his work on the "conditions of under-development" as building upon and updating the ideas of the nineteenth-century economic nationalists Friedrich List and Henry Carey. As he put it, "in an open international system, advantages once gained tend to become cumulative and handicaps to be perpetuated so that in the end poor countries may remain poor just because they were poor to begin with. This tendency—or one aspect of it—was noted very early by Carey and List."[37]

In July 1944, the prominent British think tank Political and Economic Planning (PEP) also published a report calling for the "economic development of South-East Europe" that had been prepared by "people from the countries concerned." The report argued that after the war "it would be intolerable to condemn them again to the conditions of political insecurity and economic backwardness which were their lot before the war." Focusing on Poland, Hungary, Romania, Bulgaria, Yugoslavia, and Greece, the report argued that "these countries will never attain economic security unless conditions for their inhabitants are greatly improved according to a long-term programme of economic development." Researchers from the region "had not only hammered out a way of approach but had evolved a working model for regional economic advance which was capable of application to several of the world's great backward areas."[38]

Eastern Europe and the Bretton Woods Negotiations

These various ideas were echoed by eastern European officials during the negotiations leading up to Bretton Woods. Like their US counterparts, British officials began in the second half of 1942 to consult with other countries about postwar international financial plans. These consultations initially took place with the British dominions (Canada, Australia, New Zealand, and South Africa) and India, but they soon widened to include financial officials from European Allied governments, including representatives from Poland (such as Baranski), Czechoslovakia (such as Feierabend), Yugoslavia, and Greece. At a meeting in late February 1943, Keynes described his ICU proposal to these governments for the

36. Mandelbaum 1979, 511.
37. Mandelbaum 1961 (1945), 4.
38. "Economic Development in South-East Europe," pp. 2, 1, in *Planning,* no. 223 (July 21, 1944).

first time. The response of the Greek representative, Bank of Greece governor Kyriakos Varvaressos (who would represent Greece at Bretton Woods), was that the plan would not work unless there was also a focus on postwar international financial assistance (a message he repeated to White in mid-1943).[39]

One of the Polish representatives, Hendryk Strasburger, also expressed his hope that the British would be making a statement about postwar international investment plans.[40] Reinforcing Strasburger's message, Baranski sent Keynes a paper around this time outlining his plan for "an international economic body along the lines of the Tennessee Valley Authority" that "might be useful for carrying out some fundamental capital investments in this area, as it might also be in other similar areas." His paper outlined a plan for a customs union and regional economic planning in east-central Europe to promote industrialization in the region. As he put it, "the industrialisation of the whole of East-Central Europe is the first pre-requisite of raising the standard of life of its people."[41] He also argued that industrialization was necessary for the countries of the region to become more politically independent from Germany and Russia.

Keynes responded, telling Baranski that this was "a most important paper" and that "personally, I find myself in strong sympathy with all its main proposals and conclusion." He warned that Baranski's proposals would meet many political obstacles, but also declared that "the task must be to try to make sure that nothing is done which will interfere with this line of evolution and everything possible which will encourage it."[42] Keynes then sent the paper and his comments to some colleagues, remarking that his comments to Baranski were "not intended as idle compliments. It is an impressive and interesting piece of work."[43] In a letter the next month to another British official, he commented that "Old Baranski talks in a voice and accent that makes one lose the thread unless one attends carefully. But in fact he is well worth listening to. There is no Allied representative, I think, whose observations go as deep as his."[44]

A few months later, Baranski also participated as one of the Polish representatives in White's consultations on the US Stabilization Fund proposal in

---

39. "Meeting of Finance Ministers, 26th February, 1943," NAC, RG19 v. 3981, M-1-7-1. For his memo to White, see K. Varvaressos, "The Proposal for a United and Associated Nations Stabilization Fund: The Position of Greece Under the Proposed Plan," July 13, 1943, HDWP, box 8, folder 2. In the latter memo, Varvaressos also stressed the importance of exchange controls for Greece and urged White to include provisions for a transition period.

40. "Meeting of Finance Ministers, 26th February, 1943."

41. Baranski, "East-Central Europe," p. 5, (n.d. but Keynes responded on March 15, 1943), UKT 247/97.

42. Keynes to L. Baranski, March 15, 1943, p. 1, UKT 247/97.

43. Keynes to W. Eady, H. Henderson, and D. Waley on cover of Keynes to L. Baranski, March 15, 1943.

44. Keynes to Philips, April 16, 1943, in Keynes 1980b, 241.

Washington in mid-June 1943 (as did Feierabend for Czechoslovakia). When the Polish team emphasized to White its country's need for external financial assistance after the war, White declared that "we fully appreciate the needs of a country like Poland" and these needs would have to be taken care of by other means than just the Fund.[45] Baranski followed up a week later, meeting with White to discuss his ambitious plan to double Poland's national income in nineteen years through large investments in areas such as industry, agriculture, housing, and communications.[46] When refining his IBRD plan later that fall in cooperation with other US officials, White included Poland along with other eastern European countries such as Greece, Romania, Albania, Bulgaria and Czechoslovakia, in a discussion of countries that would benefit from its lending.[47] After the United States published the IBRD plan in November 1943, the Polish finance minister also expressed his strong support for it.[48]

Baranski and Feierabend were both delegates to the Bretton Woods conference at which their respective countries, Poland and Czechoslovakia, continued to press for external financial assistance. The Polish delegation urged that the IBRD give priority to reconstruction loans, an initiative that is often seen as conflicting with the Latin American goal of giving the "development" role of the IBRD equal billing. It is worth noting, however, that the Polish delegation, when advancing its case for prioritizing reconstruction loans, also highlighted the importance of the IBRD's role in promoting economic development more generally: "We fully appreciate the necessity of creating an International Institution for the purpose of the development of all countries and of the expansion of the productive capacities and for raising the standard of living. We are well aware of this fact because our future, too, depends on the help we receive in expanding the productive capacities of our country."[49] As we have seen, this commitment to the Bretton Woods international development objectives was very genuine.

India and Bretton Woods

Like eastern European officials and analysts, many Indians were keen to see development goals included in postwar international financial planning. Most general accounts of the Bretton Woods negotiations devote relatively little attention

---

45. John Deutsch, "International Stabilization of Currencies—Informal expert discussions, US. Treasury, June 15–17, 1943," p. 55, NAC, RG19 v. 3981.

46. Baranski, "Notes on Poland's Economic Plan," June 25, 1943, HDWP, box 8, folder 3.

47. "Meeting in Mr. White's Office, November 10, 1943," HDWP, box 8, folder 4.

48. Grossfield to Morgenthau, February 4, 1944, BWCC, box 5/4.

49. Quoted in US State Department 1948, 593.

to India's role at the conference.[50] Scholars sometimes mention its initiative to address sterling balances, an initiative that was cast in development terms as noted already. Another issue sometimes discussed was India's unsuccessful effort to secure a quota as large as China's and to be included among the five countries that were guaranteed a single-member seat on the Fund's executive Board.[51] Indians also saw that initiative through a development lens. As some Indian business leaders put it at the time, a guaranteed seat for both India and China was needed to ensure that the "special requirements" of "economically backward and industrially undeveloped" countries were taken into account.[52] Important though these initiatives were, India's effort to inject development content into the Bretton Woods negotiations actually went much further.

Since India did not become independent until 1947, it was represented during the Bretton Woods negotiations by the British-run Government of India.[53] The Government of India's input into the negotiations initially took place primarily via consultation sessions that the British government held with it and the British dominions that began in late 1942 and carried through until early 1944. Not until India was invited to the drafting conference at Atlantic City in June 1944 did the Government of India have more direct contact with US negotiators. Even then, White initially refused to allow Indian delegates to this meeting unless they were part of the British team, arguing that "it would be difficult to announce to the United States public that India as well as Canada and Australia has to be represented on agenda committee."[54] He eventually agreed on the condition that two more countries from the Western hemisphere be added for balance.[55] The three representatives of the Government of India at Atlantic City were then joined by five others at the Bretton Woods conference itself.[56]

---

50. More detailed studies of India's role can be found in Simha (1970, chap. 14), Chandavarkar (2001, 1989, chap. 6) and Mukherjee (2002, 161–72). This section builds on their work while adding new archival material.

51. The top five were the United States, Britain, the Soviet Union, China, and France. India subsequently became a member of the top five when the USSR did not join the institution. Indian delegates apparently told US officials informally that they did not actually expect to receive equal quota size to China's (MD, book 749, p. 14, book 750, p. 87).

52. Quoted in Mukherjee 2002, 169.

53. India had also been one of the signatories of the Declaration of the United Nations in January 1942.

54. Telegram from Washington to Foreign Office, Viscount Halifax, No. 429 REMAC, June 3, 1944, p. 1, UKT 247/29. See also MD, book 740, pp. 84–85.

55. Telegram Washington to Foreign Office, Viscount Halifax, No. 3048, June 6, 1944, UKT 247/29.

56. The three representatives at Atlantic City were Theodore Gregory, Jeremy Raisman, and Chintaman Deshmukh (Simha 1970, 426). For the Bretton Woods delegation, see below.

The Importance of Indian Opinion

In developing its position toward the negotiations, the Government of India initially kept discussions high-level and secret from the Indian public in late 1942 and early 1943. But government officials soon recognized the need to consult broader Indian opinion because of the contentious nature of British rule in India at this time. The Government of India had entered World War II in 1939 without consulting Indian leadership in the provincial governments, the majority of which were run by the Indian National Congress Party since 1937 elections. In response, the Congress Party had asked all its elected representatives to leave their government positions and some called for open revolt against British rule. By 1942, India's strategic significance for Britain had been heightened by the Japanese military successes in Asia, India's contribution of troops to the war effort, and the accumulation of Indian sterling balances in London. In March 1942, the British government sent the Cripps mission to India to discuss some form of greater self-rule or even independence in order to enhance Indian support for the war. Soon after the Cripps mission failed to secure any agreements, the Congress Party launched its "Quit India" campaign that threatened widespread civil disobedience if the British did not withdraw from the country immediately.

In this charged political environment, it is not surprising that Indians demanded greater voice in the Government of India's policy toward the Bretton Woods negotiations. The first demand of this kind came in March 1943 from the board of the colony's central bank, the Reserve Bank of India (RBI), just as the Keynes and White plans began to circulate to various governments. The RBI's lead role in the process stemmed not just from its expertise on monetary issues but also from its composition. When the bank had been created in 1935, the British had insisted on giving it a quasi-private form in which shareholders selected eight of the twelve voting directors on the board (while the viceroy appointed the governor, the deputy governors, and the four other directors). By the time of the Bretton Woods negotiations, the shareholders had elected an Indian majority to the Board. Indeed, Chandavakar notes that "the resignation of the Congress ministries in the provinces and the absence of the Congress Party from the legislatures thrust upon the central board of the Reserve Bank the role of the only elected or representative trustees of India's economic and monetary interests."[57]

British officials were very aware that the Indian majority on the Board had, as one official in October 1942 put it, "strong Congress affinities."[58] After the

---

57. Chandavakar 1983, 795.
58. Secretary of state quoted in Mukherjee 2002, 140.

sudden death of the bank's governor James Taylor in February 1943, the nationalist orientation of many of the board members became even more evident when
they appointed the first Indian—Cambridge-educated Chintaman Deshmukh—
as head of the bank, albeit on a temporary basis. The board then rejected two
Europeans nominated by the Government of India, leading the British secretary
of state for India to intervene and allow Deshmukh to become Taylor's formal
successor in August 1943.[59]

The Government of India initially refused to share the Keynes and White plans
with the RBI. In August 1943, however, it changed course and requested the RBI's
input into the development of government policy toward postwar international
financial plans. The RBI then sent a formal comment on the US and British plans to
the government in November. Around the time that the RBI's views were solicited,
the top financial official of the Government of India, Finance Member Jeremy Raisman, also created a high-level Reconstruction Committee to hear broader Indian
perspectives—official and nonofficial—on the plans.[60] At the first meeting of its
General Policy Committee in January 1944, Raisman stated that the Government
of India had not yet taken an official view on the merits of the British and US plans,
and that "it is clearly desirable that it should take cognisance of public opinion."[61]
The economist R. K. Shanmukhan Chetty challenged Raisman to be sure that the
Government of India would represent India's interest without being dictated to by
Britain, and Raisman assured the committee that it would. Raisman also received
some criticism at the meeting for neglecting to allow Indian experts to develop an
Indian plan at the time that the Keynes and White proposals were being developed.[62]

After the release of the Anglo-American Joint Statement on the Fund in April
1944, the Government of India then conducted a wider consultation, sending
copies to provincial governments and chambers of commerce across the country
and inviting their input.[63] Although the government received fewer comments
than it expected, the official tasked with summarizing the responses concluded
that "the consensus of opinion is in favour of India participating in the scheme."[64]
This consultation process resulted in a number of specific suggestions for the
negotiators, and the RBI also sent the government a letter outlining a number of
issues that it felt needed to be addressed.[65]

---

59. Deshmukh 1974, 122; Chandavarkar 1983, 795.
60. Simha 1970, 407–14, 419.
61. "Record of the First Meeting of General Policy Committee held at New Delhi on the 17th and
18th January 1944," p. 4, NAI, File 88-P. W.R./44.
62. "Record of the First Meeting of General Policy Committee," 15, 10.
63. NAI, Finance Department, File No. 2(52)-F/uu).
64. B. K. Nehru, June 23, 1944, p. 1, NAI, Finance Department, File No. 2(77)-F/uu).
65. Simha 1970, 421.

In selecting the delegation to represent India at the Bretton Woods conference, British officials were pushed by Indian pressure to create a delegation
that allowed for Indian opinion to be expressed. Initially, the delegation was
to include Raisman (as chair), Deshmukh, and Theodore Gregory (who was a
British economic adviser to the government). But at an early May 1944 meeting
of the General Policy Committee of the government's Reconstruction Committee, there were calls for the delegation to be widened to include members outside
of the government because of India's political situation.[66]

Two individuals were then selected to participate as "non-official delegates,"
both of whom had been involved with the General Policy Committee: Chetty
and the businessman Ardeshir Darabshaw Shroff. Chetty was an obvious choice
because he had represented India at a number of international economic meetings since the late 1920s. Shroff was included because he was seen as representative of an Indian nationalist perspective. In the words of one British Treasury
official, "Raisman had told me that it was felt necessary that the Indian Delegation should include at least one person with strong nationalist views and Shroff
was 'nominated' by nationalist interests."[67] The Indian delegation also included
three other individuals: David Meek (Indian Trade Commissioner in London,
who served as an adviser), A. A. Henderson (assistant adviser), and the RBI's
director of research, B. K. Madan (who acted as the delegation's secretary).

After the conference, Chetty and Shroff complained to the *Times of India* that
"the fact that the leader of the Indian delegation at Bretton Woods was not an
Indian was embarrassing and humiliating."[68] At the conference, however, Raisman went out of his way to assign the principal roles to the Indian delegates, and
the minutes of the conference make it clear that the Indians played major roles
in representing the views of the delegation. Chandavarkar argues that "Raisman's
role at Bretton Woods was the most unsordid act of leadership actuated by a
deep sense of mission that India's permanent interests were best served by Indian
spokesmen."[69] Raisman himself believed that India should receive full dominion
status as soon as possible and had earlier groomed Deshmukh for a role in the
RBI as well as mentored Chetty.[70] Deshmukh was the most prominent Indian
delegate, playing a particularly significant role in the discussions of the Bank

---

66. George Merrell to US Secretary of State, May 12, 1944, HDWP, box 8, folder 2.
67. W. Eady to Richard Hopkins, June 14, 1944, UKT 247/28. The Government of India had in
fact intended to invite only one unofficial Indian to join the delegation but, after deciding on Shroff
for the role, they realized an invitation had already been extended to Chetty and so both were invited.
See Raisman to Jones, May 9 1944, and Jones to Raisman, May 11, 1944, NAI, Finance Department,
file: 2(74)-F/1944).
68. Quoted in Chandavarkar 2001, 2652.
69. Chandavarkar 2001, 2652.
70. Deshmukh 1974, 103; Chandavarkar 2001.

(he was nominated as chair of one of the committees developing its role).[71] He and other Indian representatives made a good impression at the conference, with Brazil's Souza Costa telling a Brazilian audience soon after the meeting that India had "brilliant representation" at Bretton Woods.[72]

Development Aspirations and the Fund's Purposes

At the core of India's contribution to the discussions at the conference was an insistence that any postwar international financial system had to favor the development ambitions of poorer countries. At this time, many Indian nationalists (Gandhi was an important exception) had become very committed to the goal of increasing Indian living standards through state-led industrialization. Attracting particular attention was the Bombay Plan, whose first component had been published in January 1944 by eight prominent Indian business leaders. The plan called for ambitious industrial investment to double the country's per capita income in fifteen years, and it envisaged the state playing a major role in the economy, financing and controlling basic industries.[73] In addition to support it garnered among Indian nationalists (although some on the left criticized it as a plan of capitalists), the viceroy even welcomed the plan a few days after its release, despite the fact that Gregory had strongly critiqued its departure from economic orthodoxy (the viceroy chose not to release Gregory's criticism publicly).[74]

Shroff was one of the eight authors of the Bombay Plan. A graduate of the London School of Economics, he was a prominent business figure as a director at the major Indian firm Tata Sons Ltd. Although he had emerged as a strong critic of Nehru's socialist views in the mid-1930s, he was associated with nationalist wing of the business community in Bombay and he was inspired by the New Deal's TVA which he felt showed what state planning could achieve.[75] In speaking to the Reconstruction Committee in early 1944, he argued that any postwar international monetary plans should be assessed on the basis of "whether it would be possible for India to raise the standard of living of her people within the next 10 to 15 years to something like double the existing standard." At the same meeting, Chetty expressed similar views, arguing that "in evaluating these schemes, the main consideration to be kept in mind was how far they would

---

71. Simha 1970, 426–27.
72. Souza Costa, speech at Escola Superior de Guerra, p. 28, FGV, CPDOC, SC pi Costa, S.1944.09.19.
73. Thakurdas et al. 1944.
74. Lokanathan 1945; Rothermund 1993, 125.
75. "A. D. Shroff, 'The Future of India as an Industrial Nation,' Record of General Meeting Held at Chatham House on 12 June 1945," pp. 4–5, RIIA, file 8/112. See also Markovits 1985.

enable us to raise the standard of life of our own people in India by increasing employment and by increasing the national wealth of the country."[76]

Deshmukh was also very keen to foster India's economic development, arguing in early 1945 that "I am more than ever convinced of the imperious necessity of planning, of the assumption of direct initiative by the State for a vast effort of development and amelioration."[77] As RBI governor, Deshmukh expanded the central bank's role to foster the development of rural credit and the creation of an Industrial Finance Corporation.[78] The developmental orientation of the RBI under Deshmukh's leadership was also apparent from its initial formal commentary on the Keynes and White plans in November 1943. It pointed out that these plans, if they were to be acceptable to poor countries such as India, had to include "the making of conscious efforts to raise the standard of living in these countries."[79] Privately, Deshmukh had written to the RBI Board in late September pointing out that the survival of the new international organizations would depend on the willingness of powerful nations to make "temporary sacrifices" of their higher standard of living to "assist in the raising of the standard of living of the poorer and less developed nations."[80]

After the Anglo-American Joint Statement appeared in April 1944 and the RBI Board had discussed its contents, Deshmukh wrote to Raisman complaining that the purposes of the Fund needed to make more explicit reference to the goal of encouraging the development of poorer countries: ". . . no international economic co-operation worth the name will succeed and lay the foundation for enduring international peace and prosperity unless the retarded development of important units like India and China receive special recognition and treatment."[81] The government's countrywide consultations about the Joint Statement had produced a similar suggestion that "the fund should specifically recognise that one of its purposes is to promote internal national development, particularly that of the backward countries."[82]

The Indian delegation to the Atlantic City conference—made up of Raisman, Deshmukh, and Gregory—succeeded in placing on the Bretton Woods agenda an amendment that would make the Fund's purposes more explicitly supportive of development goals. In the Joint Statement released before Atlantic City, one of

---

76. "Record of the First Meeting of General Policy Committee," pp. 12, 15.

77. C. Deshmukh, "Some Thoughts on Post-war Development" (speech made before the Poona Rotary Club, February 25, 1945), p. 17, CDDP, Speeches and Writings Unpublished, S.No. 43(6).

78. "Talk by Sir C. D. Deshmukh On the Bretton Woods Meetings, at the Rotary Club, Bombay on 3rd October, 1944," p. 169, CDDP, Speeches/Writings Unpublished, S.No.43(5).

79. Quoted in Simha 1970, 416.

80. Quoted in Mukherjee 2002, 164–65.

81. Quoted in Simha 1970, 421–22.

82. B. K. Nehru, June 23, 1944, p. 1.

the Fund's purposes had been "to facilitate the expansion and balanced growth of international trade and to contribute in this way to the maintenance of a high level of employment and of real income which must be a primary object of economic policy." India now proposed alternative wording: "To facilitate the expansion and balanced growth of international trade, *to assist in the fuller utilisation of the resources of economically underdeveloped countries* and to contribute thereby to the maintenance in the world as a whole of a high level of employment and real income, which must be a primary objective of economic policy."[83] At the Bretton Woods conference, the Indian delegation explained that this new wording was needed because the Joint Statement's wording seemed "to stress unduly the position of highly industrialised countries."[84] In commenting on draft US and UK proposals before the conference. Indian business leaders had similarly argued that the goal for poorer countries was how to achieve high employment in the first place rather than how to maintain it.[85]

This argument met with some sympathy at the conference. As one Australian delegate acknowledged, "we realise that there are some undeveloped countries whose problem is one of increasing production rather than maintaining employment."[86] Both Australia and Ecuador backed the Indian amendment, while a Peruvian delegate suggested that India's objective could be obtained more simply by adding the words "promote and maintain" in front of "high levels of full employment and real income." Delegates from South Africa, Brazil, the Netherlands, and the United States were much less enthusiastic about India's wording, arguing that it would confuse the Fund's objectives with those of the Bank. Echoing Peru, however, a consensus emerged that the statement of purposes should refer to both the attainment of a high level of employment and real income as well as its maintenance.[87]

The issue was then referred to a drafting committee that presented new wording the next day: "To facilitate the expansion and balanced growth of international trade and to contribute thereby to the promotion and maintenance of a high level of employment and to the development of the sources of productive

---

83. US State Department 1948, 23 (emphasis in original). In an internal memo to the RBI board, the RBI's senior economist J. V. Joshi had initially suggested adding a separate clause stating "that one of the objects of the Fund will be to help in the industrial and agricultural development of backward countries in order to raise their standards of living." (J. V. Joshi, "Note on the Joint Statement by Experts on the Establishment of an International Monetary Fund," May 4, 1944, p. 2, NAI, Finance Department, File No. 2(7)-F/44).

84. US State Department 1948, 118.

85. Mukherjee 2002, 163.

86. US State Department 1948, 836.

87. Schuler and Rosenberg 2012, 305–8; Eugênio Gudin II, Entrevista, 3/7/1979–24/08/1979, p. 131, FGV, Fita 8-B.

power in all member countries as primary objectives of economic policy." The inclusion of the phrase "productive power" was interesting since it was one that List had used and popularized. When the New Zealand delegate suggested replacing the words "productive power" with "unused resources," the Chinese committee chair, Tingfu Tsiang, objected that those words had already been rejected by the drafting committee "since they implied capitalistic development."[88] The drafting committee's wording was then approved by Committee 1 of the commission drafting the Fund's articles of agreement, although Chetty was not fully satisfied and reserved the right to object later.

The Indian delegation subsequently suggested similar text but with the following addition at the end: "with due regard to the needs of economically backward countries."[89] Chetty explained in a speech that the additional phrase was necessary in order to ensure that the reference to "the expansion and balanced growth of international trade" was inclusive of poorer countries' perspectives. As he put it, "a predominant flow of raw materials and food stuffs in one direction and highly manufactured goods in the other direction is not a really balanced international trade from this latter point of view. It is only by greater attention to the industrial needs of countries like India that you can achieve a real and rational balance."[90] In internal Indian discussions, the link between trade policy and the Bretton Woods proposals had been raised earlier. For example, a consultative group of the Reconstruction Committee made up of mostly Indian economists had urged in January 1944 that the Keynes and White plans include a "right to levy protective tariffs and to adopt measures of control for general development."[91] Chetty then ended his speech by noting India's "sad experience" with international organizations, that "the approach to every problem has been from the point of view of economically advanced countries." If his wording was accepted, Chetty argued that "less advanced countries will then have greater hopes of the possibilities of economic development than they were led to believe in the past."[92]

After further discussions, the conference finally settled on the following wording, suggested by Bernstein, for the purposes of the Fund: "To facilitate the expansion and balanced growth of international trade, and to contribute

88. Schuler and Rosenberg 2012, 328–29, 347. The members of the drafting committee were Goldenweiser (chair), Tsiang, Gudin, Jan Mladek (Czechoslovakia), Leslie Melville (Australia), Robbins, and Varvaressos. An Indian delegate was also present.
89. Schuler and Rosenberg 2012, 129.
90. US State Department 1948, 1180–81. See also Schuler and Rosenberg 2012, 129.
91. "Record of the First Meeting of the Finance Sub-committee held on January 12, 1944," p. 2, NAI, External Affairs department, File No. 83(5) P. W.R./44.
92. Schuler and Rosenberg 2012, 129–30.

thereby to the promotion and maintenance of high levels of employment and real income and to the development of the productive resources of all member countries as primary objective of economic policy."[93] Although the statement made no explicit reference to the special needs of poorer countries, some delegates interpreted the wording as endorsing the Indian goal, including in the area of trade policy. For example, Carlos Lleras Restrepo from Colombia argued that the wording implied recognition of "the right of new nations whose resources are not sufficiently developed to move forward on the road which they have already started to travel toward a more complex economy, toward a growing industrialization which may alter, and probably will alter, the volume of international trade in many commodities."[94] After the conference, Shroff also suggested that one of the IMF's objectives was "to see that the economically backward countries got suitable opportunities for rapid development, and that a substantial increase in the standard of living and real income of the people is brought about."[95]

In a speech in India in early 1945, Deshmukh acknowledged that the Indian delegation had not fully achieved its objectives with respect to the wording of the Fund's purposes, but he pointed out that the IBRD's creation reflected a clearer victory for India's goal of embedding a commitment to further the development of poorer countries within the Bretton Woods order as a whole:

> We all now apparently subscribe to the belief that poverty and plenty are infectious, in the international as well as in the national field, and that we cannot hope to keep our own side of the garden pretty if our neighbour's is full of weeds. . . . Even in highly industrialised countries, with large vested interests in world markets, the realization has been borne in all thinking sections of the populations that poor customers are never good customers and that the setting up of industries in mainly agricultural countries together with an improvement in their agricultural production, does not represent a challenge to the industrialised countries. Although the Indian Delegation to Bretton Woods conference failed to get this thought embodied among the purposes of the International Monetary Fund, in the draft agreement relating to the International Bank for Reconstruction and Development we did succeed in getting it included as among the economic goals of all nations.[96]

---

93. Schuler and Rosenberg 2012, 191, 244–45, 247; US State Department 1948, 698.
94. Schuler and Rosenberg 2012, 1186.
95. "A. D. Shroff, 'The Future of India,'" p. 5.
96. Deshmukh, "Some Thoughts," pp. 2–3.

Support for the IBRD and Exchange Rate Flexibility

The Indian delegates had indeed been very much in favor of the IBRD's creation because of the prospect of development loans.[97] In the Indian press, some concerns had been expressed that the Bank might be "merely the apparatus of a new type of colonialism and economic penetration."[98] Business leaders argued, however, the Bank's loans would provide foreign exchange to import capital goods at lower cost and with less chance of political domination than other sources.[99] Even though India was emerging from the war as a major creditor, Indian officials assumed that the country would need to borrow from abroad to help finance its industrialization goals, and they hoped postwar arrangements would ensure an adequate flow of capital to poorer countries.[100] Deshmukh thus strongly supported Latin American efforts to ensure that the Bank gave equal consideration to development projects as against reconstruction ones.[101] After the conference, he also played a lead role in convincing Indian legislators that India should become a member of the Bank after some questioned whether the country might simply end up sharing in losses of other nations' borrowing.[102]

It is worth noting that Indian officials also saw the flexibility of exchange rate commitments in the IMF's articles of agreement as furthering their development goals. During the Great Depression, the Government of India's insistence on a fixed peg to sterling had been very controversial domestically because of its severe contractionary effects at a time of collapsing world agricultural prices and Indian export earnings. At the time, Indian business leaders and nationalists had called for the rupee's devaluation and for a more active and expansionary monetary policy geared toward the internal goal of maximizing industrial growth.[103] In mid-1931, the British finance member of the Government of India (in charge of financial affairs) George Schuster had even noted privately that the government's currency policy was "one of the most important factors in the whole anti-British political movement." The issue remained politically salient at the time of the RBI's creation when Indians pushed for the new central bank to be able to adjust the colony's exchange rate.[104]

---

97. Simha 1972, 48; "Talk by Sir C. D. Deshmukh," p. 141.
98. Quote in Mukherjee 2002, 170.
99. Mukherjee 2002, 161–72.
100. Deshmukh, "Some Thoughts"; Simha 1970, 424; "A. D. Shroff, 'The Future of India.'" The Bombay Plan had also anticipated that some of the financing of Indian industrialization would come from abroad.
101. Eckes 1975, 156.
102. "Talk by Sir C. D. Deshmukh," p. 141.
103. Mukherjee 2002, chap. 4; Tomlinson 1979, 73–75, 78, 131; "Talk by Sir C. D. Deshmukh," p. 96.
104. Mukherjee 2002, 103, 129–31.

Not surprisingly, then, in its first formal comments on the Keynes and White plans in November 1943, the RBI board argued that India should not participate in postwar international monetary arrangements unless they provided for flexible exchange rates.[105] After the release of the Joint Statement, the RBI's senior economist J. V. Joshi also approved its provisions allowing exchange rate adjustments, pointing out that they would help agricultural countries such as India adjust to agricultural price changes that could cause "violent fluctuations" in the balance of payments. In addition, Joshi declared that "we desire freedom to change the par value of the rupee on the ground that India's economic plans, such as the development of her industrial and agricultural resources may introduce such disequilibrium in her balance of payments position which can only be effectively and appropriately corrected by a depreciation of the exchange value of the rupee."[106] In May 1944, even the acting finance member, C. E. Jones, endorsed flexible rates: "the exchange value of a currency must be adjusted to conform to the domestic policy of a country—say, a policy of full employment, or a policy of intensive economic development, or a policy of intensive industrialization."[107] Indian businessmen also stressed the important of exchange rate flexibility at this time. As N. R. Sarkar told the Reconstruction Committee's General Policy Committee, "countries like India and China with a large population and a comparatively low standard of life should be given special considerations in any international plan," which included the right not just to vary exchange rates but also to employ protective tariffs and foreign exchange rationing to strengthen local industry.[108]

Officials and analysts from both eastern Europe and India saw the Bretton Woods negotiations as an opportunity to create an international financial order that was supportive of their development aspirations. These aspirations were remarkably similar to those of many Latin American and Chinese officials at this time, including an interest in state-led industrialization strategies that could raise living standards, create more balanced national economies, and bolster their countries' political autonomy. Both eastern Europeans and Indians sought international

105. Simha 1970, 416–17.

106. J. V. Joshi, "Note on the Joint Statement," pp. 8–9.

107. C. E. Jones, "The New International Monetary Plan: Its Simplicity, Elasticity and Freedom," May 19, 1944, p. 7, NAI, Finance Department, File No. 2(77)-F/44). See also "Article VII Discussions with representatives of the Dominions and India. Committee on Monetary Policy. Draft Minutes of the Fifth meeting held at 10:45 a.m. on Wednesday 8th of March, 1944," March 13, 1944, p. 7, UKT 247/13.

108. "Record of the First Meeting of General of General Policy Committee," pp. 9–10. See also C. Pramaswami Aiyar, "Memorandum," May 2, 1944, NAI, Finance Department, File No. 2(77)-F/44); Mukherjee 2002, 166.

support for these strategies, arguing that this would also generate new markets for rich countries and bolster international peace. Arguments in favor of public international lending echoed those made in the inter-American context, as did the Indian case for international acceptance of trade protectionism and flexible exchange rate arrangements.

The specific influence of eastern European and Indian views on the final Bretton Woods agreements is difficult to gauge precisely. In the eastern European case, advocacy of international development lending simply reinforced existing support for this idea in the United States and elsewhere. This advocacy was also diluted by the fact that eastern Europeans lobbied at the Bretton Woods conference itself for the Bank to prioritize reconstruction over development loans. The influence of the Indians was felt more strongly at the conference through their efforts to widen the Fund's purpose and their proposals that the Bank should prioritize both reconstruction and development lending. The impact of the former was ambiguous, while the success of the latter was largely due to Latin American leadership on the issue. India's support for exchange rate flexibility also simply echoed the preferences of many other countries, including Britain.

Even if the specific influence of eastern Europeans and Indians on the content of the final agreement was limited, their voices were important in reinforcing what Rosenstein-Rodan called the general political "atmosphere" in favor of international development. Like their Latin American and Chinese counterparts, they called attention to the distinctive needs of poorer countries within the international financial system. Some of the ideas they developed—particularly those that emanated from Rosenstein-Rodan's seminar—had an important longer-term intellectual influence in generating the new field of development economics. More generally, the views of the eastern Europeans and Indians—like the perspectives of officials and analysts from Latin America, China, the Philippines and Ethiopia that we have already seen—also show clearly how the new ideas of international development found support not just in rich countries but also in poor regions of the world.

THE AFTERMATH AND
THE FORGETTING

This book has called into question some common understandings of the origins and content of the Bretton Woods system. It has shown that US policymakers explicitly sought to create a postwar international financial system that was supportive, rather than neglectful, of international development goals. White and other US officials initially had quite ambitious ideas in this area, ideas that built on US–Latin American initiatives of the late 1930s and early 1940s. These ambitions were tempered somewhat by the time of the Bretton Woods conference, but the commitment to promoting international development remained core to the US vision of the Bretton Woods system. This feature was apparent not just in US backing of various provisions of the IBRD and of the IMF's articles of agreement but also in its financial advisory activities in Southern countries at the time. Officials from several other Northern countries also favored, to varying degrees, these international development goals.

Southern countries were also much more deeply involved in the creation of the Bretton Woods system than has often been acknowledged. Most significant was the role of Latin American officials and analysts, beginning with their input into the Good Neighbor financial partnership of the late 1930s and early 1940s (which set the stage for the Bretton Woods proposals) and carrying through to their participation in the Bretton Woods negotiations and the Triffin missions. In these contexts, Latin Americans were keen to promote international initiatives that would further their development aspirations. Analysts and representatives from other Southern countries—particularly India, China, and eastern

Europe—also participated actively in the Bretton Woods negotiations. Like their Latin American counterparts, these figures also stressed the need to build an international financial order that met the distinctive development needs of poorer countries. Officials from the Philippines and Ethiopia—though they made little contribution to the Bretton Woods conference—also appreciated the link that US officials drew between the Bretton Woods system and support for development-oriented monetary reforms.

The international development content of the Bretton Woods agreements, and the North-South dialogue that produced it, represent forgotten foundations of the postwar international economic order. They have been forgotten not just by many historians of the Bretton Woods system but also by those scholars who date the invention of international development to Truman's inauguration speech of early 1949. The Bretton Woods stress on international development both pre-dated Truman's speech and went much further than what Truman proposed. Moreover, it built on a number of international development initiatives with an even deeper history, the most significant by far being those associated with the Good Neighbor financial partnership. Other precursors that influenced various Bretton Woods negotiators included the 1918 visions of Sun Yat-sen, some of the League of Nations activities, and (in the case of Britain for example) changing colonial policies. The invention of international development, in other words, took place much earlier than Truman's 1949 speech and had many more authors, among whom should be included the large number of participants in the Bretton Woods negotiations themselves.

Although the goal here has been to shed light on these forgotten foundations of Bretton Woods, one question remains: What was their fate in the postwar years? A comprehensive answer is beyond the scope of this book, but a brief exploration, focusing on the main developments, is worth while. The Bretton Woods development goals first of all fell victim very quickly after the war to changing US priorities in the context of domestic political shifts and new strategic priorities. This outcome in turn led to frustrations among many Southern policymakers which escalated by the 1970s into calls for as New International Economic Order. Southern demands resurrected many ideas discussed during the Bretton Woods negotiations, but reference to that history was rarely made either by supporters or by opponents. Although various modest international economic reforms were introduced during the 1960s and 1970s that built upon the development foundations of Bretton Woods, the ambitious NIEO project soon collapsed in the early 1980s. In the early twenty-first century, changing economic power encourages speculation about the renewed relevance of the development content of Bretton Woods.

The US Foreign Policy Shift

To understand the fate of the international development goals of Bretton Woods, it is necessary first to explore how US foreign economic policy changed quite suddenly with Truman's ascent to the presidency after Roosevelt's death on April 12, 1945. Although the Truman administration shepherded the Bretton Woods legislation through Congress, key architects of Bretton Woods quickly found themselves marginalized in the more conservative administration. One of these was Morgenthau, who resigned in July 1945. His departure also undermined White's influence in the Treasury, a development reinforced by the fact that he came under Federal Bureau of Investigation surveillance in late 1945 for possible links to Soviet espionage activities.[1] White's changed status became particularly apparent when he was passed over in the choice of the Fund's first managing director, a job many had assumed would be his.[2] The position went to Camille Gutt from Belgium, an individual Morgenthau had privately dismissed at the Bretton Woods conference as part of "a little group" supported by New York interests and with ties to the old order in international finance.[3] White accepted instead a two-year appointment as the US executive director in the IMF, but resigned that post early in March 1947 after suffering a heart attack. Then, three days after denying allegations of espionage before the House Committee on Un-American Activities in August 1948, White died of another heart attack.

In the new Truman administration, members of the New York financial community acquired much more sway in US foreign economic policy than they had had in the Roosevelt years, and they lobbied successfully for the ambitions of the Bretton Woods institutions to be scaled back. The status of the IMF and IBRD was further diminished when the Truman administration launched the Marshall Plan that placed the US government, rather than multilateral institutions, at the center of the task of constructing the postwar international economy. For the next decade, the IMF played only a marginal role in international monetary affairs as many countries took advantage of the provisions for a "transition" period to keep their currencies inconvertible. The IBRD also assumed a much more limited role in European reconstruction than many of its supporters had anticipated.

The Bank's conservative approach to development lending was equally striking. Partly because of concerns about marketing the Bank's bonds, the Truman administration had nominated a former investment banker, Eugene Meyer, as its first president. He quickly became involved in disputes over development

---

1. Black 1991, 53; Rees 1973, 362–63, 377.
2. Oliver 1961a, 22–28.
3. MD, book 755, p. 185.

loans with Collado, the first US executive director in the Bank and a veteran of the Good Neighbor financial partnership. After the first few loans of the Bank had been for European reconstruction projects, Collado urged it to agree to a Chilean request for a loan to support various projects of its public development corporation, but Meyer delayed a decision. When Meyer resigned after only six months, he was succeeded by New York investment lawyer John McCloy who refused to accept the job unless Collado—who he thought was too liberal and independent—resigned and was replaced by Chase Bank's vice president Eugene Black.[4] Collado's forced resignation left many Bank staff upset, and McCloy shocked them further with speeches in which he argued that the Bank should be closed down once it had succeeded in reviving international private investment.[5] Under McCloy's leadership, Bank loans were also blocked to countries that had not reached settlements on their external debts to foreign bondholders.[6] The contrast with the views of White and Morgenthau was stark.

The Bank's lack of development lending angered many Latin American officials, including Mexico's Monteros.[7] Urquidi, who had joined the Bank in October 1947 was also increasingly frustrated by its lack of enthusiasm for development issues and he left his position in mid-1949.[8] Latin American governments complained, too, that they had been discouraged from borrowing from the Fund. In mid-1947, one US official who had been involved with wartime Latin American financial relations, Frank Southard, even warned his Treasury colleagues that "we must take account of the danger of a Latin American exodus from the Fund and the Bank."[9] Latin American frustrations were only compounded by the refusal of the US Congress to ratify the International Trade Organization (ITO), which had included some provisions to address trade-related development issues that had been raised at Bretton Woods, such as commodity price stabilization and recognition of the right to protect infant industries. The only multilateral trade rules left were those embodied in the much less ambitious 1947 General Agreement on Tariffs and Trade (GATT) that included relatively little development content. Whereas seventeen Latin American countries had signed the ITO's Havana Charter, only three (Brazil, Chile, and Cuba) had felt sufficiently enthused to sign up to the original GATT.[10]

---

4. Kapur, Lewis, and Webb 1997, 79; Casey 2001, 141–44, 152–56; Kindleberger 1991, 46.
5. Oliver 1961a, 49, 57–58.
6. Kapur, Lewis, and Webb 1997, 81–82; Kofas 1997, 162.
7. Casey 2001, 157–60; Fuchs 1974b, 47–48.
8. Urquidi 1996, 45–46, 49.
9. Frank Southard to Snyder, July 17, 1947, p. 1, TSF, 450/81/20/07, box 28.
10. Williams 1991, 22. Article XVIII of the 1947 GATT did allow trade restrictions for economic development purposes, but subject to some conditions and the consent of the contracting parties.

Alongside these changes (and explaining some of them) was a dramatic transformation in US policy toward Latin America. Since the end of the war, Truman administration officials had declared firmly that they would no longer provide public development loans to the region. They also rejected proposals for commodity price stabilization and became quite critical of Latin American state-led development policies, arguing that Latin American governments should be doing more to create a market-friendly business climate that was attractive to private international investors. Indeed, US officials now argued that private investment flows and free trade should serve as the main engines for development in Latin America, a perspective that many regional officials viewed very skeptically.[11] Symbolizing the shift away from policies of the Good Neighbor financial partnership, the Truman administration even formally withdrew the IAB legislative proposal from Congress in April 1947, despite enduring Latin American interest in the idea.[12]

To explain the sudden shift in postwar US policy toward Latin America, it is useful to recall how US support for the Good Neighbor financial partnership emerged from a combination of strategic interests, New Deal values, and economic interests. At the end of the war, the strategic rationale for the policy collapsed as the region no longer had the same kind of importance to US security interests that it had had in the face of the Nazi threat.[13] Indeed, at the height of US interest in the partnership in 1940, some Latin American officials, such as Mexico's Suárez, had correctly predicted that US financial assistance for Latin American development might vanish at the end of the war when the region's strategic importance diminished.[14]

The shift in US policy also reflected the greater ideological conservatism of the Truman administration. The turn away from New Deal values in US policy toward Latin America was symbolized by the new influence of individuals who had been critical of the Good Neighbor financial partnership. They included not just bankers but also Spruille Braden who replaced Rockefeller as Assistant Secretary of State for American Republic Affairs after the latter was dismissed in August 1945.[15] Braden used his position (which he held until mid-1947) to attack

---

Because of these limitations, Williams (1991, 23) notes that "in practice, this article was hardly ever used" before its revision in 1954. See also Wilkinson 2006, chap. 2; Toye and Toye 2004, 33–40, 214–15; Gardner 1980, 364–68; Scott 2010.

11. Green 1971, chap. 7, 11; Gilderhus 2000, 124–25; Schoultz 1998, 332–23; Urquidi 1996, 44; Grow 1981, 91; Wallich 1948, 156; Dosman 2008, 241; Hilton 1981, 602–4; Rabe 1978.

12. *Congressional Record*, April 17, 1947, vol.,93, part 3, p. 3583. For enduring Latin American interest in the IAB, see Green 1971, 206, 284; Urquidi 1996, 33; Fuchs 1974b, 48.

13. Green 1971, chap. 7; Hilton 1981, 602–4; Rabe 1978.

14. Schuler 1998, 22.

15. Gellman 1985, 98–99.

"the virus of economic nationalism" in Latin America as well as past US public lending to the region. He emphasized for the region that "private enterprise is the best and in most circumstances the only really sound means to develop the known or unknown resources of a new country."[16] In the Chilean loan debate, Braden had also strongly opposed Bank lending until Chile settled its external debts; indeed, he also wanted the Chilean government to end exchange and tax policies that discriminated against US copper companies.[17]

Not all US officials involved in US–Latin American relations after the war shared Braden's views. For example, as we saw earlier, Triffin (who was no fan of Braden) and his Federal Reserve colleagues continued in the immediate postwar years to recommend reforms in Latin America along the Paraguayan model (although with more conservative content in two of the most prominent missions after the war involving Guatemala and Dominican Republic).[18] Even after Triffin went to the IMF in 1946, this policy endured under his successor in the Fed job, David Grove, who shared Triffin's views closely and remained in this role until the early 1950s.[19] The approach even persisted in the Philippine case despite considerable opposition from private US financial interests, a result that partly reflected the Philippines' strategic importance and the fact that reforms would reduce the need for further US financial assistance to the country. The latter consideration highlights one way in which the Federal Reserve Board's missions were in fact compatible with the new more conservative postwar US Latin American policy: they addressed Latin American economic problems through domestic reform rather than international public assistance. As we saw earlier, this had in fact been a point emphasized by Triffin to the Fed Board after his Paraguayan mission.

What about economic interests? It is interesting how private economic interests that had backed the Good Neighbor partnership—such as manufacturers— did little to rally to its defense in this period (although they played a role in the Philippine case). In attempting to account for how US policy toward Latin America could shift so suddenly, Wallich argued in 1948 that the US business lobby with an economic interest in the region's development was simply not all that substantial. As he put it, "with some exceptions, there has been a tendency on the part of manufacturing exporters to disregard Latin American needs whenever

---

16. Quotes from Grow 1981, 91, and Green 1971, 262.

17. Casey 2001.

18. For Triffin's views of Braden, see Triffin to Arthur Schlesinger, May 13, 1946, ISF, box 156.

19. For Grove's views, see for example David Grove, "The Potentialities of Monetary Policy in the Economic Development of Latin America," June 18, 1951, ISF, box 156. Chapter 3 also noted the support of the FRBNY's Wallich for the creation of Cuba's central bank in 1950 on the lines recommended by the 1942 report of the White mission.

the going became difficult or when the home pastures looked greener . . . very few of our businessmen have to regard Latin American business as their bread and butter."[20]

The Cold War and the Point Four Program

The onset of the Cold War engendered some renewed US interest in international development policies, as signaled by Truman's famous January 1949 inauguration speech that committed the United States to combat "underdevelopment." The new "Point Four" program was accompanied by considerable hype. Secretary of State Dean Acheson, for example, argued that the Point Four legislation created "economic development of underdeveloped areas for the first time as a national policy" of the United States.[21]

The analysis here has shown, however, that in spite of the many scholars who have picked up on this view, it is very difficult to square with the evidence of the extensive international development initiatives of the Good Neighbor financial partnership and the Bretton Woods negotiations. Acheson's statement was an exaggeration, as he would well have known since he had been involved various US policy discussions about promoting development during the war, including the drafting of the IBRD at Bretton Woods.[22] A more accurate assessment of the Point Four program came from Simon Hanson, an ex-Treasury official involved in developing the early stages of the Good Neighbor partnership, who wrote in early 1950 that, from a Latin American perspective, "the Point Four program represents a restatement of objectives rather than a new policy on the part of the Government of the United States. The sympathies of our Government and of our people have long been deeply engaged by the desirability of accelerating the economic development of Latin America."[23]

Other veterans of the Good Neighbor financial partnership also initially saw the Point Four program as a revival of the earlier US wartime support for Latin American development goals. For example, Rockefeller was so encouraged by Truman's speech that he became actively involved in lobbying Congress to

---

20. Wallich 1948, 158.
21. Quoted in Packenham 1973, 43–44.
22. Acheson's role in drafting the Bank should not be overstated. At the conference, he became very irritated at one point about the lead role he had been given—and even threatened to step down—because he knew so little about the proposal and was getting little staff support. MD, book 753, p. 80–81, 141–52.
23. Hanson 1950, 66. After his work at the Treasury, Hanson worked for Rockefeller's Office of Coordinator of Inter-American Affairs.

support it. He was subsequently named chair of the advisory board that administered the program.[24] Some of the US manufacturing groups that had backed the partnership and the Bretton Woods provisions for development lending also emerged as supporters of the Point Four program.[25] Interestingly, even the very idea for the Point Four program had come from an individual, Benjamin Hardy, who had worked in Brazil for the Institute for Inter-American Affairs that Rockefeller had created in 1942.[26]

It is tempting thus to see Truman's commitment to international development as building directly on earlier US policy. The degree of continuity with past policy, however, should not be overstated. To begin with, the Point Four program was focused primarily on the provision of technical advice rather than on broader international financial assistance. Even Truman's efforts to get very modest (in comparison to the Marshall Plan) financing for technical assistance met considerable resistance in Congress. Despite linking his appeal to the battle against communism, Truman's initial request for only $45 million to support the program was scaled back to $27 million and still only passed the Senate by one vote. As historian Michael Latham points out, opponents argued that public spending "was a weak and ineffective substitute for the only real engine of progress, the unregulated, capitalist marketplace."[27] In the face of this kind of resistance, Rockefeller resigned from his position in 1951, frustrated by with his inability to change US policy as much as he had hoped.[28] US officials also strongly opposed efforts by poorer countries at this time to establish international mechanisms for more concessional development assistance. In the words of Hans Singer (who experienced this opposition directly), advocates of soft aid for poorer countries—particularly if done under UN auspices—were treated as "subversive" and "as outcasts and out to weaken the Free World," particularly after Senator Joseph McCarthy's campaign against communist influence intensified.[29]

The weaker political backing for international development finance reflected not just the changed ideological atmosphere but also the new security situation. Some of the poor regions of the world that had been the focus of US development plans during the Bretton Woods discussions were no longer strategic priorities for the United States following the Soviet takeover of eastern Europe and the Chinese revolution of 1949. As US attention shifted to Cold War battlegrounds in

---

24. Rivas 2002.
25. Maxfield and Nolt 1990, 58–59.
26. Ekbladh 2010, 97.
27. Latham 2011, 31.
28. Rivas 2002, 185–88.
29. Singer 1984, 296–97 n. 47. See also Toye and Toye 2004, 173.

Europe and East Asia, Latin America's strategic importance to United States also continued to diminish. The United States did provide extensive bilateral financial assistance to poor countries at the front line of the Cold War such as South Korea, but the bulk of US assistance now went to Europe and Japan.

American development policy after 1949 also differed from that of the late 1930s and early 1940s because US officials were no longer so favorably inclined to state-led development strategies. Against a background of resurgent conservative business interests and Cold War ideology, US officials increasingly saw economic policy debates in binary terms as a struggle between supporters of free markets and those of communism.[30] For example, Raúl Prebisch found himself a victim of the hardening worldview in early 1949 after he was tentatively offered a top job at the IMF. To his great frustration (as well as that of other Latin Americans working at the Fund), US opposition scuttled the appointment for reasons that were at least partly related to the changing domestic political situation. As Dosman notes, "while not yet hysteria, a groundswell of anti-communism in the US capital demanded the greatest care in choosing senior people for the IMF and World Bank; while no one could possibly argue that Prebisch was pro-communist, he was a Latin American who used terms such as 'core' and 'periphery' and was therefore not automatically 'safe.'"[31]

The changing US views of appropriate development policies were even more apparent during the Eisenhower administration that came into office in January 1953.[32] The most striking contrast with earlier US policy came with the 1954 coup in Guatemala sponsored by the US Central Intelligence Agency that deposed Jacobo Árbenz Guzmán's government.[33] Árbenz had been defense minister in Arévalo's government that had come power in 1945 and whose reformism had been greeted with enthusiasm by Triffin and other US officials. Indeed, during his mission to Guatemala in 1945, Triffin had formed a very positive impression of Árbenz, who reminded him of a "centre-left" politician in his native Belgium whom he had admired. Árbenz had also taken a keen interest in Triffin's work, visiting him in the evening and often talking with him long into the night. Watching from afar in 1954, Triffin lamented how much US policy had shifted.[34] After the coup, Guatemala's new government introduced policies that

---

30. Maxfield and Nolt 1990, 57–59, note, however, some enduring support for ISI policies.
31. Dosman 2008, 234. The US decision was also driven in part by its effort to improve relations with Argentina's Perón who strongly opposed Prebisch's appointment. Brazil also opposed the appointment, a position that Dosman (2008, 234) attributes to Bulhões's "envy."
32. Gilderhus 2000, 139–57.
33. Latham 2011, chap. 5.
34. Triffin 1990, 28–29. For Triffin's relations with Árbenz in 1945, see also Triffin to Board of Governors, October 2, 1945, p. 2, ISF, box 221. After participating in a 1952 financial advisory mission requested by Iran's Mohammed Mosaddegh, Triffin had also been critical (just months before

were more market-friendly and replaced the head of the central bank, Manuel Noriega Morales, who had attended Bretton Woods and whose commitment to development had so impressed Triffin in 1945.[35]

Even the content of US thinking about financial advisory activities began to shift. In the immediate wake of the Truman speech, the Fed continued to send high-profile missions whose advice roughly followed the Triffin lines, such as ones to Ceylon and South Korea in 1950. By the second half of the 1950s, however, US officials began to support more conservative IMF-led stabilization programs that promoted fiscal and monetary discipline, freer trade, and the removal of multiple exchange rates and exchange controls. Interestingly, one of the first such programs was introduced in Paraguay to tackle high inflation that had been caused by excessive central bank accommodation of lending by a government-owned commercial bank.[36] As in 1943–44, Paraguay became a kind of model, but of a new kind. The 1957 Paraguayan IMF stand-by arrangement was the first to introduce policy conditionality, and its conditions were part of the Fund's new "monetary approach" to the balance of payments.[37] With this new approach, the IMF quickly became what one observer called "the bête noire of the Left" in Latin America.[38]

In sum, the impact of the initial Cold War on the politics of international development was rather different than is often portrayed in existing literature. The conventional view is that the Cold War acted as a catalyst for the birth of international development, as evidenced by Truman's inaugural speech. In fact, however, the Cold War had the effect of undermining the already existing international development project of Bretton Woods in two ways. First, US strategic attention was steered away from the poor regions of the world that had been the center of US thinking about the Bretton Woods's development goals. Second,

---

Mosaddegh's overthrow) of the unwillingness of the United States and Britain to listen to the Iranian concerns: "Iran's Negotiations Criticized," *Washington Post*, March 9, 1953.

35. Latham 2011, 128; Horace Sanford and Francis Schott, "Report on Visits to Central Banks of Mexico, Curacao, and Eleven Central and South American Countries, October and November 1955," December 1955, Part 2, p. 41, ISF, box 229.

36. Horace Sanford and Richard Dosik, "Report on the Visits to Central Banks of Argentina, Paraguay, Bolivia, Costa Rica, Nicaragua and Cuba, November–December, 1959," January 1960, p. 13, ISF, box 229, file: Foreign Missions, Latin America, Pocket. In 1945, Triffin himself had anticipated the difficulties the Paraguayan central bank was likely to have in limiting its assistance to the government. He noted that his legislation tried to minimize this risk, but argued that "in the final analysis no mere banking provisions can solve this problem . . . this will remain one of the crucial problems of Paraguay for a long time . . ."; Triffin to Board of Governors, "Second Mission to Paraguay," January 10, 1945, pp. 5–6, ISF, box 162. By contrast, at the 25th anniversary of the establishment of the Bank of Guatemala in which he had been so deeply involved, Triffin noted that it could boast since its founding of absolute stability of the exchange rate and cost-of-living increases averaging less than 1.5 percent per year (Triffin, untitled, May 1971, p. 1, RTP, box 27, file: Triffin in Guatemala.

37. Boughton 2011, 383–84; James 1996, 78–83.

38. Campos 1996, 101. Roberto Campos had been a Brazilian delegate to Bretton Woods.

the ideological polarization of the Cold War eroded US support for the kinds of interventionist development policies—international and national—discussed in the Bretton Woods negotiations.

Southern Contestation

How did Southern countries react to the US retreat from the Bretton Woods development goals? We have already seen the Latin American frustration with the changing US policy toward their region after the war. This frustration was increasingly channeled through the United Nations system where they had a large bloc of votes. Particularly important was their initiative in the late 1940s to create—despite US reluctance—a UN Economic Commission for Latin America to further their region's development.[39]

After being rebuffed for the IMF position, Prebisch assumed a leadership role in ECLA, promoting the kinds of ideas he had begun to express in the early 1940s. He challenged the "false sense of universality" of mainstream economic theory and urged activist state policies to promote more diversified, industrialized economies in Latin America.[40] In an increasingly assertive manner, Prebisch—with much Latin American backing—also called on the United States to foster the region's development with more financial assistance, support for commodity stabilization programs, and the creation of a regional development bank.[41] Across much of Latin America, his reputation and that of ECLA soared, and he was able to attract prominent economists to work for the organization, including Urquidi, who was employed in ECLA's Mexican office between 1951and 1958.

While Prebisch's ideas had been similar to those of many prominent US policymakers and analysts during the early 1940s, his demands were now rejected by US policymakers and his analyses provoked strong criticism from neoclassical economists there.[42] In the McCarthy years, ECLA even fell under the scrutiny of the FBI and CIA, which considered the organization subversive. Some more orthodox Latin American economists—including two members of Brazil's Bretton Woods delegation, Campos and Gudin—were also increasingly critical of ECLA's focus on ISI and government planning.[43] After a tour of Latin America

---

39. Dosman 2008, 236–37; Toye and Toye 2004, 138–39.
40. Quote from Dosman 2008, 249. See also chaps.11, 12, and 13.
41. Dosman 2008, 292–94.
42. Dosman 2008, 248, 292–94. Some of the critics included individuals who had favored development ideas during the Bretton Woods planning process, such as Charles Kindleberger and Jacob Viner.
43. Dosman 2008, 287–88, 282–84. Some other Southern delegates at Bretton Woods also became advocates of free-market positions, such as India's Shroff who co-founded the think tank "Forum of Free Enterprise" in 1956 to critique the interventionist policies of Nehru.

in late 1959, two FRBNY officials noted how the views of many central bankers in the region were also changing, with "a noticeable disenchantment with the results of government intervention in the economy and a tendency to allow a greater role to market forces and free enterprise generally."[44] In the late 1950s, Prebisch began to experience growing criticism from the left as well, including from the prominent Brazilian economist Celso Furtado who suggested that ISI policies were accompanied by growing inequality.[45]

Prebisch and other Latin Americans were not the only officials from the South demanding more assistance for international development. Indian policymakers also assumed a lead role after the war, as they had at Bretton Woods, in raising the profile of this issue. During the ITO negotiations, they echoed many of the Latin American demands.[46] India also emerged at this time as a prominent supporter of the proposal for a Special UN Fund for Economic Development (SUNFED) to offer longer-term concessional loans to poor countries. The idea had first been proposed in 1949 by the Indian economist V. K. R. V. Rao (who had studied with Keynes at Cambridge). In 1951, despite US opposition, the UN General Assembly voted by a two-to-one majority to set up a panel to study SUNFED's establishment.[47] At the 1950 IMF and World Bank annual meeting, Deshmukh—now India's finance minister—also called on the Bank to establish a department offering such soft development loans.[48]

At Bretton Woods, Latin American and Indian calls for international support for their development ambitions had been echoed strongly by officials from eastern Europe and China. But their participation in the Bretton Woods system now became a casualty of the Cold War. The two East European countries that had been most favorable toward development at the Bretton Woods conference, Poland and Czechoslovakia, left the Bretton Woods system soon after the USSR— which never ratified the Bretton Woods agreements—created an alternative economic bloc, Comecon, for its allies in 1949.[49] Rosenstein-Rodan was soon forced to acknowledge that "the practical value" of the detailed development plans for eastern Europe his seminar had prepared for the RIIA between 1943 and 1945

44. Sanford and Dosik, "Report," p. 3.

45. Dosman 2008, 331–33.

46. Gardner 1980, 365.

47. Murphy 2006, 59–61.

48. Prasad 1985, 21.

49. Poland withdrew voluntarily in early 1950, complaining of US domination of the system after its requests for two loans from the Bank in 1946–47 were turned down. Czechoslovakia was forced to withdraw in 1954 after the United States accused it of not providing information that was required under the Fund's charter (McKinzie 1973). After this and throughout the 1960s, the only centrally planned economy from East Europe that remained in the IMF and World Bank was Yugoslavia (Jacobson and Oksenberg 1990, 27).

had been destroyed.[50] In 1951, the RIIA chose simply to publish a short overview of his fifty-thousand-word plan, hoping that it might be of use to policymakers in other regions of the world.[51] Rosenstein-Rodan did, however, serve on the IBRD's staff between 1947 and 1952 and continued to work on development issues, although he found the Bank's narrow focus on specific project lending frustrating.[52] After serving as Poland's first executive director to the Bank, the other lead advocate of international development from the RIIA seminar, Leon Baranski, also worked for the institution on development issues in other regions of the world such as Africa.[53]

After the communist revolution in 1949, mainland China also ceased to be a member of the Bretton Woods institutions. When the KMT retreated to Taiwan, the United Nations continued to recognize it as the official representative of China, and the Bretton Woods institutions followed suit. Chou En-lai asked the IMF managing director to expel the Taipei government's representatives from the Fund in August 1950, but he did not include a request that the new People's Republic of China assume China's seat in the Fund.[54] Although Chou had appeared to support China's participation in the Bretton Woods institutions in late 1944, the political context had changed dramatically with the revolution, America's active support for the KMT government in Taiwan, and the outbreak of the Korean War. Membership in the United States–dominated bodies now held little appeal and the PRC's relations with the West more generally were largely severed over the next few years, not to be resumed until the UN General Assembly voted in 1971 to give the PRC government the right to represent China.[55] Even then, the PRC did not show a consistent interest in joining the Bretton Woods institutions until Deng Xiaoping committed the country in late 1978 to an outward-oriented development strategy (reminiscent of Sun's thinking) that focused on state-led growth and industrialization through economic linkages with the West.[56]

While Latin American and Indian promoters of international development lost the eastern European and Chinese backing that they had had at Bretton Woods, they gained new allies in the 1950s and 1960s with the rapid decolonization of Africa and Asia. Taking advantage of their growing numbers in the United

---

50. "Analysis and Method in the Study of Economic Development: Selected Papers Relating to Eastern Europe, Compiled by Dr. P. N. Rosenstein-Rodan, edited and with an introduction by A. L. Minkes," p. 1, (n.d., but with covering memo dated October 22, 1952), RIIACR 9/23qq.

51. Minkes 1951.

52. Oliver 1961c, 2; Kapur, Lewis, and Webb 1997, 128–30.

53. For his work for the IBRD in Africa in the early 1960s, see Tignor 2006, 186–89; Oliver 1961b, 19.

54. Boughton 2001b, 968.

55. Jacobson and Oksenberg 1990, 44; Jian 2001, chap. 2

56. Jacobson and Oksenberg 1990, 63–70; Vogel 2011, 808 n. 16. The PRC became China's official representative in the institutions in 1980.

Nations, a new coalition of Latin American, African and Asian countries—soon called the G77—pushed for the creation of the UN Conference on Trade and Development (UNCTAD) in 1964.[57] Prebisch was named its secretary general and began to promote similar issues as he had in ECLA, such as the need for greater development finance and commodity price stabilization. Prebisch also encouraged initiatives to improve access to Northern markets for Southern manufacturing exports, but on a nonreciprocal basis that would allow poorer countries to retain their tariffs.

In advocating these reforms, Prebisch often critiqued the Bretton Woods system for not taking account of the distinctive needs of Southern countries. As Toye and Toye put it, Prebisch argued throughout the 1960s that "the Bretton Woods/GATT system was based on a failure to recognize the fundamental differences between the industrial centers and the periphery of the world economy and thus sought to apply common principles to what was fundamentally different."[58] This was an interesting line of argument from a person who had been deeply involved in shaping Triffin's innovative efforts to further the development content of Bretton Woods through financial advisory activities that were very attentive to the distinctive conditions and goals of Southern countries.[59] Prebisch's case no doubt reflected his disillusionment with the way the Bretton Woods system had been subsequently implemented. The framing of his cause as a challenge to the Western-dominated Bretton Woods system may also have made some political sense given the anticolonial sentiments in many of the countries in the coalition he was mobilizing. Whatever the cause, Prebisch's framing contributed to a growing perception that Bretton Woods had overlooked international development issues and the needs of Southern countries.

In the face of the growing Southern pressures and prompted by fears of communist influence in poor regions of the world, the United States and other Northern governments supported several reforms of the international economic architecture. Some of these focused primarily on Latin America, particularly after the hostile reaction to Nixon's 1958 tour of Latin America and the Cuban revolution of early 1959. For example, the United States finally backed the creation of the Inter-American Development Bank (IADB), which opened its doors in early 1960 and focused much of its initial lending on industrial projects and social

---

57. Williams 1991; Toye and Toye 2004, chap. 8.

58. Toye and Toye 2004, 43.

59. Toye and Toye (2004, 43) argue that his criticism "was largely correct," but they note that Prebisch underestimated the importance of some of the concessions that poor countries gained in the negotiation of the postwar trading system. The same criticism can be made of his views of the Bretton Woods international financial order. Toye and Toye themselves downplay the role of Southern countries in the Bretton Woods negotiations (p. 23).

infrastructure. To support key allies in the region, US officials also endorsed an International Coffee Agreement that was finalized in 1963.[60] When the Kennedy administration came into office, it even reached out to Prebisch—via a veteran of the Good Neighbor policy, Adolf Berle—to help design its new Alliance for Progress initiative aimed at assisting Latin American development. Prebisch was initially enthused; his new acceptance in Washington reminded him of working with Triffin in the 1940s. But disappointment quickly followed when the ambitions for the Alliance for Progress were scaled back in the face of US business and conservative opposition.[61]

At the global level, the United States and other Northern countries finally backed—in part to block the SUNFED proposal—the creation in 1960 of a soft loan facility within the World Bank: the International Development Association (IDA).[62] New regional development banks were also established for Africa (1964) and Asia (1966). In addition, the IMF responded to calls for greater financial assistance for poorer countries facing sudden declines in export earnings by creating the Compensatory Financing Facility (CFF).[63] At the second UNCTAD meeting in 1968, Northern countries also agreed formally to a generalized system of trade preferences allowing greater access for manufactured exports from poor countries on a nonreciprocal basis, although its specific provisions were very weak.

These various initiatives were seen by many policymakers and analysts as pioneering a more development-friendly international economic order for the first time in response to a new kind of "North-South dialogue." But many of these initiatives simply built upon the original international development content of Bretton Woods that had been constructed by the now forgotten North-South dialogue of that earlier era. The IDA reinforced the widespread support that had existed at Bretton Woods for long-term international development finance, offering it on more generous terms. The CFF strengthened the commitment expressed during the Bretton Woods discussions of the IMF's waiver clause to provide greater access to IMF's loans for agricultural-exporting countries that were exposed to large balance of payments fluctuations. The International Coffee Agreement followed up on the resolution passed at Bretton Woods that recommended governments to reach agreement on ways to address international commodity price issues. The IADB also finally brought to fruition the idea of

---

60. Toye and Toye 2004, 216.
61. Dosman 2008, 357–59; Toye and Toye 2004, 175; Pollock 1978, 69–71.
62. Kapur, Lewis, and Webb 1997, 154–6.
63. The first country to use it was Brazil, the Southern country that been most forceful in pushing this issue at Bretton Woods (James 1996, 145).

an inter-American bank devoted primarily to development issues, an idea that in 1939–40 had served as a kind of first draft of the Bretton Woods institutions.

The Rise and Fall of the NIEO

Despite these various reforms, many Southern governments remained frustrated that more was not being done at the international level to further their development goals. The political context then changed dramatically when the Organization of the Petroleum Exporting Countries (OPEC) countries quadrupled the price of oil in 1973, a development that seemed to demonstrate the potential power of Southern commodity producers. Emboldened and in the context of the broader world economic crisis, a wide coalition of Southern governments used a special session of the UN General Assembly in 1974 to call for a comprehensive New International Economic Order. The NIEO proposals included many ideas Prebisch had promoted in UNCTAD (from which he had resigned by this time), such as greater financial and technical assistance to poor countries, measures to improve the terms of trade facing such countries, greater "preferential and non-reciprocal treatment for developing countries," and more influence for the South in international economic decision making.[64] The 1974 UN resolution also introduced other issues such as the regulation and supervision of transnational corporations (including the right to nationalize them), greater economic cooperation among Southern countries, and the broader protection of policy autonomy ("the right of every country to adopt the economic and social system that it deems the most appropriate for its own development").[65] UNCTAD subsequently added to the overall reform agenda more specific initiatives relating to commodity price stabilization, as well as proposals for an international debt-restructuring mechanism.[66]

The NIEO proposal was widely seen as a major challenge to the Bretton Woods order.[67] But once again, the objective to create an international economic order that was favorable to the state-led development goals of Southern countries was one that had been shared by many officials involved in the Bretton Woods negotiations, including those from United States. To be sure, many of the specific

---

64. Quote from UN General Assembly, "Declaration on the Establishment of a New International Economic Order," Sixth Session, Agenda Item 7, May 1, 1974, p. 1, http://www.un-documents.net/s6r3201.htm.

65. Quote from UN General Assembly, "Declaration," p. 1.

66. For debt, see Helleiner 2008, 104–5.

67. For the debates surrounding the new NIEO "ideology," see Murphy 1984.

NIEO proposals went much further than what the Bretton Woods negotiators had endorsed. But in its general aspirations, the NIEO proposal could be seen as an initiative that built upon the Bretton Woods foundations. Indeed, when one looks at the NIEO agenda, it is striking how many of the issues it raised had been discussed by White in his early postwar plans as well as by others during the development of the Bretton Woods agreements: long-term international development finance, short-term compensatory financing for commodity export shortfalls, an international debt-restructuring mechanism, backing for infant industry trade protection, commodity price stabilization, the regulation of capital flows, and support for national autonomy in the pursuit of state-led development policies.

In a few instances, participants in the NIEO debates seemed to recognize this. For example, in advocating for commodity agreements, the Sri Lankan official Lal Jayawardena circulated Keynes's early 1942 proposals on this topic that he had found in the British archives.[68] Prebisch also referred to Keynes's ideas on this topic and hoped that Northern countries might finally be willing to implement the famous economist's proposals.[69] For the most part, however, the rich history of the international development discussions of Bretton Woods was not mentioned by participants in the NIEO debates. Even the active participation of Southern countries in the negotiation of Bretton Woods—and their dominant numbers at the conference itself—were overlooked. For example, as part of its critique of the status quo, the 1974 UN resolution highlighted how the existing international economic system "was established at a time when most of the developing countries did not even exist as independent States."[70] This statement was of course true, but its implication—that Southern countries had little role in the creation of Bretton Woods—was not.

For most of those involved in the NIEO debates, this neglect of the Bretton Woods history may have simply reflected a lack of knowledge. Aside from Gardner's 1956 book *Sterling-Dollar Diplomacy* (which neglected the development content of Bretton Woods), there were few serious analyses of history of the Bretton Woods negotiations available at the time.[71] Indeed, Jayawardena was only able to find Keynes's proposals because the British archives had just made them available under their thirty-year rule.[72] The forgetting of the development content of the Bretton Woods negotiations may also have had some political sources. The framing of the NIEO as a frontal challenge to Bretton Woods by

68. Williamson 1977, 94; Keynes 1974.
69. Prebisch 1972, 10.
70. UN General Assembly, "Declaration," p. 1.
71. For Gardner's neglect, see the introductory chapter above.
72. Keynes 1974.

Southern supporters matched the heated rhetoric of the time. On the other side, it also allowed Northern officials who disliked the NIEO proposals to represent them as too radical a challenge to the principles of "global liberalism" that had been embodied in the international economic regimes established at the end of the war.[73]

Indeed, while Northern governments initially made some concessions to Southern countries, the position of many Northern governments hardened by the end of the decade, particularly after the election of Margaret Thatcher in Britain (1979) and Ronald Reagan in the United States (1980). Those political changes symbolized and reinforced the growing support for free-market—or "neoliberal"—ideas in the North. Many neoliberals disliked the interventionist economic ideas of the NIEO and argued that the poverty of Southern countries would be better addressed by domestic reforms that dismantled statist economic policies. By the time of the North-South summit at Cancún in 1981, it was clear that the NIEO proposal was dead.

It is worth noting that the NIEO attracted critics not just from the neoliberal camp. From the left, neo-Marxist "dependency" thinkers argued that the global capitalist system was not reformable in the way that NIEO advocates suggested. They critiqued the NIEO project as a strategy of "the Third World bourgeoisie" designed simply to promote state-led capitalist industrialization (much as Marx had critiqued List) and they urged instead a more radical "de-linking" from the capitalist Bretton Woods system altogether.[74] From an emerging "Green" perspective, the environmental and social costs of the Southern governments' quest for rapid industrial growth were increasingly questioned, including by E. F. Schumacher who had been involved in the Bretton Woods negotiations and whose 1973 *Small is Beautiful* became a core text for the Green movement.[75] This critique was not new; Schumacher was partly inspired by the ideas of Gandhi who had advanced a similar line of argument at the time of Bretton Woods. In the 1940s, Gandhi's critique of modern industrial growth was very much a minority voice, but it now found a much wider international audience, as the meaning of "development" became more hotly contested than it had been in the 1940s.

The collapse of the NIEO project also reflected the fact that the power of Southern governments had diminished rapidly by the early 1980s as their unity on various issues unraveled and as it became clear that OPEC's power was not easily emulated by other commodity exporters, particularly after the global recession of 1979–82 caused commodity prices to plummet. That recession and

---

73. Krasner (1985) describes this line of thinking.
74. Quote from Amin 1990, 115. See also Dos Santos's (1970) critique of ECLA ideas.
75. Schumacher 1973.

the sudden hiking of US interest rates also provoked severe external debt crises in many Southern countries that redirected their governments' attention away from global reform to immediate crisis management at home. While creditor banks and Northern countries formed a tight IMF-led cartel, the debtors failed to organize themselves and were left bearing the brunt of the adjustment to the crisis. The growing influence of neoliberal thinking among many policy elites in Southern countries also encouraged acceptance of the creditors' preferred solution to the crisis: the introduction in debtor countries of austerity and structural adjustment programs that ushered in free-market policies.

A consequence of this resolution of the international debt crisis of the 1980s was that the goals of the NIEO were turned upside down. Instead of increased development finance for poor countries flowing from North to South, large resource transfers flowed from South to North for most of the decade to pay off external debts. Policy autonomy was also undermined rather than strengthened as state-led development policies were dismantled under IMF and World Bank guidance. In place of greater influence in global economic decision making, Southern countries also found their voices marginalized in a world economy dominated more than ever by rich countries through the Group of Seven (G7) club. In their role as promoters and enforcers of austerity programs and neoliberal reforms, the Bretton Woods institutions also took on a very different role from that envisioned in 1944.

The increasingly worldwide spread of neoliberal policies after the end of the Cold War further marginalized those who sought to reform the global economic order along the lines of the NIEO. Even many critics of the Washington Consensus no longer saw the reformist agenda of the NIEO as a model. At the fiftieth anniversary of the Bretton Woods conference in 1994, a common slogan of protesters with an interest in development issues was "Fifty Years Is Enough." Rather than reform of the global economic order, outright rejection was coming into fashion, a stance that became even more prominent among many in the widespread antiglobalization protests of the late 1990s and early 2000s.

What Next?

In the early twenty-first century, however, echoes of the Bretton Woods development discussions have begun to be heard once again. A key catalyst has been the rising economic power of so-called emerging economies such as China, India, Brazil, Mexico, Indonesia, and South Africa. The most dramatic symbol of the new power of these countries came with the creation of the Group of 20 (G20) leaders forum at the height of the global financial crisis of 2008, a body that includes all of these large Southern economies. The G20 quickly eclipsed the G7 to become the premier forum for international economic cooperation and it provides Southern countries—albeit just a select few of them—more influence in global economic decision making than they have had since the 1970s.

As at Bretton Woods, many of the Southern G20 countries are governed by policy elites committed to state-led development goals, including some of the most powerful countries such as Brazil, China, and India. With their support, Southern governments are placing many of the international development issues affecting Southern countries that were discussed at Bretton Woods back on the global economic agenda: more long-term development finance, greater access to short-term balance of payments assistance, new mechanisms for debt restructuring, special trade provisions, measures to address commodity price volatility, regulation of international financial flows, and enhanced policy autonomy (or "policy space") for development. The prospects for significant reforms in these areas have also been enhanced by the growing criticism of neoliberal ideas in the wake of the 2008 global financial crisis.

International economic reforms demanded by Southern governments may be resisted—as they were in the 1970s—by Northern officials on the grounds that they depart too radically from the Bretton Woods ideals. The history told here, however, shows that efforts to address these issues build upon foundations established precisely at Bretton Woods. The Bretton Woods architects—from both North and South—in fact saw the reconciliation of liberal multilateralism with the state-led development priorities of Southern governments as one of the core features of the postwar settlement. The construction of initiatives on that foundation has been slow and uneven since the end of World War II. For those seeking to accelerate the building process, this forgotten history may generate some ideas and inspiration. And for those less keen on the kinds of international development goals outlined at Bretton Woods—on either the left or the right of the political spectrum—this analysis provides a sobering reminder of their deep historical grounding.

References

ARCHIVES

ALP   Ansel Luxford Papers, International Monetary Fund Archives, Washington, DC

AYP   Arthur N. Young Papers, Hoover Institution Archives, Stanford University, Stanford, CA

BOE   Bank of England Archives, London

BP   Berle Papers, Franklin D. Roosevelt Library, Hyde Park, New York

BWA   Record Group 56, General Records of the Department of the Treasury, Office of the Assistant Secretary for International Affairs, Records of the Bretton Woods Agreements, 1938–1946, United States National Archives, College Park, MD

BWCC   Bretton Woods Conference Collection, IMF Archives, Washington, DC

CDDP   Dr. C. D. Deshmukh Papers, Nehru Memorial Museum and Library Archives, New Delhi

CFHDW   Record Group 56, General Records of the Department of the Treasury, Chronological File of Harry Dexter White, Nov 1934–April 1946, United States National Archives, College Park, MD

CFR   Council on Foreign Relations Records, Public Policy Papers, Department of Rare Books and Special Collections, Princeton University Library, Princeton, NJ

CSF   Record Group 82, Records of the Federal Reserve System, Board of Governors Central Subject Files, United States National Archives, College Park, MD

DS   Record Group 59, General Records of the Department of State, United States National Archives, College Park, MD

DSDF   Record Group 59, General Records of the Department of State, Decimal Files, 1940–44, United States National Archives, College Park, MD

DSFS   Record Group 84, Records of the Foreign Service Posts of the Department of State, United States National Archives, College Park, MD

EBP   Edward Bernstein Papers, IMF Archives, Washington, DC

EKP   Edwin W. Kemmerer Papers, Public Policy Papers, Department of Rare Books and Special Collections, Princeton University Library, Princeton, NJ

FGV   Centro de Pesquisa e Documentação de História Contemporânea do Brasil, Fundação Getúlio Vargas, Rio de Janeiro

FO   Foreign Office Records, The National Archives of the United Kingdom, Kew, Richmond, Surrey

HDWP   Harry Dexter White Papers, Public Policy Papers, Department of Rare Books and Special Collections, Princeton University Library, Princeton, NJ

ISF   Record Group 82, Records of the Federal Reserve System, Board of Governors International Subject Files, United States National Archives, College Park, MD

ITM   Record Group 56, General Records of the Department of the Treasury, Intra-Treasury Memoranda of Harry Dexter White, 1934–45, United States National Archives, College Park, MD

JVP   Jacob Viner Papers, Public Policy Papers, Department of Rare Books and Special Collections, Princeton University Library, Princeton, NJ

LSE   London School of Economics Archives, London School of Economics, London

MD   Morgenthau Diary, The Papers of Henry Morgenthau Jr., 1866–1960, Franklin D. Roosevelt Library, Hyde Park, NY

MP   The Papers of Henry Morgenthau Jr., 1866–1960, Franklin D. Roosevelt Library, Hyde Park, NY

NAC, RG   National Archives of Canada, Ottawa, Record Group

NAI   National Archives of India, New Delhi

RIC   Record Group 43, Records of International Conferences, Commissions and Expositions; International Conference Records, US Delegation to the Seventh International Conference of American States, General Records, 1933–34, Reports of Delegates, United States National Archives, College Park, MD

RIIA   Royal Institute of International Affairs Archives, London

RIIACR   Royal Institute of International Affairs Committee on Reconstruction, Royal Institute of International Affairs Archives, London

RTP   Robert Triffin Papers, Manuscripts and Archives, Yale University Library, New Haven, CT

SMHDW   Record Group 56, General Records of the Department of the Treasury, Staff Memoranda of Harry Dexter White, January 1941–June 1946, United States National Archives, College Park, MD

THMC   Thomas Harrington McKittrick Collection. Baker Library Historical Collections. Harvard Business School, Cambridge, MA

TSF   Record Group 56, General Records of the Department of the Treasury, Office of the Assistant Secretary for International Affairs, Subject Files 1934–72, United States National Archives, College Park, MD

UKT   United Kingdom Treasury Records, The National Archives of the United Kingdom, Kew, Richmond, Surrey

WFP   Wesley Frost Papers, Department of State: Messages Sent by Wesley Frost 1944, Oberlin College Archives, Oberlin, OH

Acheson, Dean. 1969. *Present at the Creation*. New York: W. W. Norton.

Acsay, Peter Josef. 2000. "Planning for Postwar Economic Cooperation: US Treasury, the Soviet Union and Bretton Woods 1933–46." Ph.D. diss., Saint Louis University.

Adams, Frederick. 1976. *Economic Diplomacy: The Export-Import Bank and American Foreign Policy 1934–39*. Columbia: University of Missouri Press.

Adamson, Michael. 2002. "The Failure of the Foreign Bondholders Protective Council Experiment, 1934–1940." *Business History Review* 76: 479–514.

———. 2005. "'Must We Overlook All Impairment of Our Interest?' Debating the Foreign Aid Role of the Export-Import Bank, 1934–41." *Diplomatic History* 29 (4): 589–623.

Alacevich, Michele, and Pier Francesco Asso. 2009. "Shaping Monetary Constitutions for Developing Countries: Some Archival Evidence on the Bloomfield Missions to South Korea (1949–50)." In Leeson 2009.

Alcalde, Javier Gonzalo. 1987. *The Idea of Third World Development: Emerging Perspectives in the United States and Britain, 1900–1950.* New York: University Press of America.

American Technical Mission to Cuba. 1942. "Report to the Cuban Government of the American Technical Mission to Cuba." *Federal Reserve Bulletin* (August 1942): 774–801.

Amin, Samir. 1990. *Delinking.* London: Zed Books.

Anstey, Vera. 1943. "The Economic Reconstruction of India." *Agenda* 2 (4): 339–50.

Argote-Freyre, Frank. 2006. *Fulgencio Batista.* New Brunswick, NJ: Rutgers University Press.

Arndt, H. W. 1972. "Development Economics before 1945." In *Development and Planning,* edited by J. Bhagwati and R. Eckhaus. London: George Allen and Unwin.

———. 1987. *Economic Development: The History of an Idea.* Chicago: University of Chicago Press.

———. 1996. *Essays in International Economics, 1944–1994.* Aldershot: Avebury.

Asso, Pier Francesco, and Luca Fiorito. 2009. "A Scholar in Action in Interwar America: John H. Williams on Trade Theory and Bretton Woods." In Leeson 2009.

Babb, Sarah. 2001. *Managing Mexico: Economists from Nationalism to Neoliberalism.* Princeton, NJ: Princeton University Press.

Bagby, Wesley. 1992. *The Eagle-Dragon Alliance: America's Relations with China in World War II.* Newark: University of Delaware Press.

Becker, William, and William McClenahan. 2003. *The Market, the State and the Export-Import Bank of the United States, 1934–2000.* Cambridge: Cambridge University Press.

Bemis, Samuel Flagg. 1943. *The Latin American Policy of the United States.* New York: Harcourt, Brace and World.

Benjamin, Bret. 2007. *Invested Interest: Capital, Culture, and the World Bank.* Minneapolis: University of Minnesota Press.

Benjamin, Jules. 1977. "The New Deal, Cuba, and the Rise of a Global Foreign Economic Policy." *Business History Review,* 51 (1): 57–78.

Berle, Beatrice Bishop, and Travis Beal Jacobs, eds. 1973. *Navigating the Rapids 1918–1971: From the Papers of Adolf A. Berle.* New York: Harcourt Brace Jovanovich.

Berle, Adolf. 1941a. "The Economic Interests of the United States in Inter-American Relations." *Department of State Bulletin* (June 28) 4 (105): 756–60.

———. 1941b. "Peace Without Empire." *Survey Graphic.* (March): 103–8.

Bernstein, Edward. 1993. "The Soviet Union and Bretton Woods." In Bordo and Eichengreen 1993..

———. 1996. "The Making and Remaking of the Bretton Woods Institutions." In Kirshner 1996.

Beyen, J. W. 1949. *Money in a Maelstrom.* New York: Macmillan.

Bittermann, Henry. 1971. "Negotiation of the Articles of Agreement of the International Bank for Reconstruction and Development." *International Lawyer* 5 (1): 59–88.

Black, Stanley. 1991. *A Levite Among Priests: Edward M. Bernstein and the Origins of the Bretton Woods System.* Boulder, CO: Westview.

Blum, John Morton. 1959. *From the Morgenthau Diaries: Years of Crisis, 1928–38.* Boston: Houghton Mifflin.

———. 1965. *The Morgenthau Diaries: Years of Urgency 1938–1941* Boston: Houghton Mifflin.

———. 1967. *The Morgenthau Diaries: Years of War 1941–1945.* Boston: Houghton Mifflin.

Bonné, Alfred. 1945. *The Economic Development of the Middle East: An Outline of Planned Reconstruction after the War*. London: Kegan Paul, Trench, Trubner.

Bordo, Michael. 1993. "The Bretton Woods International Monetary System: A Historical Overview." In Bordo and Eichengreen 1993.

Bordo, Michael, and Barry Eichengreen. 1993. *A Retrospective on the Bretton Woods System*. Chicago: University of Chicago Press.

Bordo, Michael, and Anna Schwartz. 2001. *From the Exchange Stabilization Fund to the International Monetary Fund*. NBER Working Paper 100. Cambridge, MA: National Bureau of Economic Research.

Borgwardt, Elizabeth. 2005. *A New Deal for the World; America's Vision for Human Rights*. Cambridge, MA: Belknap Press for Harvard University Press.

Bose, Sugata. 1997. "Instruments and Idioms of Colonial and National Development." In Cooper and Packard 1997.

Boskey, Shirley. 1957. "Bretton Woods Recalled." *International Bank Notes* (July).

Boughton, James. 2001a. "The Case Against Harry Dexter White: Still Not Proven." *History of Political Economy* 33 (2): 219–39.

——. 2001b. *Silent Revolution: The International Monetary Revolution, 1979–1989*. Washington, DC: IMF.

——. 2002. "Why White, Not Keynes? Inventing the Postwar International Monetary System." In *The Open Economy Macromodel: Past, Present, and Future*, edited by Arie Arnon and Warren Young. Dordrecht: Kluwer.

——. 2004. "New Light on Harry Dexter White." *Journal of the History of Economic Thought* 26 (2): 179–95.

——. 2009. "American in the Shadows: Harry Dexter White and the Design of the International Monetary Fund." In Leeson 2009.

——. 2011. "Jacques J. Polak and the Evolution of the International Monetary System." *IMF Economic Review* 59 (2): 379–99.

——. 2013. "Dirtying White." *The Nation*, June 26, 42–44.

Boughton, James, and Roger Sandilands. 2003. "Politics and the Attack on FDR's Economists." *Intelligence and National Security* 18 (3): 73–99.

Braden, Spruille. 1971. *Diplomats and Demagogues*. New Rochelle, NY: Arlington House.

Broad, Lewis. 1955. *Sir Antony Eden: The Chronicles of a Career*. London: Hutchinson.

Bryce, Robert. 1943. "International Aspects of an Investment Program." In Harris 1943.

Bulhões, Otávio Gouvêa de. 1990. *Otávio Gouvêa de Bulhões: Depoimento*. Brasilia: Divisão de Impressão e Publicações do Departamento de Administração de Recursos Materiais do Banco Central do Brasil.

Bullock, Alan. 1967. *The Life and Times of Ernest Bevin*: vol. 2: *Minister of Labour, 1940–1945*. London: Heinemann.

Burley, Anne-Marie. 1993. "Regulating the World: Multilateralism, International Law, and the Projection of the New Deal Regulatory State." In *Multilateralism Matters*, edited by J. Ruggie. New York: Columbia University Press.

Campos, Roberto. 1996. "Fifty Years of Bretton Woods." In Kirshner 1996.

Carr, E. H. 1939. *The Twenty Years' Crisis*. London: Macmillan.

Casey, Kevin. 2001. *Saving International Capitalism During the Early Truman Presidency*. London: Routledge.

Chandavarkar, Anand. 1983. "Money and Credit, 1858–1947." In *The Cambridge Economic History of India*, edited by Dharma Kumar. Cambridge: Cambridge University Press.

——. 1989. *Keynes and India*. London: Macmillan.

——. 2001. "Sir (Abraham) Jeremy Raisman, Finance Member, Government of India (1939–45): Portrait of an Unsung Statesman Extraordinaire." *Economic and Political Weekly* 36 (28) (July 14): 2641–55.

Coates, Kenneth. 2009. "The Centre for Latin American Monetary Studies and its Central Bankers' Networks." In *Networks of Influence,* edited by L. Martinez-Diaz and N. Woods. Oxford: Oxford University Press.

Cobbs, Elizabeth. 1992. *The Rich Neighbor Policy: Rockefeller and Kaiser in Brazil.* New Haven, CT: Yale University Press.

Cooper, Frederick. 1997. "Modernizing Bureaucrats, Backward Africans, and the Development Concept." In Cooper and Packard 1997.

Cooper, Frederick, and Randall Packard. 1997. *International Development and the Social Sciences.* Berkeley: University of California Press.

——. 1997. "Introduction." In Cooper and Packard 1997.

Corbridge, Stuart. 2007. "The (Im)possibility of Development Studies." *Economy and Society* 36 (2): 179–211.

Cowen, M., and R. Shenton. 1996. *Doctrines of Development.* London: Routledge.

Craig, R. Bruce. 2004. *Treasonable Doubt: The Harry Dexter White Spy Case.* Lawrence: University Press of Kansas.

Cramer, Gisela, and Ursula Prutsch. 2006. "Nelson A. Rockefeller's Office of Inter-American Affairs (1940–1946) and Record Group 229." *Hispanic American Historical Review* 86 (4):785–806.

Cullather, Nick. 1992. "The United States, American Business, and the Origins of the Philippine Central Bank." *American Historical Collection* 20 (4): 80–99.

——. 1994. *Illusions of Influence.* Stanford, CA: Stanford University Press.

——. 2000. "Development? It's History." *Diplomatic History* 24 (4): 641–53.

——. 2010. *The Hungry World.* Cambridge, MA: Harvard University Press.

Dávila, Francisco Suárez. 1977. "Bosquejo biográfico." In Suárez 1977.

Dell, Sidney. 1972. *The Inter-American Development Bank.* New York: Praeger.

Degefe, Befekadu. 1995. "The Development of Money, Monetary Institutions and Monetary Policy 1941–75." In *An Economic History of Modern Ethiopia:* vol. 1: *The Imperial Era 1941–74,* edited by Shiferaw Bekele. Senegal: Codesria.

Department of State. 1940. "Inter-American Bank." *Federal Reserve Bulletin* (June 1940): 517–25.

Deshmukh, C. D. 1974. *The Course of My Life.* New Delhi: Orient Longman.

De Vries, Margaret Garritsen. 1986. *The IMF in a Changing World: 1945–85.* Washington, DC: IMF.

Diaz-Alejandro, Carlos. 1988. "Latin America in the 1930s." In *Trade, Development and the World Economy,* edited by Andres Velasco. Oxford: Basil Blackwell.

Dimand, Robert, and Mary Ann Dimand. 1990. "J. M. Keynes on Buffer Stocks and Commodity Price Stabilization." *History of Political Economy* 22 (1): 113–23.

Director General of the Pan American Union. 1942. *Report on the Third Meeting of the Ministers of Foreign Affairs of the American Republics, Rio De Janeiro, January 15–28, 1942.* Washington, DC: Pan American Union.

Dosman, Edgar. 2001. "Markets and the State in the Evolution of the 'Prebisch Manifesto.'" *CEPAL Review* 75: 87–102.

——. 2008. *The Life and Times of Raúl Prebisch, 1901–1986.* Montreal: McGill-Queen's University Press.

Dos Santos, Theodore. 1970. "The Structure of Dependence." *American Economic Review* 60 (2): 231–36.

Drake, Paul. 1989. *The Money Doctor in the Andes.* Durham, NC: Duke University Press.

Drucker, Peter. 1943. "Keynes, White, and Postwar Currency." *Harper's Magazine*, June 18, 177–85.

Eckes, Alfred. 1975. *A Search for Solvency: Bretton Woods and the International Monetary System, 1941–1971*. Austin: University of Texas Press.

Ekbladh, David. 2010. *The Great American Mission: Modernization and the Construction of an American World Order*. Princeton, NJ: Princeton University Press.

Escobar, Arturo. 1995. *Encountering Development: The Making and Unmaking of the Third World*. Princeton, NJ: Princeton University Press.

Esteva, Gustavo. 1992. "Development." In Sachs 1992.

Fajardo, Feliciano, Manuel Manansala, and Placido Borbon. 1987. *Central Banking: Focus on the Philippines*. Manila: National Book Store.

Farrell, Terrence. 1980. "Arthur Lewis and the Case for Caribbean Industrialization." *Social and Economic Studies* 29 (4): 52–75.

Finnemore, Martha. 1997. "Redefining Development at the World Bank." In *International Development and the Social Sciences*, edited by Frederick Cooper and Randall Packard. Berkeley: University of California Press.

Friedman, Max. 2003. *Nazis and Good Neighbors*. Cambridge: Cambridge University Press.

Fuchs, James. 1974a. *Oral History Interview with Arthur N. Young*, February 21. Harry S. Truman Library and Museum. http://www.trumanlibrary.org/oralhist/young.htm.

———. 1974b. *Oral History Interview with Dr. John Parke Young*, February 21. Harry S. Truman Library and Museum. http://www.trumanlibrary.org/oralhist/youngjp. htm.

Galbraith, John Kenneth. 1972. "How Keynes Came to America." In *Economics, Peace, and Laughter*. Boston: Houghton Mifflin.

Gantenbein, James. 1950. *The Evolution of Our Latin-American Policy: A Documentary Record*. New York: Columbia University Press.

Gardner, Lloyd. 1964. *Economic Aspects of New Deal Diplomacy*. Madison: University of Wisconsin Press.

Gardner, Richard. 1980. *Sterling Dollar Diplomacy in Current Perspective*. New York: Columbia University Press.

———. 1985. "Sterling Dollar Diplomacy in Current Perspective." *International Affairs*. 62 (1): 21–33.

———. 1996. "The Bretton Woods–GATT System after Fifty Years." In Orin Kirshner 1996.

Gardner, S., and J. Powelson, 1970. "Regional Banking in the Americas." *Inter-American Economic Affairs* 24 (1): 15–30.

Gellman, Irwin. 1973. *Roosevelt and Batista*. Albuquerque: University of New Mexico Press.

———. 1979. *Good Neighbor Diplomacy*. Baltimore: Johns Hopkins University Press.

———. 1985. *The Dismantling of the Good Neighbor Policy*. Austin: University of Texas Press.

Gilderhus, Mark. 2000. *The Second Century: U.S.–Latin American Relations since 1889*. Wilmington, DE: Scholarly Resources.

Gold, Joseph. 1988. "Mexico and the Development of the Practice of the International Monetary Fund." *World Development* 16 (10): 1127–42.

Gootenberg, Paul. 2004. "Between a Rock and a Softer Place." *Latin American Research Review* 39 (2): 239–57.

Gramby-Sobukwe, Sharon. 2005. "Africa and US Foreign Policy." *Journal of Black Studies* 35: 779–801.

Green, David. 1971. *The Containment of Latin America*. Chicago: Quadrangle Books.

Grey, Austin. 1944. "The Monetary Conference and China." *Far Eastern Survey* 13 (18) (September 6, 1944): 165–67.

Grove, David, and Jon Exter. 1948. "The Philippine Central Bank Act." *Federal Reserve Bulletin* 34 (8): 938–49.

Grow, Michael. 1981. *The Good Neighbor Policy and Authoritarianism in Paraguay.* Lawrence: Regents Press of Kansas.

Guerrant, Edward. 1950. *Roosevelt's Good Neighbor Policy.* Albuquerque: University of New Mexico Press.

Haglund, David. 1984. *Latin America and the Transformation of US Strategic Thought, 1936–40.* Albuquerque: University of New Mexico Press.

Hailey, Lord. 1942. "Colonial Policy and Some of Its Post-war Problems." *Agenda* 1 (2): 107–18.

Hansen, Alvin. 1944. "The Views of Alvin Hansen." In Shields 1944.

Hansen, Alvin, and Charles Kindleberger. 1942. "Economic Tasks of the Postwar World." *Foreign Affairs* 20 (3): 466–76.

Hanson, Simon. 1938. *Utopia in Uruguay.* New York: Oxford University Press.

——. 1950. "Latin America and the Point Four Program." *Annals of the American Academy of Political and Social Science* 268: 66–74.

Harris, Seymour, ed. 1943. *Postwar Economic Problems.* New York: McGraw-Hill

Harrod, R. F. 1951. *The Life of John Maynard Keynes.* London: Macmillan.

Hartendorp, A. V. H. 1958. *History of Industry and Trade of the Philippines.* Manila: American Chamber of Commerce of the Philippines.

Havinden, Michael, and David Meredith. 1993. *Colonialism and Development: Britain and Its Tropical Colonies, 1850–1960.* London: Routledge.

Haynes, John Earl, Harvey Klehr, and Alexander Vassiliev. 2009. *Spies.* New Haven, CT: Yale University Press.

Helleiner, Eric. 1994. *States and the Reemergence of Global Finance.* Ithaca: Cornell University Press.

——. 2002. "Economic Nationalism as a Challenge to Economic Liberalism?" *International Studies Quarterly* 46 (3): 307–29.

——. 2008. "The Mystery of the Missing Sovereign Debt Restructuring Mechanism." *Contributions to Political Economy* 27 (1): 91–113.

——. 2009. "Central Bankers as Good Neighbors." *Financial History Review* 16 (1): 1–21.

Henning, C. Randall. 1999. *The Exchange Stabilization Fund: Slush Money or War Chest?* Washington, DC: Institute for International Economics.

Hilton, Stanley. 1979. "Brazilian Diplomacy and the Washington-Rio de Janeiro 'Axis' During the World War II Era." *Hispanic American Historical Review* 59 (2): 201–231.

——. 1981. "The United States, Brazil, and the Cold War, 1945–1960." *Journal of American History* 68 (3): 599–624.

Hirschman, Albert. 1981. "The Rise and Decline of Development Economics." In *Essays in Trespassing.* Cambridge: Cambridge University Press.

——. 1995. "How the Keynesian Revolution Was Exported from the United States." In *A Propensity to Self-Subversion.* Cambridge, MA: Harvard University Press.

Hodge, Joseph Morgan. 2007. *Triumph of the Expert: Agrarian Doctrines of Development and the Legacies of British Colonialism.* Athens: Ohio University Press.

Horsefield, J. Keith. 1969a. *The International Monetary Fund 1945–1965: Twenty Years of International Monetary Cooperation.* Vol. 1. Washington, DC: IMF.

——. 1969b. *The International Monetary Fund 1945–1965: Twenty Years of International Monetary Cooperation.* Vol. 3. Washington, DC: IMF.

Howard, Thomas. 2003. "Franklin Roosevelt, the Caribbean and the Postcolonial World." In *Franklin D. Roosevelt and the Formation of the Modern World*, edited by Thomas Howard and William Pederson. Armonk, NY: M. E. Sharpe.

Howson, Susan, and Donald Moggridge, eds. 1990. *The Wartime Diaries of Lionel Robbins and James Meade, 1943–45*. London: Macmillan.

Ikenberry, John. 1992. "A World Economy Restored: Expert Consensus and Anglo-American Postwar Settlement." *International Organization* 46 (1): 289–321.

———. 2011. *Liberal Leviathan*. Princeton, NJ: Princeton University Press.

Inman, Samuel Guy. 1944. "Some Latin American Views on Post-War Reconstruction." *Foreign Policy Reports* 20 (1) (March 15): 2–11.

Jacobson, Harold, and Michel Oksenberg. 1990. *China's Participation in the IMF, the World Bank, and GATT*. Ann Arbor: University of Michigan Press.

James, Harold. 1996. *International Monetary Cooperation since Bretton Woods*. Oxford: Oxfrod University Press.

Jian, Chen. 2001. *Mao's China and the Cold War*. Chapel Hill: University of North Carolina Press.

Johnson, Harry. 1978. "Keynes and Development." In *The Shadow of Keynes*. Chicago: University of Chicago Press.

Kalecki, Michael, and E. F. Schumacher. 1943. "International Clearing and Long-Term Lending." *Oxford Institute of Statistics Bulletin* 5 (S5) (August 7): 29–33.

Kapur, Devesh, John Lewis, and Richard Webb. 1997. *The World Bank: Its First Half Century*. Washington: Brookings Institution Press.

Karunatilake, H. N. S. 1973. *Central Banking and Monetary Policy in Sri Lanka*. Colombo: Lake House Investment.

Kemmerer, Edwin. 1944. "The Views of Edwin W. Kemmerer." In Shields 1944.

Keynes, John Maynard. 1974. "International Control of Raw Materials." *Journal of International Economics*. 4: 299–315.

———. 1980a. *The Collected Writings of John Maynard Keynes*. Vol. 1, edited by Donald Moggridge. London: Macmillan.

———. 1980b. *The Collected Writings of John Maynard Keynes*. Vol. 25, edited by Donald Moggridge. London: Macmillan.

———. 1980c. *The Collected Writings of John Maynard Keynes*. Vol. 26, edited by Donald Moggridge. London: Macmillan.

Kimball, Warren. 1991. *The Juggler: Franklin Roosevelt as Wartime Statesman*. Princeton, NJ: Princeton University Press.

Kindleberger, Charles. 1943a. "International Monetary Stabilization." In Harris 1943.

———. 1943b. "Planning for Foreign Investment," pt. 2. *American Economic Review* 33 (1): 347–54

———. 1991. *The Life of an Economist*. Oxford: Basil Blackwell.

Kirshner, Orin, ed. 1996. *The Bretton Woods–GATT System*. Armonk, NY: M. E. Sharpe.

Kofas, Jon. 1997. "The Politics of Foreign Debt: The IMF, the World Bank, and US Foreign Policy in Chile, 1946–1952." *Journal of Developing Areas*. 31: 157–82.

Krasner, Stephen. 1985. *Structural Conflict: The Third World Against Global Liberalism*. Berkeley: University of California Press.

Laidler, David, and Roger Sandilands. 2002. "An Early Harvard Memorandum on Anti-Depression Policies." *History of Political Economy* 34 (3): 515–32.

Langer, William, and S. Everett Gleason. 1970. *The Challenge to Isolation: The World Crisis of 1937–1940 and American Foreign Policy*. Gloucester, MA: Peter Smith.

Latham, Michael. 2011. *The Right Kind of Revolution*. Ithaca: Cornell University Press.

League of Nations. 1939. *The Development of International Co-operation in Economic and Social Affairs: Report of the Special Committee*. Geneva: League of Nations.

Lee, David. 2010. *Stanley Melbourne Bruce.* London: Continuum.

Lee, J. M. 1967. *Colonial Development and Good Government.* Oxford: Clarendon Press.

Leeson, Robert, ed. 2009. *American Power and Policy.* New York: Palgrave Macmillan.

Li, Choh-Ming. 1943. "China in World Economy." *Foreign Policy Reports* 19 (16): 218–23.

Li, Tania. 2007. *The Will to Improve.* Durham, NC: Duke University Press.

Lokanathan. P. S. 1945. "The Bombay Plan." *Foreign Affairs* 23 (July): 680–86.

Love, Joseph. 1996. *Crafting the Third World.* Stanford, CA: Stanford University Press.

Luthringer, George. 1931. "The Gold-Exchange Standard in the Philippines Since 1913." Ph.D. diss., Princeton University.

Mandelbaum, Kurt. 1961 (1945). *The Industrialisation of Backward Areas.* Oxford: Basil Blackwell.

——. 1979. "'I am still the same, but . . .' A Portrait of the Economist Kurt Mandelbaum Based on an Interview with Matthias Greffrath." *Development and Change* 10 (4): 503–13.

Marcus, Harold. 1983. *Ethiopia, Great Britain, and the United States, 1941–1974.* Berkeley: University of California Press.

Markovits, Claude. 1985. *Indian Business and Nationalist Politics 1931–1939.* Cambridge: Cambridge University Press.

Mason, Edward, and Robert Asher. 1973. *The World Bank since Bretton Woods.* Washington, DC: Brookings Institution Press.

Mauri, Arnaldo. 2010. "The Re-establishment of the National Monetary and Banking System in Ethiopia 1941–1963." *South African Journal of Economic History* 24 (2): 82–130.

Maxfield, Sylvia, and James Nolt. 1990. "Protectionism and the Internationalization of Capital: US Sponsorship of Import Substitution Industrialization in the Philippines, Turkey and Argentina." *International Studies Quarterly* 34 (1): 49–81.

McCann, Frank. 1974. *The Brazilian-American Alliance 1937–1945.* Princeton, NJ: Princeton University Press.

McKinzie, Richard. 1972. Oral history interview with Roman L. Horne. Harry S. Truman Library and Museum. http://www.trumanlibrary.org/oralhist/hornerl.htm.

——. 1973. Oral history interview with Frank A. Southard. Harry S. Truman Library and Museum. http://www.trumanlibrary.org/oralhist/southard.htm.

——. 1974. Oral history interview with Emilio Collado. Harry S. Truman Library and Museum. http://www.trumanlibrary.org/oralhist/collado2.htm.

Mehrling, Perry. 1997. *The Money Interest and the Public Interest: American Monetary Thought, 1920–1970.* Cambridge, MA: Harvard University Press.

Meier, Gerald 1984a. *Emerging from Poverty.* Oxford: Oxford University Press.

——. 1984b. "The Formative Period." In Meier and Seers 1984.

Meier, Gerald, and Dudley Seers, eds. 1984. *Pioneers in Development.* Oxford: Oxford University Press.

Mikesell, Raymond. 1951. "Negotiating at Bretton Woods, 1944." In *Negotiating with the Russians,* edited by Raymond Dennett and Joseph Johnson. Boston: World Peace Foundation.

——. 1994. *The Bretton Woods Debates: A Memoir.* Essays in International Finance, no. 192. Princeton, NJ: International Finance Section, Department of Economics, Princeton University.

——. 1996. "Some Issues in the Bretton Woods Debates." In Kirshner 1996.

——. 2000. *Foreign Adventures of an Economist.* Eugene: University of Oregon Press.

Minkes, A. L. 1951. "The Economic Development of Eastern Europe." *International Affairs* 27 (1): 45–54, (3): 332–41.

Mitchell, Timothy. 2002. *Rule of Experts*. Berkeley: University of California Press.

Moggridge, Donald. 1992. *Maynard Keynes: An Economist's Biography*. London: Routledge.

Mora, Frank. 1998. "The Forgotten Relationship: United States–Paraguay Relations, 1937–89." *Journal of Contemporary History* 33 (3): 452–73.

Morgenthau, Henry, 1945. "Bretton Woods and International Cooperation." *Foreign Affairs* 23 (1): 182–94.

Mukherjee, Aditya. 2002. *Imperialism, Nationalism and the Making of the Indian Capitalist Class, 1920–1947*. London: Sage.

Murphy, Craig. 1984. *The Emergence of the NIEO Ideology*. Boulder, CO: Westview.

——. 1994. *International Organization and Industrial Change*. New York: Oxford University Press.

——. 2006. *The United Nations Development Programme: A Better Way?* Cambridge: Cambridge University Press.

Museo Numismático del Banco Nacionale de Cuba. 1980. *Cuba: Emisiones de monedas y billetas, 1915–1980*. Havana: Museo Numismático del Banco Nacionale de Cuba.

Nagano, Yoshiko. 2010. "The Philippine Currency Standard During the American Colonial Period." *International Journal of Asian Studies* 7 (1): 29–50.

Nerozzi, Sebastiano. 2009. "Building Up a Multilateral Strategy for the United States: Alvin Hansen, Jacob Viner, and the Council on Foreign Relations (1939–45)." In Leeson 2009.

Norberg, Viveca Halldin. 1977. *Swedes in Haile Selassie's Ethiopia, 1924–1952*. Uppsala: Scandinavian Institute of African Studies.

Norman Wait Harris Memorial Foundation. 1941. *The Political and Economic Implications of Inter-American Solidarity. Proceedings of the 17th Institute under the Auspices of the Norman Wait Harris Foundation, July 7 to 15, 1941*. Chicago: University of Chicago Press.

Nurkse, Ragnar. 1944. *International Currency Experience*. Geneva: League of Nations.

O'Brien, John B. 2000. "F. L. McDougall and the Origins of the FAO." *Australian Journal of Politics and History* 46 (2); 164–74.

Oliver, Robert. 1957. "The Origins of the International Bank for Reconstruction and Development." Ph.D. diss., Princeton University.

——. 1961a. Transcript of interview with Ansel F. Luxford. The World Bank/IFC Archives Oral History Program, Oral History Research Office, Columbia University, July 13. http://siteresources.worldbank.org/EXTARCHIVES/Resources/Ansel_Luxford_Oral_History_Transcript_44_01.pdf.

——. 1961b. Transcript of interview with Luis Machado. The World Bank/IFC Archives Oral History Program, Oral History Research Office, Columbia University, July 18. http://siteresources.worldbank.org/EXTARCHIVES/Resources/Luis_Machado_Oral_History_Transcript_44_01.pdf.

——. 1961c. Transcript of interview with Paul Rosenstein-Rodan. The World Bank/IFC Archives Oral History Program, Oral History Research Office, Columbia University, August 14. http://siteresources.worldbank.org/EXTARCHIVES/Resources/rosenstein-rodan_transcriptt.pdf.

——. 1971. *Early Plans for a World Bank*. Princeton Studies in International Finance, no. 29. International Finance Section, Department of Economics, Princeton University.

——. 1975. *International Economic Co-operation and the World Bank*. London: Macmillan.

——. 1985. *Bretton Woods: A Retrospective Essay*. California Seminar on International Security and Foreign Policy, Discussion Paper no.105. Santa Monica: California Seminar on International Security and Foreign Policy.

O'Sullivan, Christopher. 2008. *Sumner Welles*. New York: Columbia University Press.

Packenham, Robert. 1973. *Liberal America and the Third World*. Princeton, NJ: Princeton University Press.

Pakula, Hannah. 2009. *The Last Empress: Madame Chiang Kai-Shek and the Birth of Modern China*. New York: Simon & Schuster.

Park, James William. 1995. *Latin American Underdevelopment: A History of Perspectives in the United States, 1870–1965*. Baton Rouge: Louisiana State University Press.

Patrick, Stewart. 2009. *Best Laid Plans*. Boulder, CO: Rowman & Littlefield.

Patterson, James. 1972. *Mr. Republican—A Biography of Robert A. Taft*. Boston: Houghton Mifflin.

Pauly, Louis. 1997. *Who Elected the Bankers?* Ithaca: Cornell University Press.

Peet, Richard. 2009. *Unholy Trinity: The IMF, World Bank and the WTO*. 2d ed. London: Zed Books.

Penrose, E. F. 1953. *Economic Planning for the Peace*. Princeton, NJ: Princeton University Press.

Pérez, Louis. 1986. *Cuba under the Platt Amendment 1902–1934*. Pittsburgh: University of Pittsburgh Press.

Pike, Frederick. 1995. *FDR's Good Neighbor Policy*. Austin: University of Texas Press.

Pinho Barreiros, Daniel de. 2009. "Atuação da delegação brasileira na formulação do Acordo Internacional de Bretton Woods (1942–1944)." *História* 28 (2). http://www.scielo.br/scielo.php?pid=S0101–90742009000200018&script=sci_arttext.

Pollock, David. 1978. "Some Changes in United States Attitudes Towards CEPAL Over the Past 30 Years." *CEPAL Review* 6: 57–80.

Prasad, P. S. Narayan. 1985. *C. D. Deshmukh: His Contribution to Monetary and Economic Policy*. New Dehli: Lancer International.

Prebisch, Raúl. 1972. "A View from the Developing World." In *Bretton Woods Revisited,* edited by A. L. Acheson, J. F. Chant, and M. F. J. Prachowny. Toronto: University of Toronto Press.

——. 1991 (1944). "Conversaciones en el Banco de México, 21 de febrero, 1944." In *Obras 1919–48,* 3:189–206. Buenos Aires: Fundación Raúl Prebisch.

Pruessen, Ronald. 2009. "A Globalization Moment: Franklin D. Roosevelt in Casablanca (January 1943) and the Decolonization/Development Impulse." In *Empires and Autonomy,* edited by Stephen Streeter, John Waever, and William Coleman. Vancouver: University of British Columbia Press.

Rabe, Stephen. 1978. "The Elusive Conference: United States Economic Relations with Latin America, 1945–1952." *Diplomatic History* 2: 279–94.

Rauchway, Eric. 2013. "How the Soviets Saved Capitalism." *Times Literary Supplement,* 5740 (April 5): 12–13.

Rees, David. 1973. *Harry Dexter White: A Study in Paradox*. New York: Coward, McCann & Geoghegan.

Rist, Gilbert. 1997. *The History of Development,* translated by Patrick Camiller. London: Zed Books.

Rivas, Darlene. 2002. *Missionary Capitalist: Nelson Rockefeller in Venezuela*. Chapel Hill: University of North Carolina Press.

Rock, David. 1994. "War and Postwar Intersections." In *Latin America in the 1940s: War and Postwar Transitions,* edited by D. Rock. Berkeley: University of California Press.

Roorda, Eric. 1998. *The Dictator Next Door*. Durham, NC: Duke University Press.

Roosevelt, Franklin D. 1933. "Address by Franklin D. Roosevelt, 1933." http://www.inaugural.senate.gov/swearing-in/address/address-by-franklin-d-roosevelt-1933.

——. 1944. "Address to an International Labor Conference, May 17, 1944." In Gerhard Peters and John T. Woolley, *The American Presidency Project*. http://www.presi dency.ucsb.edu/ws/?pid=16509.

Rosenberg, Emily. 2003. *Financial Missionaries to the World*. Durham, NC: Duke University Press.

Rosenman, Samuel. 1952. *Working with Roosevelt*. New York: Harper & Brothers.

Rosenstein-Rodan, Paul. 1943. "Problems of Industrialization in Eastern and South-Eastern Europe." *Economic Journal* 53 (210/211): 202–11.

——. 1944. "The International Development of Economically Backward Areas." *International Affairs* 20 (2): 157–65.

——. 1984. "Natura Facit Saltum: Analysis of the Disequilibrium Growth Process." In Meier and Seers 1984.

Rothermund, Dietmar. 1993. *An Economic History of India*. London: Routledge.

Ruggie, John. 1982. "International Regimes, Transactions and Change: Embedded Liberalism in the Postwar Economic Order." *International Organization* 36: 379–415.

——, ed. 1983a. *The Antinomies of Interdependence*. New York: Columbia University Press.

——. 1983b. "International Interdependence and National Welfare." In Ruggie 1983a.

——. 1983c. "Political Structure and Change in the International Economic Order: the North-South Dimension." In Ruggie 1983a.

Sachs, Wolfgang. 1990. "The Archeology of the Development Idea." *Interculture* 28 (4): 2–32.

——, ed., 1992. *The Development Dictionary*. London: Zed Books.

——. 2010. Preface to the new edition. In Wolfgang Sachs, ed., *The Development Dictionary, Second Edition*. London: Zed Books.

Salant, Walter. 1989. "The Spread of Keynesian Doctrines and Practices in the United States." In *The Political Power of Economic Ideas: Keynesianism Across Nations*, edited by P. Hall. Princeton, NJ: Princeton University Press.

Sandilands, Roger. 2009. "An Archival Case Study: Revisiting the Life and Political Economy of Lauchlin Currie." In Leeson 2009.

Schaefer, Chris. 1992. "The Politics of Banking: the Bank of Abyssinia, 1905–1931." *International Journal of African Historical Studies* 25 (2): 361–89.

Schoultz, Lars. 1998. *Beneath the United States: A History of U.S. Policy Toward Latin America*. Cambridge, MA: Harvard University Press

Schuler, Friedrich. 1998. *Mexico Between Hitler and Roosevelt*. Albuquerque: University of New Mexico Press.

Schuler, Kurt, and Andrew Rosenberg, eds. 2012. *The Bretton Woods Transcripts*. New York: Center for Financial Stability.

Schuler, Kurt, and Dylan Schuler, eds., 2013. *Questions and Answers on the Bank for Reconstruction and Development, June 10, 1944*. Center for Financial Stability Paper in Financial History. New York: Center for Financial Stability.

Schumacher, E. F. 1943. "Multilateral Clearing." *Economica* 10 (38): 150–65.

——. 1973. *Small is Beautiful*. New York: Harper & Row.

Schwartz, Anna. 1997. "From Obscurity to Notoriety: a Biography of the Exchange Stabilization Fund." *Journal of Money, Credit and Banking* 29 (2): 135–53.

Schwartz, Jordan. 1987. *Liberal: Adolf A. Berle and the Vision of an American Era*. New York: Free Press.

Scott, James. 2010. "Developing Countries in the ITO and GATT Negotiations." *Journal of International Trade Law* 9 (1): 5–24.

Scott, William R. 1993. *The Sons of Sheba's Race: African Americans and the Italo-Ethiopian War, 1935–1941*. Bloomington: Indiana University Press.

Shields, Murray, ed. 1944. *International Financial Stabilization*. New York: Irving Trust Company.

Shoup, Laurence, and William Minter. 1977. *Imperial Brain Trust: The Council on Foreign Relations and United States Foreign Policy*. New York: Monthly Review Press.

Sikkink, Kathryn. 1991. *Ideas and Institutions: Developmentalism in Brazil and Argentina*. Ithaca: Cornell University Press.

Simha, S. L. N. 1970. *History of the Reserve Bank of India,* vol.1: *1935–1951*. Bombay: Reserve Bank of India.

———. 1972. "The World Bank Group." In *Economic and Social Development,* edited by S. L. N. Simha. Bombay: Vora and Co. Publishers Private Ltd.

Singer, Hans. 1984. "The Terms of Trade Controversy and the Evolution of Soft Financing: Early Years in the United Nations." In Meier and Seers 1984.

Skidelsky, Robert. 2000. *John Maynard Keynes,* vol.3: *Fighting for Britain 1937–1946*. London: Macmillan.

Skidmore, Thomas. 1967. *Politics in Brazil, 1930–1967*. New York: Oxford University Press.

Souza Costa, Artur de. 1944. *Bretton Woods e o Brasil*. Rio de Janeiro: Jornal do Commercio.

Spencer, John H. 1984. *Ethiopia at Bay*. Algonac, MI: Reference Publications.

Staley, Eugene. 1939. *World Economy in Transition*. New York: Council on Foreign Relations.

Staples, Amy. 2006. *The Birth of Development*. Kent, OH: Kent State University Press.

Steffek, Jens. 2006. *Embedded Liberalism and Its Critics*. London: Palgrave Macmillan.

Steil, Benn. 2013. *The Battle of Bretton Woods*. Princeton, NJ: Princeton University Press.

Stiller, Jesse. 1987. *George Messersmith*. Chapel Hill: University of North Carolina Press.

Suárez, Eduardo. 1977. *Commentarios y recuerdos (1926–1946)*. Mexico City: Editoria Porrúa.

Sun Yat-sen. 1922. *The International Development of China*. New York: Putnam.

Thakurdas, Purshotamdas, J. R. D. Tata, G. D. Birla, Ardeshir Dalal, Shri Ram, Kasturbhai Lalbhai, A. D. Shroff, and John Matthai. 1944. *A Plan of Economic Development for India*. New York: Penguin Books.

Tignor, Robert. 2006. *W. Arthur Lewis*. Princeton, NJ: Princeton University Press.

Tomlinson, B. R. 1979. *The Political Economy of the Raj 1914–1947*. London: Macmillan.

Toye, John. 1987. *Dilemmas of Development*. Oxford: Blackwell.

Toye, John, and Richard Toye. 2004. *The UN and Global Political Economy*. Bloomington: Indiana University Press.

Triffin, Robert. 1940. *Monopolistic Competition and General Equilibrium Theory*. Cambridge, MA: Harvard University Press.

———. 1946. *Monetary and Banking Reform in Paraguay*. Washington, DC: Board of Governors of the Federal Reserve System.

———. 1966 (1947). "National Central Banking and the International Economy." In R. Triffin, *The World Money Maze*. New Haven, CT: Yale University Press.

———. 1981. "An Economist's Career: What? Why? How?" *Banca Nazionale del Lavoro Quarterly Review* 138: 239–59.

———. 1990. "Conversation avec Catherine Ferrant et Jean Sloover." In *Robert Triffin: Conseiller des princes,* edited by Catherine Ferrant and Jean Sloover. Brussels: Editions Ciaco.

Urquidi, Victor L. 1994. "Bretton Woods: Un recorrido por el primer cincuentenario." *Comercio Exterior* 44 (10): 1–21. http://alcantara.net16.net/alcantaraunitec_archivos/archivosblog/bretonwoods.pdf.

——. 1996. "Reconstruction vs. Development: The IMF and the World Bank." In Kirshner 1996.

US Senate. 1941. *Inter-American Bank, Hearings Before a Subcommittee of the Committee on Foreign Relations, United States Senate,* 77th Congress, 1st session, May 5 and 6, 1941. Washington, DC: US Government Printing Office.

US State Department. 1948. *Proceedings and Documents of the United Nations Monetary and Financial Conference, Bretton Woods, New Hampshire, July 1–22, 1944.* Washington, DC: US Government Printing Office.

——. 1956. *Foreign Relations of the United States: Diplomatic Papers, 1938,* vol. 5: *The American Republics.* Washington, DC: US Government Printing Office.

——. 1957. *Foreign Relations of the United States: Diplomatic Papers, 1939,* vol. 5: *The American Republics.* Washington, DC: US Government Printing Office.

——. 1961. *Foreign Relations of the United States: Diplomatic Papers, 1940,* vol. 5: *The American Republics.* Washington, DC: US Government Printing Office.

——. 1962. *Foreign Relations of the United* States: *Diplomatic Papers, 1941,* vol. 7: *The American Republics.* Washington, DC: Government Printing Office.

——. 1963a. *Foreign Relations of the United States: Diplomatic Papers, 1942,* vol. 1: *General; the British Commonwealth; the Far East.* Washington, DC: US Government Printing Office.

——. 1963b. *Foreign Relations of the United States: Diplomatic Papers, 1942,* vol. 6: *The American Republics.* Washington, DC: US Government Printing Office.

——. 1967a. *Foreign Relations of the United States, Diplomatic Papers, 1944,* vol. 2: General Economic and Social Matters. Washington, DC: US Government Printing Office.

——. 1967b. *Foreign Relations of the United States: Diplomatic Papers, 1944,* vol. 6: *China.* Washington, DC: US Government Printing Office.

Van Dormael, Armand. 1978. *Bretton Woods: Birth of a Monetary System.* London: Macmillan.

Villaseñor, Eduardo. 1941. "The Inter-American Bank." *Foreign Affairs* 20 (1): 165–74.

Vinelli, Paul. 1950. "The Currency and Exchange System of Honduras." *IMF Staff Papers* 1: 420–31.

Vogel, Ezra. 2011. *Deng Xiaoping and the Transformation of China.* Cambridge, MA: Belknap Press of Harvard University Press.

Walker, J. Samuel. 1976. *Henry A. Wallace and American Foreign Policy.* Westport, CT: Greenwood Press.

Wallich, Henry. 1948. "Some Aspects of Latin American Economic Relations with the United States." In *Foreign Economic Policy for the United States,* edited by Seymour Harris. Cambridge, MA: Harvard University Press.

——. 1950. *Monetary Problems of an Export Economy: The Cuban Experience 1914–1947.* Cambridge, MA: Harvard University Press.

Wasserman, Max. 1946. "The New Ethiopian Monetary System." *Journal of Political Economy* 54 (4): 358–62.

Weinstein, Allen, and Alexander Vassiliev. 1999. *The Haunted Wood.* New York: Random House.

Weis, W. Michael. 2000. "Pan American Shift: Oswaldo Aranha and the Demise of the Brazilian-American Alliance." In *Beyond the Ideal: Pan-Americanism in Inter-American Affairs,* edited by D. Sheinin. Westport, CT: Greenwood Press.

Whitaker, Arthur P. 1944. "Politics and Diplomacy: the United States and Latin America." In *Inter-American Affairs 1943: An Annual Survey,* no. 3, edited by Arthur P. Whitaker. New York: Columbia University Press.

White, Harry Dexter. 1933. *The French International Accounts, 1880–1913*. Cambridge, MA: Harvard University Press.

White, Theodore, and Annalee Jacoby. 1946. *Thunder Out of China*. New York: William Sloane Associates.

Wilbur, C. Martin. 1976. *Sun Yat-sen: Frustrated Patriot*. New York: Columbia University Press.

Wilkinson. Rorden. 2006. *The WTO*. London: Routledge.

Williams, John. 1947. *Postwar Monetary Plans and Other Essays*. 3d. ed. New York: Knopf.

——. 1947 (1943). "Currency Stabilization: The Keynes and White Plans." In Williams 1947.

——. 1947 (1944). "The Joint Monetary Plan." In Williams 1947.

Williams, Marc. 1991. *Third World Cooperation: The Group of 77 in UNCTAD*. London: Pinter.

Williamson, John. 1977. *The Failure of World Monetary Reform, 1971–74*. Sunbury-on-Thames: Nelson.

Wilson, Theodore A., and Richard D. McKinzie. 1971. Oral history interview with Emilio Collado. July 7. Harry S. Truman Library and Museum. http://www.trumanlibrary.org/oralhist/collado1.htm.

Wood, Bryce. 1961. *The Making of the Good Neighbor Policy*. New York: Columbia University Press.

Woods, Randall Bennett. 1979. *The Roosevelt Foreign-Policy Establishment and the "Good Neighbor": The United States and Argentina 1941–1945*. Lawrence: Regents Press of Kansas.

Wu, Ching-Chao. 1943. "Internal Economic Development." *Foreign Policy Reports* 19 (16): 214–18.

Young, Arthur N. 1963. *China and the Helping Hand: 1937–1945*. Cambridge, MA: Harvard University Press.

——. 1965. *China's Wartime Finance and Inflation, 1937–1945*. Cambridge, MA: Harvard University Press.

Young, John Parke. 1950. "Developing Plans for an International Monetary Fund and a World Bank." *Department of State Bulletin*, November 13: 778–90.

Zanasi, Margherita. 2006. *Saving the Nation: Economic Modernity in Republican China*. Chicago: University of Chicago Press.

——. 2007. "Exporting Development: The League of Nations and Republican China." *Comparative Studies in Society and History* 49 (1): 143–69.

Index